GRAFFITI *as* DEVOTION

Edited by
Geoff Emberling
and Suzanne Davis

GRAFFITI as DEVOTION

Along the Nile and Beyond

Kelsey Museum Publication 16
Kelsey Museum of Archaeology
University of Michigan, 2019

The Kelsey Museum of Archaeology, Ann Arbor 48109

Published 2019

ISBN-13: 978-0-9906623-9-6
Library of Congress Control Number: 2019944110

Kelsey Museum Publication 16

Series Editor
Leslie Schramer

Cover design by Eric Campbell

This book was published in conjunction with the special exhibition *Graffiti as Devotion along the Nile: El-Kurru, Sudan*, held at the Kelsey Museum of Archaeology in Ann Arbor, Michigan. The exhibition, curated by Geoff Emberling and Suzanne Davis, was on view from 23 August 2019 through 29 March 2020.

An online version of the exhibition can be viewed at
http://exhibitions.kelsey.lsa.umich.edu/graffiti-el-kurru

Funding for this publication was provided by the University of Michigan College of Literature, Science, and the Arts and the University of Michigan Office of Research.

This book is available direct from ISD Book Distributors:
70 Enterprise Drive, Suite 2
Bristol, CT 06010, USA
Telephone: (860) 584-6546
Email: orders@isdistribution.com
Web: www.isdistribution.com

A PDF is available for free download at
https://lsa.umich.edu/kelsey/publications.html

Printed in South Korea by Four Colour Print Group, Louisville, Kentucky.

♾ This paper meets the requirements of
ANSI/NISO Z39.48-1992 (Permanence of Paper).

Contents

Contributors

Rebecca R. Benefiel is a professor of classics at Washington & Lee University, where she teaches Latin literature and Roman archaeology. She has published numerous articles focusing on Latin epigraphy and Roman social history and has been interviewed on NPR and in *Smithsonian, Forbes, The Atlantic,* and *National Geographic.* She co-edited the volume *Inscriptions in the Private Sphere in the Roman World* (Brill, 2016) and is director of the Ancient Graffiti Project (http://ancientgraffiti.org).

Ayman Damarany is an archaeologist and photographer based in Sohag, Egypt. Since 2007, he has directed, supervised, and collaborated on numerous excavations and archaeological projects throughout the greater Abydos area. He was the photographer for the American Research Center in Egypt at Luxor between 2014 and 2017, and is currently the project photographer for both the Kelsey Museum's Abydos Middle Cemetery Project and New York University's missions to Abydos.

Suzanne Davis is an archaeological conservator and the associate curator and head of conservation at the Kelsey Museum of Archaeology of the University of Michigan, Ann Arbor. She directs conservation for the International Kurru Archaeological Project and is co-curator of the exhibition *Graffiti as Devotion along the Nile.*

Geoff Emberling is an archaeologist and museum curator, currently an associate research scientist at the Kelsey Museum of Archaeology of the University of Michigan, Ann Arbor. He is co-director of the International Kurru Archaeological Project and co-curator of the exhibition *Graffiti as Devotion along the Nile.*

Fawzi Hassan Bakhiet is the head of the Department of Archaeology at the University of Neelain in Khartoum, Sudan, and was previously senior inspector in the National Corporation for Antiquities and Museums in Sudan. He received his PhD from Charles de Gaulle University – Lille 3 with a dissertation on rock art in the Middle Nile. He has since directed a number of archaeological projects in Sudan.

Jeremy Pope is an associate professor in the Department of History at the College of William & Mary. He is a member of the editorial board of *African Archaeological Review* and is the author of the 2014 book *The Double Kingdom under Taharqo: Studies in the History of Kush and Egypt c. 690–664 BC.* He has excavated at Jebel Barkal in Sudan and at the Mut Precinct of Karnak in Egypt, and his work on the Philae graffiti has appeared in *Enchoria: Zeitschrift für Demotistik und Koptologie.*

Alexandros Tsakos is the scientific director of the Manuscripts and Rare Books Collection of the Special Collections at the University Library of Bergen, Norway. His research interests are manuscript cultures, paleography, codicology, and religious practices, with a special focus on medieval Nubia. He is co-editor in chief of the Nubiological journal *Dotawo* and has co-authored and co-edited a number of books, as well as producing several articles and book chapters.

Bruce Beyer Williams was for many years a research associate at the Oriental Institute of the University of Chicago. He has authored eight volumes of results from the Oriental Institute Nubian Expedition (two further volumes are in press) and a book on early painted pottery, and has co-authored a volume on Nubian textiles. He has also written numerous articles on the archaeology and history of Nubia and has edited other works. In addition, he curated the Robert F. Picken Family Nubia Gallery in the Oriental Institute Museum. He has co-directed and participated in excavations in Sudan since 1997. He is currently a research associate of the Polish Center of Mediterranean Archaeology of the University of Warsaw and an associate at the Oriental Institute of the University of Chicago.

Bogdan Żurawski directed the Southern Dongola Reach Survey project (1997–2001) and Polish Salvage Missions to the 4th Nile Cataract (2004–2008). Since 2001 he has been directing the Polish excavations at Banganarti and from 2008 also in Selib. He is currently the head of the Department of Nubiology at the Institute of Mediterranean and Oriental Cultures of the Polish Academy of Sciences.

Overview Map

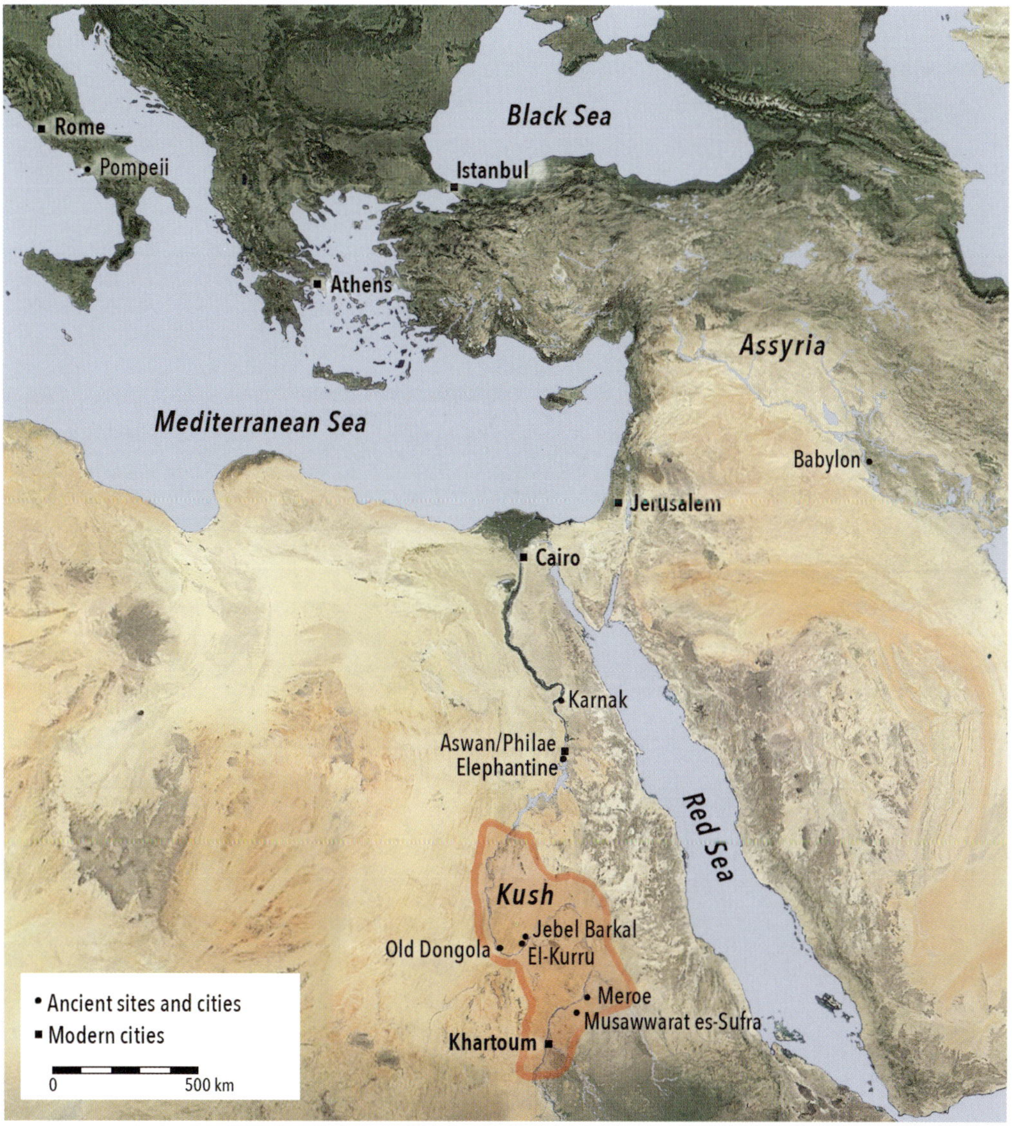

Map: Lorene Sterner

Timeline of Kush and Nubia

Dates are approximate.

	Kush and Nubia	**Egypt**
3400 BCE	**Neolithic (5000–3000)**	Predynastic (5300–3000)
3300 BCE		
3200 BCE		
3100 BCE	**Pre-Kerma / A-Group (before 3050–2700)**	
3000 BCE		
2900 BCE		Early Dynastic (3000–2686)
2800 BCE		
2700 BCE		
2600 BCE	**Early Kerma / Early C-Group (2700–2000)**	*Construction of the pyramids at Giza (2590–2500)*
2500 BCE		
2400 BCE		Old Kingdom (2686–2125)
2300 BCE		
2200 BCE		
2100 BCE		1st Intermediate Period (2160–2055)
2000 BCE	*2000 BCE the term "Kush" appears in the historical record*	
1900 BCE	**Middle Kerma / C-Group (2000–1685)**	Middle Kingdom (2055–1650)
1800 BCE		
1700 BCE		
1600 BCE	**Classic Kerma / C-Group (1685–1500)**	2nd Intermediate Period (1650–1550)
1500 BCE		
1400 BCE	**Egyptian Occupation (1500–1100)**	New Kingdom (1550–1170)
1300 BCE		
1200 BCE		
1100 BCE		

(Continued on next page)

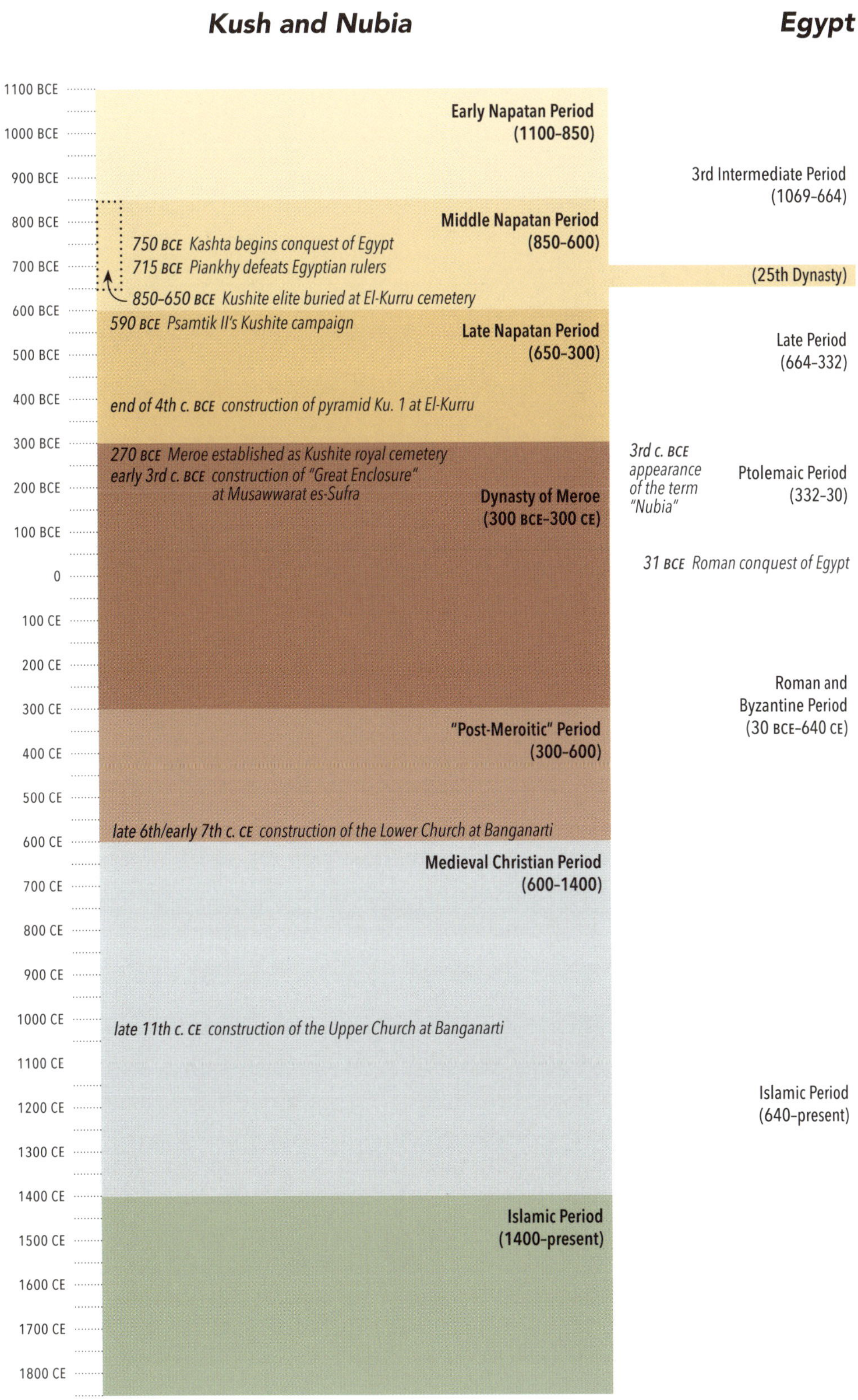
Kush and Nubia
Egypt
1100 BCE
1000 BCE
900 BCE
800 BCE
700 BCE
600 BCE
500 BCE
400 BCE
300 BCE
200 BCE
100 BCE
0
100 CE
200 CE
300 CE
400 CE
500 CE
600 CE
700 CE
800 CE
900 CE
1000 CE
1100 CE
1200 CE
1300 CE
1400 CE
1500 CE
1600 CE
1700 CE
1800 CE
Early Napatan Period (1100–850)
3rd Intermediate Period (1069–664)
Middle Napatan Period (850–600)
750 BCE Kashta begins conquest of Egypt
715 BCE Piankhy defeats Egyptian rulers
850–650 BCE Kushite elite buried at El-Kurru cemetery
(25th Dynasty)
590 BCE Psamtik II's Kushite campaign
Late Napatan Period (650–300)
Late Period (664–332)
end of 4th c. BCE construction of pyramid Ku. 1 at El-Kurru
270 BCE Meroe established as Kushite royal cemetery
early 3rd c. BCE construction of "Great Enclosure" at Musawwarat es-Sufra
Dynasty of Meroe (300 BCE–300 CE)
3rd c. BCE appearance of the term "Nubia"
Ptolemaic Period (332–30)
31 BCE Roman conquest of Egypt
Roman and Byzantine Period (30 BCE–640 CE)
"Post-Meroitic" Period (300–600)
late 6th/early 7th c. CE construction of the Lower Church at Banganarti
Medieval Christian Period (600–1400)
late 11th c. CE construction of the Upper Church at Banganarti
Islamic Period (640–present)
Islamic Period (1400–present)

Abbreviations

a.k.a.	also known as
BCE	Before the Common Era
c.	century
ca.	*circa,* about, approximately
cat.	catalog
CE	Common Era
cf.	*confer,* compare
ed.	edition, editor
e.g.	*exempli gratia,* for example
esp.	especially
fig(s).	figure(s)
fl.	*floruit,* flourished
forth.	forthcoming
ibid.	*ibidem,* in the same place
IKAP	International Kurru Archaeological Project (https://ikap.us/)
n(n).	note(s)
no(s).	number(s)
p(p).	page(s)
pl(s).	plate(s)
vol.	volume(s)

Foreword

Graffiti in Ancient Kush and Medieval Nubia: An Introduction

Geoff Emberling & Suzanne Davis

GRAFFITI — the practice of leaving unsanctioned marks in public built spaces — has ancient roots. Ancient graffiti could be textual or figural,[1] but the range of meanings was arguably similar. Some ancient marks meant "I was here" (unsurprising to modern viewers) and could also have been intended to mark ownership of territory. Other signs could be social commentary. Still others left in sanctified places could be marks of spiritual practice or devotion (perhaps more surprising today).

Graffiti was related in some times and places to traditions of rock art — images made on natural rock formations.[2] These images could be incised, drawn using pigment, or pounded on rock faces.[3]

Graffiti as privately made marks can also be contrasted with official state-sponsored public art, some carved on natural rock to mark territory. Official monuments produce official narratives that make people into subjects of the state,[4] but graffiti retain the power of being marks made by individuals.

An archaeological discovery of a new group of graffiti in an unfinished ancient temple and associated pyramid at El-Kurru in northern Sudan provided the impetus for a broader look at this practice in its ancient cultural setting, both in this volume and in the accompanying exhibition, *Graffiti as Devotion along the Nile: El-Kurru, Sudan* (23 August 2019–29 March 2020, at the Kelsey Museum of Archaeology at the University of Michigan).

The geographic area that is the focus of this volume is the Middle Nile region between Aswan (now in southern Egypt) and Khartoum (the capital of Sudan, located at the confluence of the Blue and White Nile rivers). In ancient times, much of this region was known as Kush, the local, indigenous name for the major political power in the region. Ancient Greek authors referred to the area as Aithiopia and, beginning in the 3rd century BCE, as Nubia. Nubia mostly likely meant "land of the Noba(tae)" and the term was retained by people in medieval times who spoke languages that we now call Nubian. Their descendants still live along the Nile in northern Sudan and southern Egypt.

It is clear that many of the graffiti in ancient Kush and medieval Nubia were marks of devotion rather than idle doodles. They are concentrated in particular places, have

1. Definitions of graffiti differ widely by discipline and region. The definition we propose here is common in archaeology in Sudan. In other areas, graffiti is assumed to be textual, or can apply to texts on natural rock. We do not intend to resolve these differences here, only to highlight the way we use the term.
2. For the Nile Valley, see Paner forthcoming; Fawzi Hassan Bakhiet, this volume.
3. The term "rock art" is widely used but is sometimes avoided because of the implication that "art" in these contexts has the same aims as art in Western tradition. The term "petroglyph" would be most accurate for the images on natural rock formations found in and around the ancient and medieval Nile Valley, but it is not widely used in research on these areas.
4. Harmanşah 2018, p. 50.

a symbolic repertoire that incorporates images related to offerings (offering tables and altars), to the movement associated with pilgrimage (feet, sandals, boats, and horses), and of other religious symbols (sacred animals, for example). Pilgrimage to sacred sites has ancient roots that extend before the origins of Christianity or Islam and are widespread around the world in many different traditions. It represents both a cultural practice and a highly personal encounter with the spiritual world.

Graffiti of course occur in a range of contexts, many of which are not religious or devotional in nature.[5] Yet graffiti as devotion are also a widespread practice. Devotional graffiti are also known in ancient Egypt,[6] and in a wide range of other contexts elsewhere including medieval churches in England.[7] In the Nile Valley alone, travelers through rocky cataract zones and along desert routes left inscriptions in abundance. Graffiti in quarries at Gebel el-Silsila in Egypt and near Meroe in Sudan, some argued to be devotional in nature, have also recently been investigated.[8] Graffiti on the roof of the Khonsu Temple at Karnak, Egypt, mostly dating to the 1st millennium BCE, are shown through texts to have been made by the temple priests and are mostly concerned with practices of worship.[9] And more broadly, devotional graffiti are found across the Mediterranean.[10]

In this volume, chapter one (Emberling) outlines the history of ancient Kush, the culture that dominated the Middle Nile Valley for almost 2,500 years, from before 2000 BCE to after 300 CE. It provides some historical and archaeological context for the graffiti at the site of El-Kurru, which were found in a funerary temple and on the facing stones of a pyramid, both originally constructed in the 4th century BCE. Some graffiti, particularly on the pyramid, were carved later, during the medieval Christian period of Nubian history (ca. 600–1400 CE). Chapter one also includes a brief summary of the research and documentation of figural graffiti at the site of Musawwarat es-Sufra, a pilgrimage center with a large temple complex that was built beginning in the 3rd century BCE.

The second and third essays present the graffiti at El-Kurru in detail. Chapter two (Davis and Emberling) focuses on the funerary temple, while chapter three (Williams) presents graffiti on the pyramid. These chapters on the graffiti themselves — figural images rather than text — are supplemented by a catalog with commentary at the end of the volume.

The fourth chapter (Davis) describes common preservation challenges for ancient, carved graffiti and gives an overview of the work to conserve and document graffiti at El-Kurru. It walks readers through the project's goals, the team's decision-making and, ultimately, the methods chosen to carry out the work.

Chapter five (Pope) presents an analysis of graffiti at another Nubian pilgrimage center, the Temple of Isis at Philae, located on the traditional border between ancient Egypt and ancient Nubia. It explores the relationships, similarities, and differences seen in the graffiti of El-Kurru and Philae and discusses the role of pilgrimage in graffiti from the Meroitic period (ca. 300 BCE–300 CE).

Some of the ideas behind ancient graffiti in Kush, and indeed some of the specific motifs, continued into medieval Christian times. The sixth essay (Żurawski) explores these later images and their meanings, again focusing particularly on their association with pilgrimage and religious devotion.

5. One well-known ancient case is Pompeii; see Milnor 2014; Benefiel and Keegan 2016; Benefiel and Sypniewski 2018; Benefiel, this volume.
6. E.g., Peden 2001; Frood 2013.
7. Champion 2015; Kleinitz 2018.
8. Nilsson 2015.
9. Jacquet-Gordon 2003.
10. For ancient Jewish graffiti, see Stern 2018.

A practice closely connected with inscribing graffiti is the creation of rock art. The widespread practice of hammering, incising, or painting images on rock outcrops or in caves is known throughout the world. Chapter seven (Fawzi Hassan Bakhiet) discusses rock drawings in Nubia with particular emphasis on the region of the 4th and 5th Cataracts just upstream of El-Kurru.

One of the most famous sites of ancient graffiti, Pompeii, is discussed in chapter eight (Benefiel). The graffiti of this Roman town are mostly texts, but images were also an important part of the repertoire. The contexts in which graffiti at Pompeii were inscribed were considerably broader than those of ancient Kush, attesting to greater literacy in the population. Apparent in this chapter, too, is the sense of enjoyment Pompeii's citizens had in making and looking at graffiti. This contribution to the volume makes an important point especially clear: whatever the reason for a graffito's creation — pilgrimage and religious devotion, or excitement about the outcome of a gladiatorial contest — graffiti are social. When carved, they were a responsive means of sharing a particular place and communicating a wide variety of thoughts and ideas. Today, through them, we can gain a small but satisfying glimpse into the daily lives of ancient people.

Finally, a photo essay (Damarany) documents the modern practice in Egypt of painting houses in connection with the hajj, the Muslim pilgrimage to Mecca. Too many centuries intervene between ancient and modern times for us to suggest a continuous tradition, but the images include some striking parallels that illuminate the private representation of religious pilgrimage.

References

Benefiel, Rebecca R., and Peter Keegan, eds.
2016 *Inscriptions in the Private Sphere in the Greco-Roman World.* Brill Studies in Greek and Roman Epigraphy 7. Leiden: Brill.

Benefiel, Rebecca R., and Holly M. Sypniewski
2018 "The Greek Graffiti of Herculaneum." *American Journal of Archaeology* 122 (2): 209–44.

Champion, Matthew
2015 "Medieval Ship Graffiti in English Churches: Interpretation and Function." *The Mariner's Mirror* 101 (3): 343–50.

Frood, Elizabeth
2013 "Egyptian Temple Graffiti and the Gods: Appropriation and Ritualization in Karnak and Luxor." In *Heaven on Earth: Temples, Ritual, and Cosmic Symbolism in the Ancient World,* edited by Deena Ragavan, pp. 285–318. Oriental Institute Seminars 9. Chicago: The Oriental Institute.

Harmanşah, Ömür
2018 "Graffiti or Monument? Inscription of Place at Anatolian Rock Reliefs." In Scribbling through History: Graffiti, Places and People from Antiquity to Modernity, edited by Chloé Ragazzoli, Ömür Harmanşah, Chiara Salvador, and Elizabeth Frood, pp. 49–63. London: Bloomsbury Academic.

Jacquet-Gordon, Helen
2003 *The Temple of Khonsu 3. The Graffiti on the Khonsu Temple Roof at Karnak: A Manifestation of Personal Piety.* Oriental Institute Publications 123. Chicago: The Oriental Institute.

Kleinitz, Cornelia
2018 "Graffiti of the Ancient Sandstone Quarries of Meroe: An Overview." In *The Quarries of Meroe, Sudan,* edited by Brigitte Cech, Thilo Rehren, and Abdelrahman Ali Mohammed,

vol. 1, pp. 93–117. UCL Qatar Series in Archaeology and Cultural Heritage 2. Doha: Hamad Bin Khalifa University.

Milnor, Kristina
2014 *Graffiti and the Literary Landscape in Roman Pompeii.* Oxford: Oxford University Press.

Nilsson, Maria
2015 "Non-Textual Marking Systems at Gebel el-Silsila: From Dynastic Signifiers of Identity to Symbols of Adoration." In *Non-Textual Marking Systems in Ancient Egypt (and Elsewhere),* edited by Julia Budka, Frank Kammerzell, and Sławomir Rzepka, pp. 81–105. Lingua Aegyptia, Studia Monographica 16. Hamburg: Widmaier Verlag.

Paner, Henryk
Forth. "Nubian Rock Art." In *The Oxford Handbook of Nubia,* edited by Geoff Emberling and Bruce B. Williams. New York: Oxford University Press.

Peden, Alexander J.
2001 *The Graffiti of Pharaonic Egypt: Scope and Roles of Informal Writings (c. 3100–332 BC).* Probleme der Ägyptologie 17. Leiden: Brill.

Stern, Karen B.
2018 *Writing on the Wall: Graffiti and the Forgotten Jews of Antiquity.* Princeton: Princeton University Press.

1

Geoff Emberling

A Cultural History of Kush: Politics, Economy, and Ritual Practice

The middle stretch of the Nile River, in what is now northern Sudan and southern Egypt, was the foundation of a series of kingdoms and empires from antiquity into medieval times. One of these was Kush, the earliest empire of sub-Saharan Africa. Arising along the Middle Nile River in what is today northern Sudan, its rulers controlled much of the Nile Valley for more than 2,000 years, from before 2000 BCE to about 300 CE (see the timeline on pp. x–xi). In the final phase of the empire, the Meroitic period (ca. 300 BCE to 300 CE), Kushites developed ritual practices that included pilgrimage to holy sites and graffiti at those sites — carving images and texts into the walls of temples, shrines, and other potent places in the landscape (**FIG. 1.1**). These practices would continue into medieval times.

This chapter outlines the history of Kush, emphasizing its political relations with and adaptation of cultural forms from Egypt. It focuses particularly on the area around El-Kurru, known by its ancient name as the region of Napata (**FIGS. 1.2-3**). It provides a brief overview of Kushite religion and the role of pilgrimage and graffiti in it, and briefly discusses the continuation of these practices in the medieval Christian kingdoms of Nubia.

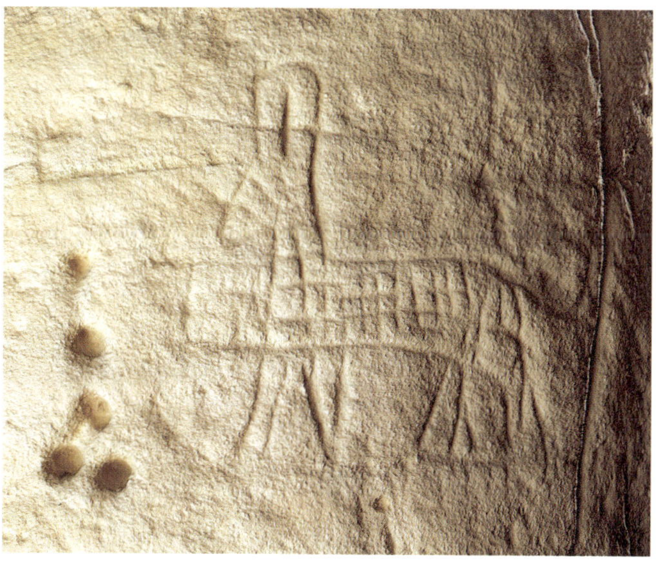

FIGURE 1.1. Graffito of a ram, symbol of the god Amun, on a column in the funerary temple at El-Kurru. Graffito T11. Meroitic period.
RTI: Suzanne Davis and Janelle Batkin-Hall / IKAP, 2016

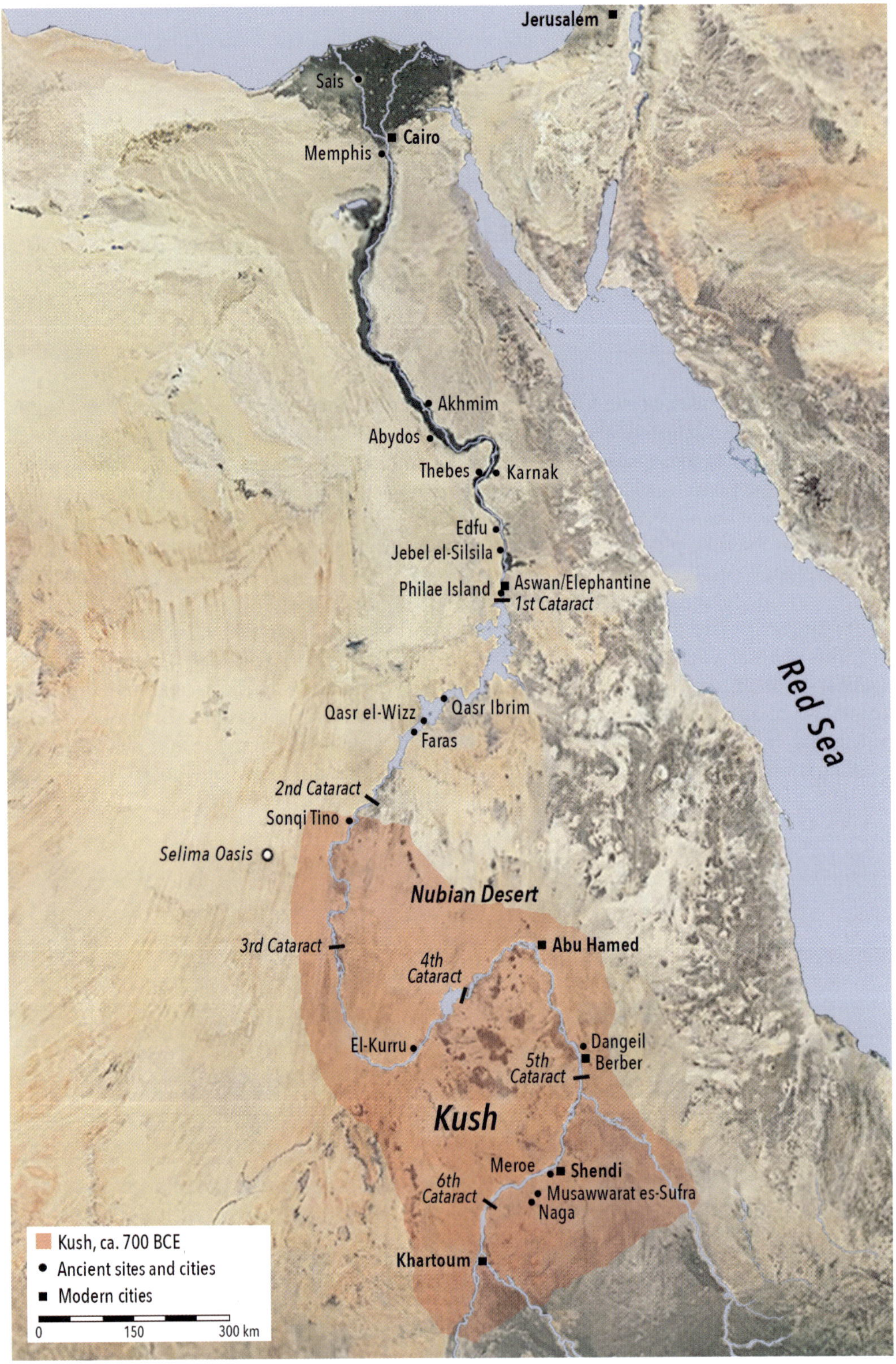

FIGURE 1.2. Map of ancient Egypt and Kush.
Map: Lorene Sterner

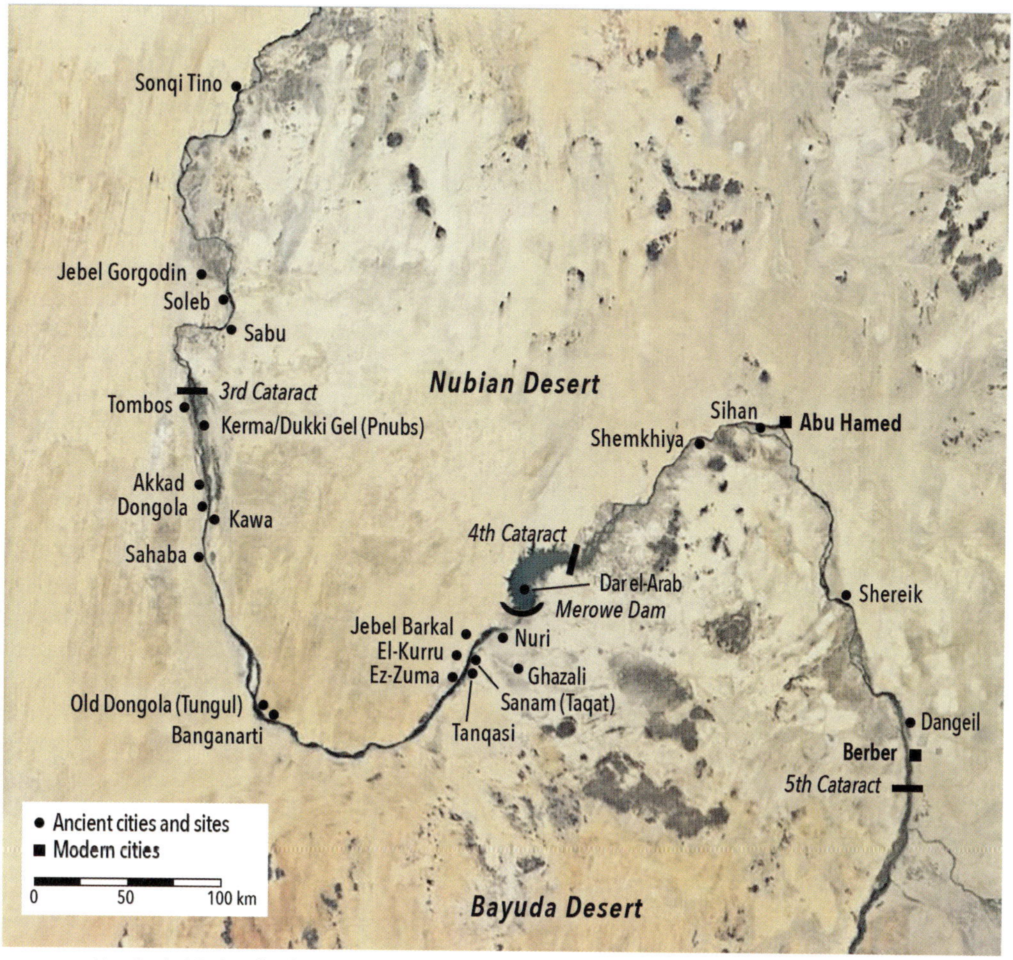

FIGURE 1.3. Heartland of Kush and Nubia.
Map: Lorene Sterner

Early History of Kush (2000–1100 BCE)

The history of Kush is tightly interwoven with that of ancient Egypt, its trade partner and military adversary to the north, with whom Kush shared a distant common origin in groups of cattle pastoralists in the Sahara Desert.[1] As the two cultures developed, however, Kush and Egypt came to be culturally different in many ways. Retaining its reliance on cattle (**FIG. 1.4**), Kush was a partially mobile society whose cities were relatively small, but whose kings appear to have commanded loyalty over large territories. Burial customs in Kush retained their traditional form — pits covered by burial mounds — and broader religious ideas and practices (about which we know frustratingly little) seem to have included worship of a god in the form of a ram with a solar disk, as well as a notion that gods lived in rock outcrops. By contrast, Egypt was a culture of massive monumental constructions (pyramids, temples, and palaces) and large cities, with distinctive religious practices, all recorded in written records.

1. Wengrow et al. 2014.

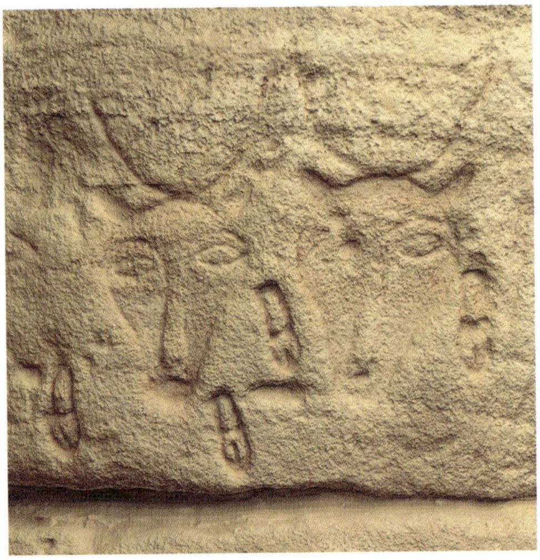

FIGURE 1.4. Cattle with human eyes from funerary temple Ku. 1500 at El-Kurru. Graffito T12. Meroitic period.
RTI: Suzanne Davis and Janelle Batkin-Hall / IKAP, 2016

The first term in Egyptian texts for what would later become Kush is *Ta-sety*, meaning "land of the bow," and archery was a specialty of people living in the Middle Nile region for millennia (**FIG. 1.5**). When the name Kush itself first appeared in the historical record in about 2000 BCE, its capital was located at Kerma, just south of the 3rd Cataract of the Nile.[2] During this time, the environment around Kerma appears to have been more like savannah than the desert it is today, and giraffes (**FIG. 1.6**) and ostriches may have lived in the area.

Kush grew in size and wealth after 2000 BCE and organized major alliances with groups in the deserts and the regions to the south that together conducted raids, looted, and threatened the existence of the Egyptian state during its Second Intermediate Period (1650–1550 BCE). Egypt, however, was ultimately victorious, regaining control of its own territory, quickly conquering Kush (by 1500 BCE) and ruling it as a colony for more than 400 years. During this colonial occupation, Kushites were exposed to Egyptian cultural practices including worship of

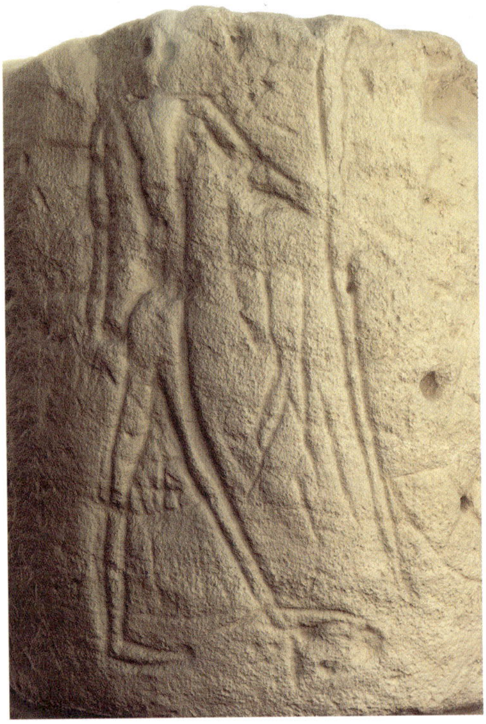

FIGURE 1.5. An archer from funerary temple Ku. 1500 at El-Kurru. Graffito T1. Meroitic period.
RTI: Suzanne Davis and Janelle Batkin-Hall / IKAP, 2016

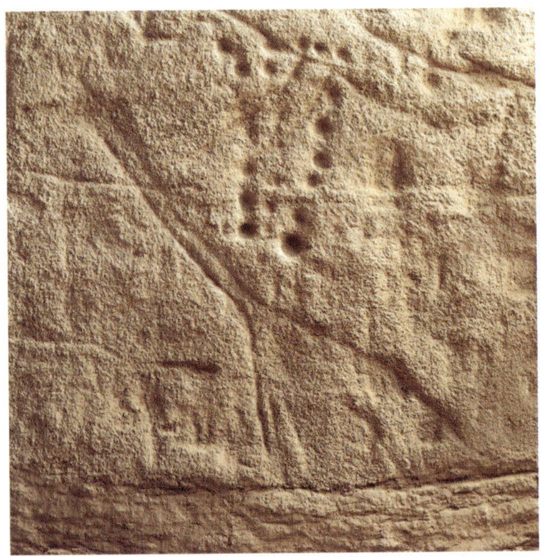

FIGURE 1.6. A giraffe from funerary temple Ku. 1500 at El-Kurru. Graffito T15. Meroitic period.
RTI: Suzanne Davis and Janelle Batkin-Hall / IKAP, 2016

2. Cataracts are stretches of the Nile Valley in which harder volcanic stones create rapids, islands, and even waterfalls that can make boat travel difficult. By convention, there are six numbered cataracts, from the 1st Cataract in the north, at Aswan, to the 6th Cataract in the south, north of Khartoum.

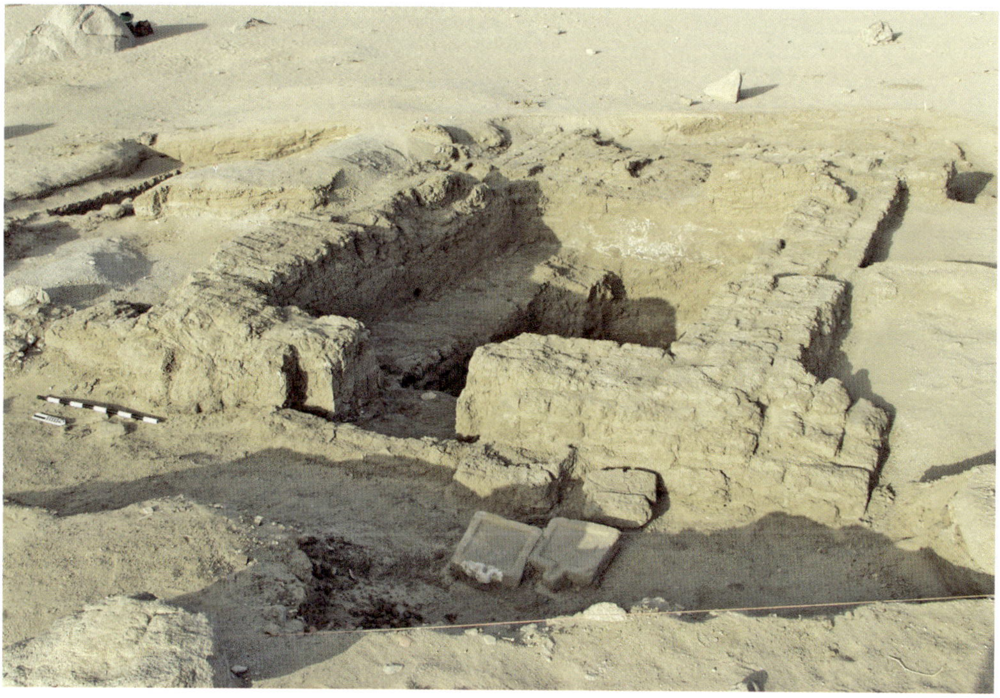

FIGURE 1.7. Two offering tables (middle foreground) outside the remains of the pyramid burial of an Egyptian official at Tombos in Kush, ca. 1400–1350 BCE.
Photo: Stuart Tyson Smith

the god Amun and elite burial under pyramids (which by this time were no longer used for royalty in Egypt), with offering tables placed outside (**FIG. 1.7**). The Egyptian empire collapsed after 1100 BCE and there followed a period of relative decentralization along the Middle Nile.[3]

The Dynasty of Napata (1100–300 BCE)

In the aftermath of the collapse of Egyptian control, a new political dynasty began to rule in Kush. The first archaeological evidence for this appears as a series of burials at a site known today as El-Kurru (**FIGS. 1.8–9**), but the dynasty's name comes from their capital city, Napata, about 10 kilometers upstream from El-Kurru.[4] Although all the burials at El-Kurru were looted in antiquity, enough survives of the tombs that we know elite burials there initially took a traditional Kushite form: pits covered by burial mounds. But the graves of this dynasty changed relatively quickly — from simple burial mounds, to mounds with chapels and enclosure walls, and finally to small pyramids.

This dynasty grew in power and around 750 BCE began to conquer Egypt under King Kashta, whose name means "the Kushite." Kashta's son Piankhy defeated Egyptian rulers in about 715 BCE, as we know from a long and highly personal inscription that describes the conquest and, among other details, expresses his contempt for an Egyptian ruler who

3. With some exceptions, including a ruling queen named Katimala; Darnell 2006.
4. Dunham 1950; Kendall 1999.

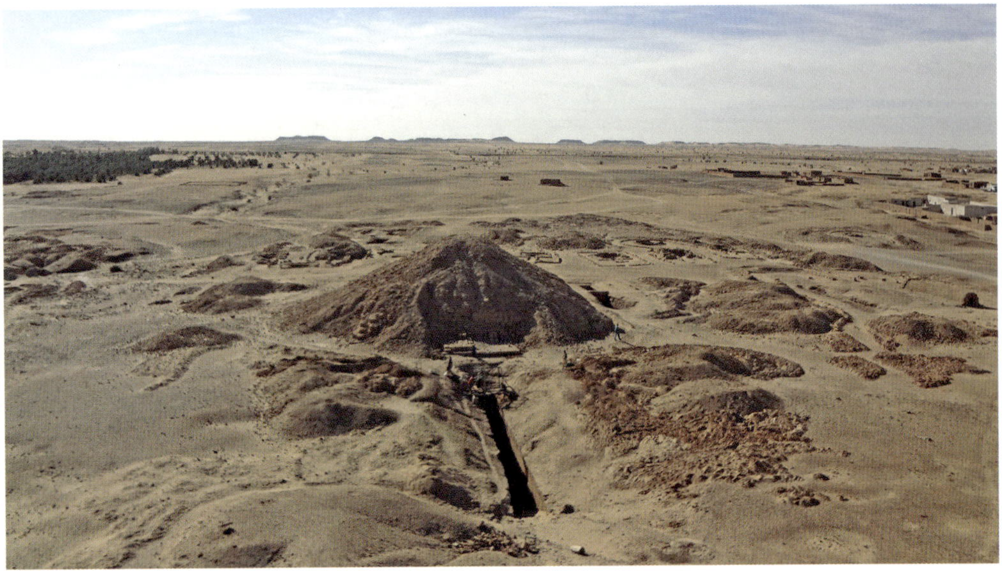

FIGURE 1.8. Kite photograph of the royal cemetery at El-Kurru. Pyramid Ku. 1 is in the center with earlier kings' tombs behind and to the right.
Photo: IKAP, 2014

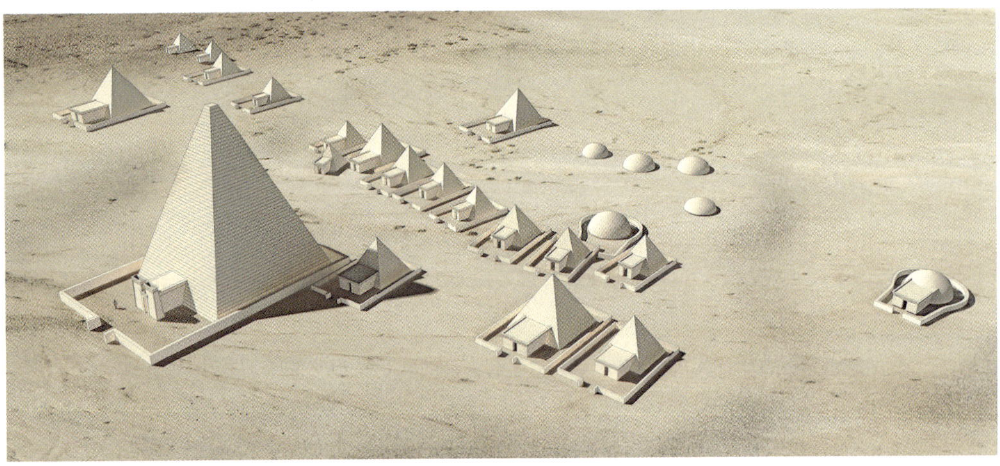

FIGURE 1.9. Reconstruction of the burials at El-Kurru. Ku. 1 is the large pyramid at center left.
Reconstruction: Franck Monnier

did not care properly for his horses (**FIG. 1.10**). Piankhy's successors Shabataqo, Shabaqo,[5] Taharqo,[6] and Tanwetamani lived in Egypt and ruled there until 653 BCE as Egypt's 25th Dynasty (**FIG. 1.11**).

During Kushite rule over Egypt, the burials at El-Kurru became more elaborate, having subterranean burial chambers entered by stairs cut into the bedrock. Originally, these chambers would have been plastered and painted with Egyptian scenes and funerary spells written in Egyptian hieroglyphs, which were adopted for the first time in Kush during this period (**FIG. 1.12**). Queens were also given their own pyramid tombs beginning in the time

5. The regnal order of these rulers has recently been reconsidered. See Bányai 2013 and, more recently, Jurman 2017.
6. Buried not at El-Kurru but at the nearby site of Nuri. His successor Tanwetamani was buried at El-Kurru.

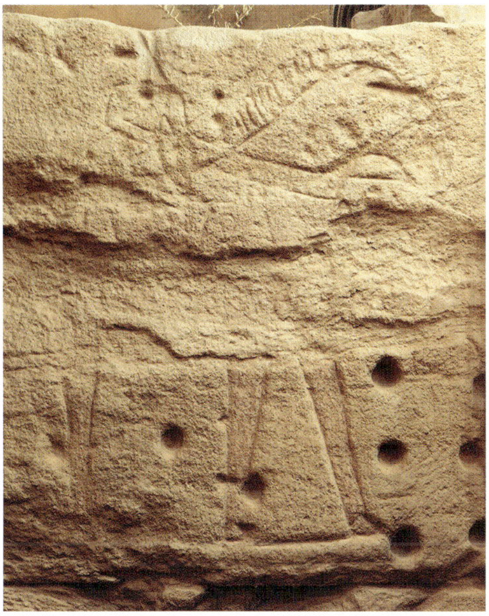

FIGURE 1.10. Graffito of a horse and rider from funerary temple Ku. 1500 at El-Kurru. Graffito T9.
RTI: Suzanne Davis and Janelle Batkin-Hall / IKAP, 2016

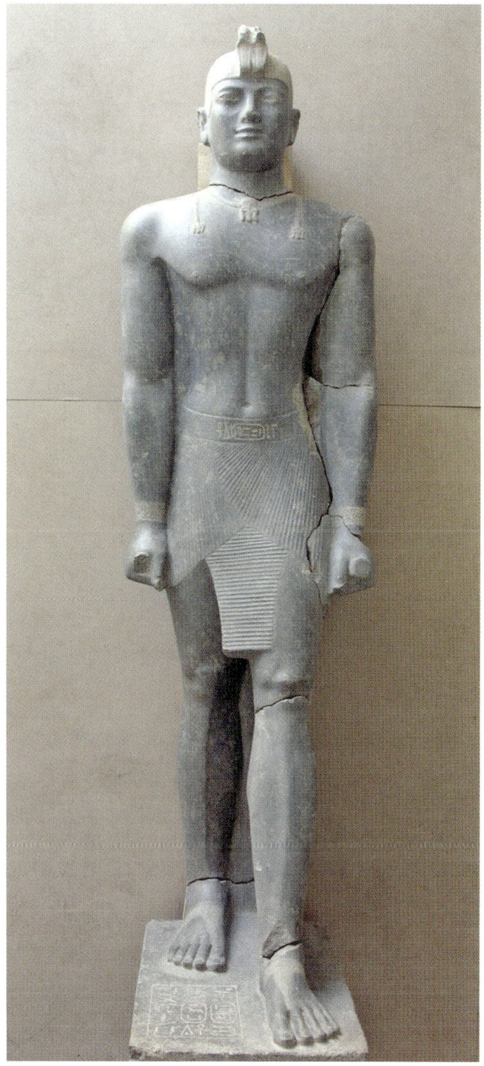

FIGURE 1.11. Life-size royal statue of Tanwetamani found at Dukki Gel, near Kerma. Kerma Museum.
Photo: Swiss, Franco-Sudanese Archaeological Mission of Kerma/Dukki Gel (Sudan)

of Piankhy; one section of the cemetery at El-Kurru was devoted to ruling queens and another area contained the less elaborate burials of secondary royal wives. Each of the last four kings interred at El-Kurru was accompanied by four horses buried at a distance of over 100 meters from their pyramid tombs. The horses were buried standing up and facing away from the tomb, as if ready to carry their king on a final journey.

The development of burial traditions at El-Kurru represents a series of steps toward more Egyptian practices that included pyramid burial, use of Egyptian hieroglyphs to write Egyptian funerary spells in the tombs, and Egyptian techniques of manufacturing elite goods, among others. How and why the Kushites took these steps is not certain. Were they taught by Egyptian priests fleeing unrest in Egypt?[7] Or by priests remaining in the Amun temples left after the collapse of the Egyptian New Kingdom? Or by Kushites who had lived in Egypt?

While we do not yet have answers to these questions, we do know that the Kushite elite were making deliberate choices to adopt these styles and traditions, and we know from their writing that they presented themselves as the inheritors of Egyptian religious practices. This was a part of the justification for their conquest of and rule over Egypt. At the same time, there were aspects of Egyptian culture that they did not adopt. They continued to be

7. Kendall 1999; Morkot 2003.

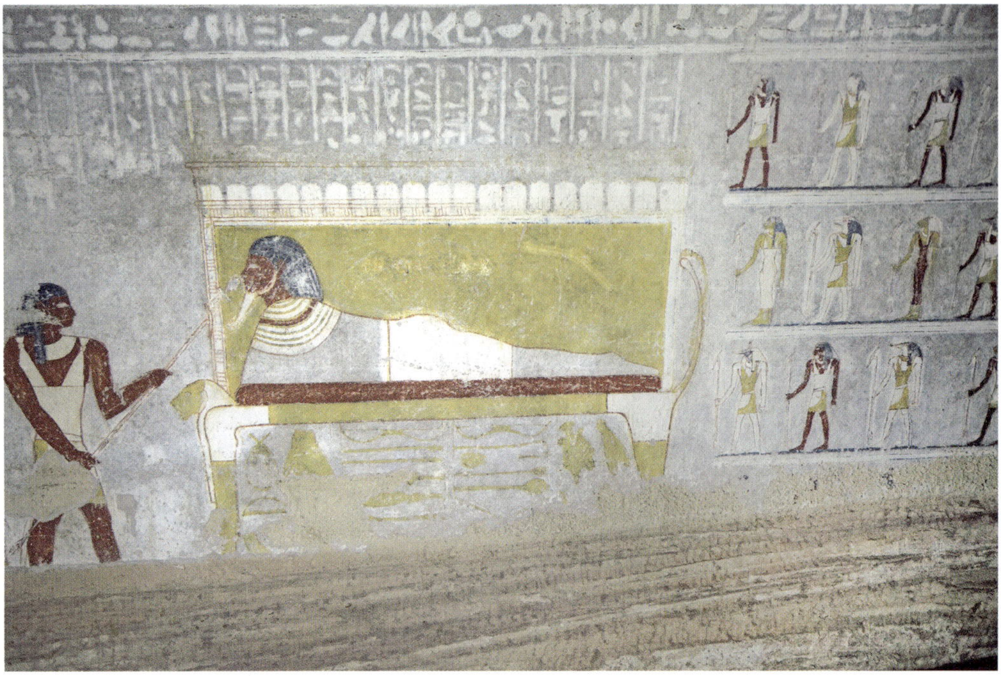

FIGURE 1.12. Painting in the burial chamber of Queen Qalhata at El-Kurru showing the queen's mummy "awakened." Napatan period, ca. 675 BCE.
Photo: Martin Thygesen Jensen

buried on beds rather than being placed on the ground, they adopted the outer trappings of mummification but not the treatment of the body and its organs, and their burials and craft objects sometimes represented distinctly local practices, as in the burial of horses for the kings.

As already noted, the dynasty of rulers that began with the burials at El-Kurru is named for their capital city of Napata, which was at the foot of a massive rock outcrop now called Jebel Barkal (an Arabic name) about 10 kilometers upstream from El-Kurru. While this outcrop was likely the site of an earlier settlement of Kush, the Egyptian conquerors had recognized Barkal as a sacred place because a pinnacle of rock on one side of the outcrop resembles a rearing cobra, the protective uraeus goddess depicted on Egyptian crowns who could spit fire or poison at enemies of the king (**FIG. 1.13**). For this reason, Egyptian occupiers built an outpost at the base of the jebel that incorporated a temple to Amun of Napata within its walls. In Egypt, Amun in human-headed form was the chief god of the Egyptian pantheon during the New Kingdom (ca. 1550–1170 BCE). Amun of Napata appeared as a ram-headed man, perhaps a syncretism with the earlier ram-god of Kush.

The city of Napata was surrounded by other sites that together formed the heartland of the empire of Kush during the Middle Napatan period (ca. 850–600 BCE), and the empire extended far beyond this core. Some 250 kilometers to the southeast of Barkal, along a route through the Bayuda Desert, was the city of Meroe.[8] Meroe during Napatan times was smaller than it would become as the later capital of Kush, but already by this time it was a center

8. Meroe was likely not regularly in connection with Napata by water because of the intervening 4th and 5th Cataracts.

for iron smelting.[9] To the northeast of Napata was the city of Kawa, a very large settlement with a walled temple precinct first built by Egyptian occupiers and later rebuilt and expanded in the reign of the Napatan king Taharqo. It lay 150 kilometers across the desert to the northwest, but the river route (about 250 km long) was more accessible. Inscriptions of the Napatan kings of Kush make clear that a new king upon his coronation had to travel along these routes and be confirmed as king in each of these cities as well as in the city of Kerma/Dukki Gel (ancient Pnubs), farther north.[10]

Napatan occupation also extended north of Kawa to sites including Soleb[11] and Tombos,[12] although the area between the 1st and 2nd Cataracts was only sparsely inhabited.[13] To the south and west, Napatan occupation extended into the deserts, along routes that extended toward Darfur and across the Bayuda Desert to the south.[14]

Napatan rule in Egypt included construction in the great temple of Amun in Karnak and tombs in the broader area of Thebes as well as in Abydos. These were burials of noble Kushite men: men who served as priests of Amun, mayors of the city of Thebes, and at least one general of the army. Royal Kushite women also participated in the occupation of Egypt as God's Wives of Amun, with chapels and tombs in Thebes.[15]

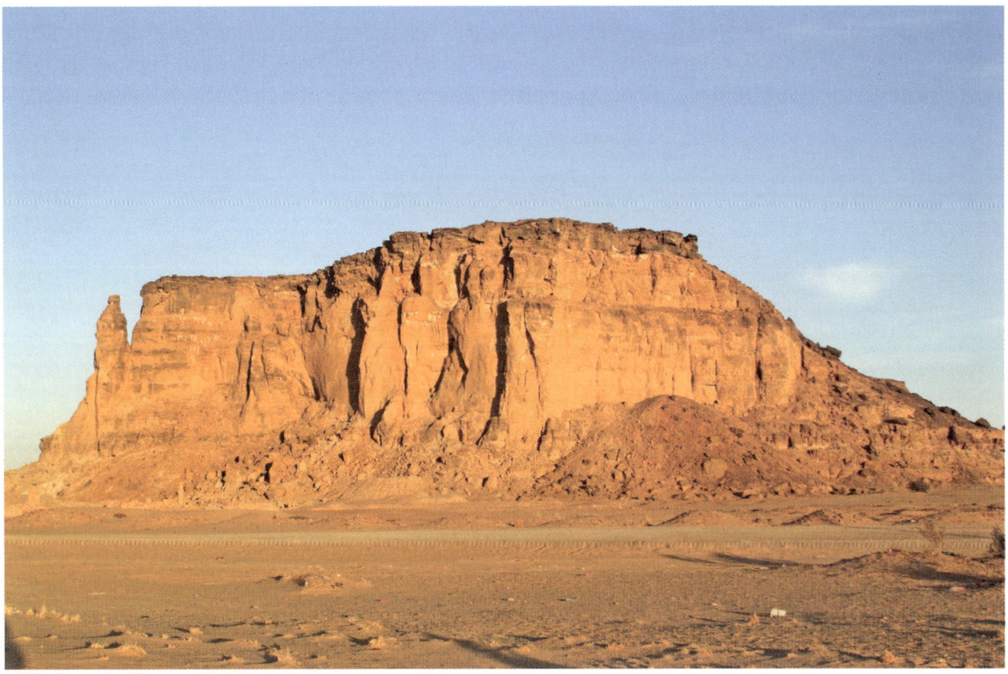

FIGURE 1.13. Profile of Jebel Barkal, the "Pure Mountain." The outcrop that resembles a rearing cobra can be seen at left.
Photo: Geoff Emberling, 2006

9. See Grzymski forthcoming; Humphris forthcoming.
10. For the coronation journey, see Török 1992; for Kerma and Dukki Gel, see Salah 1992 and 2004.
11. Schiff Giorgini 1971.
12. Buzon, Smith, and Simonetti 2016, with references.
13. Williams 1990; Heidorn 1992.
14. Jesse 2014; Kendall 2018.
15. See Budka forthcoming.

Late Napatan Kush (ca. 650–300 BCE)

Kushite rule over Egypt was short-lived, less than a century all told. Although King Taharqo (Tirhakah in the Hebrew Bible) as a general had defended Jerusalem against the armies of Assyria, as king of Egypt and Kush he was defeated by Assyria, his palace in Memphis captured and his court and family deported to Assyria. His successor Tanwetamani (see FIG. 1.11) recaptured Egypt briefly but was again defeated by the Assyrian army, which conquered as far south as Thebes, ending Kushite rule there.[16]

Assyrians supported local Egyptian rulers in establishing the 26th Dynasty in Egypt, but the Assyrian empire was soon after defeated by armies of Babylon and the Medes. The 26th Dynasty survived the defeat and ruled from its capital at Sais in the Nile Delta.[17] During the 26th Dynasty (or "Saite Renaissance"), Kushite control of Egypt was not remembered fondly. King Psamtik II led a campaign into Kush around 590 BCE that destroyed the cities of Dukki Gel, Napata, and Dangeil, including smashing royal statues of kings of Kush that had been set up there.[18] His armies also destroyed the city of Taqat (modern Sanam), leaving burned elephant tusks in the great "Treasury" building there.

After the Egyptian army returned to Egypt, the location of the Kushite capital is uncertain — perhaps it was still at Napata, but perhaps at Meroe.[19]

Archaeological evidence in the region of Napata during this period is mostly limited to pyramid burials at the site of Nuri and royal inscriptions found at Nuri and in the major Amun Temple at Jebel Barkal.[20] But during the late 4th century BCE, royal pyramids were also built at other sites in the region of Napata. Two pyramids (one for a king, one for a queen — Ku. 1 and Ku. 2, respectively) were built at El-Kurru (FIG. 1.14), each seemingly with an associated funerary temple, although neither the pyramids nor the temples seem to have

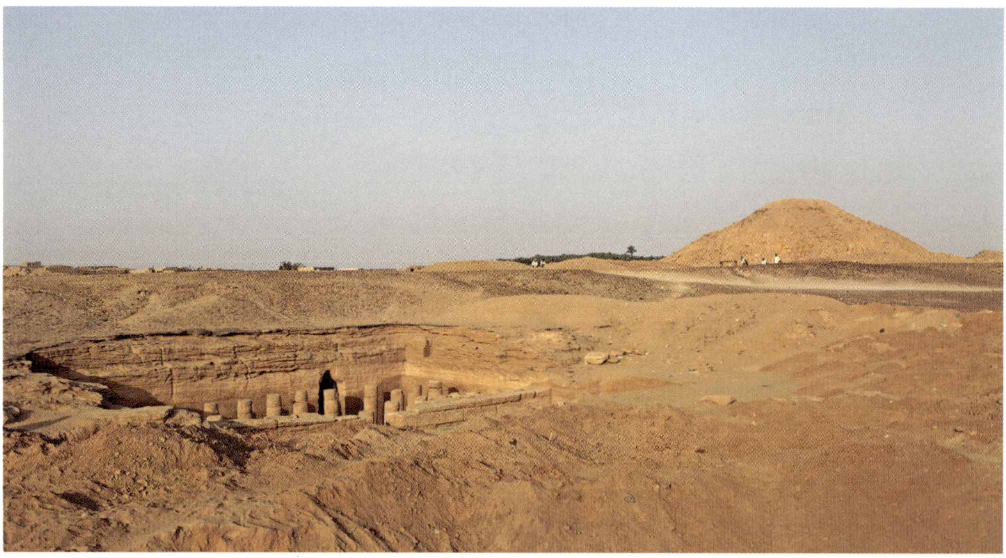

FIGURE 1.14. Pyramid Ku. 1 and associated funerary temple Ku. 1500 at El-Kurru, built in the late 4th century BCE.
Photo: Geoff Emberling / IKAP, 2014

16. For a good summary of these campaigns, see Morkot 2000.
17. See also Dodson 2012.
18. Dunham 1970; Bonnet and Valbelle 2005; Anderson and Ahmed 2009.
19. This argument is summarized in Pope 2014, pp. 5ff.
20. Dunham 1955; Eide et al. 1994, 1996.

been completed.[21] The plan of the larger funerary temple at El-Kurru was unusual;[22] the temple is partly rock-cut and is paralleled only by a nearly identical temple at Nuri,[23] which must have been built at the same time. A king's pyramid surrounded by smaller queens' pyramids was also built during the 4th century at Jebel Barkal — the earliest royal burials at Napata itself.[24] The diversity of burial locations may reflect political competition among branches of the royal family — making appeals of memory to different illustrious ancestors.

The Dynasty of Meroe (ca. 300 BCE–300 CE)

The outcome of this political struggle was eventually a relocation of the royal burial site to the city of Meroe, beginning with the pyramid of King Arkamani in 270 BCE. The greater distance of Meroe from Egypt, and the resulting lesser risk of invasion, may also have been a factor in this move. The city of Meroe, with its great temple to Amun, vast ironworking workshops, and royal pyramid cemetery (**FIG. 1.15**) was undoubtedly the capital of Kush from this point until the final collapse of the empire after 300 CE.[25]

Unlike the regions farther north, in which the Nile Valley was enclosed by desert, the region around Meroe received enough rainfall to allow settlement away from the river, particularly with the use of large reservoirs, called *hafirs*. This period sees the first

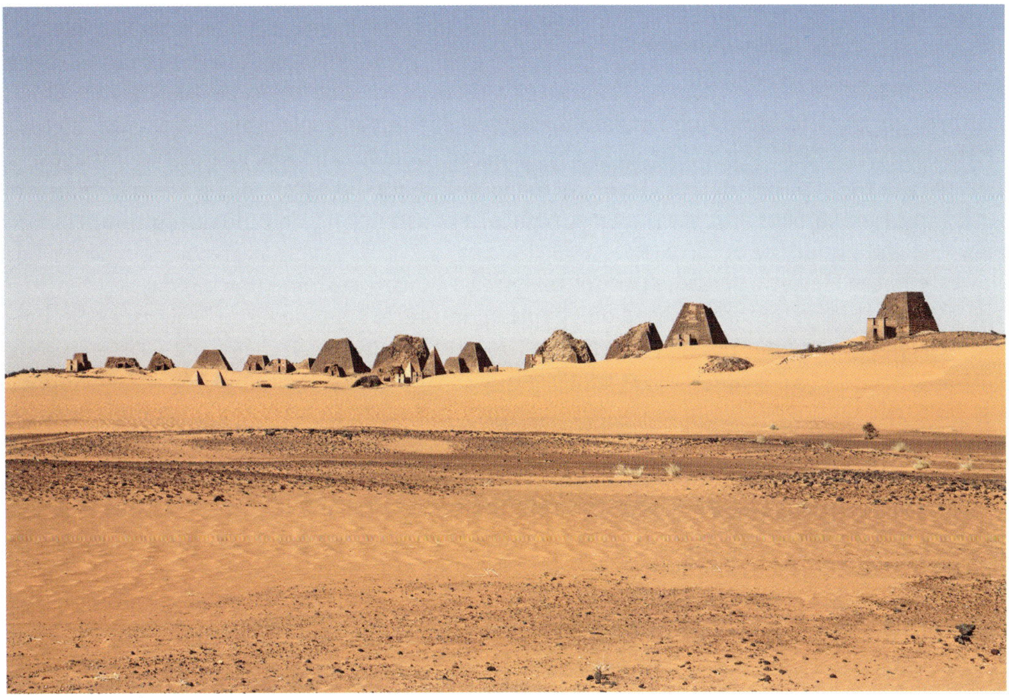

FIGURE 1.15. Royal pyramid cemetery of kings and queens of Kush at Meroe. The tops of the pyramids were removed in the late 19th century in a misguided search for treasure by an Italian doctor, Giuseppe Ferlini.
Photo: Geoff Emberling, 2012

21. Emberling 2015.
22. See Davis and Emberling, this volume.
23. Dunham 1955, pp. 271, 273.
24. Dunham 1957.
25. Grzymski forthcoming.

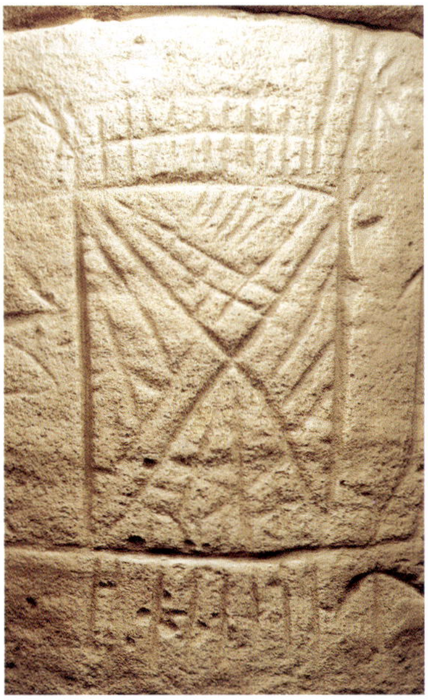

FIGURE 1.16. Graffito of a textile from funerary temple Ku. 1500 at El-Kurru. Graffito T37. Meroitic period.
RTI: Suzanne Davis and Janelle Batkin-Hall / IKAP, 2016

evidence for extensive cultivation in Kush of the African crops of sorghum and millet — in earlier periods, and farther north, wheat and barley introduced from the Middle East had been cultivated. Cultivation of cotton also began in Kush during this "Meroitic" period, perhaps in response to the demand for textiles in Roman Egypt (**FIG. 1.16**).[26]

Early in the Meroitic period, a new and enigmatic structure was built 70 kilometers southwest of Meroe, east of the Nile. This site is now known by its modern name, Musawwarat es-Sufra (see below, pp. 16–20). The main complex at the site, known as the Great Enclosure, had several shrines, some built on terraces and accessed by ramps and corridors. The sculptural decoration of the Great Enclosure includes an elephant sculpture, which has led to a suggestion that it was dedicated to the training of elephants.[27] Other interpretations have included that it was a seasonal royal hunting camp[28] and that it was a pilgrimage center.[29]

With the Roman conquest of Egypt in 31 BCE, Kush began a series of interactions with the borderlands of Egypt. A raid into Egypt recovered a bronze head of the Roman emperor Augustus Caesar, which was brought back to Meroe and buried under the entrance to a temple.[30] A Roman history refers to an attack of a Kushite army led by "a manly woman who had lost one of her eyes."[31] This period was a particularly active one for monumental building in the Meroitic empire, with King Natakamani and his queen Amanitore constructing or renovating temples and palaces throughout the empire (**FIG. 1.17**).

Late in the Meroitic period, Kushites invented a writing system known today as Meroitic. The signs of this system were based on Egyptian uniliteral ("single letter") signs, and scholars are able to sound out the texts, but since the language in which they were written is only partially deciphered, we do not yet understand all these texts. Scholars began to decipher the Meroitic language in the early 20th century but after some initial success the work stalled. In the past fifteen years progress has again been made.[32]

Kushite religion during the Meroitic period continued many practices from Napatan times, most of them adopted from the religion of Egypt. This included maintenance of temples to Egyptian gods including Amun, and the maintenance of an essentially Egyptian set of burial practices that included invocation of Egyptian gods of the underworld, particularly Osiris.[33] They also included use of offering tables (see **FIG. 1.7**) and a new kind of platform, the horned altar (**FIG. 1.18**).

26. Fuller 2014.
27. Welsby 1996, p. 146.
28. Wenig 2001, pp. 76–77.
29. Wolf 2004; Wenig 2013.
30. Opper 2014.
31. Strabo, *Geography* 17.1.53–54; see translation and commentary in Eide et al. 1998, pp. 830–35. Greek and Roman texts referred to Kush as "Aithiopia."
32. Rilly and de Voogt 2012.
33. Yellin 2012.

At the same time, Meroitic religion developed some significantly new practices, perhaps adopted from deities and rituals that have simply not previously been documented by archaeology or history. These included the introduction of worship of the lion-headed god Apedemak, whose temples are found at a range of sites in the heartland of Meroe (including Musawwarat es-Sufra, Naga, and Meroe itself), although not in the region of Napata.

The new ritual practices in the Meroitic period also included pilgrimage as a means of private devotion, which we can recognize in the archaeological record in the form of textual

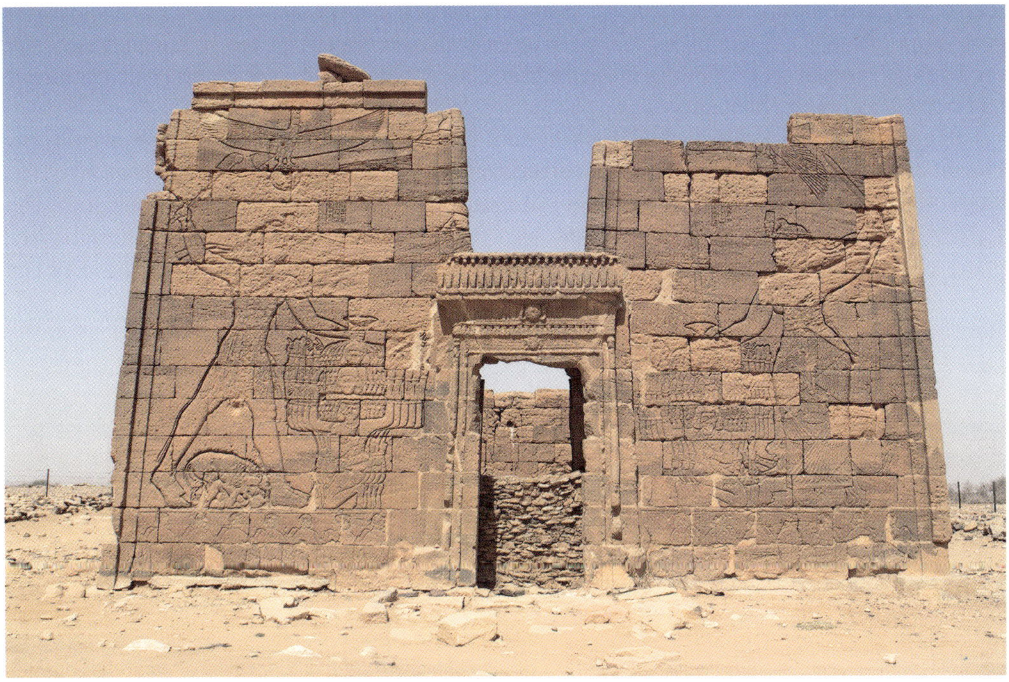

FIGURE 1.17. Natakamani and Amanitore on the pylon of the Apedemak Temple at Naga.
Photo: Raymond Silverman, 2016

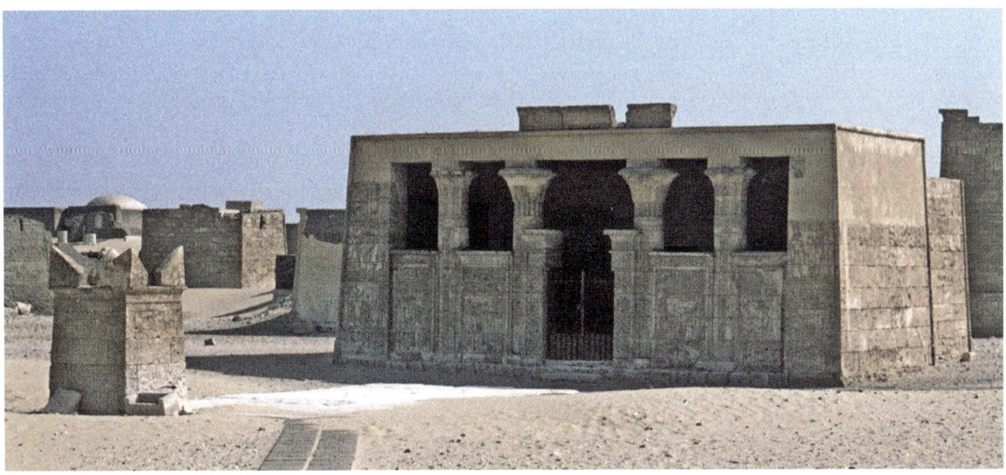

FIGURE 1.18. Reconstructed horned altar outside the mid-4th century BCE tomb of the Egyptian priest Petosiris at Tuna el-Gebel (ancient Hermopolis).
Photo: Bruce Beyer Williams, 1979

and figural graffiti. Two sites in the Meroitic world have long been known as focal points of graffiti: the Great Enclosure at Musawwarat es-Sufra[34] and the Egyptian temple of Isis at Philae, located at the traditional border between Kush and Egypt.[35] More recent publications have outlined a wealth of Meroitic graffiti from a temple at Qasr Ibrim in Lower Nubia.[36]

The Region of Napata during the Medieval (Christian) Period

With the collapse of the Meroitic empire after 300 CE, the Napata region appears to have seen a significant shift in occupation. There are no settlement sites of the "post-Meroitic" period (ca. 300–600 CE) in this region, although two huge concentrations of burial mounds at the sites of Tanqasi and Ez-Zuma indicate that concentration of wealth and political power had not entirely left the region.[37]

Beginning in the 6th century, the kingdom of Makuria with its capital at Tungul (now known as Old Dongola) officially converted to Christianity. It would remain a Christian kingdom for about 900 years. The rise of Makuria coincided with the introduction of the waterwheel to the region of Napata and, as a result, settlements expanded dramatically, many of them growing around churches and fortified strongholds extending along the

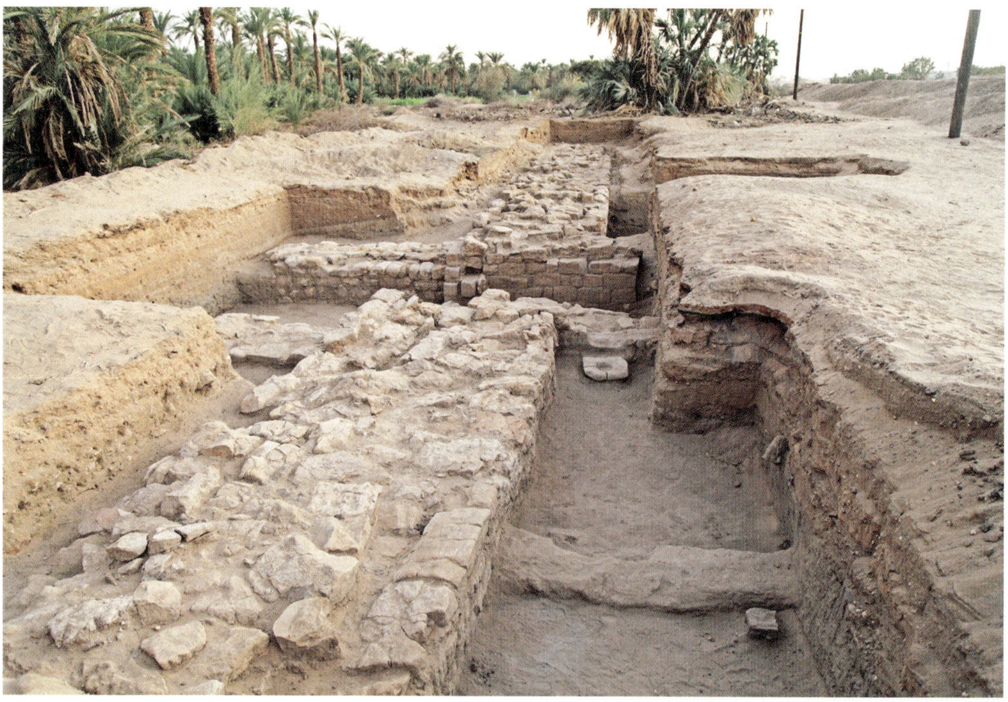

FIGURE 1.19. A portion of the medieval (Christian) town wall at El-Kurru, built with stone taken from the El-Kurru pyramids. *Photo: Geoff Emberling / IKAP, 2014*

34. Kleinitz 2014; see Musawwarat es-Sufra excursus, pp. 16–20 herein.
35. Dijkstra 2012; Cruz-Uribe 2016; Pope, this volume.
36. Wilson 2007.
37. El-Tayeb 2012; El-Tayeb, Skowrońska, and Czyżewska 2016.

Nile. Several monasteries were also established in the region, notably one at Ghazali.[38] The fortifications suggest some level of conflict, most likely between people living in the Nile Valley and nomads in the desert (**FIG. 1.19**).[39]

Pilgrimage continued as a religious practice during Christian times in Nubia[40] and in Egypt. A concentration of Christian textual graffiti near the site of Qasr Ibrim shows that a rock outcrop outside the settlement could be a place of prayer and that graffiti could still be part of that devotional practice.[41]

Conclusion

This historical sketch situates the Meroitic and medieval graffiti found in a partially abandoned funerary temple and nearby pyramid at El-Kurru. It provides the background to the construction of the temple and pyramid, the local historical and political context. It also indicates how the practice of marking graffiti fit within new Meroitic practices of pilgrimage, and how those practices continued in medieval (Christian) times. Many of these subjects are discussed in greater detail in the remainder of this volume.

Significantly, it also demonstrates that major historical trends are visible through graffiti. In the Meroitic graffiti at El-Kurru, we can see syncretic Kushite/Egyptian religious practices in images of the ram of Amun, offering tables, and horned altars. The "land of the bow" is clearly visible in carvings of archers with bows. An interest in cattle, horses, and other animals is apparent, and we see signs of a different, earlier climate in graffiti of giraffes. Boats show that people were moving along the Nile. What we know from the historical and archaeological record, graffiti make visible at a personal, individual level. Graffiti like those at El-Kurru are not inscriptions of language, but they are important parts of the historical record. Graffiti tend to be understudied and underreported in archaeological literature. This volume, we hope, will help make the case that they deserve greater attention.

38. See Obłuski 2018.
39. Żurawski 2013.
40. See, for example, Żurawski 2014; also Żurawski, this volume.
41. Łajtar and van der Vliet 2013.

Excursus: Meroitic Graffiti in the Great Enclosure at Musawwarat es-Sufra

Suzanne Davis

No volume on graffiti in ancient Kush would be complete without at least a brief description of the site of Musawwarat es-Sufra, which is home to a large, enigmatic architectural complex carved with thousands of Meroitic graffiti (**FIG. E.1**). These graffiti include Meroitic inscriptions, animals (including animals not seen at El-Kurru, such as lions, elephants, and baboons), people, gods, mythical creatures, and religious objects.[1]

Unlike El-Kurru, Musawwarat es-Sufra is located outside the Nile Valley, about 25 kilometers east of the river. The site's location is dramatic; its impressive sandstone buildings are situated in a wide basin and appear to be framed by surrounding, higher rock outcrops. The site seems to have been a major religious center with at least seven buildings interpreted as temples, three of which are located within an architectural complex known as the Great Enclosure.

Measuring about 55,000 square meters in area, the Great Enclosure is a huge and confusing complex of buildings. It is built on a series of raised

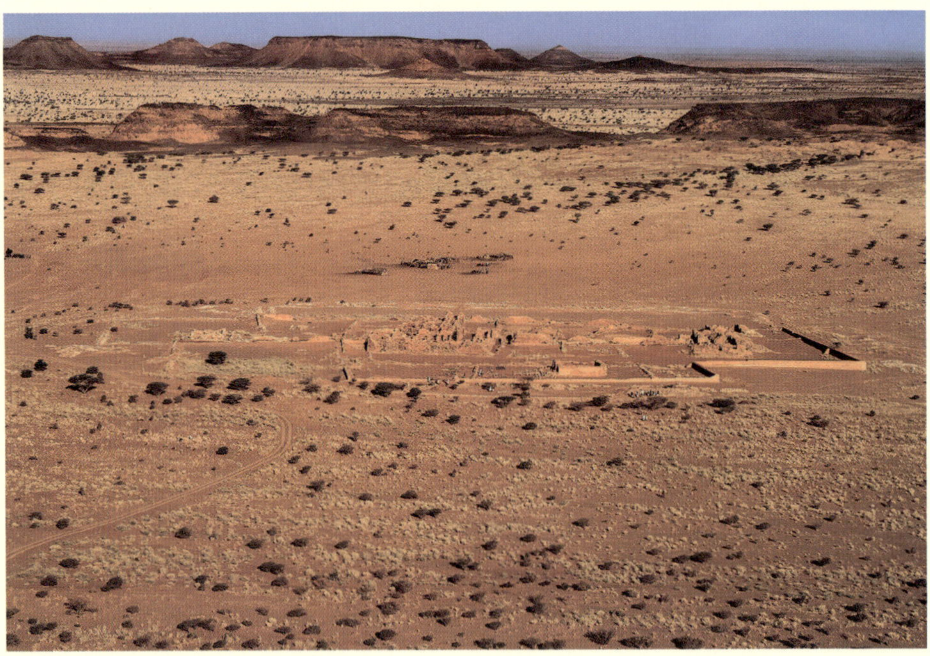

FIGURE E.1. Aerial view of Musawwarat es-Sufra.
Photo: Thomas Scheibner, 2008

1. Kleinitz 2014.

Graffiti at Musawwarat es-Sufra

terraces and, in addition to the three temples, it contains chapels and other small buildings, open plazas, and courtyards with gardens. Many of the structures within the complex are linked by corridors and ramps. The gardens have been identified by the discovery of planting pits containing Nile silt, and because they have irrigation systems utilizing water supplied from large reservoirs or rainfall catch-basins known as *hafirs*.[2] The largest known *hafir* in Sudan is located at Musawwarat es-Sufra.

Musawwarat es-Sufra was first explored by the Egyptologist Richard Lepsius in the mid-19th century, and the site was excavated in the 1960s by the archaeologist Fritz Hintze from Humboldt University in Berlin. A team from Humboldt began work at the site again in the mid-1990s, and since then it has been the subject of a regular program of excavation-based research. These excavations have documented various aspects of the Great Enclosure's construction and possible functions. Construction appears to have begun as early as the Napatan period (ca. 1100–300 BCE),[3] but the majority of buildings now visible were first constructed during the Meroitic period (ca. 300 BCE–300 CE).[4] The Great Enclosure also seems to have undergone multiple "renewal" or rebuilding phases, some of which involved demolition of existing structures. Ideas about the site's function have varied and different kinds of evidence, such as pottery workshops, have been uncovered. But archaeologists generally agree that the site's primary purpose was as a religious or cult center, and it seems to have been the focus of religious pilgrimage. Both Egyptian and local Kushite gods are represented at Musawwarat.[5]

Musawwarat es-Sufra's graffiti have been of great interest to archaeologists working at the site. Because many of the graffiti date to the same time period as the Great Enclosure, selected subsets have been used to support various theories about the complex's function. For example, graffiti of elephants have been used to suggest that the Great Enclosure was a training center for elephants,[6] and erotic imagery to argue that the Great Enclosure was linked to fertility rituals for the Kushite king and queen.[7] More recent research, however, notes that these arguments ignore the huge variety of graffiti at the site.[8]

Several attempts have been made to systematically document Musawwarat's graffiti. In the 1960s, about 700 graffiti in the Great Enclosure were photographed. In the 1990s, another 2,500 were photographed.[9] Little information about the graffiti was published as part of these campaigns, however. The most recent documentation effort, the Musawwarat Graffiti Project, began in 2007 and has proceeded under the direction of Cornelia Kleinitz. It has resulted in at least two publications as well as, significantly, an online graffiti archive that aims to make complete data sets about the

2. Karberg 2010; Näser 2010; Wenig 2008.
3. Wenig 2001.
4. Näser 2011; Karberg 2010.
5. Edwards 2004, pp. 150–53.
6. Shinnie 1967.
7. Wenig 2008.
8. Kleinitz 2014.
9. Wolf 1999.

Graffiti at Musawwarat es-Sufra

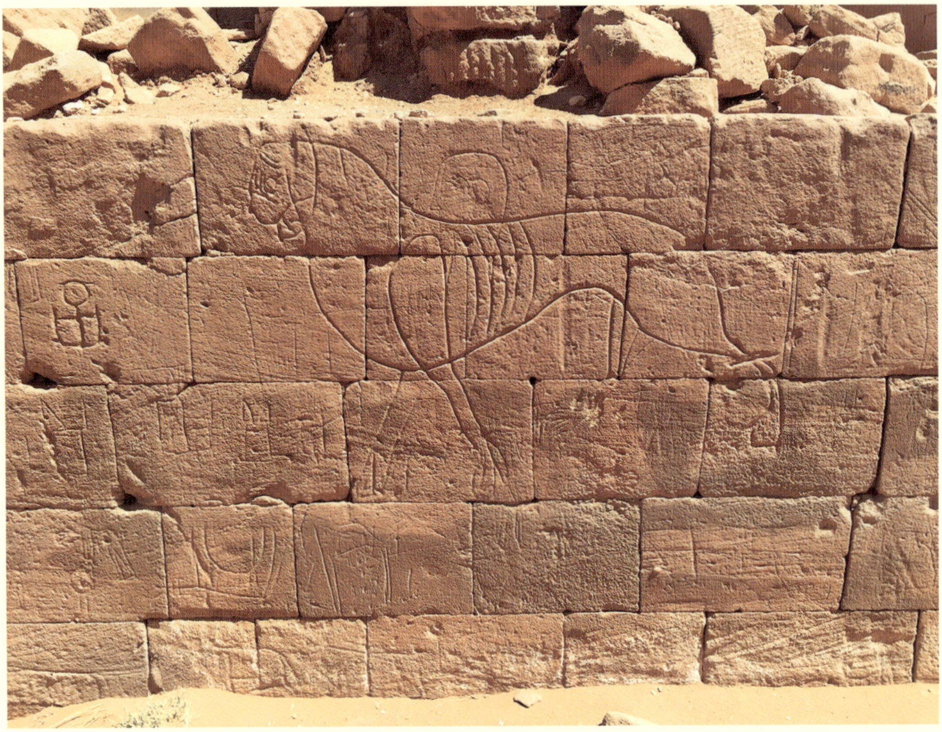

FIGURE E.2. Lion graffito from Musawwarat es-Sufra.
Photo: Suzanne Davis, 2016

site's graffiti publicly available.[10] Masons' marks, which relate to the Great Enclosure's original construction, are not categorized as graffiti but have also been the focus of recent study.[11]

Kleinitz published a preliminary overview of her work in 2014, and this publication is important not only for what it reveals about Musawwarat's graffiti but also for its in-depth discussion of documentation methodology. As at El-Kurru,[12] Reflectance Transformation Imaging (RTI) proved to be the most useful technique for documenting individual graffiti. RTI is a computational photographic technique that records surface texture with a high degree of accuracy. But at Musawwarat, the team added additional layers of documentation. Blocks were drawn and described, and photographs were taken to document the graffiti in the context of entire walls, individual blocks, and groups of graffiti. To record individual graffiti, photographs were taken with strong raking or side light as a supplement to the RTI.[13]

10. Kleinitz 2013, 2014; Musawwarat Graffiti Archive, http://musawwaratgraffiti.mpiwg-berlin.mpg.de/, accessed 9 April 2019.
11. Karberg 2010.
12. See Davis, this volume.
13. Kleinitz 2014.

Graffiti at Musawwarat es-Sufra

For descriptive purposes, the project classifies each graffito into one of three categories: inscription, pictorial, or "markings." The latter category describes the same kinds of cupules observed at El-Kurru (graffiti T53–T55); places where the stone was carved away or gouged out, perhaps to produce powder, but not to create a linear design. The inscriptions include Meroitic cursive script, Latin, Old Nubian, Greek, and Arabic, as well as inscriptions from explorers and visitors during the past 200 years. The pictorial graffiti cover a huge range of subjects: geometric symbols, religious symbols, architectural features, objects, plants, animals, hybrid creatures, and humans. As at El-Kurru, the "markings" or cupules at Musawwarat are sometimes grouped and other times carved singly.[14]

A wide variety occurs within the pictorial graffiti categories. The humans depicted are primarily men, but some of these graffiti are detailed enough to identify the figures as priests or other elite members of society, based on their hairstyles, jewelry, clothing, and other attributes. Animals include dogs, horses, cattle, and camels, but also lions, baboons, elephants, and giraffes. There are also religious animals like the double-crowned ram of Amun and the winged lion of Apedemak. Hybrid creatures include sphinxes, and religious motifs include horned altars, barks, and symbols like the winged sun disk.[15]

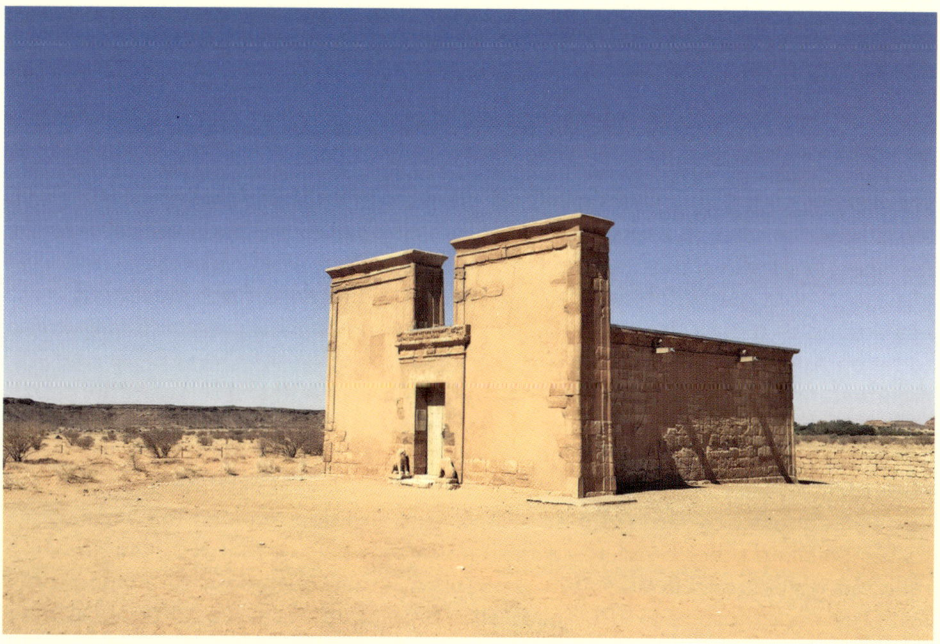

FIGURE E.3. The Lion Temple at Musawwarat es-Sufra.
Photo: Suzanne Davis, 2016

14. Ibid.
15. Ibid.

Graffiti at Musawwarat es-Sufra

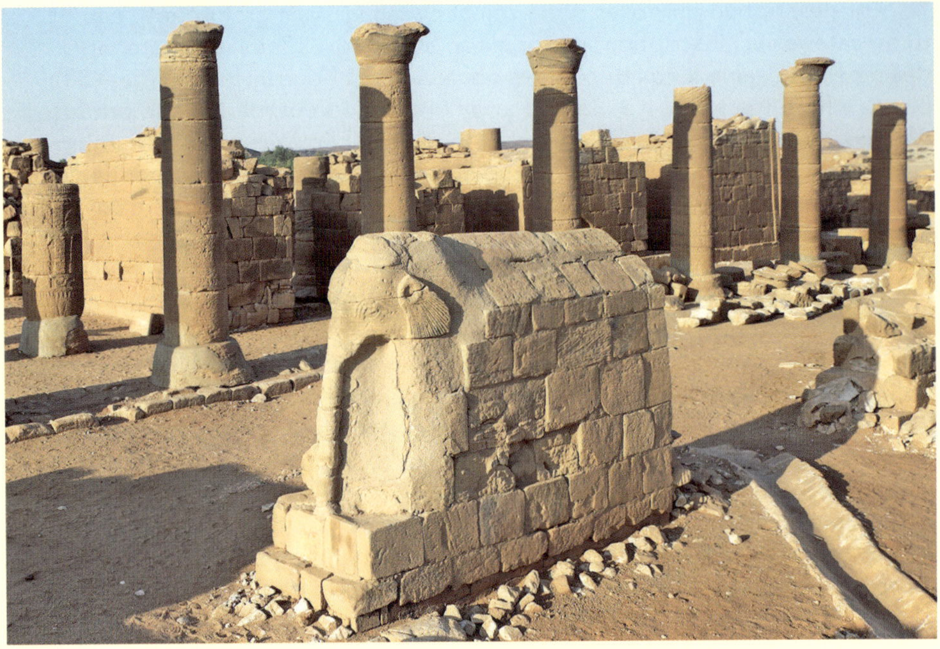

FIGURE E.4. Elephant sculpture on the Central Terrace of the Great Enclosure at Musawwarat es-Sufra.
Photo: Claudia Näser, 2015

Analysis of the graffiti and where they appear on site has not yet been fully published. Kleinitz does, however, note several important observations. Based on their varying states of preservation, graffiti seem to have been carved over multiple centuries, and the earliest may date to the 3rd century BCE. It also seems clear that the carving of graffiti did not impede the function of the site's structures. Temples at Musawwarat are typically carved on exterior, not interior, surfaces, suggesting that the interiors were less accessible to pilgrims. Kleinitz also notes that graffiti of lions (**FIG. E.2**) make logical sense since Musawwarat has a temple to the Kushite lion-headed god Apedemak (**FIG. E.3**) and is thought to be an Apedemak cult center. She also observes that the Great Enclosure's architectural decoration included elephants (**FIG. E.4**), and she relates graffiti of elephants and giraffes to the larger world of Meroitic religious imagery.[16]

In summary, the graffiti add layers of information to existing knowledge about Musawwarat es-Sufra and its function. They reveal that the site was visited frequently by large numbers of visitors and that marking the walls of its temples and other buildings was an important part of that visit. Images of religious objects and figures are common, as is religious and natural imagery from the wider Kushite world. The graffiti project at Musawwarat demonstrates the value of studying and publishing graffiti. Graffiti form an important dataset for archaeological discovery, and this can be especially useful for interpreting enigmatic sites and structures like those of the Great Enclosure at Musawwarat.

16. Ibid.

References

Anderson, Julie R., and Salah eldin Mohamed Ahmed
2009 "What Are These Doing Here above the Fifth Cataract?!! Napatan Royal Statues at Dangeil." *Sudan & Nubia* 13: 78–86.

Bányai, Michael
2013 "Ein Vorschlag zur Chronologie der 25. Dynastie in Ägypten." *Journal of Egyptian History* 6 (1): 46–129.

Bonnet, Charles, and Dominique Valbelle
2005 *Des pharaons venus d'Afrique: la cachette de Kerma.* Paris: Citadelles & Mazenod.

Budka, Julia
Forth. "Nubians in Egypt during the 25th Dynasty." In *The Oxford Handbook of Nubia*, edited by Geoff Emberling and Bruce B. Williams. New York: Oxford University Press.

Buzon, Michele R., Stuart Tyson Smith, and Antonio Simonetti
2016 "Entanglement and the Formation of the Ancient Nubian Napatan State." *American Anthropologist* 118 (2): 284–300.

Cruz-Uribe, Eugene
2016 *The Demotic Graffiti from the Temple of Isis on Philae Island.* Material and Visual Culture of Ancient Egypt 3. Atlanta: Lockwood Press.

Darnell, John C.
2006 *The Inscription of Queen Katimala at Semna: Textual Evidence for the Origins of the Napatan State.* Yale Egyptological Studies 7. New Haven: Yale University Press.

Dijkstra, Jitse H. F.
2012 *Syene I. The Figural and Textual Graffiti from the Temple of Isis at Aswan.* Beiträge zur Ägyptischen Bauforschung und Altertumskunde 18. Mainz: Philipp von Zabern.

Dodson, Aidan
2012 *Afterglow of Empire: Egypt from the Fall of the New Kingdom to the Saite Renaissance.* Cairo: American University in Cairo Press.

Dunham, Dows
1950 *El Kurru.* The Royal Cemeteries of Kush 1. Cambridge, MA: Harvard University Press.
1955 *Nuri.* The Royal Cemeteries of Kush 2. Boston: Museum of Fine Arts.
1957 *Royal Tombs at Meroë and Barkal.* The Royal Cemeteries of Kush 4. Boston: Museum of Fine Arts.
1970 *The Barkal Temples.* Boston: Museum of Fine Arts.

Edwards, David N.
2004 *The Nubian Past: An Archaeology of the Sudan.* London: Routledge.

Eide, Tormod, Tomas Hägg, Richard Holton Pierce, and László Török, eds.
1994 *Fontes Historiae Nubiorum: Textual Sources for the History of the Middle Nile Region between the Eighth Century BC and the Sixth Century AD,* Volume 1: *From the Eighth to the Mid-Fifth Century BC.* Bergen: Department of Classics, University of Bergen.
1996 *Fontes Historiae Nubiorum: Textual Sources for the History of the Middle Nile Region between the Eighth Century BC and the Sixth Century AD,* Volume 2: *From the Mid-Fifth to the First Century BC.* Bergen: Department of Classics, University of Bergen.
1998 *Fontes Historiae Nubiorum: Textual Sources for the History of the Middle Nile Region between the Eighth Century BC and the Sixth Century AD,* Volume 3: *From the First to the Sixth Century AD.* Bergen: Department of Classics, University of Bergen.

El-Tayeb, Mahmoud
2012 *Funerary Traditions in Nubian Early Makuria.* African Reports 9. Gdańsk: Gdańsk Archaeological Museum.

El-Tayeb, Mahmoud, Ewa Skowrońska, and Ewa Czyżewska
2016 "Early Makuria Research Project: The Results of Three Seasons of Excavation at El-Zuma Cemetery, 2013, 2014 and 2015." *Sudan & Nubia* 20: 110–26.

Emberling, Geoff
2015 "A Mortuary Temple at El-Kurru." *Sudan & Nubia* 19: 65–67.

Fuller, Dorian Q.
2014 "Agricultural Innovation and State Collapse in Meroitic Nubia: The Impact of the Savannah Package." In *Archaeology of African Plant Use*, edited by Chris J. Stevens, Sam Nixon, Mary Anne Murray, and Dorian Q. Fuller, pp. 165–77. Walnut Creek: Left Coast Press.

Grzymski, Krzysztof
Forth. "The City of Meroe." In *The Oxford Handbook of Nubia*, edited by Geoff Emberling and Bruce B. Williams. New York: Oxford University Press.

Heidorn, Lisa
1992 "The Fortress of Dorginarti and Lower Nubia during the Seventh to Fifth Centuries BC." Doctoral dissertation, Chicago: Department of Near Eastern Languages and Civilizations, University of Chicago.

Humphris, Jane
Forth. "Iron Production at Meroe." In *The Oxford Handbook of Nubia*, edited by Geoff Emberling and Bruce B. Williams. New York: Oxford University Press.

Jesse, Friederike
2014 "On the Borders of Kushite Power: The Gala Abu Ahmed Fortress in Lower Wadi Howar, Northern Sudan." In *The Fourth Cataract and Beyond: Proceedings of the 12th International Conference for Nubian Studies*, edited by Julie R. Anderson and Derek A. Welsby, pp. 545–55. British Museum Publications on Egypt and Sudan 1. Leuven: Peeters.

Jurman, Claus
2017 "The Order of the Kushite Kings According to Sources from the Eastern Desert and Thebes. Or: Shabataka Was Here First!" *Journal of Egyptian History* 10 (2): 124–51.

Karberg, Tim
2010 "Musawwarat el-Sufra: A Meroitic Terrace Temple in a Nubian Perspective." In *Between the Cataracts: Proceedings of the 11th Conference for Nubian Studies, Warsaw University, 27 August–2 September 2006.* Part 2, Fascicle 2: *Session Papers*, edited by Włodzimierz Godlewski and Adam Łajtar, pp. 571–75. Polish Archaeology in the Mediterranean Supplement Series, 2.2/2. Warsaw: University of Warsaw Press.

Kendall, Timothy
1999 "The Origin of the Napatan State: El Kurru and the Evidence for Royal Ancestors." In *Studien zum Antiken Sudan*, edited by Steffen Wenig, pp. 3–117. Meroitica 15. Wiesbaden: Harrassowitz.
2018 "Archaeological Explorations in the Bayuda Desert: Al-Meragh and the Wadi Muqaddam between Tamtam and Korti (1999–2000)." In *Bayuda Studies: Proceedings of the First International Conference on the Archaeology of the Bayuda Desert in Sudan*, edited by Angelika Lohwasser, Tim Karberg, and Johannes Auenmüller, pp. 359–422. Meroitica 27. Wiesbaden: Harrassowitz.

Kleinitz, Cornelia
2013 "Die Sekundärbilder und -inschriften der Großen Anlage von Musawwarat es Sufra und das 'Musawwarat Graffiti Project.'" In *Die Kulturen Nubiens, ein afrikanisches Vermächtnis*, edited by Steffen Wenig and Karola Zibelius-Chen, pp. 399–413. Dettelbach: J. H. Röll.
2014 "The Graffiti of Musawwarat Es-Sufra: Current Research on Historic Inscriptions, Images and Markings at the Great Enclosure." *Sudan & Nubia* 18: 93–103.

Łajtar, Adam, and Jacques van der Vliet
2013 "A View from a Hill: A First Presentation of the Rock Graffiti of 'Gebel Maktub.'" In *Qasr Ibrim, between Egypt and Africa: Studies in Cultural Exchange*, edited by Jacques van der Vliet and J. L. Hagen, pp. 157–66. Egyptologische Uitgaven 26. Leuven: Peeters.

Morkot, Robert G.
2000 *The Black Pharaohs: Egypt's Nubian Rulers.* London: Rubicon.

2003 "On the Priestly Origin of the Napatan Kings: The Adaptation, Demise and Resurrection of Ideas in Writing Nubian History." In *Ancient Egypt in Africa,* edited by David B. O'Connor and Andrew Reid, pp. 151–68. London: UCL Press.

Näser, Claudia

2010 "The Great *Hafir* at Musawwarat Es-Sufra, Fieldwork on the Archaeological Mission of Humboldt University Berlin in 2005 and 2006." In *Between the Cataracts: Proceedings of the 11th International Conference on Nubian Studies, Warsaw University, 27 August–2 September 2006.* Part 2, Fascicle 1: *Session Papers,* edited by Włodzimierz Godlewski and Adam Łajtar, pp. 39–46. Polish Archaeology in the Mediterranean Supplement Series, 2.2/1. Warsaw: University of Warsaw Press.

2011 "Early Musawwarat." In *La pioche et la plume: autour du Soudan, du Liban et de la Jordanie; hommages archéologiques à Patrice Lenoble,* edited by Vincen Rondot, Frédéric Alpi, and François Villeneuve, pp. 317–38. Paris: Presses de l'Université Paris-Sorbonne.

Obłuski, Artur

2018 "El-Ghazali — a Royal Monastery in Northern Sudan?" *Sudan & Nubia* 22: 155–66.

Opper, Thorsten

2014 *The Meroë Head of Augustus.* London: The British Museum.

Pope, Jeremy

2014 *The Double Kingdom under Taharqo: Studies in the History of Kush and Egypt, c. 690–664 BC.* Culture and History of the Ancient Near East 69. Leiden: Brill.

Rilly, Claude, and Alex de Voogt

2012 *The Meroitic Language and Writing System.* Cambridge: Cambridge University Press.

Salah el-din Mohamed Ahmed

1992 *L'agglomération napatéenne de Kerma: enquête archéologique et ethnographique en milieu urbain.* Paris: Éditions Recherche sur les civilisations.

2004 "A Meroitic Temple at the Site of Doukki Gel (Kerma): A Preliminary Report (Seasons 96–97, 97–98 and 98–99)." In *Nubian Studies, 1998: Proceedings of the Ninth Conference of the International Society of Nubian Studies, August 21–26, 1998, Boston, Massachusetts,* edited by Timothy Kendall, pp. 205–13. Boston: Department of African-American Studies, Northeastern University.

Schiff Giorgini, Michela

1971 *Soleb 2. Les nécropoles.* Florence: Sansoni.

Shinnie, P. L.

1967 *Meroe: A Civilization of the Sudan.* Ancient Peoples and Places 55. New York: F. A. Praeger.

Török, László

1992 "Ambulatory Kingship and Settlement History: A Study on the Contribution of Archaeology to Meroitic History." In *Études nubiennes: conférence de Genève. Actes du VIIe Congrès international d'études nubiennes, 3–8 Septembre 1990,* edited by Charles Bonnet, vol. 1, pp. 111–26. Geneva: Société d'études nubiennes.

Welsby, Derek A.

1996 *The Kingdom of Kush: The Napatan and Meroitic Empires.* London: British Museum Press.

Wengrow, David, Michael Dee, Sarah Foster, Alice Stevenson, and Christopher Bronk Ramsey

2014 "Cultural Convergence in the Neolithic of the Nile Valley: A Prehistoric Perspective on Egypt's Place in Africa." *Antiquity* 88: 95–111.

Wenig, Steffen

2001 "Musawwarat Es-Sufra: Interpreting the Great Enclosure." *Sudan & Nubia* 5: 71–86.

2008 "Ten Years of Excavations at Musawwarat Es Sufra, 1995–2004." In *Between the Cataracts: Proceedings of the 11th Conference for Nubian Studies, Warsaw University, 27 August–2 September 2006.* Part 1: *Main Papers,* edited by Włodzimierz Godlewski and Adam Łajtar, pp. 239–47. Polish Archaeology in the Mediterranean, Supplement Series, 2.1. Warsaw: University of Warsaw Press.

2013 "Musawwarat es Sufra. Ein antikes Pilgerzentrum und Nationalheiligtum." In *Die Kulturen Nubiens, ein afrikanisches Vermächtnis,* edited by Steffen Wenig and Karola Zibelius-Chen, pp. 363–82. Dettelbach: J. H. Röll.

Williams, Bruce B.
1990 *Twenty-Fifth Dynasty and Napatan Remains at Qustul: Cemeteries W and V.* Oriental Institute Nubian Expedition 7. Chicago: The Oriental Institute.

Wilson, Penelope
2007 "The Meroitic Temple Graffiti." In *The Meroitic Temple Complex at Qasr Ibrim,* edited by Pamela J. Rose, pp. 105–70. Egypt Exploration Society, Excavation Memoir 84. London: Egypt Exploration Society.

Wolf, Pawel
1999 "Arbeitsbericht über die Dokumentation der Sekundärbilder und Sekundärinschriften von Musawwarat es Sufra," *Der Antike Sudan. Mitteilungen der Sudanarchäologischen Gesellschaft zu Berlin* 9: 44–51.
2004 "Toward an Interpretation of the Great Enclosure of Musawwarat Es-Sufra, Sudan." In *Nubian Studies, 1998: Proceedings of the Ninth Conference of the International Society of Nubian Studies, August 21-26, 1998, Boston, Massachusetts,* edited by Timothy Kendall, pp. 436–45. Boston: Department of African-American Studies, Northeastern University.

Yellin, Janice
2012 "Nubian Religion." In *Ancient Nubia: African Kingdoms on the Nile,* edited by Marjorie M. Fisher, Peter Lacovara, Sue D'Auria, and Salima Ikram, pp. 125–44. New York: The American University in Cairo Press.

Żurawski, Bogdan
2013 "Strongholds on the Middle Nile: Nubian Fortifications of the Middle Ages." In *The Power of Walls: Fortifications in Ancient Northeastern Africa. Proceedings of the International Workshop Held at the University of Cologne, 4th-7th August 2011,* edited by Friederike Jesse and Carola Vogel, pp. 113–43. Colloquium Africanum 5. Cologne: Heinrich-Barth-Institut.
2014 *Kings and Pilgrims: St. Raphael Church II at Banganarti, Mid-Eleventh to Mid-Eighteenth Century.* Warsaw: Neriton and Institute of Mediterranean and Oriental Cultures of the Polish Academy of Sciences.

2

Suzanne Davis & Geoff Emberling

Graffiti at El-Kurru: The Funerary Temple

The building we call the funerary temple at El-Kurru was first excavated in 1918 and 1919 by the American archaeologist George Reisner (**FIG. 2.1**). Reisner designated the structure Ku. 1500 and associated it with the pyramid Ku. 1 about 100 meters to the west,[1] interpreting it as temple to sustain the memory of the king who was meant to be buried in pyramid Ku. 1. He uncovered the temple's two exterior rooms, but his exploration was cursory and the structure was not mentioned in the final report of work on the site.[2] He also did not mention that the walls and columns of the outer rooms were adorned with abundant graffiti, which are the focus of this chapter.

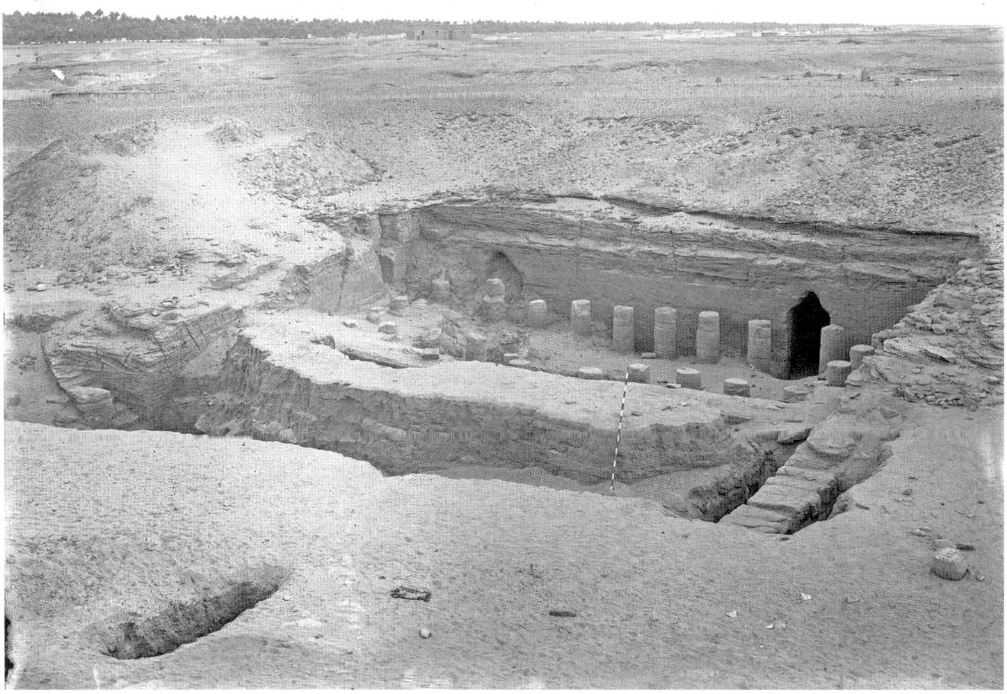

FIGURE 2.1. The funerary temple Ku. 1500 at the end of George Reisner's 1919 excavation.
Photo: © Museum of Fine Arts, Boston

1. See Williams, this volume.
2. Dunham 1950.

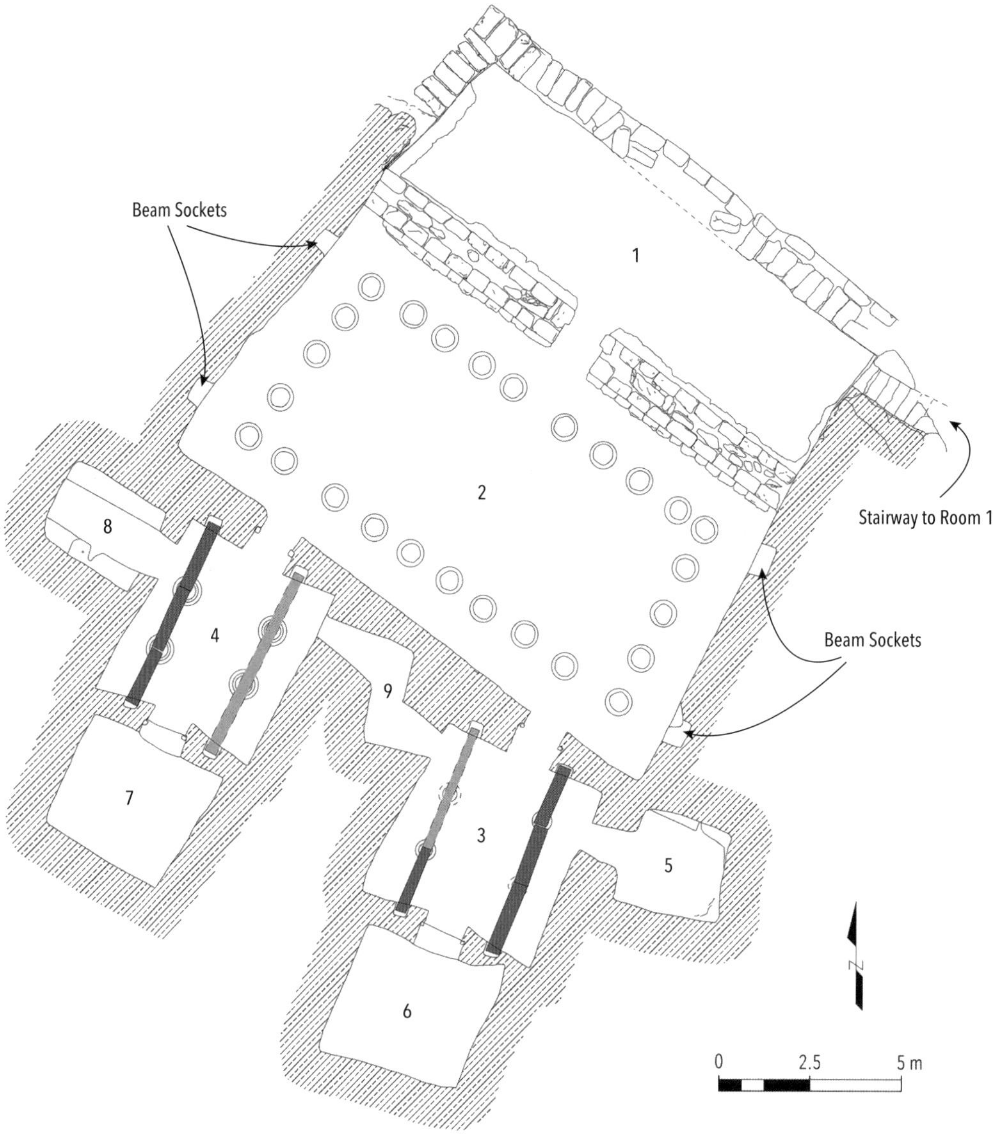

FIGURE 2.2. Plan of funerary temple Ku. 1500. For column and wall labels, see fig. C.1 on p. 144.
Plan: Jack Cheng and Martin Uildriks, 2015

The International Kurru Archaeological Project began to excavate the temple in 2013, making a number of discoveries, including hundreds of ancient figural graffiti. This work showed that the rock-cut temple (**FIGS. 2.2-3**) had been built in a sandstone quarry that presumably had been the source of much of the stone used in the royal pyramids at the site. The two rooms discovered by Reisner (rooms 1 and 2) were divided by a wall of cut sandstone blocks. The outer, northern room was entered by a staircase on the eastern side and was

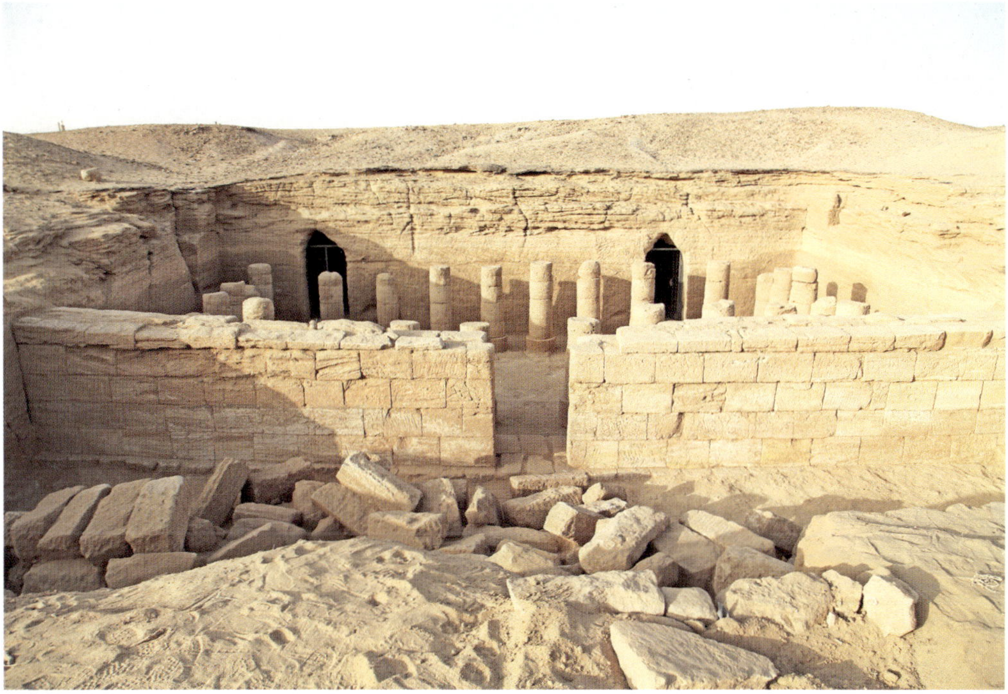

FIGURE 2.3. View of the funerary temple from the northeast, with the outer room (room 1) in the foreground (with collapsed wall visible) and columned room 2 visible beyond.
Photo: Geoff Emberling / IKAP, 2014

bounded on the north by another masonry wall of cut stone blocks.[3] There was no evidence that this outer room was roofed. The inner room — which measures roughly 16 meters long × 5 meters wide — had 26 columns around its inner perimeter. It also had beam sockets cut into the tops of the east and west walls and was most likely roofed around the perimeter with a central courtyard open to the sky. From this room, two doorways had been cut into the rock of the southern wall. These doorways led to two sets of three rooms, connected by a corridor. In each set of underground rooms, the doorway opened into an elaborate central room that was ornamented with four columns and decorative stone beams (**FIGS. 2.4–5**). Farther back into the rock was another room with emplacements to secure a door (**FIG. 2.6**). Each set of rooms also had a small side chamber (rooms 5 and 8). While the doorways cut into the rock are visible in Reisner's photo, he does not note them in his field diaries, nor did he record the complex of underground rooms accessed through these doorways.

The form of pyramid Ku. 1 suggests it was built during the later 4th century BCE, and column capitals in the underground room of the temple have their closest parallel in Alexandria of the later 4th century BCE. Ku. 1500 was almost certainly built during that time.

Although Reisner had identified Ku. 1500 as a funerary temple associated with pyramid Ku. 1, its intended function is in fact not certain. While the overall plan of the structure is highly unusual both for Kush and for ancient Egypt, it is paralleled by a building at the nearby royal Kushite pyramid burial site of Nuri that Reisner also interpreted as a funerary temple.[4] Like the temple at El-Kurru, the Nuri temple has two outer rock-cut

3. Funerary temple Ku. 1500 is not perfectly aligned with the cardinal points. Therefore what in this chapter is called "north" in relation to the temple is actually north-northeast, "south" is south-southwest, "east" is east-southeast, and "west" is west-northwest.

4. Termed Nu. 400; Dunham 1955, p. 271.

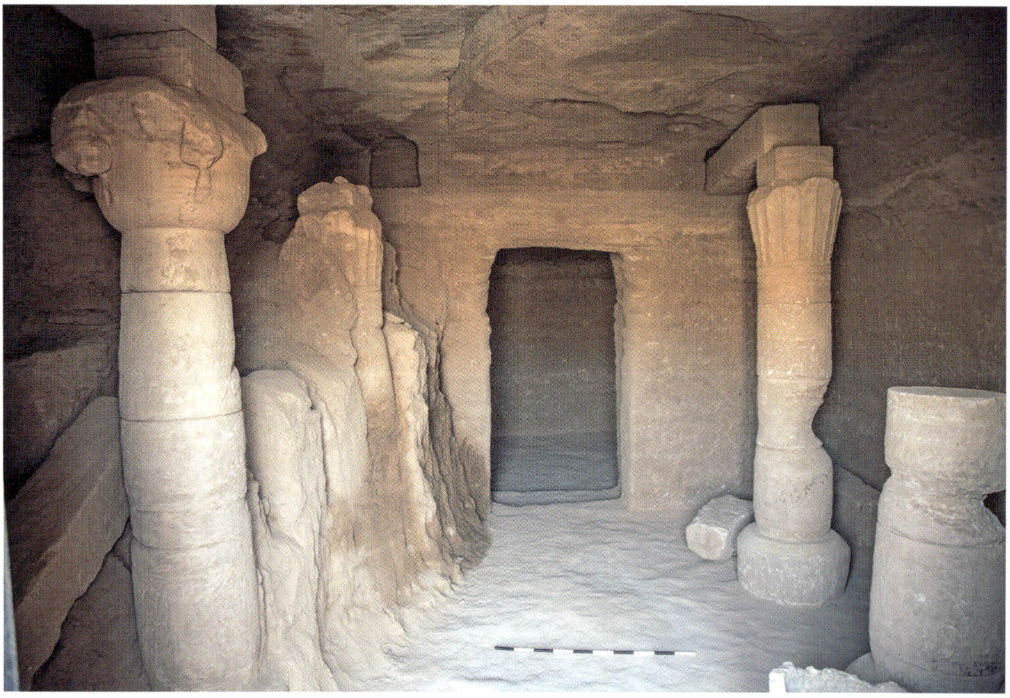

FIGURE 2.4. The eastern underground room (room 3, looking into room 6) with columns and stone beams during excavation in 2014. Two column capitals have palm frond decoration and two are ornamented with volutes.
Photo: Kathryn Howley / IKAP, 2014

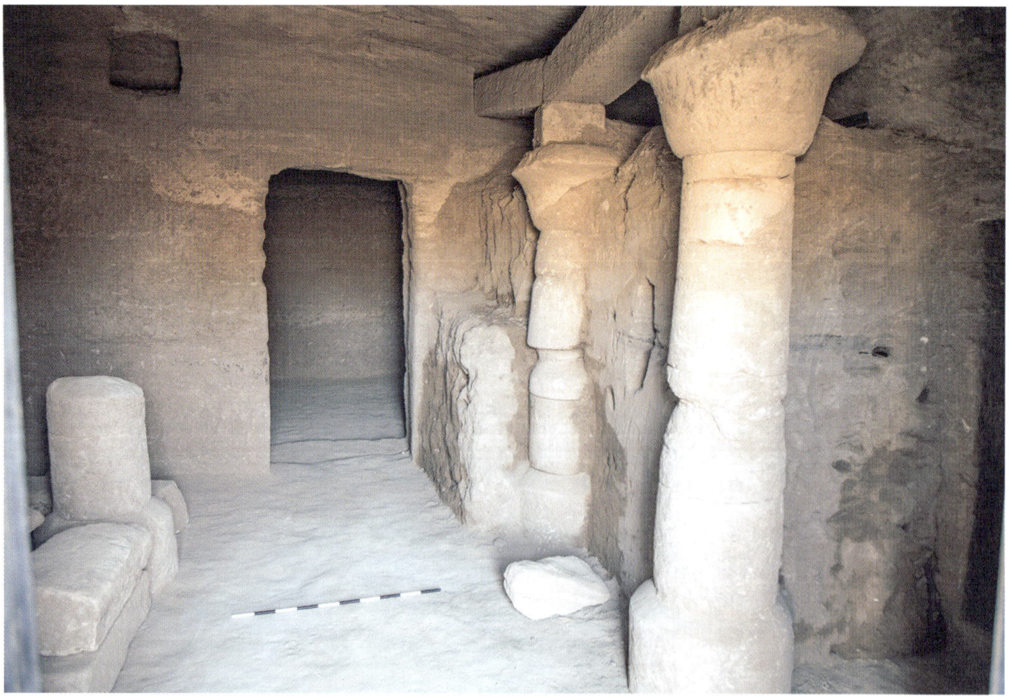

FIGURE 2.5. The western underground room (room 4, looking into room 7) with columns and stone beams during excavation in 2014. The column capitals are in the form of an open lotus flower.
Photo: Kathryn Howley / IKAP, 2014

rooms, one with columns, and a network of underground rooms. Both temples were likely built at about the same time. Thus, these structures were associated with royal burials, but in what way? The interpretation of the building as a funerary temple is complicated by the fact that the pyramids at El-Kurru appear to have had funerary chapels in which the memory of individual kings and queens could be honored. At Nuri, the situation is still more confused because a number of the pyramids there had been expanded and their chapels were no longer accessible. Was this structure intended to serve as a funerary chapel for the dynasty? At the same time, the underground rooms with elaborate decoration and unusual locking doors might suggest an intended function as a kind of treasury building for the funerary cult, as has been suggested for roughly contemporary buildings at Karnak.[5]

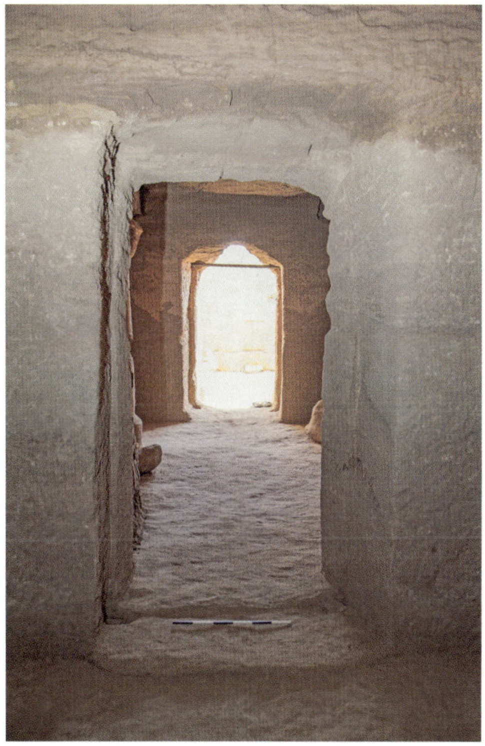

FIGURE 2.6. View from room 7 through room 4 to the courtyard. Note the door sockets and sills cut into the stone. *Photo: Kathryn Howley / IKAP, 2014*

Unlike in the temple at Nuri, however, decorative reliefs had not been carved on the interior wall of cut stone blocks in Ku. 1500. Stones defining the outer wall of the outer room had been set in place but had not received their finishing treatment.[6] Furthermore, no artifacts contemporary with its construction were found in the temple at El-Kurru. Thus, it seems this funerary temple was not completed and, like the pyramid Ku. 1, was never used.

At some time after the construction of the building, the northern wall of the outer room collapsed (see **FIG. 2.3**).[7] This wall faces a wadi (dry riverbed), and although the area is quite arid, rare but sometimes powerful storms can cause torrential flooding. It is likely that such a storm caused the collapse of this wall.

Several centuries later, however, people returned to Ku. 1500. They broke the bottoms off large jars and set them upside down around the exterior of the two outer rooms for use as braziers (**FIGS. 2.7–8**), a common practice in Meroitic Nubia.[8] The burned material likely included incense — the burning was not intense or extensive enough to have been for cooking — but the fire could also have provided light in the temple. The jars themselves are Meroitic in date, and radiocarbon dates from the burned materials suggest at least two episodes of burning between 100 BCE and 100 CE.[9] It is likely, but not possible to prove, that some graffiti in the two outer rooms of the temple were carved when the fires were lit in the temple in two discrete episodes. But some graffiti are certainly later in date (particularly

5. Traunecker 1987. Thanks to Neal Spencer for this reference.
6. Marks likely carved in the quarry were still visible on these stones; Karberg 2015.
7. This collapse was also not noted by Reisner. In fairness to Reisner, who was normally an exemplary excavator, he appears to have been suffering from illness during his time at El-Kurru, and this certainly affected his energy and enthusiasm.
8. Näser 2016.
9. Emberling 2015.

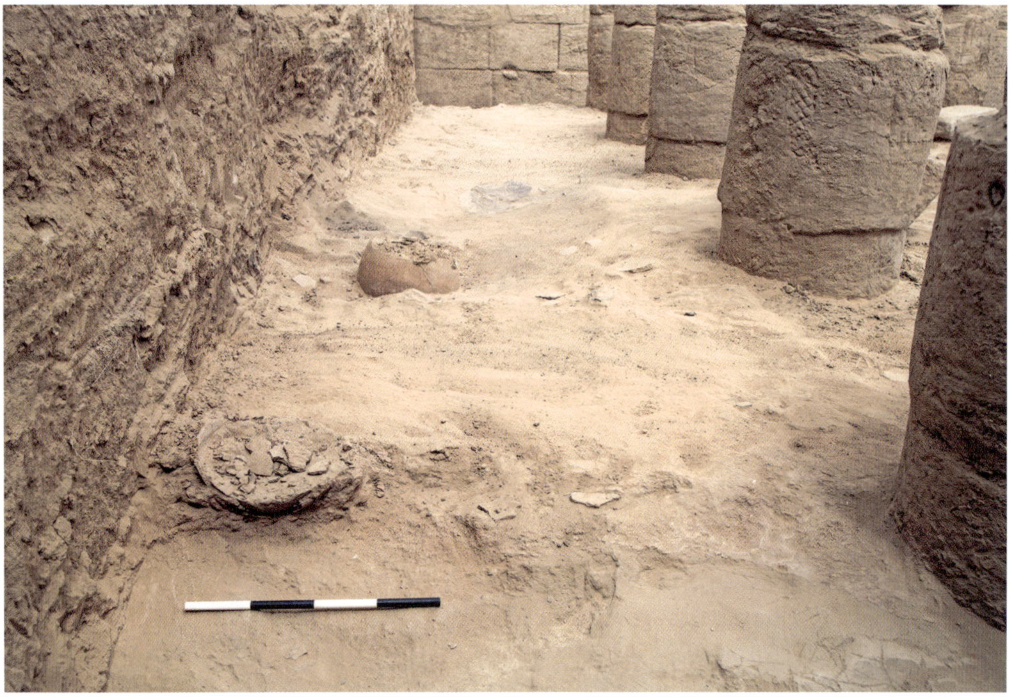

FIGURE 2.7. Pot with base broken off in situ in the El-Kurru temple (note the graffito of a sandal, T40, on the column behind).
Photo: Kathryn Howley / IKAP, 2014

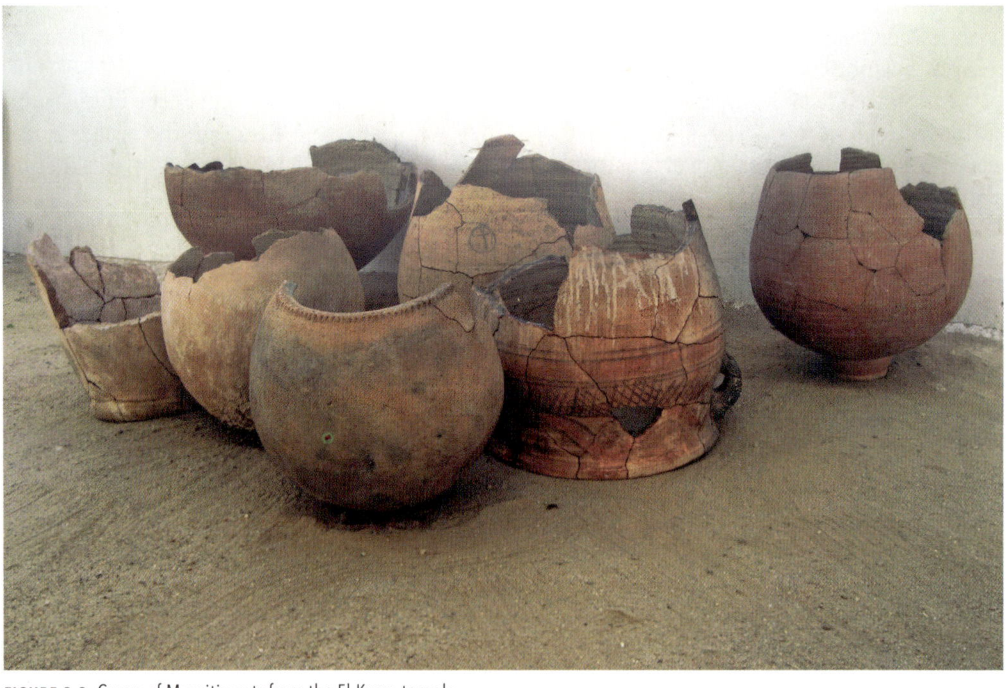

FIGURE 2.8. Group of Meroitic pots from the El-Kurru temple.
Photo: Suzanne Davis / IKAP, 2014

ones with Christian imagery), and it is also possible that many or most of the graffiti were carved during intermittent pilgrimages to the temple.

The Graffiti

To date, 643 ancient graffiti have been found in the temple.[10] The majority are located on the columns and on the masonry wall between the temple's two outer rooms; 529 are carved on columns, while 102 are located on the wall. Most of the latter — fifty-nine in total — are on the south side of the wall, facing the colonnaded courtyard, and of these fifty-nine, most are located to the west of the doorway between the two rooms. Only one graffito, showing a group of birds (graffito T24; see the catalog of at the end of this volume), is located on one of the rock-cut, or quarry, walls. This, again, is on the western wall. An additional eleven carved designs — all of which appear to be masons' marks — are located on fallen blocks in the temple's outer room. No graffiti have been found in the underground chambers.

Most graffiti are carved at heights between 1 and 1.7 meters from the original floor surface — roughly chest height for an adult. On columns, this means that most graffiti are found on the third drum. On the wall, most are carved on the third or fourth course of blocks. A few, however, are carved higher, and many columns have one or more graffiti on their fourth drum. These are too high to be reached from the temple's floor, so it is likely that they were carved after the temple had been partially filled in with windblown sand or silt brought by floods.

The same may be true for other graffiti as well. The Meroitic pots that had been inverted and used as braziers were discovered at a height substantially above the original floor level (see FIG. 2.7). If graffiti were carved at the same time these pots were being used to burn incense — as some of them undoubtedly were — people might have carved them while sitting down.

The concentration of graffiti in the temple is an indication that it was a special place in the built landscape, but the high number of graffiti is also linked, at least in part, to how easy it is to carve the local stone. The temple is constructed from soft, granular sandstone that can be scratched easily with a stick, although a stone or metal tool would make faster work of carving a graffito. The stone is too soft to retain tool marks, so it is not possible to say what kinds of tools were used.

The distribution of the graffiti on the wall has already been noted: most graffiti are concentrated on the western half of the wall, and the large majority are on the side of the wall that faces the courtyard. On the columns, graffiti are incised on all sides, but more face a northerly direction — that is, toward the wall — than in any other direction. Graffiti carved into the doorway are primarily on the western side of the door. This seems to suggest that there might have been something special about both the courtyard and the western half of the wall that faces into it. But why these areas were particularly attractive for graffiti is unclear. Perhaps the northwest quadrant of the temple's courtyard was important for some reason — a ritual was conducted there, or someone was thought to be buried there, or it was more attractive because it is closer to the pyramid. Or perhaps this stretch of wall and the northern-facing aspects of the columns were simply more accessible than other

10. Although most of these graffiti were documented in 2015 and 2016, a few "new" images are noticed each year; as the angle of the sun changes throughout the day, the visibility of individual graffiti can alter dramatically. The horned viper (graffito T25) is quite difficult to see and was first noticed at dusk one day in 2017. Graffito T19, which depicts a dog chasing a hare, was first seen in 2018. So we can expect the total number of ancient graffiti at El-Kurru to rise slowly over time, as long as archaeologists continue to work at the site.

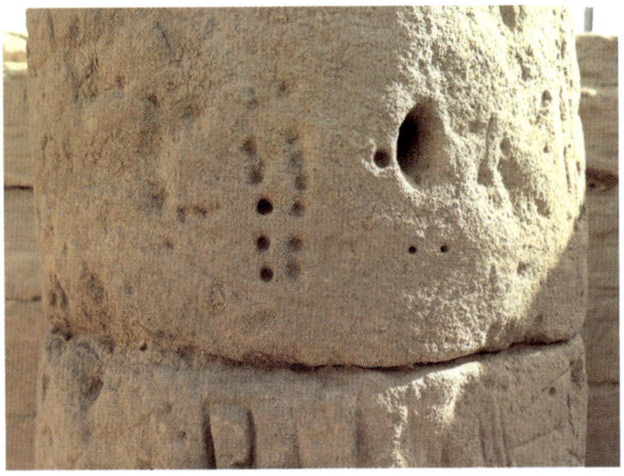

FIGURE 2.9. Holes on column A08. Graffito T53.
Photo: Suzanne Davis / IKAP, 2017

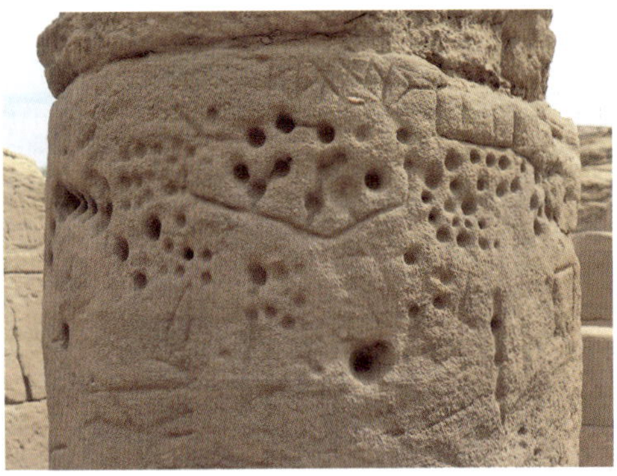

FIGURE 2.10. Holes on column A04.
Photo: Suzanne Davis / IKAP, 2017

areas. It is also possible that the area, once it had multiple graffiti, developed a sort of critical mass that encouraged even more to be carved nearby. The total absence of graffiti in the underground chambers, and the near absence on the rock-cut walls, also seems strange. Had the temple partly silted in due to wadi flooding, making these areas inaccessible? Or were they less attractive for some other reason?

The graffiti themselves take two basic forms: holes or cupules, where the soft stone has been scooped out; and images or pictorial graffiti cut into the stone. Of the two types, cupules are far more common: almost two-thirds of the graffiti are of this type (408 of the 643 total ancient graffiti; see graffiti T52–T55). Although the holes could be an ancient version of "I was here," many are deep and may have served instead as collection sites for stone powder. Column A08 has a deep hole as well as a grouped arrangement of smaller, shallow cupules (**FIG. 2.9**). The idea seems to have been that stone from an ancient, powerful monument had magical protective and healing powers. Similar behavior is seen at other ancient sites in Sudan and Egypt.[11] The practice continues into the present day, and Ku. 1 remains a popular site for removing stone powder to aid in fertility, healing, and bringing about favorable outcomes for important life events such as marriage. Although most cupules in the temple exist singly, at least fourteen different sets are grouped into patterns. A view of column A04 in the temple demonstrates how numerous these cupules are in some areas and how they are often clustered together (**FIG. 2.10**).

The temple's 235 pictorial graffiti consist of seven basic categories of images, listed here in order of their quantity in the temple: symbols (115), objects (33), masons' marks (32), animals (30), humans (16), unknown (6), and plants (3). Many of the images have clear meanings that relate to religion and ritual in Kush, while others are not recognizably connected — but that could be the result of our incomplete knowledge of Kushite religion.

The symbols (graffiti T42–51), most of which are geometric, range from very simple to quite complex. There are crosshatched designs, arrangements of parallel and perpendicular lines, and complicated yet unidentifiable compositions of shapes (see graffito T45).

There are fifteen designs consisting of an X bounded by a box (graffiti T7, T42–T46; **FIG. 2.11**), a motif with uncertain meaning. It was originally interpreted as a mason's mark[12] but might instead be intended to represent an altar or perhaps a textile.[13] Two of these Xs-in-

11. Kristensen 2015; Żurawski, this volume.
12. Karberg 2015.
13. Pope, this volume.

boxes exist as part of a more complex design that depicts a horned altar[14] and they might be part of a human figure. An additional twenty-seven Xs, unbounded by boxes, also appear in the temple.

Another symbol is clearly an ankh, an ancient Egyptian symbol of life (graffiti T47 and T48). It is interesting that within the larger group of geometric symbols, those that can be identified are religious in nature. Although impossible to prove, it seems likely that many of the unidentifiable symbols also have a deeper meaning, whether religious or otherwise, and are not simply random "doodles" on the stone.

The thirty-three graffiti representing objects and architecture depict boats, textiles, crosses, offering tables, arrows, and a sandal. This category also includes a small graffito that may represent a church. The twelve boats vary in execution. Some have multiple carved details, like masts and oars (T33; **FIG. 2.12**), while others are described with a few faint lines (T32). More than one type is depicted; in addition to the examples above, which have masts, there are a few small, rowboat-like vessels (T31) and others that seem to have a cabin or cargo on deck (T34), most conforming to boat types 2 and 3, as defined by Williams (this volume). None of the boats in the temple, however, match the size or descriptive detail seen in those on the Ku. 1 pyramid.[15] The seven textiles vary in size and level of detail. All have fringe, most have details depicting woven designs or embroidered decoration, and one appears to have tassels (T37; **FIG. 2.13**).

In the "object" subcategory there are also three images of offering tables, two of which are shown alongside a palm frond (T28–T29). Palm fronds are used in weddings and in funerary rituals in the area even today.[16] The six crosses and five arrows are carved simply, with just a few lines. The sandal is

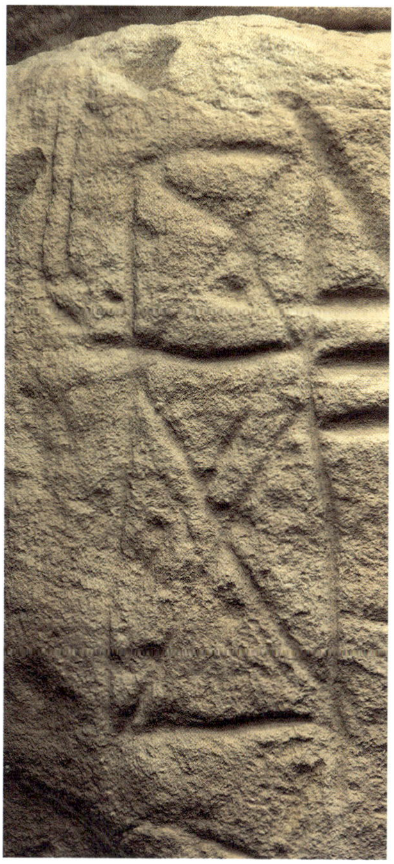

FIGURE 2.11. Example of an X in a box. Graffito T7.
RTI: Suzanne Davis and Janelle Batkin-Hall / IKAP, 2016

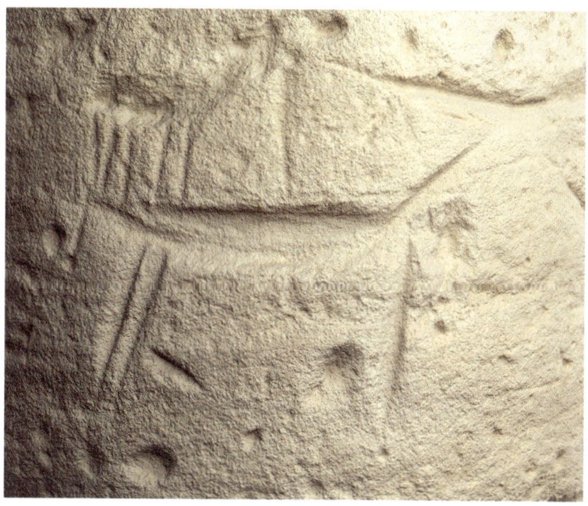

FIGURE 2.12. Boat with mast and oars. Graffito T33.
RTI: Suzanne Davis and Janelle Batkin-Hall / IKAP, 2016

14. Macadam 1955, vol. 2, pls. 11 and LXIX for horned altars from Kawa, dated to the 1st century BCE (Macadam 1955, vol. 1, p. 26). Soukiassian 1983 for horned altars in Egypt of the 1st millennium BCE.
15. Williams, this volume.
16. See essays in Kennedy 1978; also Török 2011; Bumbaugh 2011.

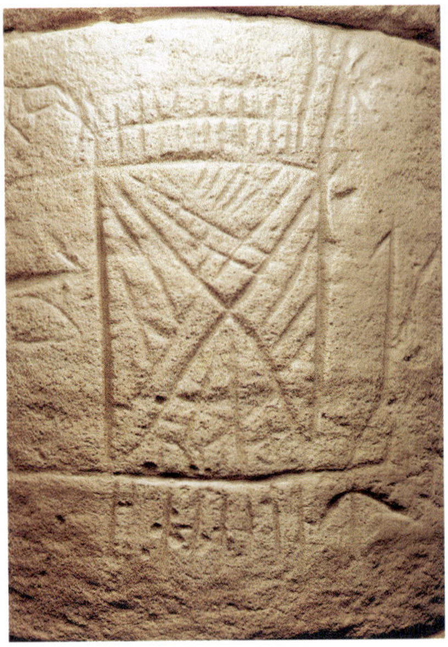

FIGURE 2.13. Fringed textile. Graffito T37.
RTI: Suzanne Davis and Janelle Batkin-Hall / IKAP, 2016

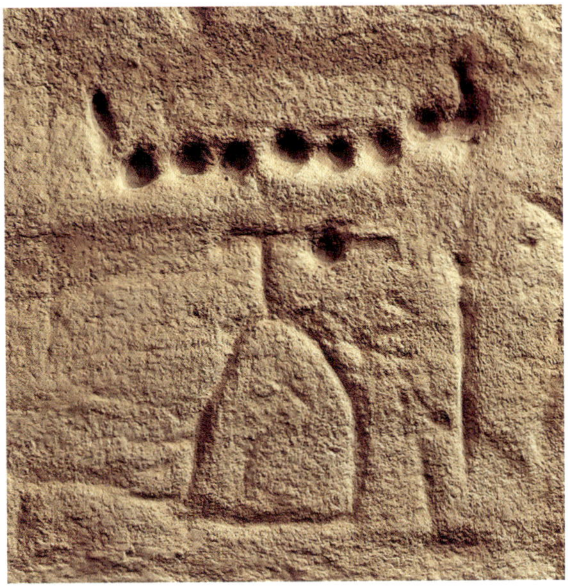

FIGURE 2.14. A possible church. Graffito T41.
RTI: Suzanne Davis and Janelle Batkin-Hall / IKAP, 2016

large and patterned with a crosshatched design (T40). The church graffito (T41; **FIG. 2.14**) is shaped like a pentagon, with a very faint cross appearing from the top point. If it is indeed a church, it is the only representation of architecture at El-Kurru.

For the purposes of our categorization, the thirty-two designs we believe are masons' marks are treated and cataloged separately from geometric symbols, but they, too, are geometric in appearance, consisting of a triangle or V shape bisected by a straight line. They exist primarily on the masonry walls and on fallen blocks in the temple's outer room. Only one is found on a column.

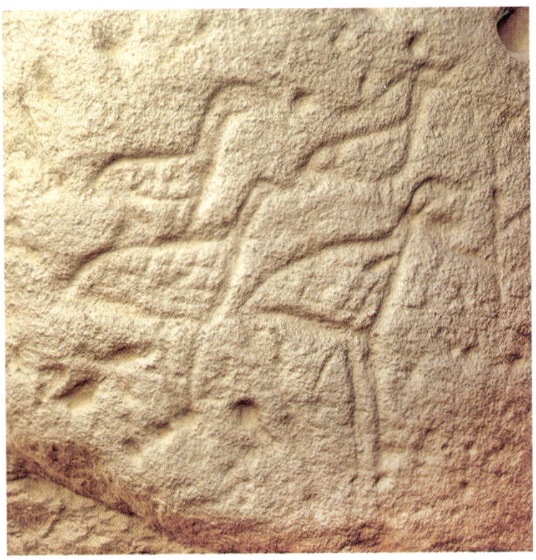

FIGURE 2.15. Group of four birds. Graffito T23.
RTI: Suzanne Davis and Janelle Batkin-Hall / IKAP, 2016

Of all the figural graffiti in the temple, the thirty animal images are probably the most varied. Although some are carved in a simple, linear fashion, many are carefully outlined and contain deftly carved, descriptive details. The most common depictions are birds, of which there are thirteen; one shows a group of four, carved together, with a delicate crosshatch pattern on their bodies to indicate their fluffy, feathered texture (T23; **FIG. 2.15**). These birds all appear to be guinea fowl, a bird that is widespread in Africa, both wild and domesticated. Guinea fowl are also depicted in paint on Meroitic ceramic vessels. It has been suggested that these birds are so often represented because they are figures in the folklore of Meroitic Kush.[17]

There are four horses and two of these, shown running (graffiti T13 and T14; **FIG. 2.16**), are very distinct. Carved deeply, side by side, they are beautifully equine. In the rightmost horse, a faint detail is visible: a series of curved parallel lines that suggest a rider. Carved with a similar high attention to detail are the images of two bull or cattle heads (T12). These small heads are horned, have human eyes, and are each accompanied by two small hooves. A table-shaped design is placed to their right. A horned viper, now extremely worn, was also carved with this level of care (T25). The horned viper, a deadly snake found in Egypt and northern Sudan, was associated with the underworld by the ancient Egyptians. It was also a hieroglyph for the sound "f." Another animal graffito with clear religious symbolism is a ram who wears the double crown of Amun (T11). This is also finely carved, with a crosshatched design across the body to indicate fleece. A gazelle, now somewhat damaged by modern over-carving, shows a similar level of artistry (T17). Two scenes of dogs chasing hares (T18 and T19) are identifiable as such because they also appear in somewhat greater numbers at Musawwarat es-Sufra. These, like the guinea fowl images, may be a reference to Kushite folklore, or they may just be images of daily life. There are more simply carved graffiti depicting a group of giraffes (T16) and two solo giraffes (T15). Finally, an additional six quadrupeds are very worn and no further attribution is possible.

There are sixteen graffiti representing human figures. The two most detailed depictions are of archers (T1) and of a seated figure holding a staff or scepter (T8). The archers are depicted in profile and striding to the right. The larger figure in the foreground stands with the right leg forward and a bow held outward in the right hand. Although this graffito is quite eroded, details of the archer's kilt are still visible. The faint outline of a second, similar figure can be seen between the archer's body and the bow. A more complex scene is depicted in graffito T2. At least two humans are carved in outline (and now quite worn), with unidentified geometric designs to the lower left and upper right. There are also simple "stick" figures (T3, for example), although one of these is riding a quadruped (T10).

Of the remaining pictorial graffiti, three are of plants: two palm fronds (T28 and T29) and one papyrus frond or lotus bud (T26). Notably, the palm fronds both appear with offering tables. Finally, six graffiti are classified as "unknown." These carvings are all obviously intentional and vaguely organic (as opposed to geometric) in appearance, but unidentifiable.

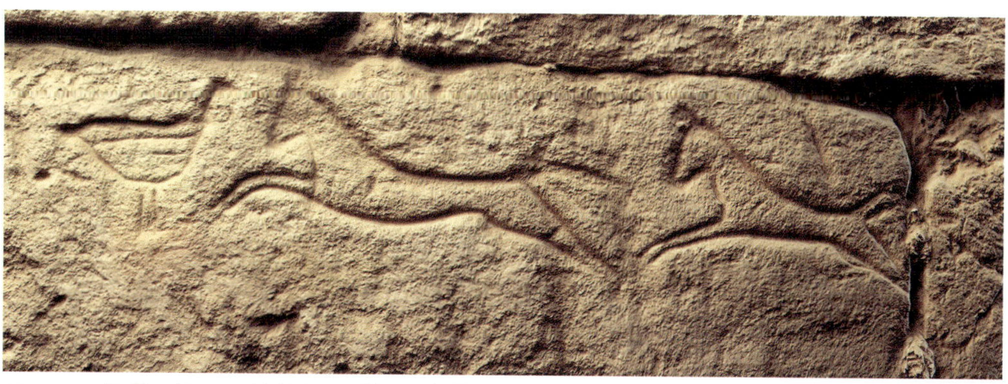

FIGURE 2.16. Graffito of horses with bird, on wall face E. Graffiti T22, T13, and T14.
RTI: Suzanne Davis and Janelle Batkin-Hall / IKAP, 2016

17. Hofmann 1988.

This overview of the graffiti demonstrates two clear themes: religion and daily life. Religious images include altars and offering tables, the ankh symbol, the Amun ram, and, perhaps, the horned viper and the small bulls' heads with human eyes, which might represent demons. The sandal may represent the foot of a pilgrim.[18] Religious pilgrimage, belief, and activity are also apparent in the huge number of gouged cupules, where visitors are both marking the temple to show that they visited and taking away with them some of its power in the form of powdered stone. Daily life is represented by animals like birds, horses, giraffes, and other quadrupeds; and also by images of people, activities like archery, and objects like boats.

But questions remain. In comparison to animals, why are there so few plants? And why are both palm fronds depicted alongside offering tables? Could the textiles — most of which are meticulously detailed — have been carved later than the Meroitic period and have been intended to represent Muslim prayer rugs? Or do they represent a special cloth or some other item from the Meroitic period? As with the questions about the graffiti's locations and orientation, no answers are immediately apparent.

The dates of the graffiti are difficult to determine. Some images can be approximately dated — images closely related to Kushite religion are likely to be pre-Christian, for example, and images that incorporate Christian imagery must postdate the introduction of Christianity into Nubia in the 6th century. Other images appear elsewhere — at other sites or in other media like painted ceramic vessels — and this can provide more precise dating.

Another approach to dating is the physical qualities of the carved images themselves. The images are incised to different depths — some very deep, others quite shallow. But it is difficult to say if the shallower graffiti are older and more worn, or if they were not carved as deeply. In this volume's chapter on the rock drawings of Sudan, Dr. Bakhiet argues that the patina or weathering of rock art can be a guide to its age. For his study of carvings on granite, a very hard rock, this is true. Granite typically has a darker appearance when weathered, so that new carvings appear "fresh" and light in color by contrast. But for the El-Kurru graffiti, which are carved into a very soft, light-colored sandstone that erodes readily, the surface weathering provides fewer clues. The rock is generally a uniform color throughout, with the surface only slightly darker than the interior. It does, however, seem obvious that the graffiti on the upper drums of the columns are newer, since these areas of the columns would have been accessible only after the temple's floor level had risen by several feet. It is worthwhile to note that the graffiti on the upper drums of the columns are also the most severely eroded because, while they must be newer, they were also exposed to the elements for much longer as the rock-cut temple was slowly buried.

As noted above, at some later point the temple was damaged and filled in by flooding from the nearby wadi. The flooding in the temple was severe enough that it broke columns in the underground rooms about one meter above the floor, and then filled the entire temple with sand and silt. The cycles of flooding may also occasionally have exposed portions of the structure, but when we came to the site to excavate in 2013, the building was entirely filled in (**FIG. 2.17**). Between the 2013 and 2014 excavation seasons, the building filled in again.

Discussion of the temple's more recent history would not be complete without a brief mention of the thirty-two modern graffiti. These primarily consist of names in Arabic script, some with dates, but there is also one geometric design, one human figure, a gazelle (carved near the ancient gazelle, seemingly in imitation), and one small pair of scissors. As discussed further in Suzanne Davis's chapter on conservation and documentation, many of these are about one meter off the ground — an easily accessible height for elementary to middle-

18. See Pope, this volume.

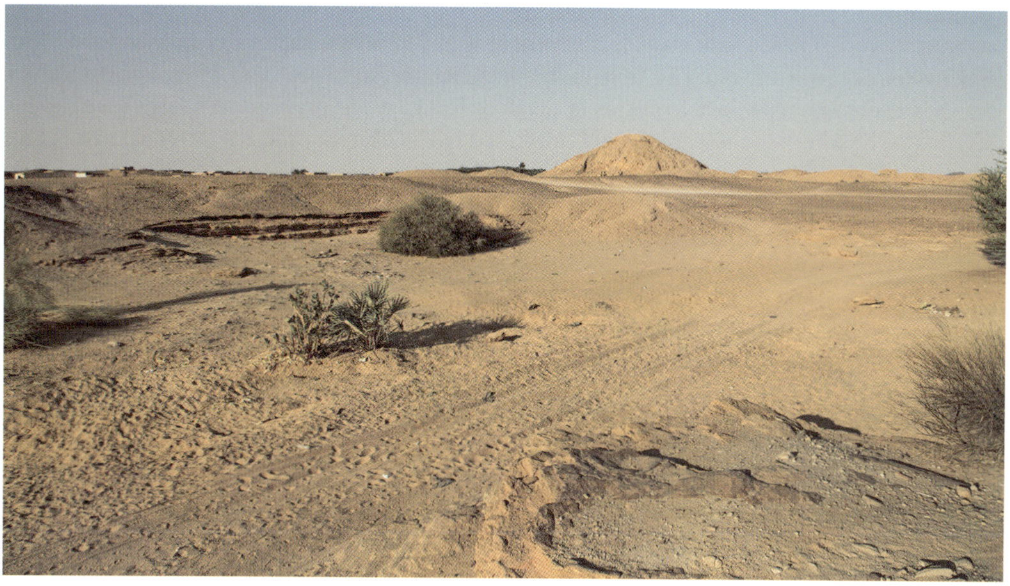

FIGURE 2.17. Funerary temple Ku. 1500 before excavation, showing the temple filled in with wash from the adjacent wadi (the temple is underneath the green bush in the center of the photograph).
Photo: Geoff Emberling / IKAP, 2013

school age children.[19] The Ku. 1 pyramid also has multiple modern graffiti, and the practice of carving graffiti remains prevalent at other sites in Sudan as well.

We should also note that while the pyramid cemetery of El-Kurru was clearly a pilgrimage site in Meroitic and medieval Christian times, the site has retained ritual significance in more recent times, too. Leaving aside archaeological and heritage tourism as a kind of ritual pilgrimage, the site has become associated in Sudanese lore with local spirits (*jinn*) known as the "daughters of the sheikh" (*banat esh-sheikh*). According to the local story, a religious figure named Sheikh el-Aghbash married a woman who turned out to be possessed by a *jinn*. They had seven daughters — the *banat esh-sheikh* — and the spirits of those daughters still appear to people, especially women, in El-Kurru village. They can provide help with fertility and illness and can give signs of the future, but they need to receive offerings so that their involvement is helpful rather than harmful. Offerings are made to the *banat esh-sheikh* at feasts, but they are also made in the pyramid cemetery at El-Kurru, specifically outside the tomb of Queen Qalhata. Hers is the only one of the queens' tombs that has its original wall paintings still preserved (see **FIG. 1.12**). Stone powder is still gouged from the pyramid, too, and local women believe that ingesting it can assist with fertility, healing, and favorable outcomes for major life events, like childbirth and marriage.

The graffiti in the temple show features that relate to ritual practice: concentration in a particular space and concentrations of images. It is reasonable, therefore, to conclude that the graffiti were a part of the practice of pilgrimage and private devotion. Some images relate to ritual, including altars, offering tables, and palm fronds, and images evoking deities including Amun and perhaps Ptah. Graffiti that relate to travel — boats, horses, and the single image of a sandal, for example — may be representations of pilgrimage, as they are at other sites, particularly the Isis Temple at Philae.[20]

19. See Davis, this volume.
20. See Pope, this volume.

But not all the graffiti in the temple are related to devotion in ways that are clear to us today. Some of these less clear images include the representations of guinea fowl, dogs chasing hares, giraffes, and the textile images that are so far unparalleled at other sites. Whether these images relate to cycles of myth or folktales, or perhaps to things seen during pilgrimage, or whether they are simply unrelated to devotional practice is not known at this time. Although our understanding of the graffiti is incomplete, they nevertheless animate the temple, forging a link between us and the people who carved them and giving us small but concrete clues into their world.

References

Bumbaugh, Solange

2011 "Meroitic Worship of Isis at Philae." In *Egypt in Its African Context*, edited by Karen Exell, pp. 66–69. BAR International Series 2204. Oxford: Archaeopress.

Dunham, Dows

1950 *El Kurru*. The Royal Cemeteries of Kush 1. Cambridge, MA: Harvard University Press.

1955 *Nuri*. The Royal Cemeteries of Kush 2. Boston: Museum of Fine Arts.

Emberling, Geoff

2015 "A Mortuary Temple at El-Kurru." *Sudan & Nubia* 19: 65–67.

Hofmann, Inge

1988 *Hase, Perlhuhn und Hyäne — Spuren meroitischer Oralliteratur: ein Beitrag zur afrikanischen Komponente der meroitischen Kultur*. Beiträge zur Sudanforschung, Beiheft 4. Vienna: Mödling.

Karberg, Tim

2015 "Some Remarks on Stonemasons' Marks in the Mortuary Temple." *Sudan & Nubia* 19: 68–69.

Kennedy, John G.

1978 *Nubian Ceremonial Life: Studies in Islamic Syncretism and Cultural Change*. New York: American University in Cairo Press.

Kristensen, Troels Myrup

2015 "Pilgrimage, Devotional Practices and the Consumption of Sacred Places in Ancient Egypt and Contemporary Syria." *International Journal of Heritage Studies* 21 (4): 354–68.

Macadam, M. F. Laming

1955 *The Temples of Kawa II. History and Archaeology of the Site*. 2 vols. London: Oxford University Press.

Näser, Claudia

2016 "Hugging the Wall: New Insights into the Building History and the Uselife of the Great Enclosure at Musawwarat." *Der Antike Sudan. Mitteilungen der Sudanarchäologischen Gesellschaft zu Berlin* 27: 7–18.

Soukiassian, Georges

1983 "Les autels 'à cornes' ou 'à acrotères' en Égypte." *Bulletin de l'Institut Français d'archéologie Orientale* 83: 317–33.

Török, László

2011 *Hellenizing Art in Ancient Nubia, 300 BC–AD 250, and Its Egyptian Models: A Study in "Acculturation."* Culture and History of the Ancient Near East 53. Leiden: Brill.

Traunecker, Claude

1987 "Les 'temples hauts' de basse époque: Un aspect du fonctionnement économique des temples." *Revue d'Égyptologie* 38: 147–62.

3

Bruce Beyer Williams

Boat Graffiti on the El-Kurru Pyramid

The recent discovery of graffiti depicting riverboats on one of the pyramids at El-Kurru represents a new milestone in gathering evidence for cultural developments in the Middle Nile region in the late 1st millennium CE.

Ku. 1, Its Excavation, and the Discovery of Graffiti

The pyramid designated Kurru 1, or simply Ku. 1, the largest monument at El-Kurru, measures some 26.65 meters square at its base. Its three subterranean chambers are accessed

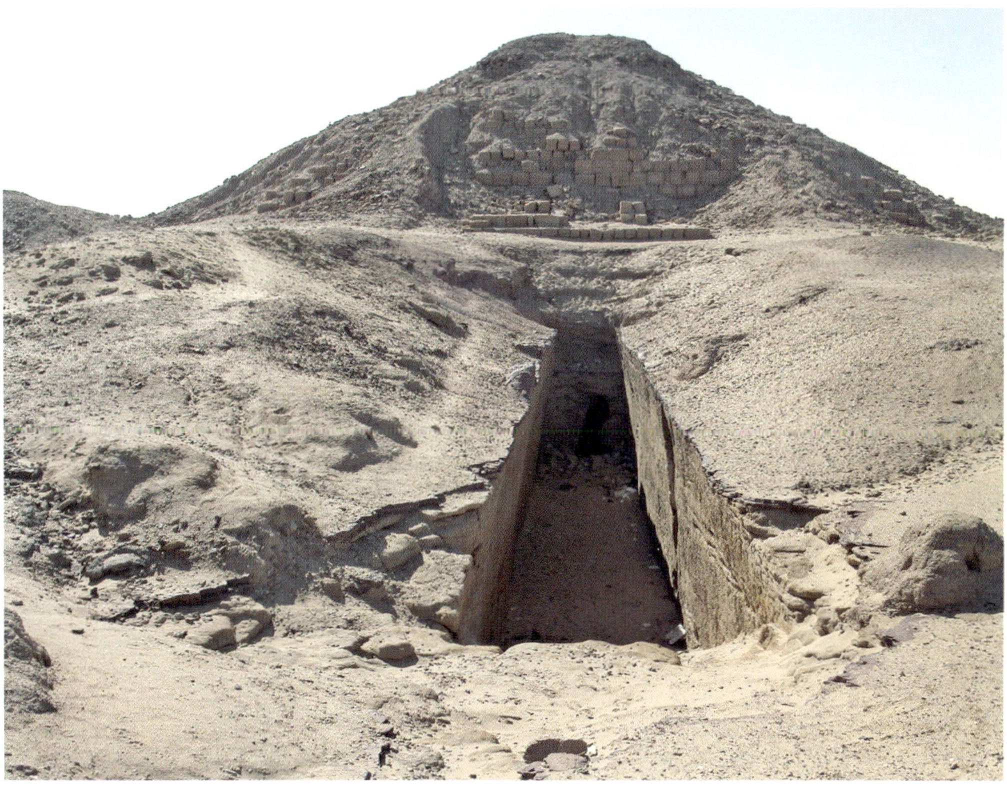

FIGURE 3.1. Pyramid Ku. 1 before excavation.
Photo: Bruce Beyer Williams, 2006

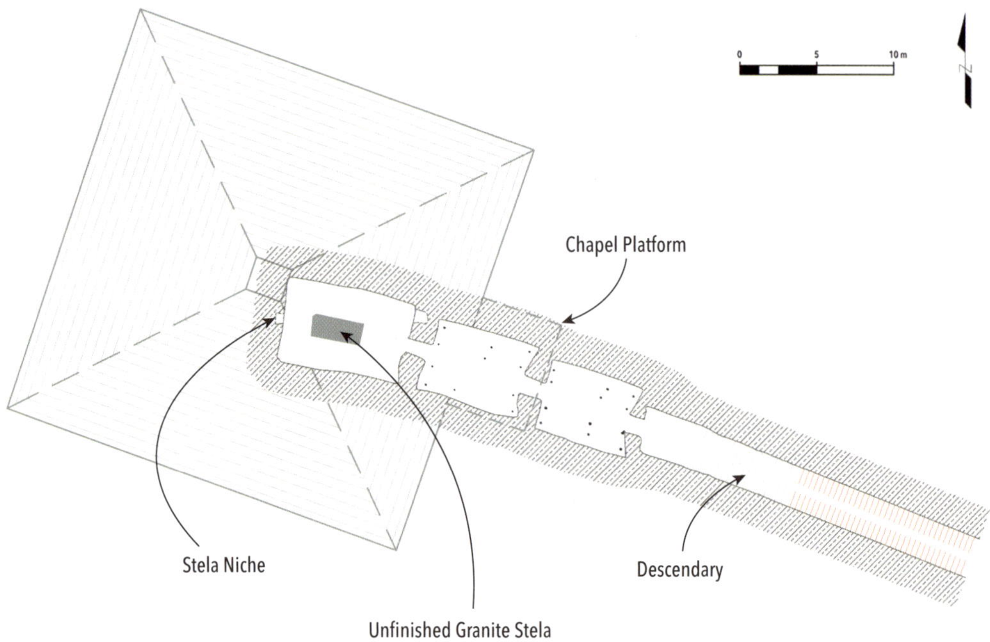

FIGURE 3.2. Plan of pyramid Ku. 1. Red indicates areas of modern restoration.
Plan: Martin Uildriks and Rob Rosa / IKAP, 2015

by a long descendary, or entrance staircase, extending toward the river (**FIGS. 3.1-2**).[1] It occupies a central position in the cemetery extending from the front row of tombs in the center (see **FIG. 1.9**) and, though now in ruins, still dominates the site. It was constructed near the end of the 4th century BCE of roughly quarried sandstone blocks, generally with deep grooves on the surface of the interior blocks. The lowest course served as a kind of plinth extending outward, and on top of this, exterior blocks called casing stones were smoothed to an angle on the face and the sides, each set back slightly from the one below to make a steep pyramid (**FIG. 3.3**). A small chapel was attached to the east side of the pyramid. The unfinished state of the burial chamber is strong evidence that the pyramid was never finished or used for its intended purpose.

Sometime in the Christian period, perhaps in the 9th or 10th century,[2] many of the casing blocks in the lower courses of Ku. 1 were carved with graffiti. The carvings concentrate on the east, river-facing, side of the pyramid,[3] on either side of the chapel as well as on the chapel itself. They consist of depictions of boats, a few animals, Christian symbols, and "monograms," stylized letters in different scripts that represented the initials of saints or archangels. Because all the pyramid blocks are individually cut and fitted, those that bear the graffiti vary considerably in size.

1. Emberling 2015, p. 60. See also Emberling and Dann 2013; Dann and Emberling 2016; and Tucker and Emberling 2016.
2. Corresponding to the date of the wall of the town. See sources in n. 1.
3. Ku. 1 is not perfectly aligned with the cardinal points. Therefore what in this chapter is called "north" in relation to the pyramid is actually north-northeast, "south" is south-southwest, "east" is east-southeast, and "west" is west-northwest.

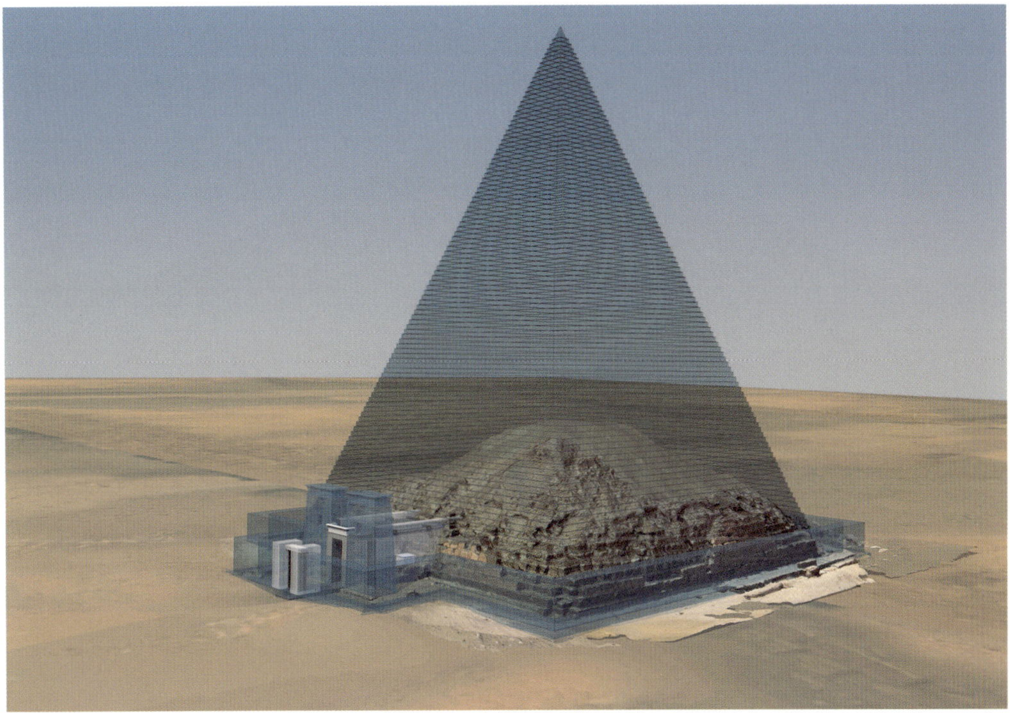

FIGURE 3.3. Rendering of pyramid Ku. 1 with reconstruction of its original form in blue.
Photo model and reconstruction: Nadejda Reshetnikova / IKAP, 2019

Many of the casing blocks were later removed and used to build a wall around the town (see **FIG. 1.19**). After, possibly long after, the blocks were removed, rock fill from the structure's core gradually spilled out and covered the base so that the pyramid took on the appearance of a low mound of rubble. This may have begun in the Christian period, for there are Arabic graffiti higher up. Of the blocks that are left many are broken. Only the bottom one, two, or three courses remain near the corners; at the corners themselves none have survived. Near the center of each side, more is preserved on the east (chapel) and north sides, up to six courses on the east and seven on the north. On the south side, only a maximum of three courses remain (see **FIGS. C.4–16** in the catalog at the end of this volume).

In 1918 and 1919, George Reisner of the Harvard University–Museum of Fine Arts, Boston Expedition excavated at El-Kurru, during which time he explored Ku. 1, partially clearing the underground chambers, the chapel, and blocks on the east side and the four corners of the pyramid. The graffiti at the corners would have been visible to Reisner and his team,[4] but they were not studied and exposed surfaces subsequently acquired more graffiti.

In 2015 and 2016, a University of Michigan Expedition cleared rubble and sand from the north, east, and south sides of the pyramid, exposing core and casing blocks (**FIGS. 3.4–6**) and revealing the graffiti.[5] At the time of excavation, many photographs were made of the graffiti, especially the boats, and some general notes were recorded. Since then, further graffiti have been added to the blocks, but the medieval carvings are still legible.

4. Of the graffiti from Ku. 1 presented in the catalog at the end of this volume, P8, P11, P12, P16, and P18 were exposed by Reisner.

5. For recent excavations, see Emberling, Dann, and Mohamed-Ali 2015; Dann and Emberling 2016. For Reisner's original work, see Dunham 1950, pp. 8, 10. For the pyramid and objects, see ibid. pp. 23–24.

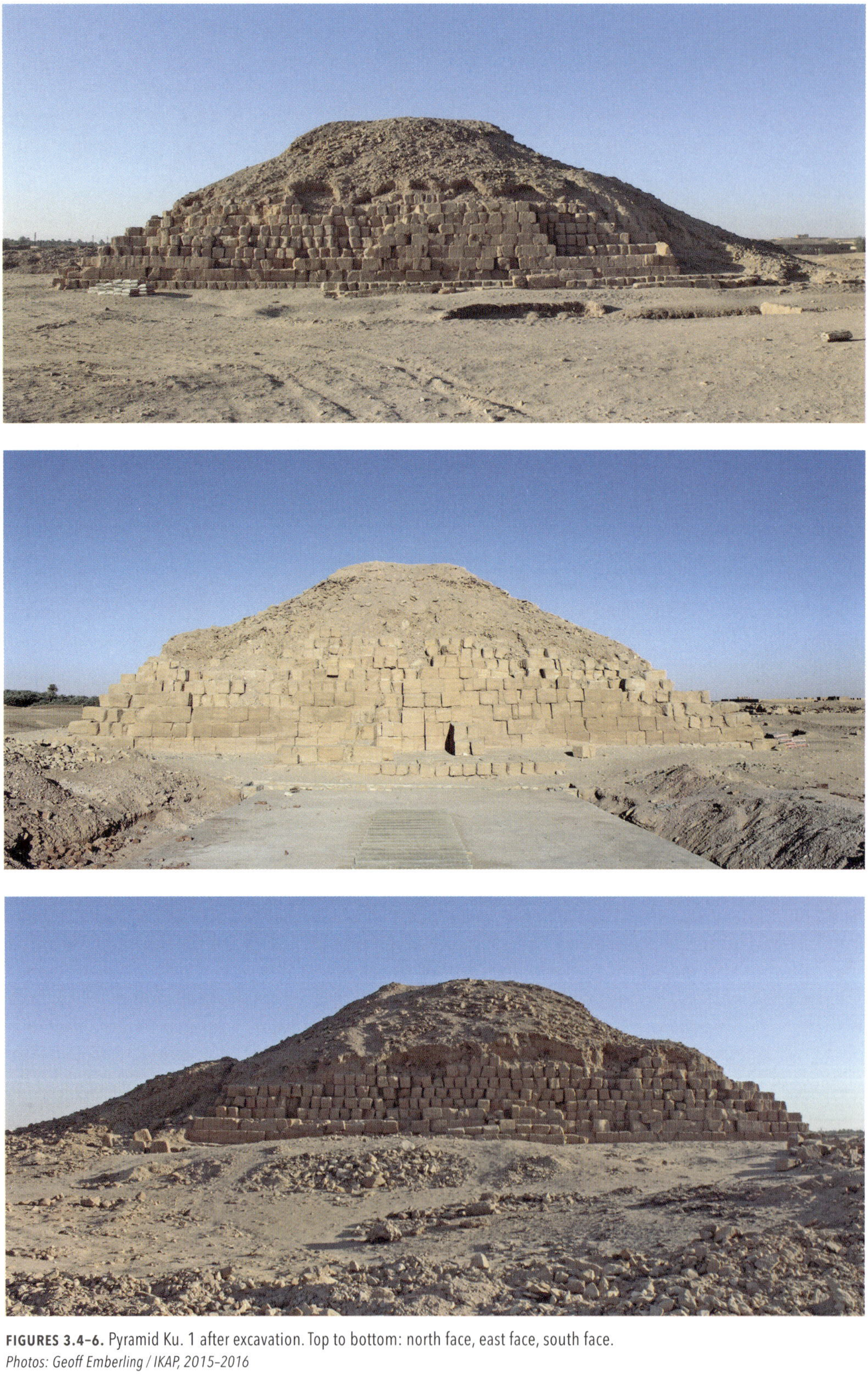

FIGURES 3.4–6. Pyramid Ku. 1 after excavation. Top to bottom: north face, east face, south face.
Photos: Geoff Emberling / IKAP, 2015–2016

Recording the Graffiti

In 2018, at the invitation of the director of the Michigan expedition, Geoff Emberling, I began recording the monument's graffiti photographically, with the intention of creating 3D images. In three weeks, I photographed details of all exposed sides of the pyramid and recorded all the graffiti I could identify, cataloging them according to their location on the pyramid. These photographs and numerous others made previously for planning purposes should, with some exceptions noted below, allow recovery of almost all inscriptions, the bulk of which are modern. Documentation of the medieval and early modern graffiti I believe to be essentially complete. For the most part, they are carved deeply enough and are of simple enough design to be clear in photographs, especially the 3D images.

Two technical issues bedeviled the project. First, the light on the pyramid differed for each face, requiring many visits to find blocks with usable lighting. Second, the medieval and modern graffiti often occupy the same space, and it can be difficult to distinguish the different carving events. To assist in visualizing the older graffiti, I made three-dimensional photo models using a high-quality camera and PhotoScan, an excellent but clumsy tool.

The large number of Arabic and some Latin script graffiti were a confusing element at Ku. 1. Some appeared patinated and some graffiti obscured earlier ones. I did not individually record these, something that would require a specialist in Arabic graffiti. At the northeast corner, the letter Φ is deeply incised with H and M (?), the sole remnants of Old Nubian or Greek. A deeply incised A (graffito P28) could be the Old Nubian/Greek/Coptic letter, but the crossbar is not slanted in a manner normally found in medieval lapidary inscriptions. There are, however, a few well-organized incisions I take to be Christian monograms or attempts at monograms (P28–P29). Other Christian graffiti include crosses and a couple of other simple shapes (P24, P26–P27).

There are remarkably few animals. These include, for example, four camels (P17–P20), two simple incised quadrupeds (P21–P22), and a possible ostrich (P23).

Boat Graffiti on Ku. 1

The bulk of the identifiable graffiti on Ku. 1 are boats, sixteen of which are included in the catalog at the end of this volume (graffiti P1–P16). Five boats are located on the pyramid's north face, fifteen on the east face (five on the left side of the chapel and ten on the right side), and two on the exterior of the chapel's north wall. Two of the boats are very simple and possibly conjectural, but the rest are quite clear. The vessels have a certain resemblance to each other, but each is unique in a manner that suggests that they were carved by different persons. They also vary greatly in elaboration.

Based on parallels discussed below, the boat graffiti are assignable to the Christian period and are probably contemporary with the El-Kurru town site near the river. The location not being sacred to Christianity, it seems likely that some kind of river procession is commemorated here, with a parallel at the rock art site of Sahaba, south of Dongola (see FIG. 3.13).[6] It should be clear from their placement that the graffiti on Ku. 1 are all related in time and purpose.

Three categories of boats represented in the Ku. 1 graffiti can be distinguished by the shape of the hull (FIG. 3.7). The following sections describe the types, illustrated by examples

6. See Jacquet-Gordon 2003, cat. nos. 297–305B, for boats of this general period she believes belonged to processions.

from the catalog. At the outset, I must stress that these are types of representation, and do not necessarily indicate the types of vessel actually in use, a topic that is discussed below.

Type 1

Type 1 is the simplest boat type (**FIG. 3.7A**). The hull is a single curve that recurves sharply to make a stern that continues above the hull. Graffito P1 is the only example at El-Kurru, and it would be difficult to call it a boat were it not surrounded by other examples. A diagonal line behind the stern with splayed lines at the end may indicate a rudder. In the center, a vertical line may be a mast and a horizontal one may indicate a cabin. At the bow, a vertical line ends in an inverted V that may be an anchor. Other scratches nearby probably have nothing to do with the boat.

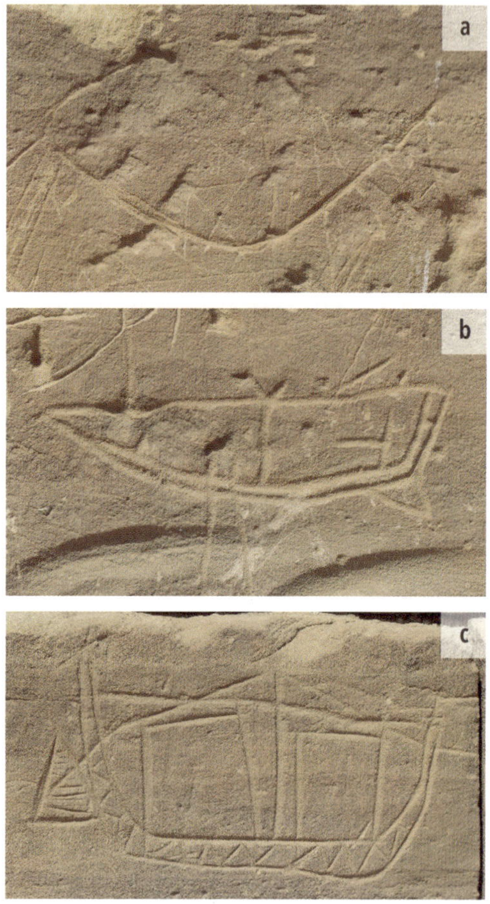

FIGURE 3.7. Examples of the three categories of boats represented in the Ku. 1 graffiti: (*a*) Type 1 (graffito P1); (*b*) Type 2 (graffito P3); (*c*) Type 3 (graffito P9).
Photos: Bruce Beyer Williams / IKAP, 2018

Type 2

Type 2 boats have a simple, curved hull that bends from the prow to a high stern (**FIG. 3.7B**). Of the five examples included here, three have relatively simple hulls. One (graffito P2) has no mast or other superstructure.

In another (P3), the outlined hull curves and tapers to a pointed bow. The stern is bent upward and is broader toward the top. The triangular rudder is attached to the hull tip-down and the tiller is a horizontal bar attached to a line extending up from the hull. The mast is far forward and has a crutch near the top. The yard extends from bow to stern, resting in a forked crutch amidships. Just forward of the crutch, two long oars extend across the hull to triangular blades, base downward (see also **FIG. 3.17**). A badly worn line curves from aft of the mast toward the forward oar, apparently a structure or load. This graffito appears to show a vessel going downstream, using oars not for propulsion but to maintain steerage.

Graffito P4 has a hull, rudder, helm, and oars similar to graffito P3. The stout mast amidships has a V-shaped crutch near the tip. Two horizontal spars are held by approximately 12–14 lines that probably represent lashings for the furled sails. A number of large structures fill the entire deck. A long line that may or may not be part of the composition extends forward from the bow.

Graffiti P6 and P7 are also related to each other. They are larger and fill the blocks on which they are incised. If not exactly graceful, the hulls are shaped to give a slightly more boat-like impression. Graffito P6 has an outlined hull that broadens near the stern and tapers to a pointed bow. The stern bends sharply forward near the tip, then a single line projects up and forward again in a curve. The triangular rudder is curved at the tip and a simple line indicates the helm. Large, rectangular structures occupy the deck between the stern and the mast. The mast has no spar, but one angled line near the top indicates a crutch. Three lines angling down from the mast and a triangular structure in the bow are probably later additions to the graffito.

Graffito P7 is transitional to type 3. The low, pointed prow expands to a rather thick hull that narrows and curves sharply but smoothly to form the stern. The stern is high and narrow and terminates in a cruciform tip with arms splayed as the cross pattée (see further below). The triangular rudder is shown as though attached to the stern by its long side. On the deck a rectangular structure extends from the stern to forward of the mast, which stands within it. At the top of the mast is a small, nearly rectangular structure, below which four lines descend: two extend to the tips of a broad V-shaped yard, and two support a lower yard extending from bow to stern. The mast is shown extending to the bottom of the hull.

Type 3

Type 3 boats have a high stern, slightly curved hull, and a bow that is bent upward but at a lower angle than the stern (FIG. 3.7C). Most of the hulls are outlined, although a few are simple lines. Often, the hull is filled in with zigzags. Most of the vessels presented here have masts, triangular rudders, and many have rigging, sometimes elaborate. There are often rectangular deck structures.

Graffito P9 has a relatively high prow. The hull is filled with a zigzag pattern that extends onto the stern, which terminates in a cross with splayed arms. The large triangular rudder is attached to the hull by a single line, which seems to extend beyond it to make a tiller. A mast is amidships with two lines running to bow and stern and there are rectangular deck structures fore and aft. Extending in front of the bow is a long line with vertical lines attached to it, likely indicating some kind of mooring.

Graffito P10 has a simple line for the hull, which bends up at the long, angled prow and at the stern. Both the prow and stern are straight. A single short line extends backward from the stern, making a crutch. The rudder is curved but clearly related to the triangular rudders seen elsewhere, and the line defining it continues across the hull as an exaggerated tiller. There is a simple square cabin amidships. An incomplete vertical forward of the cabin is possibly a mast and the long horizontal above it probably a yard.

Boats in Graffiti and Chronology at El-Kurru

Unlike formal art that is often widespread, allowing chronological comparisons, much graffiti and rock art is quite localized, especially in medieval times, making comparisons difficult. For example, a boat at Kirbekan in the 4th Cataract not far from El-Kurru differs in most details despite a general resemblance (FIG. 3.8) This circumstance we can remedy at least partly by using the details themselves. Apart from hull design, they include articulation and structures of stern and bow, deck structures, mast and rigging (especially masthead structures), and rudder.

Hull Fill

The small boat to the left of graffito P11 displays horizontal and vertical lines that could indicate planking; another boat (not illustrated) has vertical lines.[7] Several boats have hulls filled with zigzags (P5, P9, P12).[8] Normally this might be taken for binding, especially as the sail on P5 also has this feature, but it seems improbable for this kind of large boat.

Stern-tip Structures[9]

Some boats have a structure at the top of the stern that bends sharply forward, up, and forward again (P6, P13, and P14).

Three boats have cruciform stern tops. The stern of graffito P15 terminates in a simple cross. The crosses on the sterns of P7 and P9 have arms that are splayed as in the cross pattée (see also **FIG. 3.8**). The top of the high stern of graffito P9 is damaged, but the worn lines clearly indicate that it was cruciform.

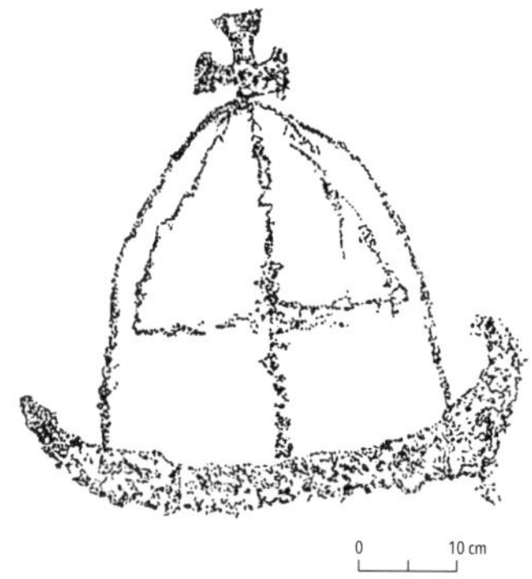

FIGURE 3.8. Christian graffito of a boat with cross pattée masthead structure from Kirbekan, in the 4th Cataract region. *After Budka 2010, fig. 8 upper right (KIR 174)*

Deck Structures

Cube or cuboid deck structures, apparently cabins, are indicated by rectilinear lines. At their simplest (P10), these structures consist of a square box behind the mast. There can be two boxes, one fore, and one aft of the mast (P9, P13, P14). Very long cabins, possibly with more complex structures, extend almost from bow to stern (P4), while shorter ones extend from aft of the mast to the stern (P6) or just before the mast to the stern (P7). As discussed below, large boats can have simple structures, such as one or two box-like cabins, but vessels with very long cabins (P15) appear to belong to the specialized category of traveling boats or barges, which I surmise were also used ceremonially.

Masthead Structures[10]

Graffiti P4 and P5 have a V-shaped crutch below the masthead, a well-known feature.[11] In addition, graffito P7 has at the top of its mast a rectangular shape with the top and bottom bent inward.

7. Červíček 1974, fig. 364, photo 11; Sadek 1972, cat. nos. 3486, 3491.
8. Sadek 1972, cat. no. 3118 a; b, d, and e are crosshatched. Also cat. no. 3122 left.
9. For other Late Antique and medieval stern-tip structures, see Bernand 1969, pp. 314 and 385, crescent crossing stern below tip, fig. 21a. Almagro Basch and Almagro-Gorbea 1968, fig. 235; Červíček 1974, fig. 53. Rectangle across the stern: Červíček 1974, fig. 55. Horned circle with central horn also and streamers and balls(?): Dijkstra 2012, cat. no. 67, Elephantine, 9th/10th century; also cat. nos. 71, 72, 73 (more like a trident), 74 (also three-horned), Late Antique or later; cat nos. 354–56, second half of 6th century. Very simple, possibly horned: Sadek 1972, cat. no. 3337; flag-like: ibid., cat. no. 3472, also Epigraphic Survey 1981, Khonsu 304.
10. For additional complexes of triangle and angled rectangles, see Almagro Basch and Almagro-Gorbea 1968, fig. 233. Circle: Červíček 1974, photo 11. Possible V fork with fill: Dijkstra 2012, cat. no. 73, Elephantine, Late Antique or later. Two arms crossing: Epigraphic Survey 1981, Khonsu 300.
11. "Crutch" is the term used by Hornell (1942, p. 7). For parallels, see Červíček 1974, fig. 55, right.

Rigging

The sail of P8 has a rectilinear grid of lines that must indicate a net-like reinforcement (see FIG. 3.10). The sail is triangular but is mounted as a square sail.

Rudder, Triangular

A distinctive feature of the El-Kurru boats is a triangular or sub-triangular rudder. Most are shown as though attached to the stern, but this was probably because they were visible from only one side (e.g., graffito P11) (see FIG. 3.9).[12] Sometimes the triangle of the rudder is shown behind and adjacent to the stern, as in graffito P9; in this case with the horizontal lines and the shaft leading at a slight curve from the tip, it might bend forward to form a tiller. In two cases, P13 and P14, the rudder is a right triangle, truncated across the hypotenuse at the base of the stern. In neither case is the shaft of the tiller preserved.

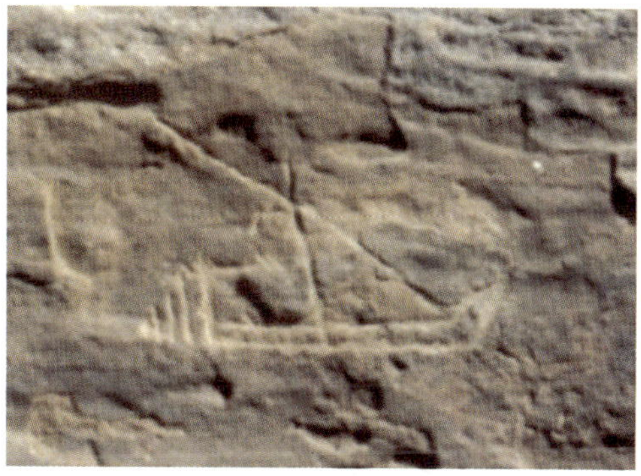

FIGURE 3.9. *Felucca* with triangular rudder, from Sabu. *Photo: Bruce Beyer Williams*

In P9 the rudder appears as a separate object, attached to the hull by a long shaft that extends across and past the stern. The blade is an isosceles triangle with horizontal lines that must indicate planks. The rudder of P8 is depicted by five lines that splay downward behind the stern, making a rough isosceles triangle attached by a shaft that extends at an angle into the vessel.[13]

Rudder, Rectangular[14]

Graffito P16, one of the cruder type 3 vessels, has a rectangular rudder that is hatched parallel to the hull and crossed by two lines, one of which extends to the masthead as part of the rigging.

Comparisons for Dating

Despite the individuality of most representations, a number of dated groups of boats in graffiti can be used to indicate the date of the Ku. 1 vessels. Most of the boats cited here have a curved hull, with no sharp bends at bow or stern. Thus the details described above are the main links between the boats of El-Kurru and the dated groups, which consist of the following.

12. For examples of triangular rudders on graffiti boats from other sites, see Červíček 1974, figs. 53, 364; Dijkstra 2012, cat. nos. 72 and 355, Elephantine, second half of the 6th century; Sadek 1972, cat. nos. 3324, 3118, four examples, three of which have a tiller arm at right angles to the shaft.
13. For parallels, see Bernand 1969, pp. 314, 385; and Philae Kiosk vessel of Annianos https://commons.wikimedia.org/wiki/Category:Graffiti_in_the_Temple_of_Philae, for example.
14. Dijkstra 2012, cat. no. 72, Elephantine, Late Antique or later.

Roman Period, 1st Century BCE and Later

The Nile Mosaic of Palestrina, dating from about the 1st century BCE and later, depicts many Roman-period boats, among them two that are of interest to this discussion (FIG. 3.10).[15] Both have a high, heavy stern to which a curved shape is attached. The hull of each boat curves to the bow, which terminates in a figure. The sail on the smaller vessel has a net reinforcement. The use of a large vessel for hunting hippopotamus appears somewhat fanciful but does have parallels from early Egypt. It is worth noting that ancient Egyptian riverboats do not commonly have high sterns or prows.

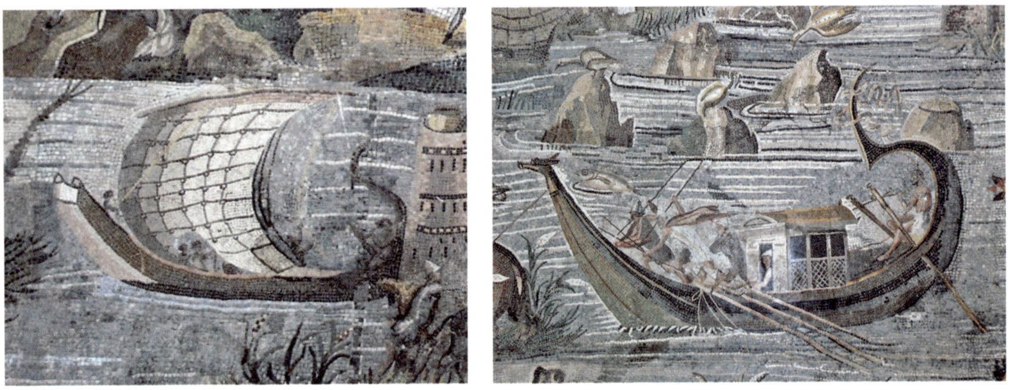

FIGURE 3.10. Details of the Nile Mosaic. Left: small boat with net reinforcement. Right: larger boat engaged in a hippopotamus hunt. (The hindquarters of the unfortunate animal can be seen at the picture's left edge, just in front of the boat.)
Camelia Boban / Wikimedia Commons

Late Antique and Later, 3rd–7th Centuries CE

Jitse Dijkstra has been able to date a number of boat graffiti in the Khnum Temple at Elephantine, Egypt, to roughly the Late Antique period and later, probably well after the conversion to Christianity.[16] A number of graffiti incised on a quay wall at Elephantine can be dated to the second half of the 6th century; a church was built above the quay at about the same date.[17] Since the styles found in these depictions differ from those noted for El-Kurru, the similarities are general.

Ca. 9th–10th Centuries CE

Again at Elephantine, Dijkstra was able to date a number of boat graffiti with horned stern and bow figures to the 9th–10th centuries (FIG. 3.11).[18] A very distinctive type of boat with horned bow and stern was incised in mud plaster at Qasr el-Wizz (FIG. 3.12),[19] and very close

15. The Nile Mosaic, now housed at the National Archaeological Museum of Palestrina in central Italy, is a large late Hellenistic floor mosaic depicting the Nile in its passage from the Blue Nile to the Mediterranean.
16. See Dijkstra 2012, pp. 73–75, for a discussion of boats in graffiti generally, cat. nos. 71–74 for the group in the temple called "Late Antique and later." Note the triangular rudder on cat. no. 72, but also 355, which is considered second half of the 5th century. Triangular rudders also appear at Thebes (Sadek 1972, cat. nos. 3324 and 3118; note the monogram c).
17. Dijkstra 2012, appendix 1.
18. Dijkstra 2012, cat. nos. 67–69, 75–84. Many of the boats are more damaged and fragmentary, and some painted and not illustrated in this context.
19. The long, low vessel has pairs of horns at prow and stern, with vertical center-projections. Forward, two pairs of oars angle downward, and there is a triangular rudder. As at Sahaba (see FIG. 3.13), weighted cords depend from the bow and stern. The long cabin with supporting poles and panels has a man holding a cross

parallels are carved into the rock face at Sahaba (**FIG. 3.13**).[20] The type makes here a coherent group of barges with a horned face or round figure on the prow, a long, low curved hull, long deckhouse, and pendant lines, probably with weights, at the bow and stern, which is indicated at El-Kurru by a fork in the bow and stern of graffito P15.

Some of the parallels cited above refer to graffiti that are not easily dated. Those noted from Sadek 1972, Jacquet-Gordon 2003, and especially Dijkstra 2012 are decisive in dating the boat graffiti on Ku. 1 to the Christian period, no earlier than the 7th century, and possibly continuing into the 11th or 12th century, parallel to the date of the Christian town at El-Kurru.

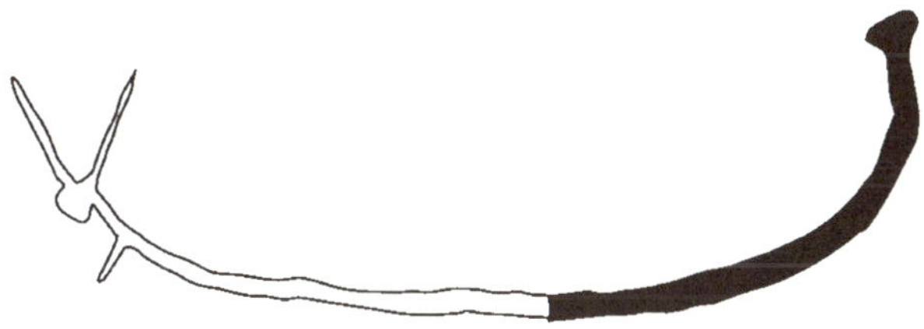

FIGURE 3.11. A long, simple hull with a horned orb or face at the prow. Aswan, 9th–10th century CE or later.
After Dijkstra 2012, cat. no. 75

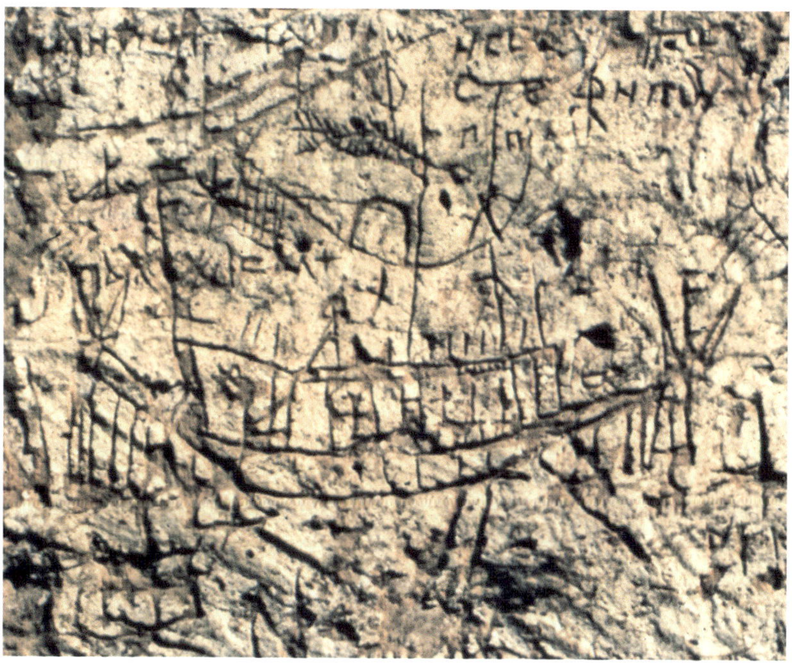

FIGURE 3.12. Depiction of a large ceremonial barge incised in mud plaster on a wall at the Monastery of Qasr el-Wizz, Egyptian Nubia.
Photo: George Scanlon / Oriental Institute Nubian Expedition, 1969

on the roof. On the rear panel is an eight-pointed sacred symbol common in Nubian Christian pottery painting. A panel near amidships bears a footed cross, while the long panel or open space forward may depict a seated figure. On the foredeck is a cat, which appears in a graffito of a barge at Aswan.

20. For the Sahaba boat, see Smith 2003, p. 166 and fig. 8. The Christian parallel for this boat was not known at the time Smith wrote his article, but exists, exact at Qasr el-Wizz and generally at Aswan (**FIG. 3.11**, herein).

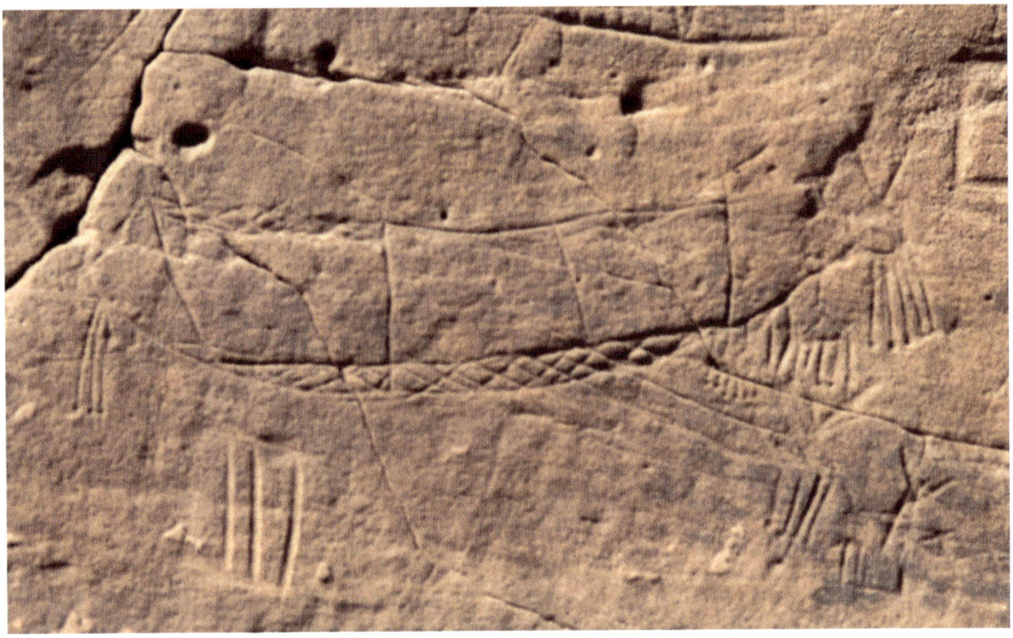

FIGURE 3.13. Ceremonial barge with a horned orb at the prow and possibly the stern, from Sahaba.
Photo: Bruce Beyer Williams

Excursus:
Terms for Boats and Navigation in Old Nubian

ALEXANDROS TSAKOS[1]

In the small corpus of texts where Old Nubian (the local language of the medieval centuries in Sudan) was used, there are preserved several terms relating to navigation, but here I will only present those directly relevant for the boats depicted in the graffiti examined by Bruce Williams. The most important observation is that there is only one term for ship or boat: ⲁⲩⲉⲗ̄. Such vessels were of various sizes and types, since they could have a rudder (ⲥⲁⲩⲯⲟ), a sternpost or tiller (ⲧⲟⲣⲓ, literally "axle"), a hold (ⲁⲥ), and a mast or spar (ⲅⲁⲕⲕ, literally "pole"). On that last element, sails could be raised, as apparently testified by the verb ⲟⲩⲁ̄ⲟⲩ, meaning "to sail." There has also been attested a verb for traveling downstream on the Nile (ⳟⲁⲕ), as well as a term for a haven or port (ⲟⲩⲧ(ⲧ)ⲟⲥⲇⲉⲣ).[2] From this very brief lexicographical survey,[3] I leave out all terms relating to the crew of these boats, which offer, however, interesting insights into navigation and naval hierarchy in medieval Nubia.

1. I would like to thank Vincent van Gerven Oei for his useful comments.
2. A composite form consisting of the verb ⲟⲩⲧ, meaning "to put," the aspect marker ⲟⲥ and the nominalizer ⲇⲉⲣ.
3. For all terms, see Browne 1996.

The Ku. 1 Boat Graffiti and River Traffic on the Medieval Middle Nile

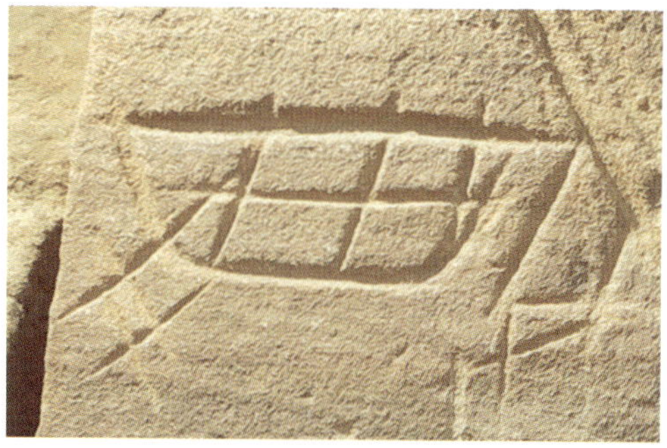

FIGURE 3.14. Rowboat from graffito P11.
Photo: Bruce Beyer Williams / IKAP, 2018

Although the rowboat shown in P11 (**FIG. 3.14**) is clearly small — much smaller than the boat that tows it — there is no clear indication of size for most vessels shown on the Ku. 1 pyramid, other than the fact that they have masts, sails, and often cabins. It is therefore useful to try to compare these boats with known vessels or clearer representations to attempt to identify them. I will restrict the comparisons to the Roman period and later, but particularly concentrate on 19th- or early 20th-century descriptions of traditional Nile craft.

Below, I present a number of Arabic terms that are applied to various vessels in different places. These terms have been applied colloquially and they vary from region to region. It is likely that they have varied from time to time and certainly from place to place within a region. For example, the term *gyassa* or *gaiassa* is also used in the eastern Mediterranean for cargo barges, while *felucca* designates a fishing boat with lateen rig used as far away as San Francisco Bay.

Shipping boat types depicted in the Nile Valley before modern times very often have a high stern and a more or less curved hull to a raised, but lower, prow. However, because of the particular configuration of the El-Kurru boats, it is not easy to distinguish them by any distinctive feature from many of the rock-drawn vessels of various ages, as early as the Naqada Period/A-Group (late 4th millennium BCE).[21] In the period after Augustus (reigned 27 BCE–14 CE), the hulls generally are curved from stern to prow, without a bend at either end. This certainly raises an issue for comparing the El-Kurru boats to other representations. There is another issue, comparing these vessels with more recent types of river transport on the Nile, which was first reliably depicted by Frederick Louis Norden, who traveled through Egypt and Nubia in the 1730s.

There are clear differences between the river craft represented in graffiti and other art from ancient times and recent traditional river craft. The technology of construction and sail propulsion has developed considerably, making a radical difference in the appearance of the vessels.[22] However, James Hornell, an ethnographer of traditional boat-building, studied Middle Nile boats in detail in the 1930s and 1940s, and some significant points of continuity can be raised. First and most important, the construction of modern Nile boats in Sudan is the same as that found in ancient times, that is to say, without a frame (see **FIG. 3.16**).[23] Hornell also noted two general classes of utility boat. Upstream of the 4th Cataract, large cargo *nuggars* could be more than 18 meters long × 7 meters wide, while smaller fishing and ferry boats (*gharab*) were mostly about 8–9 × 3–3.5 meters (**FIG. 3.15**).[24] The smaller boats

21. See Williams 1986, pp. 139–40, for this distinctive stern profile that belongs only to sacred barks of the Naqada IIIa.
22. Add to this the presence of ceremonial barks and barges in ancient art, which can be difficult to distinguish in simple graffiti or rock art. For the general conditions for navigation of the Middle Nile, see Page 1919. Most of his discussion is of steam, but sailing boats are described on pp. 305–06, and he points out that the sail with both yard and boom aids sailing near high banks. Page also asserts that a boat he designed and built at Aswan in 1903 influenced the shape of sailing boats south of Shellal (ibid., p. 303).
23. Hornell 1942, p. 1; Hornell gives the typology (p. 2), and the details of construction at Omdurman (pp. 2–5).
24. Ibid., see tables on pp. 6 and 10 for details.

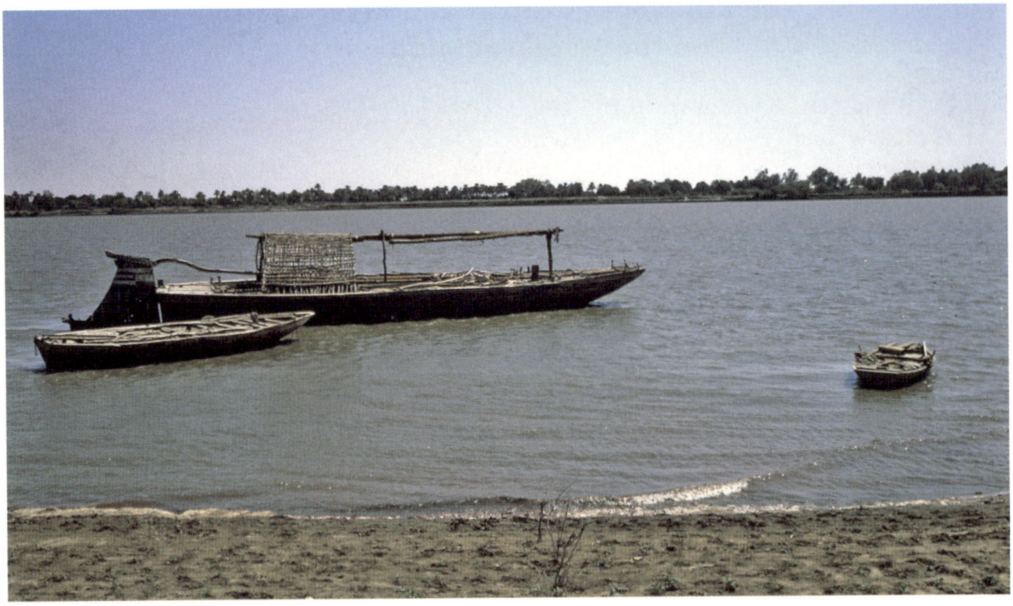

FIGURE 3.15. Khartoum *nuggar* with *felucca* tender, and smaller boat to right.
Photo: James E. Knudstad / Oriental Institute Nubian Expedition, 1964

could be used as tenders, or *felucca*, for the larger vessels. In Dongola, Sudan, the cargo boat was known as a *markib* ("boat") (**FIG. 3.17**). While Hornell does not provide overall measurements, planks in English sizes were about 72 × 12 × 2.25–2.5 inches (182.8 × 30.5 × 5.7–6.3 cm). Hornell considered the double-yard lateen sail of the Dongola boat (**FIG. 3.16**) remarkable and paralleled only in the Malay Archipelago,[25] but it could be the double-yard square sail seen on ancient and medieval vessels turned at an angle.[26] One further useful comparison is the square cabin forward of the mast of the traveling boat-shop (*kantin*), ca. 8–9 feet (2.4–2.7 m) high,[27] which furnishes a useful perspective for structures found on the El-Kurru boats.

Although the technology of sailing depicted in the graffiti appears to differ from later times,[28] the navigation system shown in the graffiti appears very much like that of the later Middle Nile, with its various classes of boat. There are four general categories of boat to consider in the graffiti, discussed here from small to large. These provide information about navigation on the Nile during this early period.

Rowboats

The smallest is a boat sometimes used for fishing and sometimes as a tender for a larger vessel. Graffito P11 introduced the rowboat, clearly being towed and used as a tender by its

25. Ibid., p. 17.
26. Pryor and Jeffreys (2006, pp. 153–61) believed the square sail disappeared from the Mediterranean until reintroduced from northern Europe in the 14th century. Given the presence of Northmen and their longships and *knars* as well as crusaders from the north, it's difficult to believe that there was a complete disappearance.
27. Hornell 1942, p. 27 and pl. II. The Egyptologist James Henry Breasted (1908, p. 25) was furnished two such boats by C. H. Page at Kareima; he refers to these boats as *nuggars*. The larger was just over 15 meters long and had a larger cabin and a smaller cabin, which was used as a darkroom. The boats both passed the Kajbar cataract in January (ibid., pp. 49–50). The larger boat was holed and repaired only with difficulty.
28. As discussed in Hornell 1942.

larger boat (see FIG. 3.14). This size is also seen next to large *markib*-type boats photographed not far south of Sahaba (FIG. 3.17). Other photographs show crafts of this size used for fishing in addition to the next larger size considered here, *feluccas.*

Feluccas

Next in size are those that Hornell indicated could be used as ferries or for fishing, roughly the size of the modern-day ferry at Tombos, Sudan (FIG. 3.16). A lateen rig would be especially useful for ferries, which sail back and forth across the wind.[29] Hornell also noted that this size and the smaller version of the cargo boats (see below) was also useful for fishing.[30] The type was normally decked fore and aft, but not amidships. They could be called *feluccas* because of the rigging. The type was apparently not present at Ku. 1, but lateen-rigged boats of intermediate size are depicted Qasr el-Wizz and Sabu (FIG. 3.9).

Cargo Boats

The third size, probably fully decked, could carry large cargo or have cabins. It is this size that is depicted in most rock art and on Ku. 1 (FIG. 3.15 but without cabin; graffiti P7 and P9, for example). The Arabic terms for these boats in Dongola or the Middle Nile above the 4th Cataract are difficult to use because both the technology of the rigging and design of the

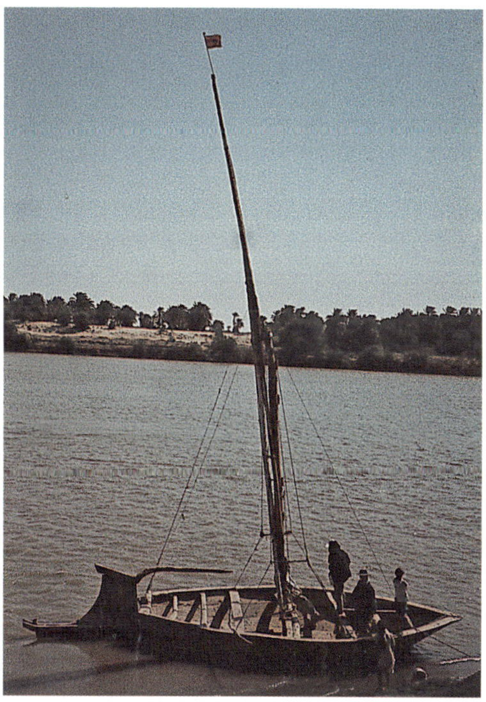

FIGURE 3.16. Tombos *felucca* ferry.
Photo: Bruce Beyer Williams, 2000

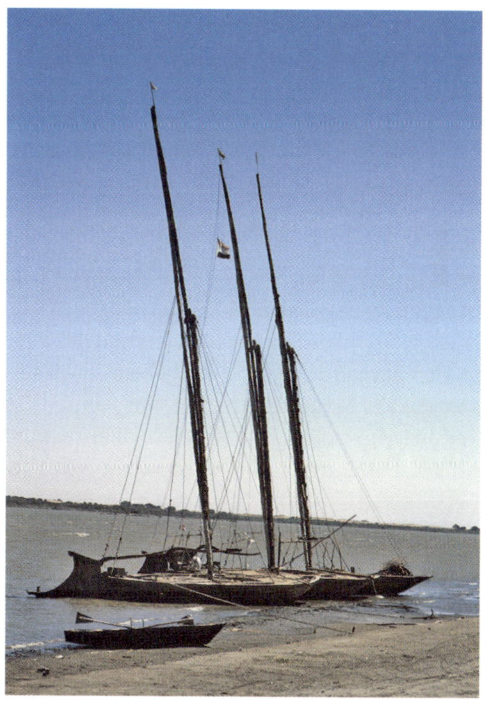

FIGURE 3.17. Dongola *markib* with tender. Note the tender's triangular oar blades.
Photo: Bruce Beyer Williams, 1997

29. Hornell (1942, p. 7) noted that the ferries of the Khartoum region had square sails.
30. Ibid., pp. 5–6.

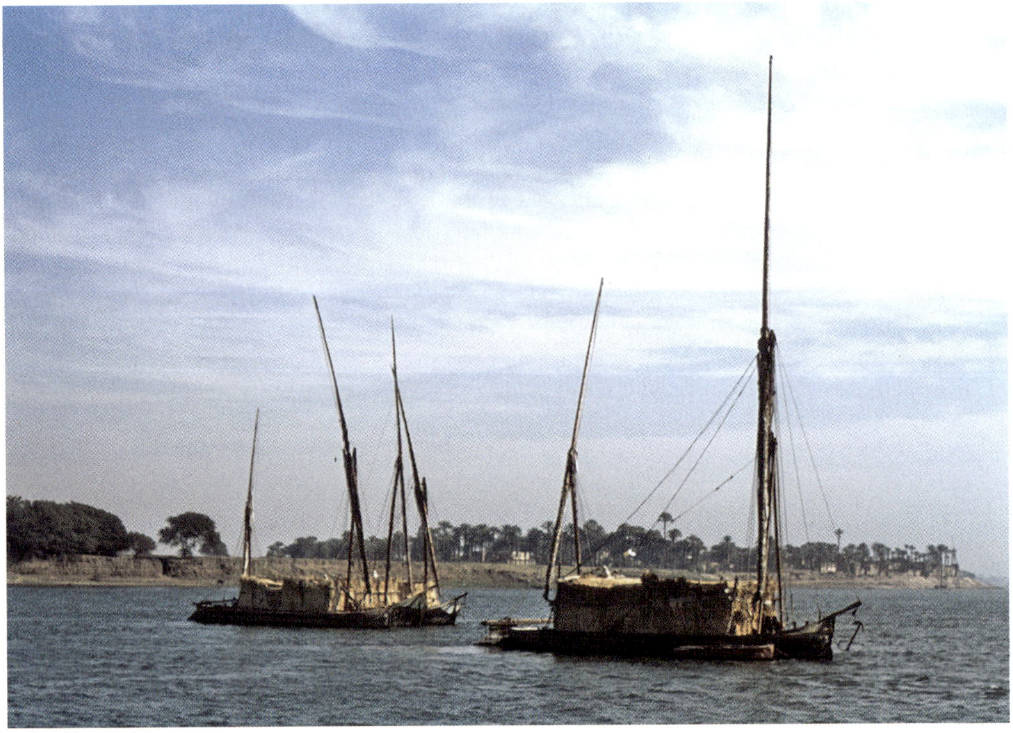

FIGURE 3.18. Egyptian *gyassa* used for grain transport.
Photo: Bruce Beyer Williams, 1972

hulls differ,[31] although they do correspond in size and function to the *nuggar* of the latter region and the *markib* of the former. With square cabins, they were decked as modern *markib* (**FIG. 3.17**) and were clumsy enough to run aground and to need tenders, at least from time to time, as noted for P10. At its largest, it could have been the size of a modern *gyassa*, widely used in Egypt for heavy or bulky cargo (**FIG. 3.18**). This range of vessels along with a variety of riggings is shown in Frederick Louis Norden's *Travels in Egypt and Nubia* (**FIG. 3.19**), illustrating a continuity in river navigation over more than two centuries. Norden was a captain in the Danish Navy and had the advantage of traveling on the Nile in 1737 and 1738, over sixty years before the Napoleonic expedition. He was an acute observer and a skilled artist, and his work is a valuable historical resource. It appears that most of the boats represented on Ku. 1 belong to this class, although the nature of representation makes distinguishing between this and the next class sometimes difficult.

Barges, Traveling or Ceremonial

The last of the riverboats considered here, the barges (P5, P8, P15, possibly P7, P13, P14), appear larger, or at least longer. The clearest (P5) has a long hull relative to bow and stern. Vertical lines from the hull to the mast perhaps indicate a very long cabin, and the bow has a forked structure that recalls certain boats depicted at Aswan (**FIG. 3.11**), but especially

31. There is a certain fluidity in the way terms are applied in any case. For example, *gyassa* or *gaiassa* can mean a flat-bottomed lighter or boat used in the eastern Mediterranean or the Red Sea, as well as a similar but larger boat on the Nile in Egypt that has a shallow draft but is not necessarily flat-bottomed. Both are used for heavy cargo.

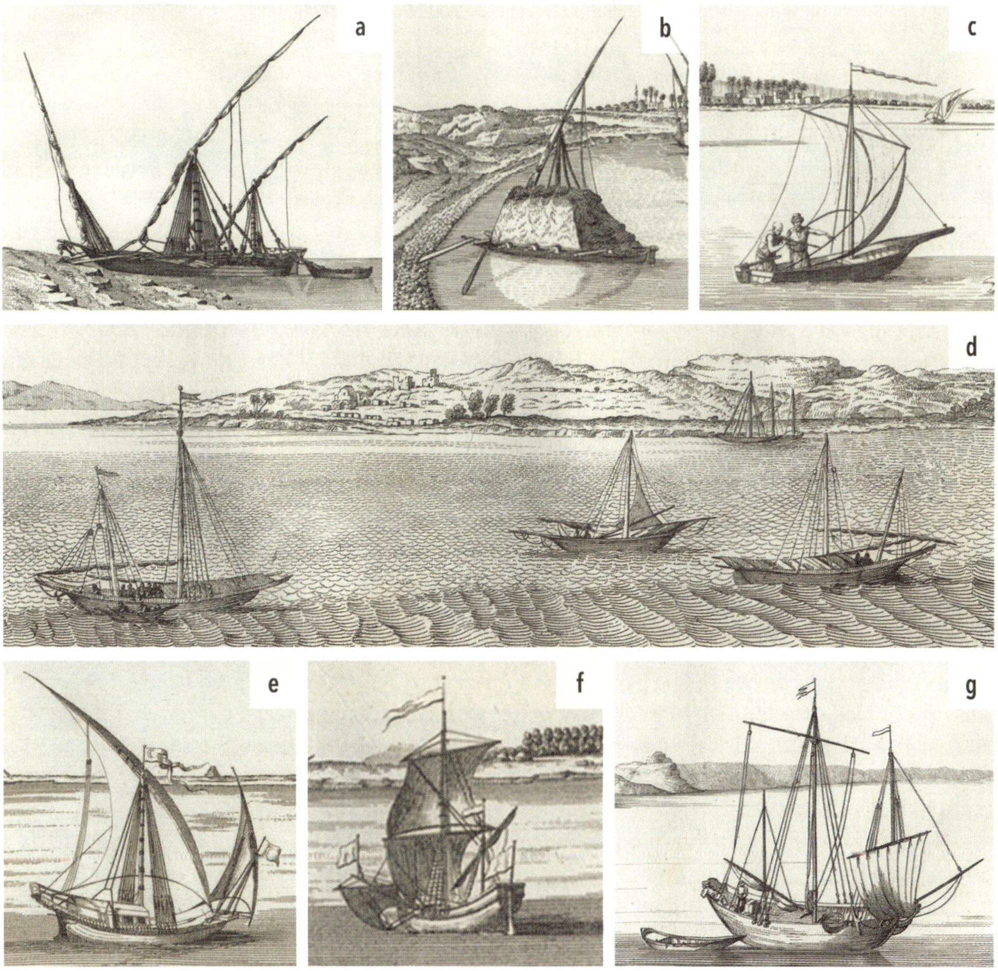

FIGURE 3.19. Nile shipping as depicted in Norden 1757. Image (*a*) is called by Norden "*merkeb*"; (*b*) resembles a *gyassa*; (*e*) is similar to a *dahabiyya*.
After Norden 1757, pls. XXXI, XXXV, XXXVI, CL, LXIII, LXXXIV, CXIX

those of Qasr el-Wizz (**FIG. 3.12**) and Sahaba (**FIG. 3.13**). This and its comparisons do not appear particularly robust in design, and they have very large cabins that occupy most of the vessel. In this, they have a strong resemblance to the *dahabiyya* used for luxury travel in 19th- and 20th-century Egypt and earlier (**FIG. 3.19E**).[32] The size is also comparable — with no need for great strength to handle heavy cargo, some are up to 40 meters in length, and are relatively narrow and of shallow draft.[33] In these graffiti we are introduced to a boat type not previously well documented in Nilotic history. As noted, large ceremonial barges are known from other sites, Sahaba and Qasr el-Wizz with horns at the prow and sometimes the stern, but at El-Kurru, graffito P15 is the most likely example, also with horns; P8 is included because of its proportions and the others because of the cabins.

32. Now revived; search "dahabiyya" in an internet search engine for tour information.
33. For less detailed versions of this type of boat in Nubia, see Shinnie and Shinnie 1978, fig. 8.

Discussion and Conclusions

The Ku. 1 boat graffiti make up a unique body of such representations from Nubia. Their number, and the fact that they can be arranged in a general order related to their placement on the pyramid and have a general date, is also unique.

Based on dated parallels, the boat graffiti on Ku. 1 are assignable to the Christian period (ca. 600–1400). There was a town along the Nile at El-Kurru during that time, and the graffiti are probably contemporary with this. Although the Nile is not currently visible from the site due to trees along the bank, the Christian town was directly in front of the pyramid and in medieval times would have been visible from it if vegetation on the bank was low. Boat and ship carvings are well known on churches and in some monasteries spread widely in the Christian world and their significance has been discussed. In this case, however, the location is not sacred to Christianity, and it seems likely that the graffiti commemorate some kind of river procession and were placed on the closest available rock face to the town, pyramid Ku. 1. A parallel for this exists at Sahaba, which is a natural rock face (FIG. 3.13).

Boat types 1–3 differ considerably from one another, and although no two boats are alike, certain groups can be pointed out so there was change over time. The event depicted could not have been yearly or there would have been many more carved boats. Perhaps the best guess as to the reason for the existence of the boat graffiti on Ku. 1 is that they commemorate events that happened at the installation of a king or a high ecclesiastical official of Dotawo, the Nubian name of the kingdom called Makuria in Greek, with its capital at Old Dongola between the 3rd and 4th Cataracts. As yet we have no written record to illuminate this problem, or to explain the astonishingly ornate barge carved at Sahaba (FIG. 3.13) or the even more ornate one at Qasr el-Wizz (FIG. 3.12), which are the same type as P15, represented more simply here, but it is another testimony to the high complexity of the state in Dotawo.

By themselves, the El-Kurru boats make up a significant body of evidence for navigation on the Nile in the Christian and probably early Late Christian periods. In comparing them to dated groups of graffiti and evidence from Sahaba in the Dongola Reach between the 3rd and 4th Cataracts, Sabu in Mahas in the region of the 3rd Cataract, and Qasr el-Wizz north of Faras, we have an even more comprehensive set of information.

Final Note

Boats and ships appear often in the art of the world, and we should not dismiss the aesthetics of boats on the Nile. In fact, even today the people on the Nubian Nile often show appreciation for daily-life vessels such as the Tombos ferry (FIG. 3.16), and express it in local folk art, such as painted panels on the sides and rear of trucks. I close with one example from Kareima: a truck that shows a sailing boat in the 4th Cataract (FIG. 3.20).

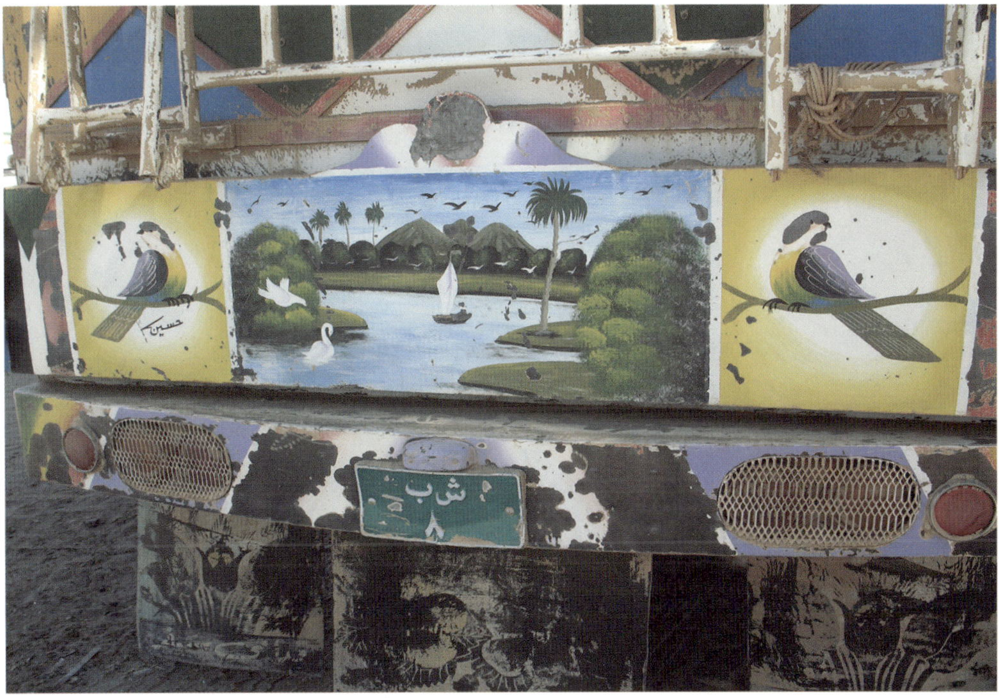

FIGURE 3.20. Truck at Kareima with a 4th Cataract Nile scene.
Photo: Bruce Beyer Williams

References

Almagro Basch, Martín, and Martín Almagro-Gorbea

1968 *Estudios de arte rupestre nubio 1. Yacimientos situados en la orilla oriental del Nilo, entre Nag Kolorodna y Kars* [sic] *Ibrim (Nubia Egipcia).* Memorias de la Misión arqueológica española en Egipto 10. Madrid: Ministerio de Asuntos exteriores.

Bernand, Étienne

1969 *Les inscriptions grecques et latines de Philae,* Volume 2: *Haut et Bas Empire.* Paris: Centre national de la recherche scientifique.

Breasted, James Henry

1908 "Oriental Exploration Fund of the University of Chicago. Second Preliminary Report of the Egyptian Expedition." *The American Journal of Semitic Languages and Literatures* 25 (1): 1–110.

Browne, Gerald M.

1996 *Old Nubian Dictionary.* Corpus Criptorum Christianorum Orientalium 556. Leuven: Peeters.

Budka, Julia

2010 "Humboldt University Nubian Expedition Riverbank Group: Summary of Three Seasons in the Fourth Cataract Area (2004–2006)." In *Between the Cataracts: Proceedings of the 11th International Conference on Nubian Studies, Warsaw University, 27 August–2 September 2006,* Part 2, Fascicle 1: *Session Papers,* edited by Włodzimierz Godlewski and Adam Łajtar, pp. 119–34. Polish Archaeology in the Mediterranean Supplement Series, 2.2/1. Warsaw: University of Warsaw Press.

Červíček, Pavel

1974 *Felsbilder des Nord-Etbai, Oberägyptens und Unternubiens.* Ergebnisse der Frobenius-Expeditionen 16. Wiesbaden: Steiner.

Dann, Rachael J., and Geoff Emberling, eds.

2016 "El Kurru 2015–16: Preliminary Report." *Sudan & Nubia* 20: 35–49.

Dijkstra, Jitse H. F.

2012 *Syene I. The Figural and Textual Graffiti from the Temple of Isis at Aswan.* Beiträge zur Ägyptischen Bauforschung und Altertumskunde 18. Mainz: Philipp von Zabern.

Dunham, Dows

1950 *El Kurru.* The Royal Cemeteries of Kush 1. Cambridge, MA: Harvard University Press.

Emberling, Geoff

2015 "A Mortuary Temple at El-Kurru." *Sudan & Nubia* 19: 65–67.

Emberling, Geoff, and Rachael J. Dann, eds.

2013 "New Excavations at El-Kurru: Beyond the Napatan Royal Cemetery." Sudan & Nubia 17: 42–60.

Emberling, Geoff, Rachael J. Dann, Abbas Sidahmed Mohamed-Ali, eds.

2015 "In a Royal Cemetery of Kush: Archaeological Investigations at El-Kurru, Northern Sudan, 2014–15." *Sudan & Nubia* 19: 54–70.

Epigraphic Survey

1981 *The Temple of Khonsu 2. Scenes and Inscriptions in the Court and the First Hypostyle Hall.* Oriental Institute Publications 103. Chicago: The Oriental Institute.

Hornell, James

1942 "The Frameless Boats of the Middle Nile." *Sudan Notes & Records* 25 (1): 1–36.

Jacquet-Gordon, Helen

2003 *The Temple of Khonsu 3. The Graffiti on the Khonsu Temple Roof at Karnak: A Manifestation of Personal Piety.* Oriental Institute Publications 123. Chicago: The Oriental Institute.

Norden, Frederick Louis

1757 *Travels in Egypt and Nubia.* 2 vols. London: Davis & Reymers.

Page, C. H.

1919 "Inland Water Navigation of the Sudan." *Sudan Notes & Records* 2 (4): 293–306.

Pryor, John H., and Elizabeth M. Jeffreys

2006 *The Age of the Δρομων: The Byzantine Navy, ca. 500–1204.* The Medieval Mediterranean 62. Leiden: Brill.

Sadek, A. A.

1972 *Graffiti de la montagne thébaine III, 4: Facsimilés.* Cairo: Centre de documentation et d'études sur l'ancienne Égypte.

Shinnie, Peter L., and Margaret Shinnie

1978 *Debeira West, a Medieval Nubian Town.* Warminster: Aris & Phillips.

Smith, Stuart Tyson

2003 "The University of California Dongola Reach Expedition, West Bank Reconnaissance Survey: 1997–1998." *Kush* 18: 157–72.

Tucker, Gregory, and Geoff Emberling

2016 "Settlement in the Heartland of Napatan Kush: Preliminary Results of Magnetic Gradiometry at El-Kurru, Jebel Barkal and Sanam." *Sudan & Nubia* 20: 50–56.

Williams, Bruce B.

1986 *Excavations between Abu Simbel and the Sudan Frontier: The A-Group Royal Cemetery at Qustul; Cemetery L.* Oriental Institute Nubian Expedition 3. Chicago: The Oriental Institute.

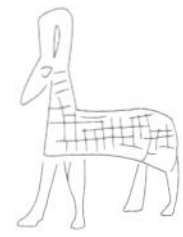

4

Suzanne Davis

Conservation and Documentation of Graffiti at El-Kurru

The royal cemeteries of ancient Kush were grand, carefully constructed landscapes of monumental funerary architecture. El-Kurru is no exception, and although it retains few standing monuments today, the site remains home to two immediately impressive features: the large, standing pyramid Ku. 1, and Ku. 1's companion funerary temple. Both monuments can be entered and explored by visitors to the site, providing experiences that are relatively rare. In the case of Ku. 1, it is the only pyramid in Sudan with a burial chamber open to visits by tourists. The temple, in turn, has only one known parallel: a funerary temple that lies buried and inaccessible upriver at the site of Nuri. But El-Kurru's Ku. 1 pyramid and funerary temple are also interesting to visitors and scholars for a reason beyond their architectural significance; their surfaces are carved with hundreds of small graffiti.

Unlike El-Kurru's monumental architecture, the site's graffiti exist on a very human scale. They are small, scratched symbols of what someone was thinking about, or hoping for, or they are simply meant to say, "I was here." They are individual and personal, and they are usually carved at a height that makes it easy for them to be noticed and appreciated. Some are instantly recognizable as familiar things, others are mysteriously ambiguous. Visually interesting and evocative, El-Kurru's many small graffiti collectively pose a big conservation challenge, because they are carved into very soft sandstone.

Archaeologists tend to think of stone as "sturdy" and, compared to most other historic materials, this is true. But as relatively strong as stone is, it can suffer from a wide variety of problems, and this has big implications for graffiti. For graffiti drawn or written in chalk, charcoal, ink, or paint, both the graffiti's media and the surface on which they are drawn can deteriorate, increasing the risk of loss. But even for incised graffiti, like those found at El-Kurru, the designs are only as stable as the rock into which they are carved. Stone can crack and break from all kinds of physical stressors, including compression and shear forces and thermal stress from sunlight and heat. It can be eroded by wind and water, attacked by fungi, and sedimentary rock containing clays can swell and dissolve if exposed to regular moisture.

Some stones, simply because of their chemical and physical composition, are especially susceptible to deterioration. Conservators have a term for this kind of compositional problem — we call it "inherent vice." The sandstone bedrock at El-Kurru, the same stone that makes up El-Kurru's monuments and into which the site's graffiti are scratched, suffers from inherent vice; the quartz grains are held together by a soft, poorly cemented matrix that breaks down readily. In other words, the "sand" is barely bound by the "stone," and the result is a sandy, easily damaged rock.

The sandstone at El-Kurru, and throughout much of northern Sudan, is prone to the following problems due to its composition: sanding, or granular disintegration, in which the surface breaks down (as if the stone is turning back into sand); delamination, where thin sheets of the surface crack and flake away; coving, where curved chunks are lost in a similar fashion; and scaling, where large sections of the rock's surface progressively crack and detach (**FIG. 4.1**). The deterioration of the stone is accelerated by multiple factors onsite: infrequent but heavy rains, windblown debris, and thermal stress from the rapid heating and cooling of the rock between Sudan's hot, sunny days and cool, desert nights. Needless to say, as the surface of the rock is lost by any of these means, so are the graffiti carved into it. The rock's inherent softness puts it at risk of another type of damage, too: modern defacement. Because it is so easy to carve, some visitors — continuing the long tradition of graffiti at El-Kurru — scratch their names into the stone (as shown in **FIG. 4.2**).

There are three basic approaches to address the kinds of damage and risk listed above. The first is reburial, where the soil excavated from inside or around the monument is used to rebury it. Conservation intervention or "treatment," that is, applying a substance to the surface of the stone to strengthen it, is the second option. The third is careful documentation coupled with a willingness to accept ongoing deterioration. Of these options, the first — reburial — is by far the best at ensuring long-term physical preservation. In most situations, reburial with the same dirt or sand that was excavated will do much more for long-term preservation of graffiti (and other archaeological remains) than any conservation treatment. But at El-Kurru, as at many sites with graffiti, reburial is not a real possibility. As an important UNESCO World Heritage site, El-Kurru is a popular destination for

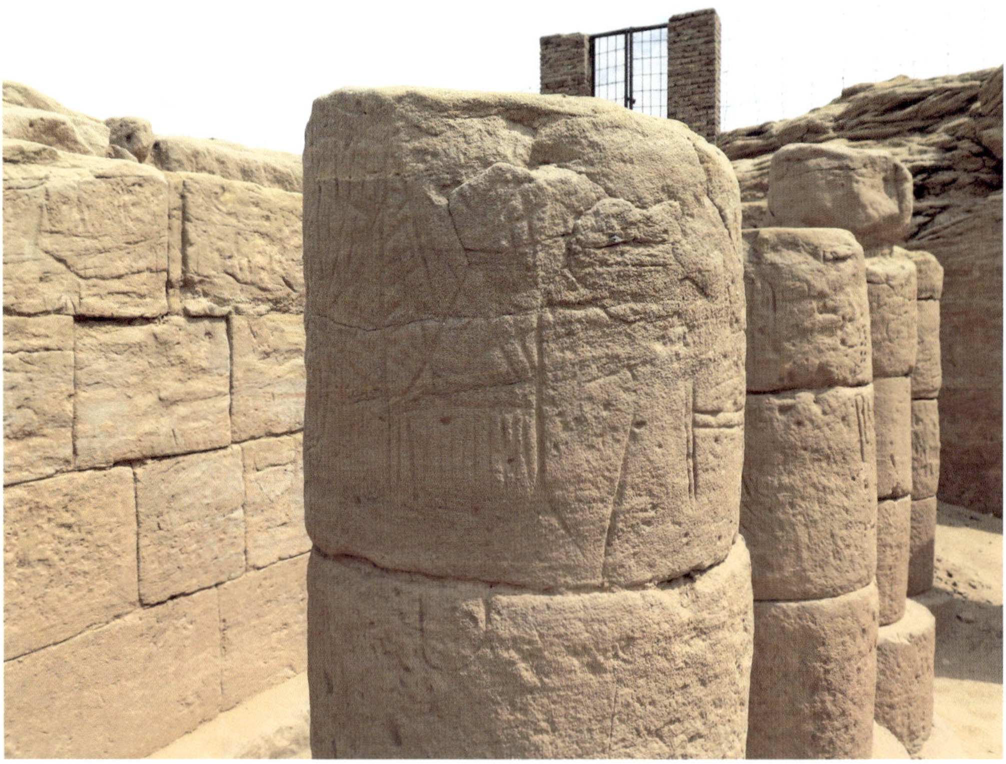

FIGURE 4.1. A column in the El-Kurru funerary temple, showing sanding, cracking, and scaling.
Photo: Suzanne Davis / IKAP, 2017

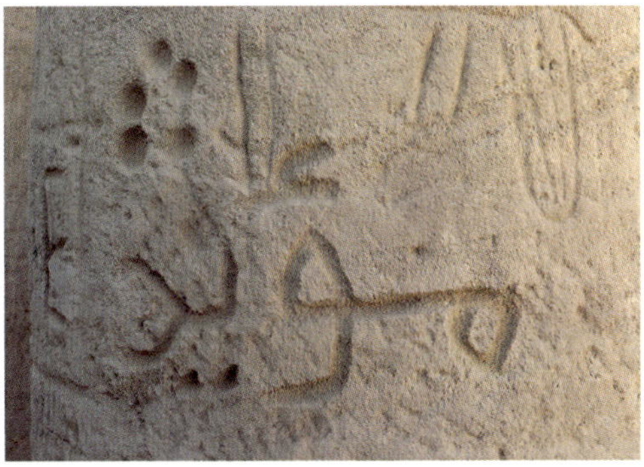

FIGURE 4.2. An example of modern Arabic graffiti, scratched into a column in the funerary temple.
Photo: Suzanne Davis / IKAP, 2017

both Sudanese and international tourists. Reburial and backfill of its most important monuments would ensure preservation but completely prohibit access.

Our objectives going into the graffiti conservation project were, therefore, to balance the seemingly opposing goals of preservation and access. This essay gives an overview of the University of Michigan team's efforts to preserve and document the graffiti, but please note that a more complete technical description of the project has also been published in the *Journal of the American Institute for Conservation.*[1]

Conservation Investigation and Treatment

The graffiti conservation project at El-Kurru began with a survey of all the graffiti. The goals of this survey were to identify which factors were most problematic for the graffiti, determine which graffiti were most at risk, and use the survey to follow them over time to see how much their condition changed from year to year. Data gathered from the survey would then be used to create a conservation plan. Designed by conservators at the Kelsey Museum, the survey used a 0–4 numeric scale tied to previously determined condition descriptors. For example, a ranking of "1" meant that the graffito had lost more than 25 percent of its original surface from problems such as granular surface disintegration; cracking, flaking, or detachment of stone; and/or modern defacement. A ranking of "4," on the other hand, indicated a graffito in excellent condition, with no signs of continuing deterioration. Using a numeric scale allowed us to conduct the survey quickly onsite, an important advantage since El-Kurru has hundreds of graffiti. The survey was also relatively low-tech. The graffiti had previously been cataloged in the project's FileMaker database,[2] so we simply added a few additional fields. One field let conservators enter the condition ranking, while others allowed us to note descriptions of the types of damage and to record when and how a graffito had been photographed. Onsite, two conservators worked together to determine the condition ranking for a graffito, take a record photograph, and enter the appropriate data in the database.

The results of the condition survey, which has now been conducted annually over a period of four years, have been somewhat surprising. In the first year of the survey, we identified sixty-nine graffiti as being at high risk due to a variety of factors. Our assumption was that the primary risk factor would be erosion due to the stone's inherently fragile composition, and we expected the graffiti to be easily subject to damage from weathering. But the survey data proved these assumptions wrong. Despite the softness of the stone, the surface condition of the graffiti changes very little from year to year, and the rate of loss is significantly slower than we expected. Although erosion and surface disintegration is occurring, it is doing so on an almost invisible scale. Instead, the major problem seems to be sub-surface scaling, where water enters the stone through cracks in the sides or top of the blocks and progressively causes large chunks of the rock to detach and fall away. Modern

1. Davis, Roberts, and Batkin-Hall 2018.
2. Anstis 2015.

defacement also proved to be a serious issue at first, much more so than we had expected. Conservation plans therefore began to shift as we acquired progressively more data from the condition survey.

In the beginning, when we assumed that surface loss from erosion would be the biggest ongoing risk, we investigated conservation treatment approaches to strengthen and stabilize the stone's surface. Elemental analysis of the stone was conducted first, and knowledge of the stone's composition allowed us to identify compatible conservation materials. A material frequently used to stabilize sandstone — a product called a silane consolidant — was then tested on the El-Kurru sandstone. Silanes work by creating chemical and physical bonds between silica in the stone, without impacting the stone's natural porosity. They are applied to the stone in liquid form and allowed to soak into the surface. Over time, as the silane cures, it forms a consolidating "gel" or network in the silica-rich stone.[3] Silanes are not easy to use in an arid climate like Sudan's because they require high humidity to fully cure. Archaeological conservators have, however, found adaptations to work with silanes in the field.[4]

Using the silane consolidant Conservare OH100, we conducted lab tests at the Kelsey Museum on samples of the El-Kurru sandstone, and then followed these with field tests onsite in the temple. Both the lab and field tests had good results; the surface of the stone became harder, more coherent, and less prone to disintegration. We observed surface discoloration in the lab tests, but the appearance of the stone was unchanged in the field tests. To evaluate the silane's penetration into the stone, we cut into the samples at the University of Michigan and were able to see that it had soaked into the rock to a depth of one inch, which seemed adequate for stabilizing the carved graffiti. But while these test results were promising, we also encountered an obstacle: silanes were not available for purchase in Sudan, and the international sanctions program against the country made their import difficult and expensive. Small amounts could be brought in easily, but the large quantity necessary for stabilizing El-Kurru's inscribed surfaces would be difficult, if not impossible, to achieve.

At the same time we were pondering the difficulty of import, I began to encounter reports of long-term issues with the use of silanes. For example, some studies report that the consolidating gel has a service life of fifteen to twenty years, after which the stone requires retreatment.[5] I also heard several disturbing stories about damage related to silane treatment of stone in outdoor settings. In these situations, chunks of surface were lost as the stone cleaved along the line between the outer, silane-treated layer and the inner, untreated rock. In each anecdotal report of this problem, the damage had occurred more than a decade after treatment, for unknown reasons. At the El-Kurru temple, I knew from environmental monitoring that the stone experienced huge temperature variations between night and day, with daytime temperatures as high as 140°F (60°C) due to solar heating, and nighttime temperatures of around 60°F (15.5°C). It seemed possible that these kinds of temperature shifts, which can be expected to cause differential expansion and contraction of the rock as it rapidly heats and cools, could cause the type of damage being reported. For all these reasons — the difficulty and expense of importing silanes, the unsustainability of the retreatment cycle if the consolidating gel did break down, and the possibility that treatment might cause us to lose the very surfaces we were trying to preserve — we began to rethink surface conservation of the graffiti.

Information from the condition survey also altered our thinking about conservation treatment priorities. The survey showed that the stone's surface condition was changing

3. Wheeler 2005; Doehne and Price 2010.

4. Hamann 2009; Kariya 2014.

5. Martin et al. 2002.

very slowly, but that large sections of columns and blocks were at high risk due to water ingress through cracks. Near-term conservation measures therefore shifted to sealing these cracks. We prioritized treatment of graffiti-decorated surfaces, and began with the areas at greatest risk (FIG. 4.3). The original intention was to grout the cracks with a lime mortar made with locally available materials. Lime mortars are a good choice for archaeological building materials because they are more permeable, softer, and weaker than cement. Using a grout or mortar that is stronger and harder than the stone can create new stress in the rock and cause damage.[6]

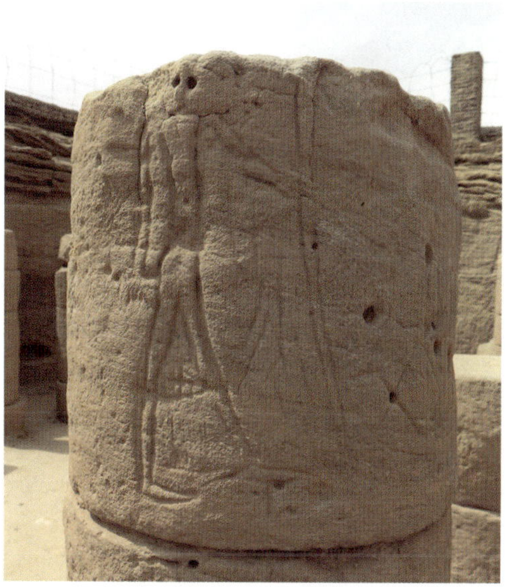

FIGURE 4.3. This important graffito depicting archers was at high risk due to cracking. Graffito T1.
Photo: Suzanne Davis / IKAP, 2017

In the 2015 season, in a project unrelated to the graffiti, we tested lime mortars as a wall-capping strategy. These mortars were made using locally available powdered lime from several different suppliers and in general they performed well. We went on to use lime mortars and grouts in other, smaller applications onsite, and even tested a version similar to the local lime-wash, in which liquid gum arabic is added (FIG. 4.4). But in 2018, when we were ready to grout cracks in association with the graffiti project, we again made test batches of grout with locally available powdered lime and found, unfortunately, that it would not cure. After more than twenty different batches failed to set, a Sudanese colleague, Mahmoud Suliman, secured a supply of quicklime, still in rock form. When slaking the quicklime, we found that some of the rocks were highly hydraulic, or reactive with water, while others were not. This variability made it difficult to consistently achieve a functional lime putty; some of the resulting grout mixtures eventually cured, others did not.

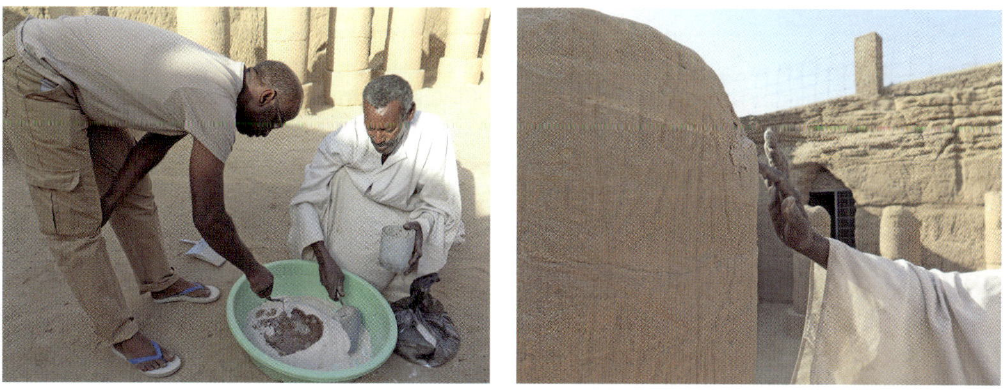

FIGURE 4.4. Left: archaeologist Sami Elamin and El-Kurru site guard Es-Sadeq Mohammed Saleh (seated) mixing sand and lime with liquid gum arabic. Right: the grout being smoothed following application.
Photos: Suzanne Davis / IKAP, 2017

6. Fidler 2006.

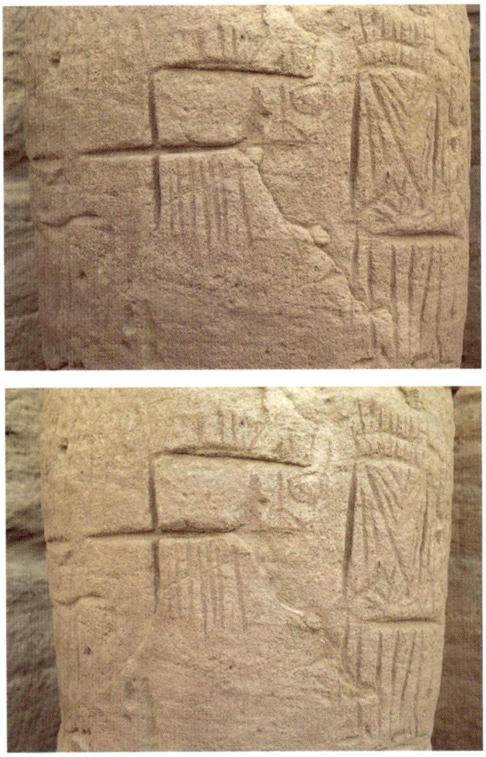

FIGURE 4.5. A cracked graffito before (top) and after (bottom) fine-grouting with Voidspan.
Photos: Suzanne Davis / IKAP, 2018

We have not abandoned local lime mixtures and continue to test and refine the composition of grout and mortar made onsite with local materials.

In 2018, however, because of the functional variability in locally available materials, we ultimately chose to use a commercial product from the United States, Voidspan. This product is made from natural hydraulic lime (limestone that is naturally reactive with water) and pozzolanic (ceramic) material. It cures slightly harder than the local grouts we had been testing at El-Kurru, but — when tested onsite at El-Kurru — we found that it cured quickly and reliably. We used the injection grout, which was appropriate for filling the size of the cracks we were grouting, and tinted it with dry pigments so that it would be close to the color of the sandstone (**FIG. 4.5**). Voidspan is not available in Sudan, and its use would be problematic for a site that needed to produce large amounts of lime mortar for architectural reconstruction or major conservation treatment. But because relatively small amounts were needed during this phase of the project, it was logistically simpler and, in the end, much faster to use a product with a known, reliable outcome.

Sealing the cracks with grout will prevent water ingress, which in turn will help stabilize large chunks of detaching stone. But without surface consolidation, the graffiti will continue to erode. Although the survey demonstrated a slow rate of damage from erosion, we remained concerned about how the graffiti would fare over a long time horizon. For this reason, we considered constructing a protective shelter over the temple.

Ideally, such a shelter would provide protection from rain, decrease windblown abrasion, and improve security for the temple. Shelters can be problematic, however. They alter the landscape and can cause environmental problems like increased temperature and relative humidity inside the structure, and they can cause wind funneling effects that increase erosion. All of this can have negative consequences for the archaeological structures they are designed to protect.[7] And yet, the stone at El-Kurru is so soft and vulnerable to damage that a shelter seems to be one of the few real options to ensure both long-term preservation and continued access.

The temple's vulnerability to another kind of damage — modern defacement — was addressed in a different way. El-Kurru's dedicated site guards felt certain that the new carving was being added during visits by large school groups, and the height and types of new graffiti seemed to confirm this (the new graffiti were usually about chest high for a middle-school child and consisted primarily of boys' names). The guards began to speak

7. Becherine et al. 2016; Rizzi 2008; Stanley-Price and Jokilehto 2002.

explicitly with teachers and students about the importance of not carving anything into the stone, and the incidence of new graffiti dropped dramatically.

Documentation

Conservation — including investigation, active treatment, and preventive strategies like the shelter — was only one part of the project. We also wanted to document the graffiti carefully. There were two primary goals for this documentation. One was to be able to track any change to the graffiti over time, and the other was to have a visual record of all the figural and geometric graffiti on site. Ideally, this record would not only allow us to monitor and study the graffiti, it would also allow us to make them widely accessible by publishing a virtual catalog online.

Three methods are commonly used in archaeology for documenting graffiti and rock art: laser scanning, photogrammetry, and reflectance transformation imaging (RTI). We assessed each for its ease of use, sustainability, and ability to record small surface details.

Laser scanning has been widely used for documenting graffiti and rock art and, in general, it is considered to be a highly effective and accurate technique for imaging both the carving and the stone's surface condition. The necessary equipment is expensive, however, and it requires an experienced technician to operate the scanner.[8] It can also be difficult to import, especially in countries with restrictions like Sudan's.

Photogrammetry, on the other hand, is easy to learn and requires only a digital camera and processing software, yet it can take days to process the images into a final file.[9] Reflectance transformation imaging is similarly low-tech, requiring only a camera and processing software, but it is much faster to capture the images and process the files.

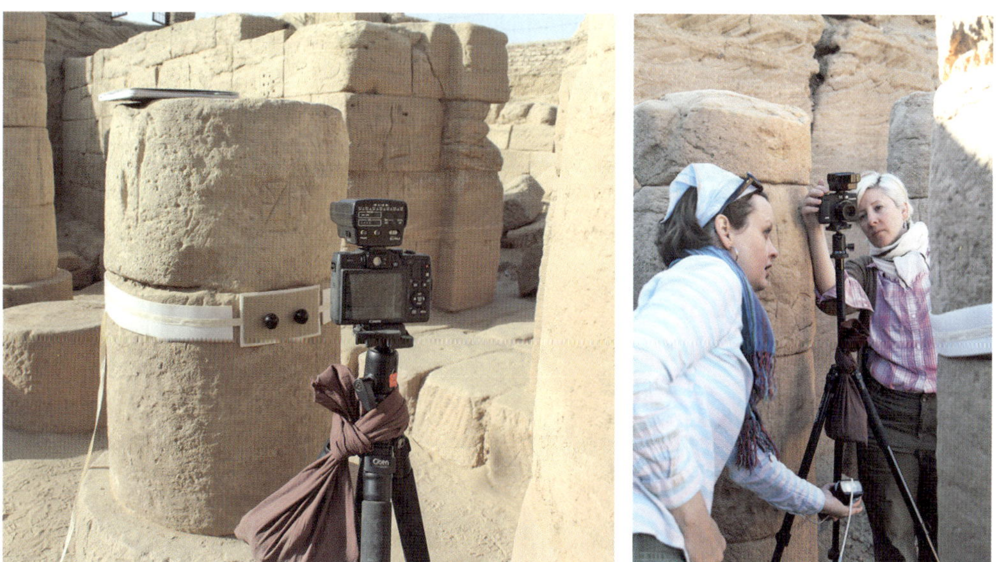

FIGURE 4.6. Left: the camera setup for RTI capture. Right: RTI capture in process.
Photos: (left) Suzanne Davis / IKAP, 2016; (right) Walter de Winter / IKAP, 2016

8. Karas, Beaubien, and Fitzhugh 2010; Kottke, Matero, and Hinchman 2011; Güth 2012; Kleinitz 2014; Alexander, Pinz, and Reinbacher 2015; Lymer 2015.
9. Martin Uildriks, email to author, 6 February 2017.

Unlike laser scanning and photogrammetry, RTI cannot produce three-dimensional image files, but it is a good technique for capturing surface texture and is considered to be 2.5 dimensional.[10] It works by having the camera remain stationary, while the surface of the graffito is lit from about fifty different angles using a detached flash. A photograph is taken at each of these angles. Two reflective spheres, also stationary, are placed in the image frame to allow the camera to record the precise angle of light from the flash (**FIG. 4.6**). Software is used to then combine the images into a single file that allows the viewer to play light across the surface of the image from any direction.

Onsite, photography for each graffito could be completed quickly, in about fifteen minutes, and the images were processed later the same day using a free software download available from Cultural Heritage Imaging.[11]

But choosing a workable documentation technique was only the beginning; other methodological questions quickly arose. Should we document single graffiti, or should we attempt to photograph an entire unit of construction, like a masonry block or a column drum? The latter approach has been adopted at the graffiti-rich site of Musawwarat es-Sufra, where masonry blocks seem to have functioned like canvases for ancient graffiti artists.[12] At El-Kurru, this choice was less clear; many graffiti extend around columns and they sometimes seem to span more than one block. Yet graffiti are not usually carved in isolation, and in some cases multiple images seemed to be arranged in a deliberate group, like the four birds shown in graffito T23, or the bull heads shown in graffito T12. In other instances, graffiti might have been intentionally arranged to tell a story, as seen in the group T22-T13-T14, where a bird appears to the left of two horses (**FIG. 4.7**), although it is equally possible that the horses and bird were carved at different times, by different hands.

It quickly became apparent that there was no single, correct answer to these questions. Documenting entire units of construction, like blocks or column drums, would make it possible to visualize graffiti in relationship to each other, but would also make it more difficult to catalog and describe an individual graffito, and column drums are impossible to document in the round using RTI. We developed a sort of hybrid approach, cataloging individual graffiti, but photographing apparent groups of graffiti together.

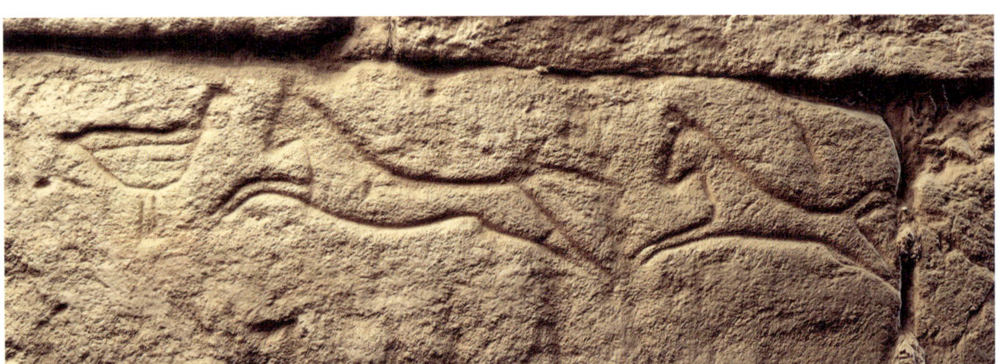

FIGURE 4.7. Graffito of two horses and a bird. Graffiti T22, T13, T14.
RTI: Suzanne Davis and Janelle Batkin-Hall / IKAP, 2016

10. Earl, Martinez, and Malzbender 2010; Miles et al. 2014; Cosentino, Stout, and Scandurra 2015; Díaz-Guardamino et al. 2015.
11. Cultural Heritage Imaging 2010, 2011.
12. Kleinitz 2014; see the excursus on pp. 16–20, herein.

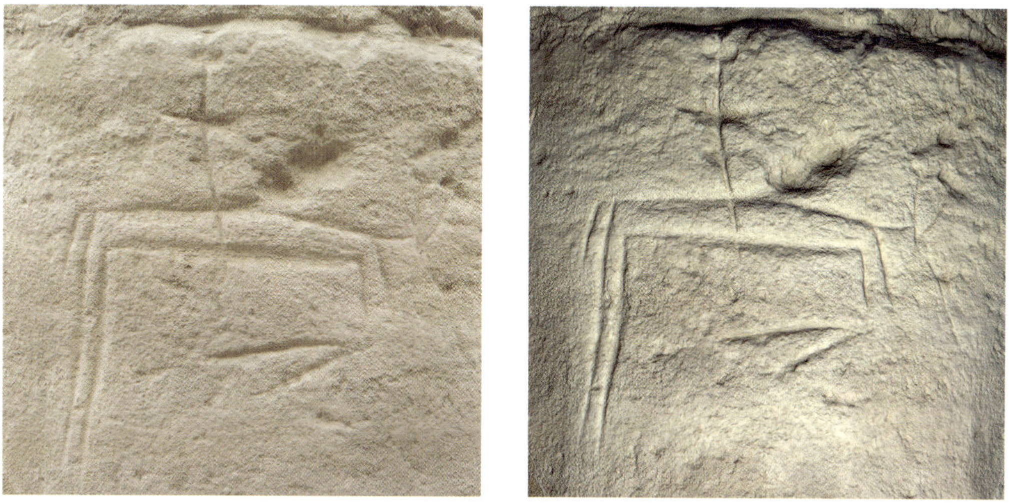

FIGURE 4.8. The eroded state of this graffito (left) and its location facing the back wall of the temple made it difficult to see under ambient lighting conditions. It had been classified as a geometric symbol. RTI imaging (right) revealed details that allowed it to be reclassified as a human riding a quadruped. Graffito T10.
Images: Suzanne Davis and Janelle Batkin-Hall / IKAP, 2016

The original goal of the graffiti documentation was to preserve them virtually, in a way that would allow us to monitor their condition over time and make them accessible to a broad audience. The RTI files have been useful for examining and tracking any surface changes, and because the files can easily be converted for web-based platforms, we can also share them online so that others can study them as well.[13]

But the work had an additional, beneficial outcome: the RTI files allowed us to see and understand some of the graffiti in a different way. Images previously classified as geometric designs became legible as humans riding quadrupeds (**FIG. 4.8**). Faint, unclassifiable graffiti became boats with masts and sails, and arrow-shaped designs suddenly had clearly delineated heads, hands, and feet. The RTI files also meant that the graffiti could be explored and studied remotely, once team members were no longer onsite at El-Kurru but back in their home institutions.

Conclusion

The graffiti conservation project has been an exercise in patience and adaptability. Although the primary goals of preservation and access never shifted, our ideas about how these would be best achieved have undergone multiple revisions. Our understanding of the vulnerabilities and risks to the stone have evolved as we followed the condition of the graffiti over time. Potential conservation and documentation strategies often seemed promising at first, yet later proved to be unworkable or impractical.

In general, when presented with decisions between a more complex plan and a simpler one — whether simpler meant less invasive, less expensive, or simply more efficient — we have chosen the simpler approach. Conservation treatment for the graffiti has, as a result, been minimal thus far, consisting of grouting major cracks with a lime mortar. The decision

13. A virtual version of the Kelsey Museum special exhibition *Graffiti as Devotion along the Nile: El-Kurru, Sudan* can be found at http://exhibitions.kelsey.lsa.umich.edu/graffiti-el-kurru.

not to consolidate the stone's surface still feels surprising, especially after a year-long testing campaign to make sure it would work, and yet a minimally invasive approach feels like the wisest course at present.

One of the best outcomes of the project has been the documentation of the graffiti. Again, the approach was one of the simplest possible; RTI is only a small step up from standard documentation photography, but it has allowed us to experience the graffiti in a new way and enables us to share them with a much wider audience. Those viewers, whether or not they ever travel to El-Kurru, will be able to explore the graffiti like archaeologists and conservators do, by experimenting with the online RTI files.

If there are broader lessons to be learned from this conservation and documentation project, they are on the same personal and human scale occupied by the graffiti; the project has been an exercise in slow but continuous progress through what at the time felt like a series of frustratingly tiny steps. One important takeaway, as we learned multiple times, is that there is no one correct solution to any problem. Often, the first seemingly "right" approach turned out not to be the best way forward. Finally, practicality and sustainability are just as important for long-term conservation as scientific analysis and technical knowledge.

References

Alexander, Craig, Axel Pinz, and Christian Reinbacher

2015 "Multi-Scale 3D Rock-Art Recording." *Digital Applications in Archaeology and Cultural Heritage* 2 (2): 181–95. https://doi.org/10.1016/j.daach.2015.02.003.

Anstis, Sebastian

2015 "Meroitic Graffiti in the Mortuary Temple." *Sudan & Nubia* 19: 67–68.

Becherini, Francesca, JoAnn Cassar, Mario Galea, and Adriana Bernardi

2016 "Evaluation of the Shelters over the Prehistoric Megalithic Temples of Malta: Environmental Considerations." *Environmental Earth Sciences* 75 (14): 1079. https://doi.org/10.1007/s12665-016-5875-z.

Cosentino, Antonino, Samantha Stout, and Carmelo Scandurra

2015 "Innovative Imaging Techniques for Examination and Documentation of Mural Paintings and Historical Graffiti in the Catacombs of San Giovanni, Syracuse." *International Journal of Conservation Science* 6 (1): 23–34.

Cultural Heritage Imaging

2010 "Reflectance Transformation Imaging: Guide to Highlight Image Capture v1.1." *Cultural Heritage Imaging.* http://culturalheritageimaging.org/What_We_Offer/Downloads/RTI_Hlt_Capture_Guide_v1_1.pdf.

2011 "Reflectance Transformation Imaging: Guide to Highlight Image Processing v1.4." *Cultural Heritage Imaging.* http://culturalheritageimaging.org/What_We_Offer/Downloads/rtibuilder/RTI_hlt_Processing_Guide_v14_beta.pdf.

Davis, Suzanne L., Caroline Roberts, and Janelle Batkin-Hall

2018 "A Comprehensive Approach to Conservation of Ancient Graffiti at El Kurru, Sudan." *Journal of the American Institute for Conservation* 57 (1–2): 1–18. https://doi.org/10.1080/01971360.2018.1424601.

Díaz-Guardamino, Marta, Leonardo García Sanjuán, David Wheatley, and Víctor Rodríguez Zamora

2015 "RTI and the Study of Engraved Rock Art: A Re-Examination of the Iberian South-Western Stelae of Setefilla and Almadén de La Plata 2 (Seville, Spain)." *Digital*

Applications in Archaeology and Cultural Heritage 2 (2): 41–54. https://doi.org/10.1016/j.daach.2015.07.002.

Doehne, Eric Ferguson, and C. A. Price
2010 *Stone Conservation: An Overview of Current Research.* 2nd ed. Research in Conservation. Los Angeles: Getty Conservation Institute.

Earl, Graeme, Kirk Martinez, and Tom Malzbender
2010 "Archaeological Applications of Polynomial Texture Mapping: Analysis, Conservation and Representation." *Journal of Archaeological Science* 37 (8): 2040–50. https://doi.org/10.1016/j.jas.2010.03.009.

Fidler, John
2006 *Stone Building Materials, Construction and Associated Component Systems: Their Decay and Treatment.* English Heritage Research Transactions 2. Sterling: Earthscan.

Güth, Alexandra
2012 "Using 3D Scanning in the Investigation of Upper Palaeolithic Engravings: First Results of a Pilot Study." *Journal of Archaeological Science* 39 (10): 3105–14. https://doi.org/10.1016/j.jas.2012.04.029.

Hamann, Jan
2009 "Naga-Projekt SUDAN." In *KulturGUTerhalten: Standards in der Restaurierungswissenschaft und Denkmalpflege. Beiträge des Internationalen Kolloquiums "Standards in der Restaurierungswissenschaft und Denkmalpflege" vom 23.–25. April 2009 an den Staatlichen Museen zu Berlin,* edited by Uwe Peltz, pp. 171–77. Mainz: Philipp von Zabern.

Karas, Basiliki Vicky, Harriet F. Beaubien, and William F. Fitzhugh
2010 "Documenting Mongolia's Deer Stones: Application of 3D Laser Scanning Technology to Archaeological Conservation." In *The Conservation of Archaeological Materials: Current Trends and Future Directions,* edited by Emily Williams and Claire Peachy, pp. 103–12. BAR International Series 2116. Oxford: Archaeopress.

Kariya, Hiroko
2014 "Conservation of Inscribed Sandstone Fragments at Luxor Temple in Egypt: Case Study." *American Institute for Conservation of Historic & Artistic Works, Objects Specialty Group Postprints* (21): 283–303.

Kleinitz, Cornelia
2014 "The Graffiti of Musawwarat Es-Sufra: Current Research on Historic Inscriptions, Images and Markings at the Great Enclosure." *Sudan & Nubia* 18: 93–103.

Kottke, Jessica, Frank Matero, and John Hinchman
2011 "Terrestrial Laser Scanning: Imaging, Quantifying, and Monitoring Microscale Surface Deterioration of Stone at Heritage Sites." *Change Over Time* 1 (2): 268–87.

Lymer, Kenneth
2015 "Image Processing and Visualisation of Rock Art Laser Scans from Loups's Hill, County Durham." *Digital Applications in Archaeology and Cultural Heritage* 2 (2): 155–65. https://doi.org/10.1016/j.daach.2015.01.002.

Martin, B., D. Mason, J.-M. Teutonico, S. Chapman, R. Butlin, and T. Yates
2002 "Stone Consolidants: BrethaneTM Report of an 18-Year Review of BrethaneTM-Treated Sites." In *Stone: Stone Building Materials, Construction and Associated Component Systems; Their Decay and Treatment,* edited by John Fidler, pp. 3–18. English Heritage Research Transactions 2. London: James & James.

Miles, James, Mike Pitts, Hembo Pagi, and Graeme Earl
2014 "New Applications of Photogrammetry and Reflectance Transformation Imaging to an Easter Island Statue." *Antiquity* 88 (340): 596–605.

Rizzi, Gionata
2008 "Sheltering the Mosaics of Piazza Armerina: Issues of Conservation and Presentation." Archaeological Institute of America's "Heritage, Conservation & Archaeology" Series 2008: 1–3. https://www.archaeological.org/sitepreservation/hca.

Stanley-Price, Nicholas P., and Jukka Jokilehto
2002 "The Decision to Shelter Archaeological Sites: Three Case-Studies from Sicily." *Conservation and Management of Archaeological Sites* 5 (1–2): 19–34.

Wheeler, George
2005 *Alkoxysilanes and the Consolidation of Stone.* Research in Conservation. Los Angeles: Getty Publications.

5

Jeremy Pope

Figural Graffiti from the Meroitic Era on Philae Island

To the non-specialist reader, the island of Philae in Egypt (FIG. 5.1) may seem a world apart from El-Kurru in the Kushite heartland of Upper Nubia. The two sites are separated by more than 800 kilometers as the crow flies across the Nubian desert — and far more through the bends and cataracts of the Nubian Nile. Unlike Kurru, the monuments of Philae also display an elaborate program of relief decoration commissioned mostly by Ptolemaic kings and Roman emperors,[1] along with more than a thousand specifically textual

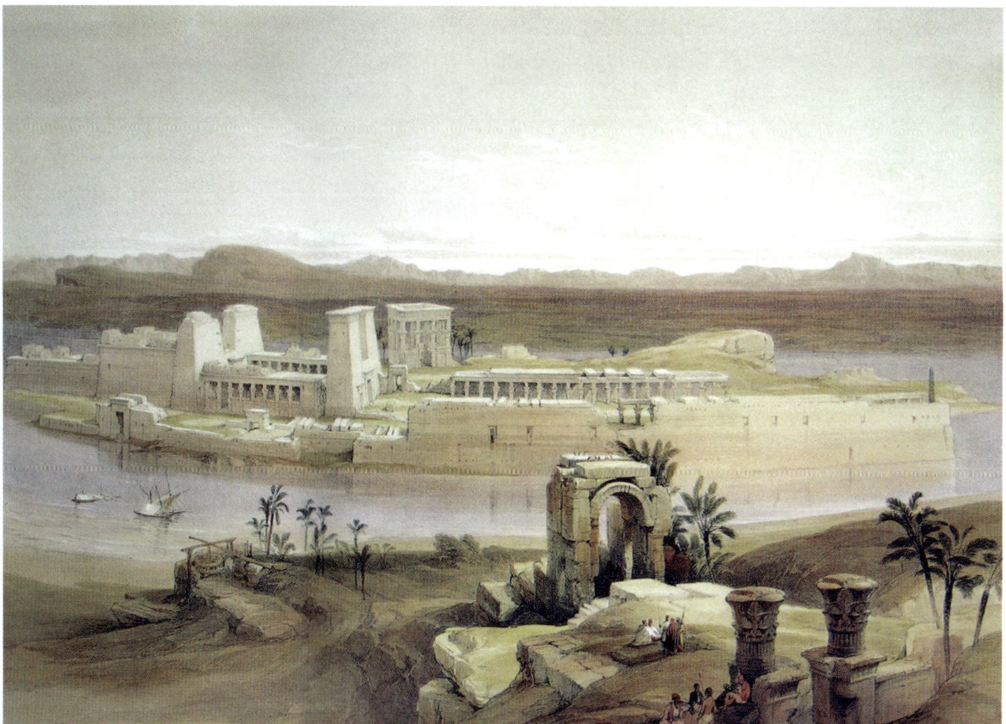

FIGURE 5.1. The island of Philae as it appeared to David Roberts in 1838, before the monuments' relocation to neighboring Agilkia. *Wikimedia Commons*

1. Porter and Moss 1970, pp. 203–56.

graffiti that find few parallels at Kurru.[2] Even if one narrows the scope of analysis to figural graffiti, Philae would seem to belong to a very different milieu from that of Kurru. Whereas the Upper Egyptian and Lower Nubian environs of Philae abound in both rock art and graffiti on royal monuments,[3] Upper Nubia at and above the 4th Cataract has yielded far less evidence in either category.[4] On these grounds, Philae and Kurru appear to be points of contrast rather than context.

Yet the cultural distance between Philae and Kurru is somewhat illusory. So far as can be determined, the architectural history of Philae began with a construction ordered by Taharqo, a Kushite pharaoh whose dynastic line was interred at Kurru.[5] Authors during the Ptolemaic and Roman eras struggled to find a coherent Egyptian etymology for the island's name, so Kockelmann has tentatively derived it instead from the Meroitic language spoken by the Kurru kings.[6] The entrance of Philae's Great Temple of Isis likewise opened toward Nubia and was later fronted by chapels devoted to the Nubian gods Arsenuphis and Mandulis.[7] Unlike the region's earlier dominant temple for Khnum at Elephantine, the temples at Philae could be accessed by travelers from the south without traversing the river's difficult 1st Cataract.[8] Most significantly, some of the textual graffiti for which Philae is famous were commissioned by visitors from Nubia who explicitly stated that they had been sent there by the Kushite king in Upper Nubia,[9] and several of the texts were written in the Meroitic language and script.[10] The two most extensive studies of the Philae graffiti in recent years have both concluded that the site's priesthood during the final centuries of the Roman era was actually appointed from distant Meroe at the southernmost fringe of Upper Nubia.[11] Indeed, Philae seems to have been as important to Upper Nubia as Upper Nubia was to Philae: analyses of Meroitic politics have concluded that patronage of Philae was essential to the sacred legitimation of the Kushite royal house.[12] This link may well be echoed in Maximinus's later insistence that his treaty with the Nubians farther south be ratified in Isis's temple at Philae.[13] As Philae was evidently a familiar haunt of Nubian elites, any differences between its graffiti and those of Kurru cannot be easily attributed to a chasm of culture.

Differences in such informal decoration at the two sites also cannot be attributed simply to contrasting "genres" or "registers." There is little justification for treating the texts of Philae as a corpus distinct from Nubian figural graffiti there and elsewhere, and we should not assume that texts and figures consistently varied in inverse proportion across northeast Africa.[14] The two forms of expression were frequently designed to interact with one another,[15] and presumed centers of ancient literacy in Egypt simultaneously manifest some of the highest concentrations of anepigraphic (non-textual) graffiti.[16] Any attempt to sharply differentiate the two would be artificial;[17] as Cruz-Uribe has explained, "[h]ieroglyphs — in

2. Griffith 1937; Bernand 1969; Burkhardt 1985; Cruz-Uribe 2016.
3. Huyge 1998; Cruz-Uribe 2008a, p. 1.
4. Hintze 1979, p. 135.
5. Weigall 1907, p. 49; Griffith 1931; Winter 1976; Farag, Wahba, and Farid 1979; Dunham 1950.
6. Kockelmann 2012, p. 1; cf. Rutherford 1998, p. 233; Rilly 2007, 2010; Rilly and de Voogt 2012.
7. Rutherford 1998, p. 231.
8. Cruz-Uribe 2002, p. 167.
9. E.g., Pope 2008, 2014.
10. Leclant 2000, pp. 212–81.
11. Cruz-Uribe 2016 pp. 39, 42–43; Ashby forthcoming.
12. Edwards 1996, pp. 85, 87; Fuller 2003; Cruz-Uribe 2002, p. 172.
13. Eide et al. 1998, pp. 1153–58.
14. Cruz-Uribe 2008b, p. 196.
15. E.g., Griffith 1912, pl. XVIII; Eide et al. 1998, pp. 1024–31; Jacquet-Gordon 2003, p. 8.
16. Huyge 1998, p. 1385 n. 22.
17. E.g., Peden 2001.

which text and picture are one — are thus, in a sense, an advanced form of figural graffiti."[18] Pictures etched into the stones of Kurru would therefore seem to belong to the same cultural and semiotic continuum as the figures and texts of distant Philae.

In fact, a case could be made that Philae provides an exceptionally valuable comparison for Kurru — not only due to their cultural and semiotic links, but also because of epistemological conditions. Unlike the rock art that covers Lower Nubia and the surrounding deserts,[19] most of the figural graffiti at Philae have indisputable *termini post quem*: put simply, a graffito upon the Gateway of Hadrian cannot have been inscribed any earlier than the reign of Hadrian.[20] Compared to many Egyptian and Lower Nubian temples, the monuments of Philae are also relatively late, further restricting the chronological range of its informal decoration. A few of Philae's figural graffiti are even explicitly paired with an inscription giving the regnal year of a specific Kushite king and/or Roman emperor — allowing text, figure, and style to be dated with unusual precision.[21] Moreover, we may reasonably expect some points of synchronism between the graffiti at Philae and those associated with the Kurru 1 pyramid and the Kurru funerary temple,[22] because chronological study of the latter has already postulated some overlap with a period of increasing Nubian traffic at Philae.[23] Lastly, the most revealing of the available texts at Philae describe their purposes in generous detail,[24] illuminating not only an adjacent figure but also potentially the functions of any comparable images from farther afield at Kurru or elsewhere. Because of these advantages, Philae reveals chronological patterns more clearly than would sites without such a profusion of firm data points. The Philae corpus facilitates exactly the kind of analysis which Dirk Huyge has recommended as "definitely the surest methodological path to follow" — namely, an "historical exegesis" of figural graffiti "founded on *contemporaneous* materials and sources."[25]

Nevertheless, research into the figural graffiti of Philae is still in its infancy. When Francis Llewellyn Griffith surveyed the island in 1929, he consistently passed over figures in favor of Demotic Egyptian texts, tracing only a handful of the former that adjoined the latter;[26] the same method was followed by André Bernand in his later study of the island's Greek and Latin graffiti.[27] The occasional allusions to unrecorded graffiti in Griffith's publication[28] then piqued the curiosity of Eugene Cruz-Uribe, who traveled to Philae in 2004 and again with Steve Vinson in 2009 to discover 534 new Demotic texts and an array of accompanying figures. In 2016, Cruz-Uribe published tracings, transliterations, and translations of the texts, with concise but often groundbreaking historical discussion, and he likewise copied and discussed some of the figural graffiti that were directly associated with those new texts.[29] Most crucially, he made available online his archive of 502 digital color photographs, many of them showing figures absent from the book.[30] Beyond Cruz-Uribe's archive, additional images consulted during my own research were kindly provided by Steve Vinson and Solange Ashby. Most recently an excellent, forthcoming book manuscript by Ashby

18. Cruz-Uribe 2008a, p. 4.
19. Huyge 2003, p. 59. See Fawzi Hassan Bakhiet, this volume.
20. E.g., Červíček 1982, p. 58.
21. E.g., Pope 2008; Cruz-Uribe 2016, p. 38.
22. Anstis 2015.
23. Emberling 2015, p. 66; Cruz-Uribe 2016, p. 14.
24. E.g., Pope 2008, 2014.
25. Huyge 2003, p. 70–71, emphasis added.
26. Griffith 1937, pls. XIII, XXIII, LVII, LXIX–LXX.
27. Bernand 1969, pp. 313–15; Cruz-Uribe 2012, p. 74.
28. E.g., Griffith 1937, p. 62.
29. Cruz-Uribe 2016.
30. http://webapp1.dlib.indiana.edu/images/splash.htm?scope=egypt/VAD4445 (accessed 17 June 2019).

has performed the hard labor of weaving from the site's Nubian graffiti some coherent narrative threads of political and cultural change over time.[31] As a result of the efforts and generosity of Cruz-Uribe, Vinson, and Ashby, we are suddenly in a much better position to contextualize Philae's figural graffiti than was possible just a few years ago. At the same time, the study of figural graffiti and rock art has now lost three of its most distinguished scholars, with the passing of Pavel Červíček (1942–2015), Eugene Cruz-Uribe (1952–2018), and Dirk Huyge (1957–2018) in quick succession. One ventures into their field with some feeling of inadequacy.

A comprehensive inventory of the informal decoration at Philae lies in any case far beyond the appropriate scope of this chapter. What follows is instead a more selective and ultimately tentative foray into this newly opened line of inquiry, focused primarily upon the Meroitic era and organized by broad categories of figural graffiti that are attested at both Philae and Kurru: inanimate objects, anthropomorphs, fauna, and flora.

Inanimate Objects

The most enigmatic of figural graffiti are arguably those with the greatest degree of geometric stylization — for example, the "X in a box" that appears repeatedly in the Kurru funerary temple (graffiti T7, T27, T37, T38, T42, T43, T44, T50). Philae offers at least two varieties of this decoration on inanimate objects of markedly different function, thereby cautioning against a uniform interpretation. On the blocks of the West Colonnade, several graffiti show an X enclosed by a square whose lower edge is interrupted by a single protrusive opening (FIGS. 5.2–3). The many parallels for this shape in graffiti of the Meroitic era would indicate that the image of an offering table was intended.[32] The protruding spout is absent from most of the graffiti at Kurru (except possibly T28 and T30), but a general votive character for these examples at Kurru is nevertheless suggested by the placement of an enclosed X beside (T7, T27, T49) and upon (T8) what appear to be horned fire altars — many of which were shown with precisely such an X at other Egyptian and Nubian sites.[33] A second variety of the enclosed X symbol at Philae appears clearly upon flags, one flying from a lone pole (FIG. 5.4) and the other from the deck of a boat (FIG. 5.5). These examples would seem entirely consistent with the interpretation of graffiti T36, T37, and T38 at Kurru as textiles, and they may therefore give a glimpse of the designs that adorned perishable materials at both sites. Unfortunately, the surviving evidence does not clarify any totemic, magico-religious, aesthetic, or other function that the symbol may have served in its historical context.[34]

Yet the most common inanimate objects depicted in Philae's graffiti are the boats. On the great majority of these, bow and stern are not ornamented with a god's head and no shrine appears on board, so they are best interpreted as river craft, rather than as divine barks to be carried in a ritual procession.[35] Cruz-Uribe noted two separate concentrations of these boat graffiti, each displaying a different form of vessel. Those on the Kiosk of Augustus he characterized as "large traveling barges, usually towed by other boats," and he proposed that such barges docked there at the kiosk and "were used to ferry the image of the goddess

31. Ashby forthcoming.
32. Červíček 1974, pp. 184 n. 726, 193.
33. Rose 2007, pp. 125, 127–28; Cruz-Uribe 2008b, pp. 57, 59–60.
34. Huyge 1998, p. 1390; Cruz-Uribe 2008a, p. 1. Adolf Erman and Heinrich Schäfer evidently recognized the "X" as a common design on ancient Egyptian textiles, for their hieroglyphic font included such an "X" in the sign representing a textile (S 32): see Erman and Schäfer 1908, p. 957.
35. Cruz-Uribe 2012, p. 73; contra Castiglione 1970, pp. 126–27.

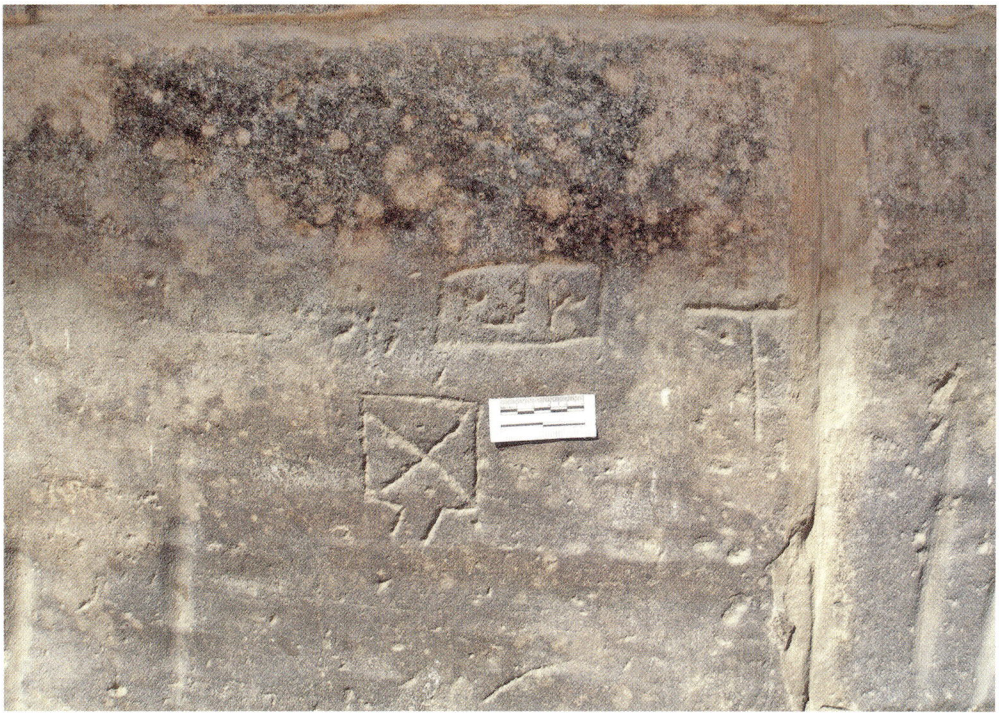

FIGURE 5.2. Offering table drawn between windows 5 and 6 of Philae's West Colonnade.
Photo: Eugene Cruz-Uribe

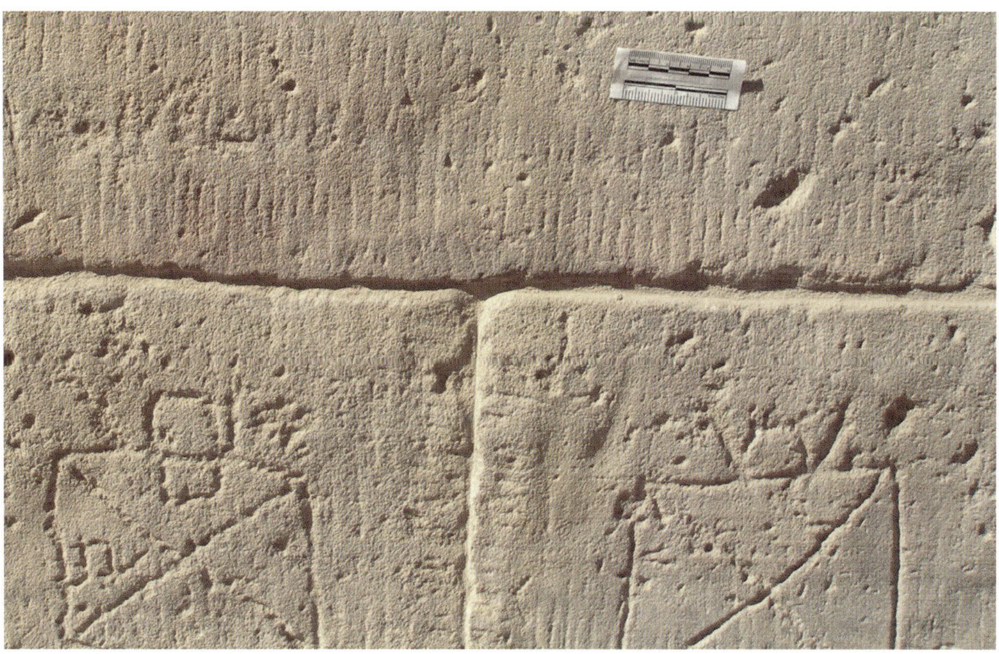

FIGURE 5.3. Two offering tables drawn between windows 3 and 4 of Philae's West Colonnade. Though the lower spout of the table is not shown in this photo, two other partial images in Cruz-Uribe's archive show a spout on the same form of table in graffito GPH 554 between windows 4 and 5 and again near Demotic graffito GPH 570 between windows 5 and 6.
Photo: Eugene Cruz-Uribe

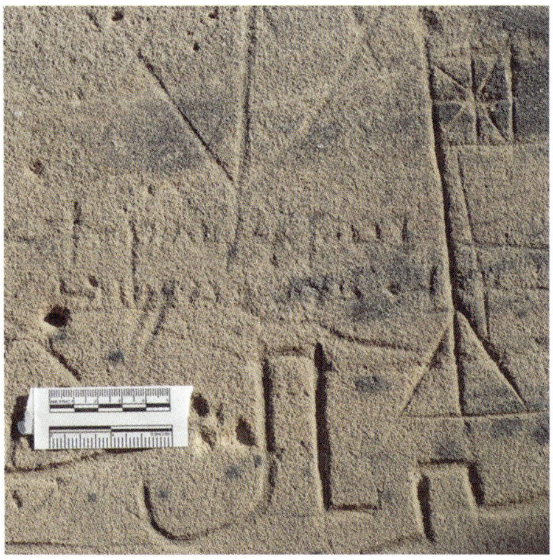

FIGURE 5.4. Decorated flag depicted on the west wall of the northwest tank upon the roof of Philae's Temple of Isis.
Photo: Steve Vinson, 2019

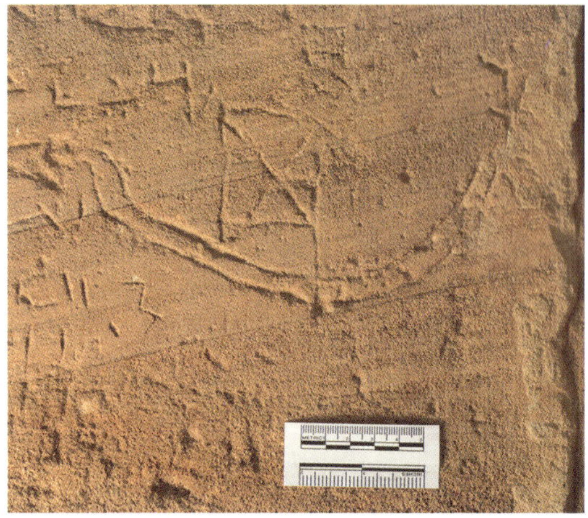

FIGURE 5.5. Decorated flag flying from the deck of a boat, as drawn upon a screen between columns 4 and 5 of the Mammisi's east colonnade at Philae.
Photo: Steve Vinson, 2019

Isis down to Nubia for her regular travels to that area."[36] Unfortunately, no clear example of this form is shown in his online archive of photographs, where only images of boats adjacent to Demotic graffiti were uploaded (e.g., **FIG. 5.6** here, a very schematic drawing[37]). A possible historical context for such barges is nevertheless well established by Maximinus's aforementioned treaty, which specified that peoples of the Dodecaschoenus would be granted access to the statue of Isis so that they could transport it by river to various temples throughout that larger region.[38] With due reservation, I would propose a similar size and form for a few of the boats depicted at pyramid Ku. 1 (graffiti P4, P6, and P16) with their elaborate rigging and, in one case, the possible appearance of a smaller vessel nearby (P11).[39] However, the examples from Kurru appear to belong to the Christian period,[40] so any parallels in boat form at Philae may have derived from an earlier and possibly very different ritual context.

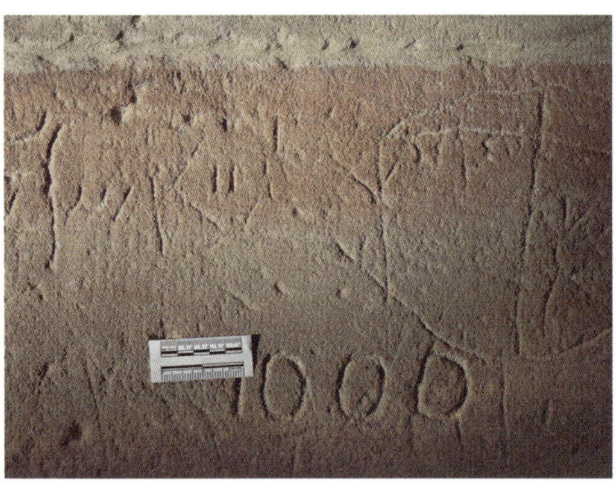

FIGURE 5.6. Boat drawn upon panel 4, course 1, of the interior south wall of the Kiosk of Augustus.
Photo: Eugene Cruz-Uribe

The second concentration of boat graffiti noted by Cruz-Uribe at Philae is better represented in his online archive, as many appear alongside Demotic text. These took the form of "much smaller single-masted boats" inscribed upon the West Colonnade near windows 3 through 9 (e.g., **FIGS. 5.7–8**); only a few of the boat graffiti at Kurru have a comparable shape (perhaps P7, P8, and P13). At Philae, the clustered depictions of small boats beside windows on the island's western edge suggests that the artists may have witnessed there a short riverine trip of special significance to them. On this point, Philae's written evidence is particularly

36. Cruz-Uribe 2016, p. 13.
37. Cf. Bernand 1969, pl. 88, no. 314.
38. Eide et al. 1998, pp. 1153–58; Pope 2014.
39. See Červíček's "Typus XXIV" in 1974, pp. 136–37.
40. Bruce B. Williams, personal communication, 19 December 2018.

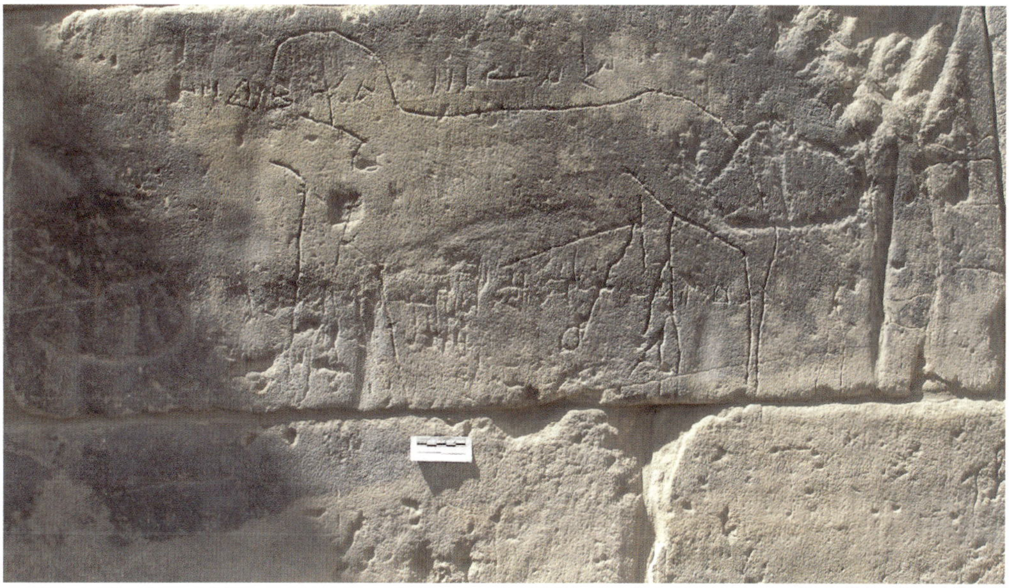

FIGURE 5.7. Boat (at viewer's upper right, behind quadruped) drawn between windows 4 and 5 of Philae's West Colonnade. A second boat appears in the shadow at viewer's lower left.
Photo: Eugene Cruz-Uribe

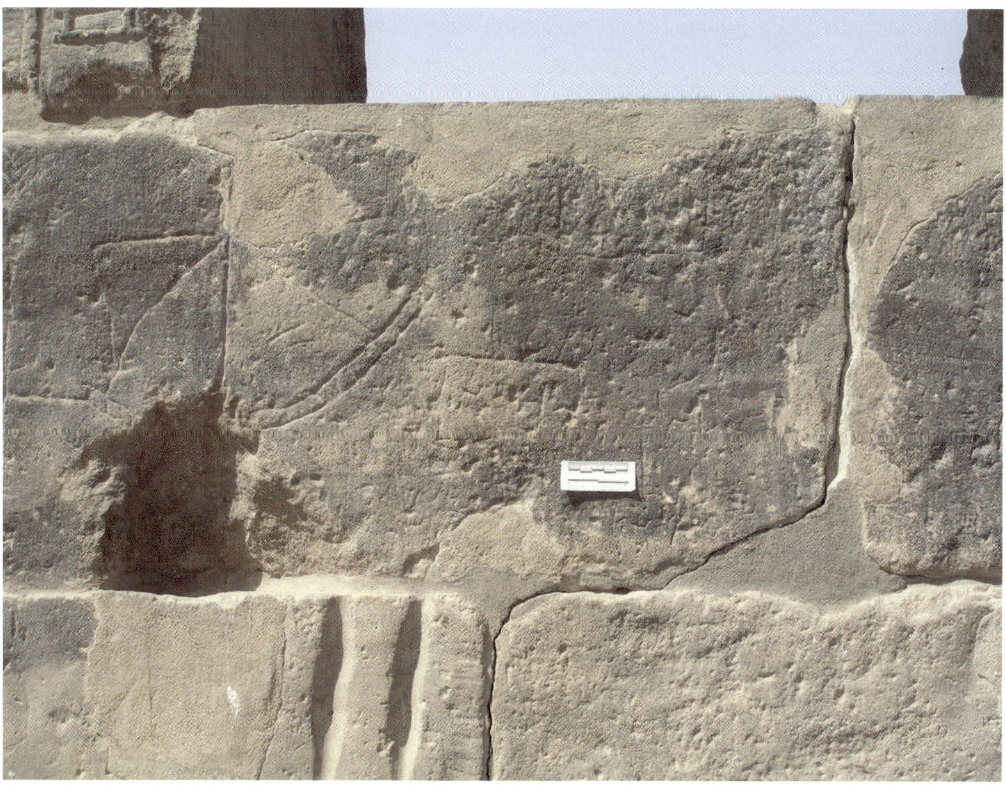

FIGURE 5.8. Boat drawn below window 4 of Philae's West Colonnade.
Photo: Eugene Cruz-Uribe

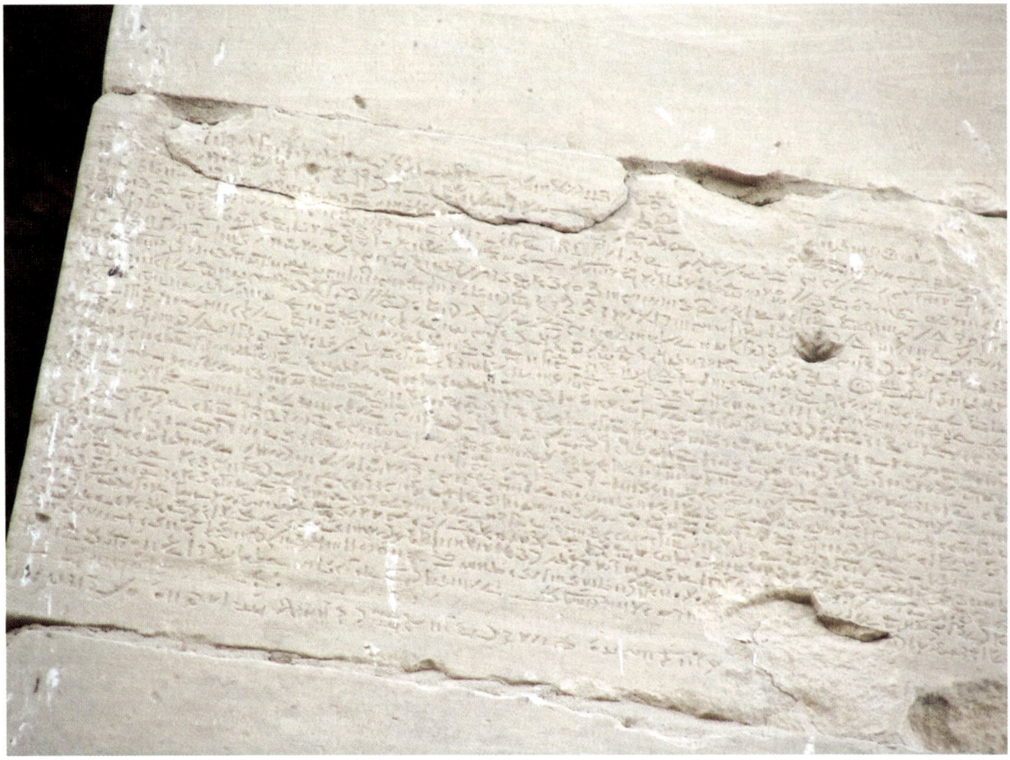

FIGURE 5.9. Demotic graffito 416 inscribed upon the southwest jamb of Hadrian's Gateway at Philae.
Photo: Solange Ashby

illuminating, as both royal inscriptions and private textual graffiti of the 3rd century CE repeatedly describe a ritual of the annual Khoiak festival in which Isis's statue was ferried from the western quay beneath Hadrian's Gateway to the neighboring island of Bigga, so that the goddess could visit her husband, Osiris.[41] One graffito from that gateway was written on the 10th of April in 253 CE for a Meroitic court official named Sasan, the "great envoy to Rome"; it records his delivery of royal donations and successful execution of "the work of Isis" upon "High Mount" (Bigga) "in the name of Pharaoh, our lord," followed by a lengthy banquet of "wine, beer, and meat, while the populace of the town in its entirety was in jubilation and making obeisance to Pharaoh, their overlord" (FIG. 5.9).[42] Prolonged emphasis is given in the text to the implied perils of Sasan's arduous trip, during which Isis "heard our prayers and brought us to Egypt safe" when Sasan was "lost and crying out" to her:

> My lady, ... [listen] to me, so that I might be brought to Meroe, the beautiful town of your beloved son, and cause that I might prosper upon this High Mount, with the things for which I came, in order to take them to your beloved son, [Pharaoh Taqere]ramani, and bring me to Egypt together with my brother, Horudja, ... the great envoy to Rome.... My lady,... Isis, you are the Mistress of the Road.... Our hearts are entrusted to you upon the way, to bring us to the way of life, while we call to you on every occasion, saying, "Listen to us." I am (you)r good servant, Isis... My heart is left to you <in> Egypt, in Meroe, and in the mountains. Isis, this is the only brother I have. I am going to leave him, and I say to you: "Keep him safe until you bring me back to Egypt."

41. Junker 1913; Pope 2008, 2014; Cruz-Uribe 2016, pp. 37–39, 42.
42. Pope 2008.

The contemporaneous graffito of Tami, the Meroitic king's "tax collector" and "envoy" at Philae ca. 261 CE, suggests that these Meroitic pilgrimages to Philae were not always brief sojourns; Tami explained that "no way presented itself for going south," so he "spent three years" at Philae and, despite local resistance from Elephantine, secured Meroitic supremacy within the Philae priesthood.[43] Such poignant testimony from Sasan and Tami gives historical context to the neighboring colonnade's numerous boat graffiti, and it serves as a reminder that the mute pictures scrawled on the walls of Philae and elsewhere were not necessarily "the outcome of casual pastimes or exercises by sculpture apprentices,"[44] nor simply a boast or demarcation of territorial boundaries.[45] Figural graffiti at Philae could also memorialize highly personal moments of piety, ambition, anxiety, affection, and gratitude.[46]

Anthropomorphs

Sasan's Demotic graffito at Philae is also accompanied by an apparent self-portrait of the man that is labeled with his name — a prime example of a "composer" image (FIG. 5.10).[47] A graffitist drew several such visitors from the south on walls behind the East Colonnade, and, though the accompanying texts in Meroitic script have defied a continuous translation, many personal names and titles can be discerned.[48] Cruz-Uribe has interpreted these images as the commemoration of a specific delegation that negotiated control of the Isis priesthood during the second half of the 3rd century CE.[49] However, portraits of private individuals are more the exception than the rule at Philae, as most pilgrims opted instead to leave feet graffiti with accompanying text (FIG. 5.11). They did so presumably in order to secure their eternal presence near or within sacred space, in a fashion analogous to private stelae on Osiris's Abydene processional route or to private statues in Karnak Temple. It is at least conceivable that graffito T2 may have served a similar function at Kurru, but it is altogether devoid of identifying features. At neither Philae nor Kurru does Huyge's label of "parasite" graffiti seem adequate,[50] as the etching of one's standing image, feet, or autobiographical text was ultimately a sign of the continued life of the temple and

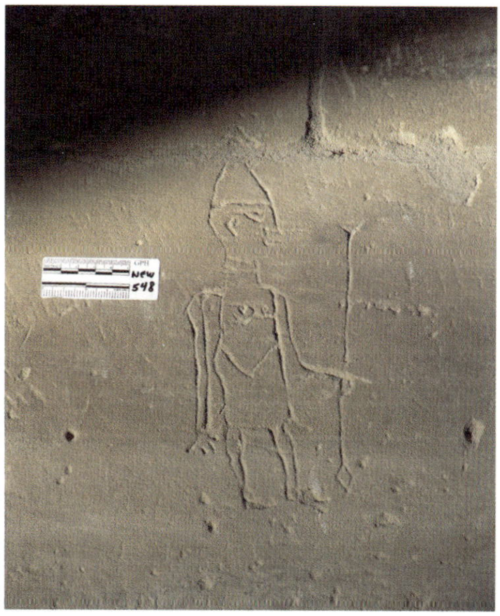

FIGURE 5.10. Image drawn upon the southwest jamb of Hadrian's Gateway at Philae, depicting Sasan, Meroe's "great envoy to Rome" and the subject of Demotic graffito 416 (fig. 5.9, above).
Photo: Eugene Cruz-Uribe

43. Eide et al. 1998, p. 1012; Cruz-Uribe 2015.
44. Huyge 2003, p. 70.
45. Cruz-Uribe 2008a, p. 1.
46. Rose 2007, p. 117; Cruz-Uribe 2012, p. 73.
47. Cruz-Uribe 2008a, p. 2.
48. Eide et al. 1998, pp. 1024–31.
49. Cruz-Uribe 2010.
50. Huyge 1998, p. 1385.

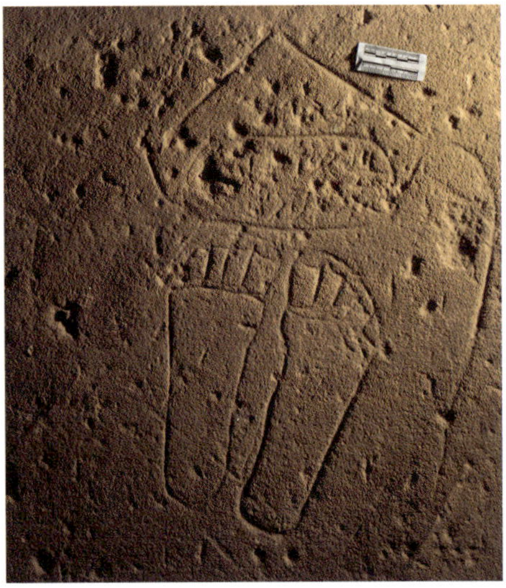

FIGURE 5.11. Foot graffiti with accompanying Demotic text on the roof "tank" of Philae's Mammisi.
Photo: Steve Vinson, 2019

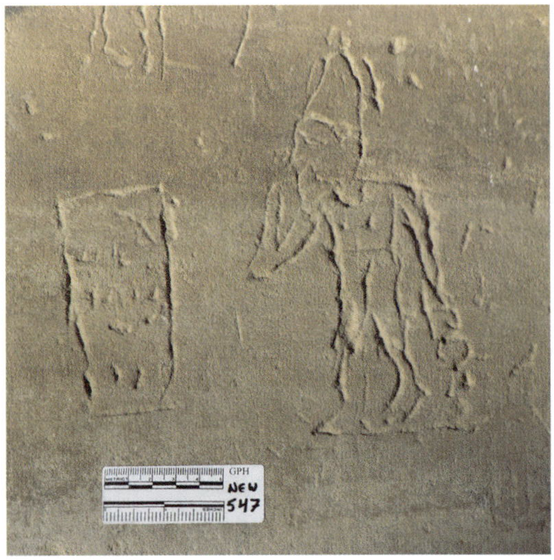

FIGURE 5.12. Standing figure with White Crown and ankh upon the southwest jamb of Hadrian's Gateway at Philae.
Photo: Eugene Cruz-Uribe

thus its symbiosis with pilgrimage.[51] At least in northeast Africa, ancient temples were less museums than palimpsests.

More commonly, anthropomorphic graffiti at Philae depict either gods or kings. On the same block with Sasan's portrait (**FIG. 5.10**, above), we see the image of another man (**FIG. 5.12**) wearing the White Crown while holding an ankh in his left hand and lifting his right hand to his mouth. The text box in front of the figure has not been read with certainty, but Cruz-Uribe logically proposed that it may identify the Meroitic sovereign whom Sasan served, Taqereramani (a.k.a. Teqorideamani).[52] Interestingly, such royal images do not seem to be paralleled among the newly discovered graffiti at Kurru — unless the seated figure in graffito T8 were meant to represent a king.

A final category of anthropomorph at Philae is the standing archer so well known from Nubian rock art.[53] In one case, a figure with bow drawn hovers above the deck of an elaborately detailed river vessel bearing three other passengers (**FIG. 5.13**). At Kurru, a bowman likewise holds his weapon before him, albeit with his off-hand resting at his side (T1), and another may hold a weapon at his waist (T3). Yet the similarity to Philae's human figures would seem superficial at best, and the available photos from Philae show little direct interaction between humans and animals that could be directly compared to the graffiti at Kurru (T9 and possibly T10).

Fauna

Animal graffiti reveal in this case a fundamental difference between sites: fauna shown at Philae were consistently symbolic of a god, whereas those at Kurru seldom were (notably T11). There is, however, an exceptional case of possible stylistic alignment across far-flung

51. Cruz-Uribe 2008b, p. 197.
52. Cruz-Uribe 2016, p. 38; see Pope 2008, pp. 85–86.
53. Cf. Červíček 1974, pp. 156–57.

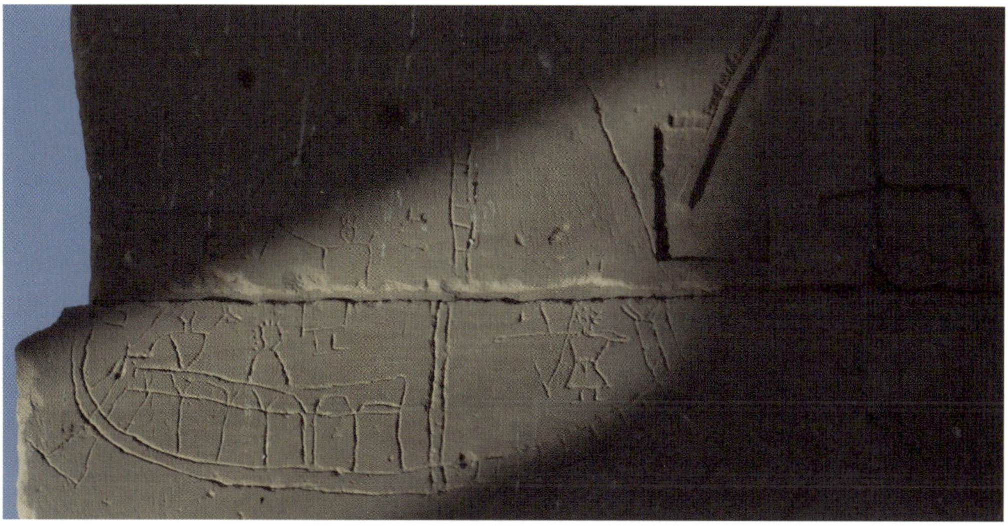

FIGURE 5.13. Boat with passengers, including archer at viewer's right. Philae, exact location unrecorded.
Photo: Steve Vinson, 2019

sites that were all within the ambit of Nubian pilgrims. At Kurru, we find an elegant rendering in sunken relief of hoofprints surrounding two bull heads with raised ears (T12), and likewise at Musawwarat an image of what appears to be a lion head with raised ears *en face*;[54] these should be compared with a small depression at Philae whose outline likewise seems to bear the shape of an animal's face with raised ears (**FIG. 5.14**). Whether any graffitist actually intended this image, a mere cupule, or instead nothing at all is unfortunately difficult to ascertain, as the result at Philae has all the determinacy of a Rorschach blot, and the neighboring Demotic graffito of "[P]asher-[... son of] Pakhnu[m]" appears in any case to have been inscribed at a separate moment.[55] As for the function of faunal graffiti, it is certainly noteworthy that the head at Musawwarat seems to depict Apedemak, the principal deity of that site.[56] As Darnell has noted, comparison with the more explicit testimony of textual graffiti would suggest that informal decoration often served an apotropaic function, invoking divine protection for both the composers and audience of graffiti.[57]

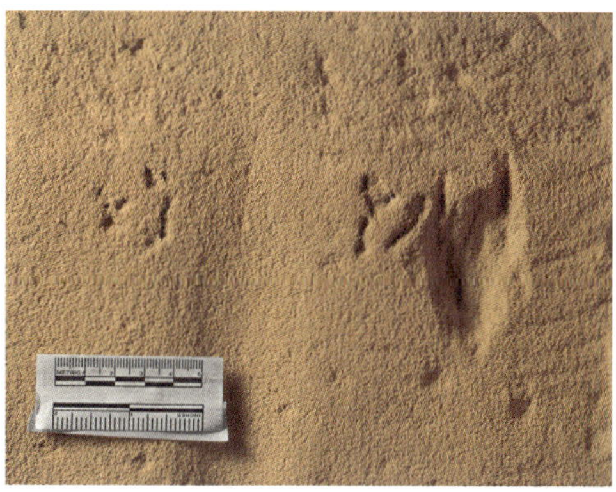

FIGURE 5.14. Depression at Philae resembling the head of an animal with raised ears, found at the north end of the west wall upon the roof "tank" of Philae's Mammisi.
Photo: Steve Vinson, 2019

The more typical representation of an animal among the graffiti at Philae uses incised lines to show a substantial amount of internal detail on a theriomorphic (animal-shaped) god. For example, three such images of the same composite deity

54. Kleinitz 2014, fig. 1.
55. Cruz-Uribe 2016, p. 218.
56. Kleinitz 2014, pp. 100–01.
57. Darnell 2002, p. 886.

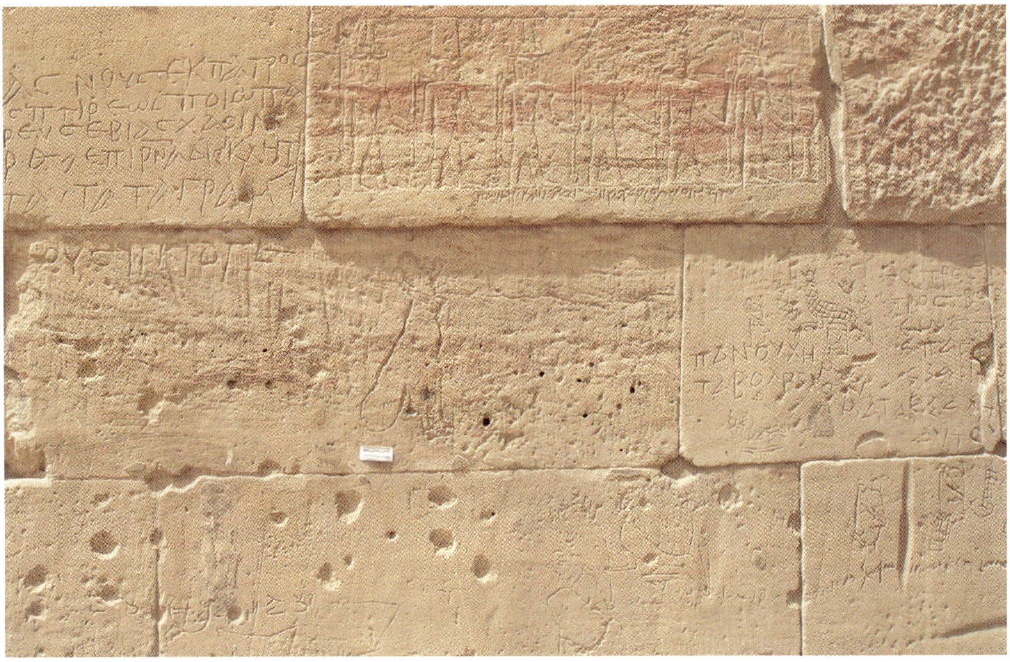

FIGURE 5.15. Deities in the form of a composite animal holding an *Isisblume* (two at viewer's right beside Greek graffiti and again one in center block of bottom row), as depicted upon the exterior east wall of Philae's East Colonnade.
Photo: Eugene Cruz-Uribe

appear on the exterior east wall of the East Colonnade (e.g., **FIG. 5.15**). Observing the proximity of this scene to the Kiosk of Augustus, Cruz-Uribe posited that "pilgrims coming from the south would see this section of the exterior of Philae Temple first" after disembarking at the quay.[58] Thus, Philae provides again rather exceptional possibilities for the establishment of historical context: the juxtaposition of textual and figural graffiti within a landscape of firmly dated monuments has at least mitigated our reliance upon conjecture.

Flora

The plants surrounding those animals on the East Colonnade are similarly instructive and especially characteristic of Philae's larger corpus of graffiti. Projecting from the animal's back is a single lotus bud, comparable to one found recently at Kurru (T26). Yet the more diagnostic plant on Philae's East Colonnade is the bouquet in the animal's claw. Identical bouquets are held by the Meroitic delegation depicted on the opposite face of the same wall (see discussion of anthropomorphs, above); their popularity was, in fact, limited to this specific category of pilgrims and priests within a narrow temporal span across a quite restricted stretch of the Nile. A recent survey by Tsubasa Sakamoto has located sixty-four scenes depicting these bouquets across Philae and the Dodecaschoenus region of Lower Nubia.[59] He posits that these *Isisblumen* (Isis blooms) signified Meroitic patronage during precisely the interval when control of Philae's priesthood was ceded to the Nubians

58. Cruz-Uribe 2016, p. 19.
59. Sakamoto 2017.

— beginning around 253 CE and then fading in the 4th and 5th centuries. The bouquet therefore manifested an inter-regional exchange on a local scale: it was a symbol evidently chosen by (or for) visitors from as far away as Upper Nubia that was nevertheless employed, not in Upper Nubia itself, but instead at the distant border of Egypt. Among Philae's figural graffiti during the Meroitic era, it would be difficult to find any example more representative of the corpus as a whole.

Conclusion

At the outset of this discussion, it was emphasized that Kurru and Philae were part of a shared cultural continuum. The temples at Philae seem to have been initiated by a Nubian king, were frequented by Nubian pilgrims for the next millennium, and were even staffed by Nubian priests during the twilight years of the Isis cult. As hieroglyphic script and its cursive derivatives were essentially "an advanced form of figural graffiti,"[60] there was also a semiotic continuum linking Philae's texts with drawn images farther afield. In fact, the unusual confidence with which Philae's pictures can be dated and their original functions explained holds some untapped potential to elucidate informal decoration at other sites. Flags depicted in the Philae graffiti do resemble the designs of textiles and horned altars at Kurru, and the offering tables shown at both sites belong to a common and recognizable type. The drawing of a disembodied animal head in frontal view at Philae also finds parallels at Kurru and Musawwarat. With further study, these data points may contribute to a useful chronological matrix for comparison across multiple locales.

Yet even this brief comparison of figural graffiti at Philae and Kurru has revealed several differences between the two sites. There are few craft shown at Kurru so small as the boats depicted during the Meroitic era on the West Colonnade at Philae, and Kurru's images of larger vessels seem, in any case, to date to the Christian period. Anthropomorphs and fauna at Philae are also more clearly and consistently identifiable with named people and gods than are their counterparts at Kurru. Among the flora depicted at the two sites, only a single lotus bud provides a clear match, but there is no parallel at Kurru for the *Isisblumen* so ubiquitous at Philae and the Dodecaschoenus. Indeed, the differences outnumber the similarities across most categories of figural graffiti.

Such results are not so much contradictory as they are complicated. After all, we know that Upper Nubians were frequenting the island of Philae during the Meroitic era, but this fact in no way requires that they would have left identical graffiti across the whole of Nubia. Styles and motifs unique to Philae and its environs would seem to be a product of either local cultic significance, change over time, the statuses of their composers, or some combination of these and other factors — and the same should be equally true of Kurru. This conclusion may not satisfy our positivistic itch to find exact stylistic matches, attribute unambiguous functions, and assign absolute dates, but it illustrates well the internal complexity of those cultural phenomena that we term broadly as "Nubian."

60. Cruz-Uribe 2008a, p. 4.

References

Anstis, Sebastian

2015 "Meroitic Graffiti in the Mortuary Temple." *Sudan & Nubia* 19: 67–68.

Ashby, Solange

Forth. *Calling Out to Isis: The Enduring Nubian Presence at Philae.* Piscataway: Gorgias Press.

Bernand, André

1969 *Les inscriptions grecques de Philae,* Volume 1: *Époque ptolémiaque.* Paris: Centre national de la recherche scientifique.

Burkhardt, Adelheid

1985 *Ägypter und Meroiten im Dodekaschoinos: Untersuchungen zur Typologie und Bedeutung der demotischen Graffiti.* Meroitica 8. Berlin: Akademie Verlag.

Castiglione, Ladislas

1970 "Vestigia." *Acta Archaeologica Academiae Scientarum Hungaricae* 22: 95–132.

Červíček, Pavel

1974 *Felsbilder des Nord-Etbai, Oberägyptens und Unternubiens.* Ergebnisse der Frobenius-Expeditionen 16. Wiesbaden: Steiner.

1982 "Notes on the Chronology of Nubian Rock Art from the End of the Bronze Age Onwards." In *Nubian Studies: Proceedings of the Symposium for Nubian Studies, Selwyn College, Cambridge, 1978,* edited by John Martin Plumley, pp. 57–63. Warminster: Aris & Phillips.

Cruz-Uribe, Eugene

2002 "The Death of Demotic at Philae, a Study in Pilgrimage and Politics." In *A Tribute to Excellence: Studies Offered in Honor of Erno Gaál, Ulrich Luft, László Török,* edited by Tamás A. Bács, pp. 163–84. Studia Aegyptiaca 17. Budapest: Université Eötvös Lorand.

2008a "Graffiti (Figural)." In *UCLA Encyclopedia of Egyptology,* edited by Willeke Wendrich. Los Angeles. https://escholarship.org/uc/nelc_uee.

2008b *Hibis Temple Project,* Volume 3: *The Graffiti from the Temple Precinct.* San Antonio: Van Siclen Books.

2010 "The Death of Demotic Redux: Pilgrimage, Nubia and the Preservation of Egyptian Culture." In *Honi soit qui mal y pense: Studien zum pharaonischen, griechisch-römischen und spätantiken Ägypten zu Ehren von Heinz-Josef Thissen,* edited by Hermann Knuf, Christian Leitz, and Daniel von Recklinghausen, pp. 499–506. Orientalia Lovaniensia Analecta 194. Leuven: Peeters.

2012 "Hieroglyphic and Demotic Texts." In *Syene I. The Figural and Textual Graffiti from the Temple of Isis at Aswan,* by Jitse H. F. Dijkstra, pp. 111–52. Beiträge zur Ägyptischen Bauforschung und Altertumskunde 18. Mainz: Philipp von Zabern.

2015 "Nubian Religious Expansion in Philae during the Roman Period." Paper presented at the 66th Annual Meeting of the American Research Center in Egypt, Houston, TX.

2016 *The Demotic Graffiti from the Temple of Isis on Philae Island.* Material and Visual Culture of Ancient Egypt 3. Atlanta: Lockwood Press.

Darnell, John C.

2002 Review of *The Graffiti of Pharaonic Egypt: Scope and Roles of Informal Writings (c. 3100–332 B.C.),* by A. J. Peden. *Journal of the American Oriental Society* 122 (4): 885–86.

Dunham, Dows

1950 *El Kurru.* The Royal Cemeteries of Kush 1. Cambridge, MA: Harvard University Press.

Edwards, David N.

1996 *The Archaeology of the Meroitic State: New Perspectives on Its Social and Political Organisation.* Cambridge Monographs in African Archaeology 38; BAR International Series 640. Oxford: BAR International.

Eide, Tormod, Tomas Hägg, Richard Holton Pierce, and László Török, eds.

1998 *Fontes Historiae Nubiorum: Textual Sources for the History of the Middle Nile Region between the Eighth Century BC and the Sixth Century AD,* Volume 3: *From the First to the Sixth Century AD.* Bergen: Department of Classics, University of Bergen.

Emberling, Geoff

2015 "A Mortuary Temple at El-Kurru." *Sudan & Nubia* 19: 65–67.

Erman, Adolf, and Heinrich Schäfer

1908 "Der angebliche ägyptische Bericht über die Umschiffung Afrikas." *Sitzungsberichte der königlichen Preußischen Akademie der Wissenschaften, Gesamtsitzung vom 30. Juli* 39: 956–67.

Farag, Sami, Gamal Wahba, and Abdel Farid

1979 "Inscribed Blocks of the Ramesside Period and of King Taharqa, Found at Philae." *Oriens Antiquus* 18: 281–89.

Fuller, Dorian Q.

2003 "Pharaonic or Sudanic? Models for Meroitic Society and Change." In *Ancient Egypt in Africa*, edited by David B. O'Connor and Andrew Reid, pp. 169–84. Encounters with Ancient Egypt. London: UCL Press.

Griffith, Francis Llewellyn

1912 *Meroitic Inscriptions*, Part 2: *Napata to Philae and Miscellaneous.* Archaeological Survey of Egypt, 20th Memoir. London: Egypt Exploration Society.

1931 "Four Granite Stands at Philae." *Bulletin de l'Institut français d'archéologie orientale* 30: 127–30.

1937 *Catalogue of the Demotic Graffiti of the Dodecaschoenus.* Oxford: Oxford University Press.

Hintze, Ursula

1979 "The Graffiti from the Great Enclosure at Musawwarat Es Sufra." In *Africa in Antiquity: The Arts of Ancient Nubia and the Sudan. Proceedings of the Symposium Held in Conjunction with the Exhibition, Brooklyn, Sept. 29-Oct. 1, 1978*, edited by Fritz Hintze, pp. 135–50. Meroitica 5. Berlin: Akademie Verlag.

Huyge, Dirk

1998 "Art on the Decline? Egyptian Rock Drawings from the Late and Graeco-Roman Periods." In *Egyptian Religion, the Last Thousand Years: Studies Dedicated to the Memory of Jan Quaegebeur*, edited by Willy Clarysse, Antoon Schoors, and Harco Willems, pp. 1377–92. Orientalia Lovaniensia Analecta 84. Leuven: Peeters.

2003 "Grandeur in Confined Spaces: Current Rock Art Research in Egypt." In *Rock Art Studies: News of the World 2, Developments in Rock Art Research, 1995-1999*, edited by Paul G. Bahn and Angelo Fossati, pp. 59–73. Oxford: Oxbow Books.

Jacquet-Gordon, Helen

2003 *The Temple of Khonsu 3. The Graffiti on the Khonsu Temple Roof at Karnak: A Manifestation of Personal Piety.* Oriental Institute Publications 123. Chicago: The Oriental Institute.

Junker, Hermann

1913 *Das Götterdekret über das Abaton.* Österreichische Akademie der Wissenschaften, Philosophisch-Historische Klasse 56. Vienna: A. Hölder.

Kleinitz, Cornelia

2014 "The Graffiti of Musawwarat Es-Sufra: Current Research on Historic Inscriptions, Images and Markings at the Great Enclosure." *Sudan & Nubia* 18: 93–103.

Kockelmann, Holger

2012 "Philae." In *UCLA Encyclopedia of Egyptology*, edited by Willeke Wendrich. Los Angeles. https://escholarship.org/uc/nelc_uee.

Leclant, Jean, ed.

2000 *Répertoire d'épigraphie méroïtique: corpus des inscriptions publiées*, Volume 1: *REM 0001 à REM 0387.* Paris: de Boccard.

Peden, Alexander J.

2001 *The Graffiti of Pharaonic Egypt: Scope and Roles of Informal Writings (c. 3100-332 BC).* Probleme der Ägyptologie 17. Leiden: Brill.

Pope, Jeremy

2008 "The Demotic Proskynema of a Meroïte Envoy to Roman Egypt (Philae 416)." *Enchoria: Zeitschrift für Demotistik und Koptologie* 31: 68–103.

2014 "Meroitic Diplomacy and the Festival of Entry." In *The Fourth Cataract and Beyond: Proceedings of the 12th International Conference for Nubian Studies,* edited by Julie R. Anderson and Derek A. Welsby, pp. 577–82. British Museum Publications on Egypt and Sudan 1. Leuven: Peeters.

Porter, Bertha, and Rosalind L. B. Moss

1970 *Topographical Bibliography of Ancient Egyptian Hieroglyphic Texts, Reliefs, and Paintings,* Volume 6: *Upper Egypt: Chief Temples.* Re-Issue. Oxford: Griffith Institute.

Rilly, Claude

2007 *La langue du royaume de Méroé: un panorama de la plus ancienne culture écrite d'Afrique subsaharienne.* Bibliothèque de l'école des hautes études. Sciences historiques et philologiques 344. Paris: Champion.

2010 *Le méroïtique et sa famille linguistique.* Collection Afrique et langage 14; Société d'études linguistiques et anthropologiques de France 454. Leuven: Peeters.

Rilly, Claude, and Alex de Voogt

2012 *The Meroitic Language and Writing System.* Cambridge: Cambridge University Press.

Rose, Pamela J.

2007 *The Meroitic Temple Complex at Qasr Ibrim.* Egypt Exploration Society, Excavation Memoir 84. London: Egypt Exploration Society.

Rutherford, Ian

1998 "Island of the Extremity: Space, Language, and Power in the Pilgrimage Traditions of Philae." In *Pilgrimage and Holy Space in Late Antique Egypt,* edited by David Frankfurter, pp. 229–56. Religions in the Graeco-Roman World 134. Leiden: Brill.

Sakamoto, Tsubasa

2017 "'Isisblumen' au Pays de Kouch: Bilan et perspectives." *Journal of the American Research Center in Egypt* 53: 91–103. http://dx.doi.org/10.5913/jarce.53.2017.a004.

Weigall, Arthur E. P.

1907 *A Report on the Antiquities of Lower Nubia.* Oxford: Hiersemann.

Winter, Erich

1976 "Die Tempel von Philae und das Problem ihrer Rettung." *Antike Welt* 7 (3): 2–15.

6

Bogdan Żurawski

Discourses with the Holy: Text and Image Graffiti from the Pilgrimage Churches of Saint Raphael the Archangel in Banganarti, Sudan

The 6th century CE witnessed the emergence, consolidation, and conversion to Christianity of the three kingdoms on the Middle Nile: Nobatia in the north, Alwa in the south, and Makuria in between them. The kingdom of Makuria with its capital at Tungul (modern Old Dongola) stretched from the 3rd to the 4th Cataract, and perhaps even farther beyond (**FIG. 6.1**). Although the Acts of the Apostles (8:26–40) recount the baptism of a eunuch in charge of the treasury of the *kandake* (queen of Kush) by Philip the Evangelist in the year 37, there is no firm archaeological evidence for the presence of Christianity in the Nile Valley south of Aswan before the collapse of the kingdom of Kush.

The story of emergence, floruit, decline, and fall of the kingdom of Makuria is implicitly written in the texts preserved on the walls of the churches dedicated to the Archangel Raphael, in the fortified settlement at Banganarti. Most of these texts are pilgrim graffiti.

Banganarti ("Locust Island" in Nubian) sits on the bank of a dried-up channel of the Nile, 7 kilometers upriver from Tungul. When the Christian king of Tungul ruled the Middle Nile, the network of churches in the heartland of Makuria was quite dense. On the right bank alone the next church downriver from Banganarti was in the southern outskirts of Tungul; the nearest church upriver was in Selib, 9 kilometers away. Farther upstream churches were reported in the fortified settlements of Abkur, Diffar, Deiga, and Bakhit. None of these has been excavated, and only a plan of the Bakhit church is known today.

The last season of excavations in Banganarti (2018/2019) ascertained the presence of a monastery there. The monastic complex around the earliest church there was followed upriver by two monasteries, on Kom H and Kom D in Old Dongola and one in Hambukol, 8.5, 9.3, and 13 kilometers, respectively. Most visitors to the Banganarti churches who left written testimonies of their visits were the monks and clerics from Tungul, Hambukol, and other Middle Nile centers as far as Pachoras (Faras) in the north and Nuri in the south.

The church of Saint Raphael the Archangel (the "Raphaelion") in Banganarti was one of the most important pilgrimage centers on the Middle Nile until the 15th century. It is known for its unusual architecture, the twelve portraits of sacrosanct kings of Makuria painted in its seven eastern chapels, and the many hundreds of inscriptions scratched onto its walls by pilgrims.[1] These inscriptions paint a picture of a well-organized, religiously homogeneous society within the medieval kingdom of Makuria. However, a more complete picture of the social order, popular religion, and psychological climate of Makuria can be gained by also looking at the many figurative drawings scratched on the walls of the Raphaelion by other,

1. Łajtar forthcoming a.

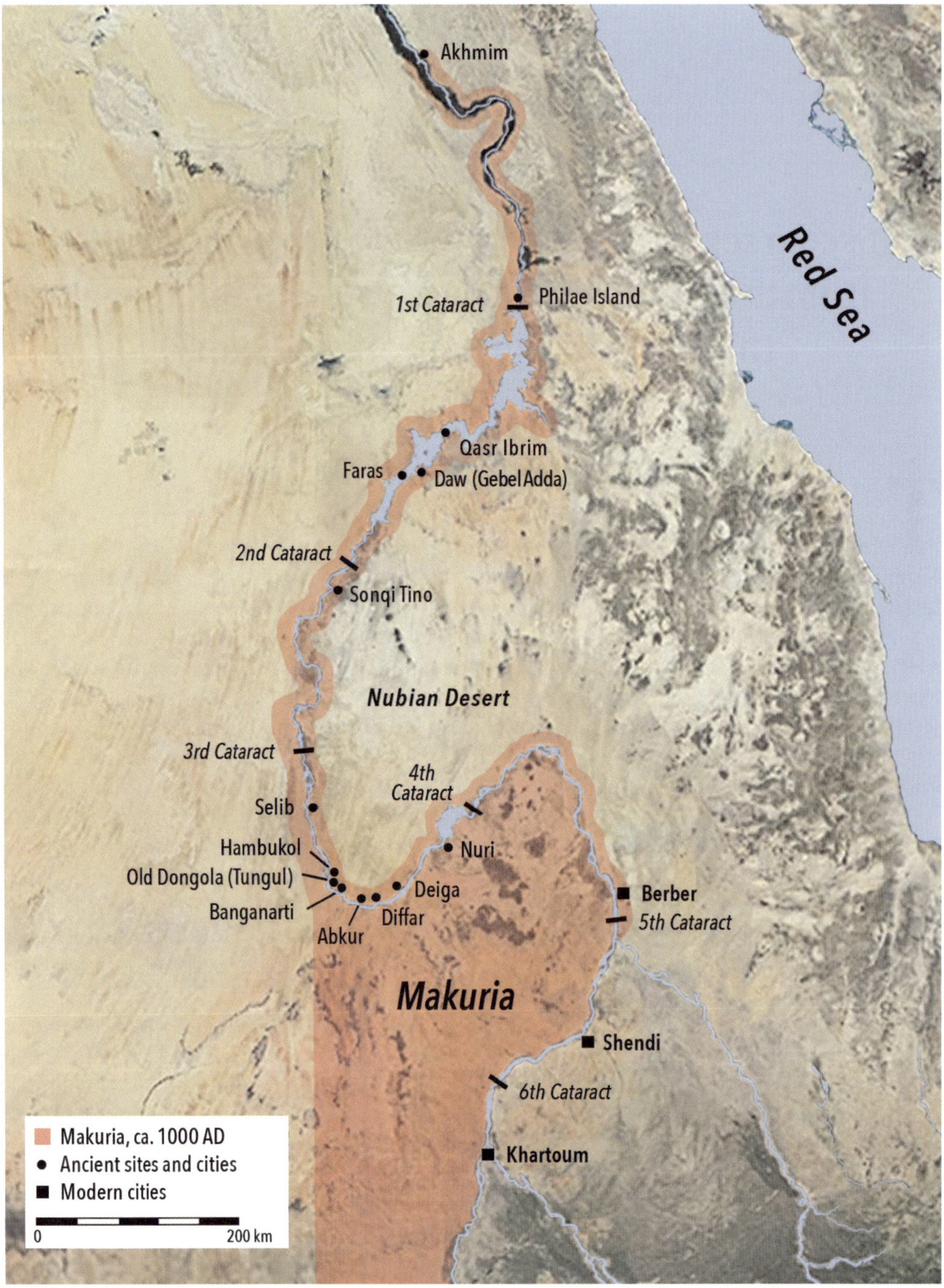

FIGURE 6.1. Map of sites discussed in the text.
Map: Lorene Sterner

not necessarily Christian, visitors. In-depth epigraphic and iconographic analyses have proved beyond doubt that these images were created simultaneously and to some extent interchangeably with the text graffiti. Are these figurative drawings prayers without words? Saint Gregory the Great answered the question in simple words: *Quod legentibus scriptura hoc idiotis praestat picture cernentibus: quia in ipsa ignorantes vident, quod sequi debeant, in ipsa legunt, qui litteras nesciunt.*[2]

The problem is more complex than that 6th-century pope could imagine. The reasons that pilgrims scratched mementos of their visits — whether text or picture — on the walls of a sacred place are not so obvious as might be expected. Why they chose one and not the other way of communicating with the holy is also puzzling, as are their motives for including or omitting certain biographical details in the inscriptions they left.

To shed some light on the various associations between text and image in the realm of the Raphaelion graffiti, let me start with some background on the church itself (**FIGS. 6.2-4**). The structure underwent two major construction phases. The so-called Lower Church was actually a sequence of three churches built one on top of the other, largely on the same cruciform plan. The first church was erected in the late 6th/early 7th century and was destroyed around 650 CE. It is plausible that already at this early phase the church was dedicated to the Archangel Raphael. The second building phase occupied the next hundred years, and it is at this time that the church began to be a center of pilgrimage. The third phase of the Lower Church was erected after 836 and destroyed in the mid-11th century. Its surviving fabric was leveled in preparation for the construction of the Upper Church.

The Upper Church was constructed in the second half of the 11th century, partly on the ruins of the Lower Church and partly on sand. It was organized around a central square space covered by a dome supported by four pillars. This church was a place of pilgrimage

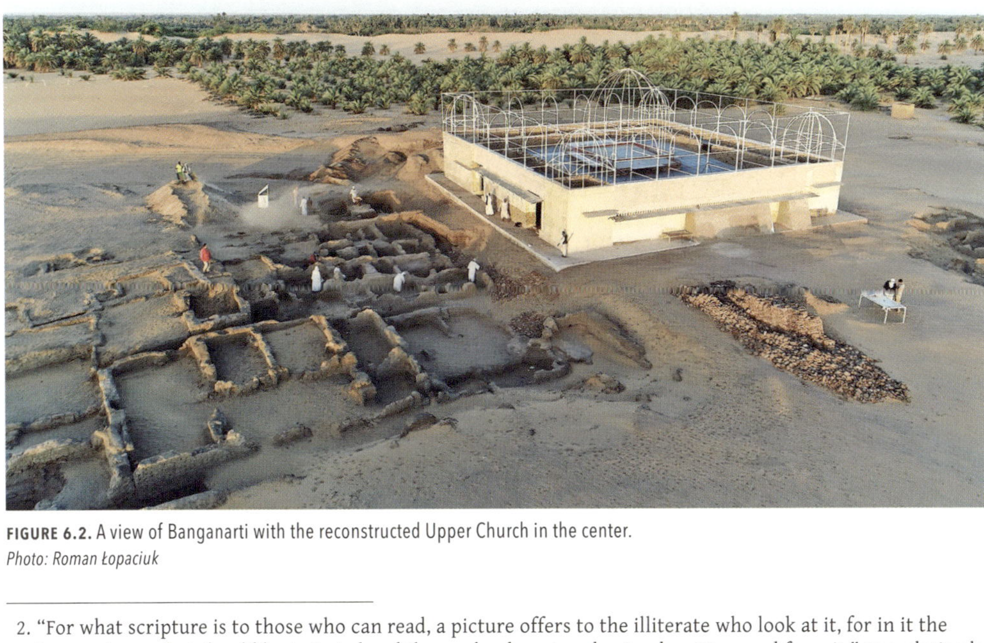

FIGURE 6.2. A view of Banganarti with the reconstructed Upper Church in the center.
Photo: Roman Łopaciuk

2. "For what scripture is to those who can read, a picture offers to the illiterate who look at it, for in it the ignorant see what should be imitated and those who do not understand writing read from it." Translation by D. Norberg, after Raw 2004, p. 103.

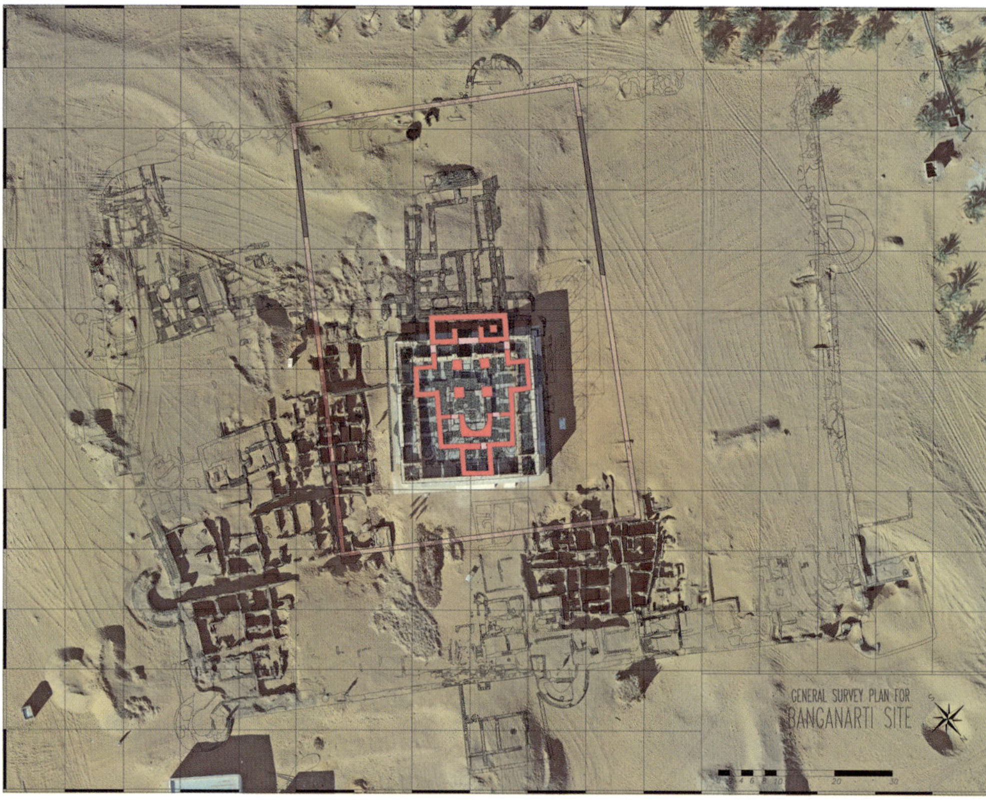

FIGURE 6.3. Aerial photograph of the Raphaelion (Upper Church) with a plan of the Lower Church marked in red.
Photo: Roman Łopaciuk

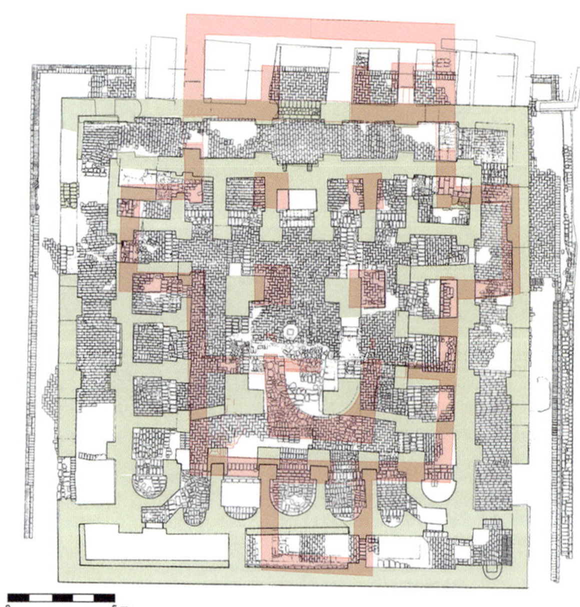

FIGURE 6.4. Overlay plans of the Lower Church (red) and Upper Church (green).
Plan: Roman Łopaciuk, Marta Momot, Mariusz Drzewiecki, and Bogdan Żurawski

on a large scale, perhaps connected with the cult of relics kept there and the healing powers attributed to its patron saint, Archangel Raphael. The Upper Church survived a series of construction disasters caused by errors made by builders, who had probably been brought from Byzantium, in estimating the stability of the sandy ground.[3]

Excavations in this most important medieval Nubian pilgrimage center were conducted between 2001 and 2019 and resulted in the discovery of more than sixty wall paintings and nearly a thousand inscriptions, distributed unevenly between the Lower and Upper Church (**FIG. 6.5**). While the exploration of the Upper Church yielded 969 inscriptions, the partial unearthing of the Lower Church produced only twenty-seven texts,[4] a mere three of which qualify as visitors' mementos.[5] What motivated visitors to the Upper Church to leave testimonials of their visits, and why did those who visited the Lower Church not feel the same compulsion? This difference suggests a fundamental change in pilgrim behavior at the turn of the millennium, probably reflecting a shift in pilgrims' objectives as well as a transformation of the sacral topography caused by leveling of the Lower Church and construction of the Upper Church.

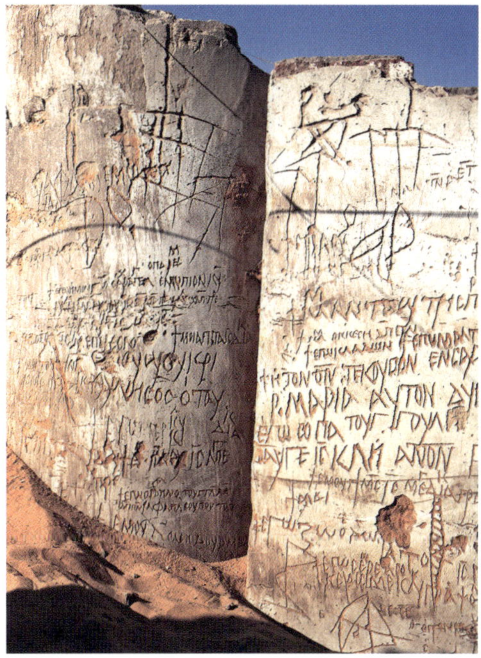

FIGURE 6.5. An example of the graffiti scratched on the walls of the Upper Church.
Photo: Bogdan Żurawski

Pilgrims to the Lower Church in the 8th and 9th centuries were likely drawn to the site by two tombs constructed outside the church's eastern wall. Those who came to see these sepulchers did not leave written mementos of their visits in the church itself, but nevertheless left traces of their presence in the form of hollows abraded in the sandstone wall of the church near one of the tombs.[6] It is unlikely that they entered the Lower Church in a substantial number since it could not accommodate crowds.

At the end of the 1st millennium, pilgrims' expectations and forms of communicating with the holy underwent a substantial change. At the newly constructed Upper Church at Banganarti, three entrances and two staircases allowed crowds of pilgrims easy access to the nave, the galleries, and, above all, to the ultimate focal point: the analogion beneath the central dome.[7] This was a low, octagonal structure on which icons, the book of Gospels, and perhaps relics were placed for veneration by the faithful.

Of the 996 textual graffiti recorded at Banganarti, the overwhelming majority (969, 97%) come from the Upper Church.[8] The walls of the Upper Church also yielded figural

3. Żurawski 2014, p. 236.
4. Deptuła 2018, p. 23.
5. Ibid., p. 27.
6. Żurawski 2012, pp. 377–79; see similar hollows, called pilgrim scrapes, on the wall of the cathedral in Qasr Ibrim; Aldsworth 2010, p. 58 and pl. 99.
7. Significantly, they walked around the analogion in the same way Muslims perform the circumambulation of the Kaaba during hajj and umrah.
8. Łajtar 2003a, 2003b, 2008a, 2008b, 2010; Deptuła 2018.

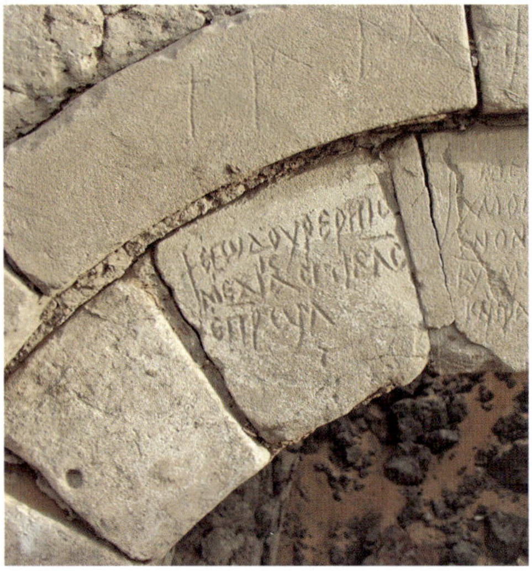

FIGURE 6.6. Graffiti on the voussoirs of the northern entrance to the Upper Church.
Photo: Bogdan Żurawski

graffiti, including forty-four animals,[9] a hunting scene (see **FIG. 6.13**), a multi-oared galley, a warrior with an oval shield (in the lower right of **FIG. 6.10**) and a pilgrim (in the upper left of **FIG. 6.10**). Graffiti left by the visitors are almost unknown from the Lower Church. The rare exception to the rule is a graffito containing the name of Antonnios or Antonnis written in black ink on the eastern wall of the passage behind the apse. The text reads, "Preserve the most holy priest Antonnios in peace, zeal, and in love."[10]

Graffiti are evenly distributed throughout the walls of the Upper Church with no obvious reference to its sacral topography. However, one can discern a general pattern in that figural graffiti tend to concentrate in the western part of the church, closer to the entrances, whereas the text graffiti dominate in the eastern part, near the seven chapels that are each decorated with a mural representing a king flanked by apostles and protected by an archangel. On the whole, epigraphic vandalism is very rare — the inscriptions occur mainly on undecorated parts of walls, very rarely interfering with the murals.[11] Some graffiti were cut into the ferruginous sandstone voussoirs and blocks used in the south and north portals (**FIG. 6.6**).

Two and in some places three layers of plaster attest to a long tradition of inscribing graffiti at the Upper Church. When a wall became full, it was whitewashed to be used again as writing space. With rare exceptions, only the graffiti on the final layer of plaster are visible. This layer — corresponding also to the final period of the Raphaelion's use as a pilgrimage center — can be dated to the last quarter of the 13th and first half of the 14th centuries.[12] The mention of King Siti of the Nubian kingdom of Dotawo in two graffiti suggests the 1330s as the most plausible date for the creation of at least some of the Banganarti graffiti.[13]

The quality of the inscriptions varies from elegant to crude. We can conjecture that many graffiti were applied to the walls by local scribes on behalf of the visitors, although literate pilgrims had a chance to do it themselves while awaiting their turn to sleep in one the rooms around the central nave, a curative practice known as incubation.

The language of everyday communication in the medieval kingdom of Makuria was Old Dongolawi and the use of Old Nubian was restricted to the written documents. Greek was the language of liturgy in the church. Needless to say, the majority of textual graffiti at the Raphaelion are in Greek or Old Nubian or a blend of these two. There is one inscrip-

9. Osypińska and Żurawski 2014.
10. Łajtar 2008a, p. 401.
11. Żurawski 2014, pp. 125–68.
12. Łajtar 2014, pp. 261–62. Apart from the graffiti left by King Siti (on which, see below) there is another graffito in the Upper Church which contains a date, written by a visitor named Teeita. We do not know whether Teeita was man or woman because Old Nubian does not recognize a gender, but we know that he or she visited the church on the 18th of November 1280. The exact date of the visit was brilliantly calculated by Adam Łajtar on the basis of three chronological indications contained in the text. Because the inscription was covered with plaster, it provides an *ante quem* date for the laying of the last coat of plaster, on which most of the inscriptions were written (Łajtar 2008b, p. 327).
13. Łajtar 2008b, p. 328.

tion in Coptic and one in Catalan/Provençal.[14] Of the two Arabic-language graffiti, one, the famous "Ali the guest" graffito, was rendered with Greek letters (see below). The other was accidentally destroyed by a French television team in 2002. That there are only two Arabic graffiti among a thousand or so Greek and Greek-Nubian ones is somewhat disappointing. This bias seems to be more understandable if we realize that most of the Banganarti texts were written by clerics from nearby churches.

In the medieval mentality, a person's name was considered a part of his or her identity, being the person's substitute, of a sort. Thus the benefits from a visit to a holy place were extended in time by leaving a graffito, which stayed forever in the holy place and stood in for the pilgrim through the virtue of their name, origin, occupation, and other details contained in the accompanying text. A pilgrim's name represented in a graffito guaranteed the "presence" of the individual in the holy place as long as it endured.

However, anonymous graffiti are common in Banganarti and at Christian pilgrimage centers at Faras, Sonqi Tino, and Tungul (Old Dongola). Intentionally omitting the supplicant's name in graffiti is usually explained by the requirement of modesty in the face of God.[15] When the supplicant's name is not mentioned in the text, they are either introduced as the one "whose name is known to the God" or simply by the Greek word *kago*, crasis for *kai ego*, "and myself."[16] In such cases, it is presumed that the pilgrim wanted to remain anonymous to the local inhabitants while being, of course, known to God.

Thanks to the study of Banganarti inscriptions we know that the original Nubian name of Dongola was Tungul. A graffito that provides this piece of information is applied to the western wall of the corridor leading to the northern entrance (**FIG. 6.7**). It accompanies the only royal representation in the Upper Church which is scratched, not painted. It is also the only one showing a mounted king. The scene is dramatic and not entirely clear.[17] It presents two mounted men riding from right to left. The rider on the right, apparently pursuing an opponent in front of him, is named by the inscription as Paper, the "small king" of the town of Tungul. In none of the four inscriptions containing his name is there even a hint of the time of his reign. The title small king (*basileus brephos*) suggests that he was ruling over the town of Tungul and an unspecified surrounding territory after the kingdom of Makuria split into small political entities governed by kinglets titled *mukkuk* (singular *mekk*). Paper's royalty is indicated by the Nubian horned headgear he wears. He holds the reins in his hand and appears to be grasping the end of a lasso tied around the rider in front of him. The latter brandishes a sword, his round shield resting on his horse's back.[18]

The question must be asked whether the episode illustrated by this graffito refers to a historic event known from literary sources. The medieval Egyptian historian al-Maqrizi, in his narrative of the events that happened in Tungul in the year 1365, describes an episode most fitting to the scene.[19] If these events indeed correspond, Paper would have been the son of the sister of the king of Tungul. In the last episode of a period of political turmoil he took the capital and massacred his opponents, the Bani Ja'd Arabs, to finally become reconciled with the regent residing in Lower Nubian Daw (also known as Gebel Adda) on the condition

14. Łajtar 2014, p. 261; Łajtar and Płóciennik 2011.
15. Łajtar 2015, p. 349 and n. 16.
16. In a graffito found at a recently discovered church in Old Dongola, the so-called Northern Church, the Arabic word *isim*, "name," substitutes for the name of the supplicant (Adam Łajtar, personal communication).
17. Łajtar forthcoming a, cat. no. 64; for King Paper, see ibid., commentary to cat. no. 67. See also Łajtar 2005, p. 311; 2008a, pp. 329–30, fig. 6; 2009, pp. 95–96; Żurawski 2005, p. 321.
18. Łajtar 2008a, p. 330.
19. Al-Maqrizi in Vantini 1975, pp. 698–703.

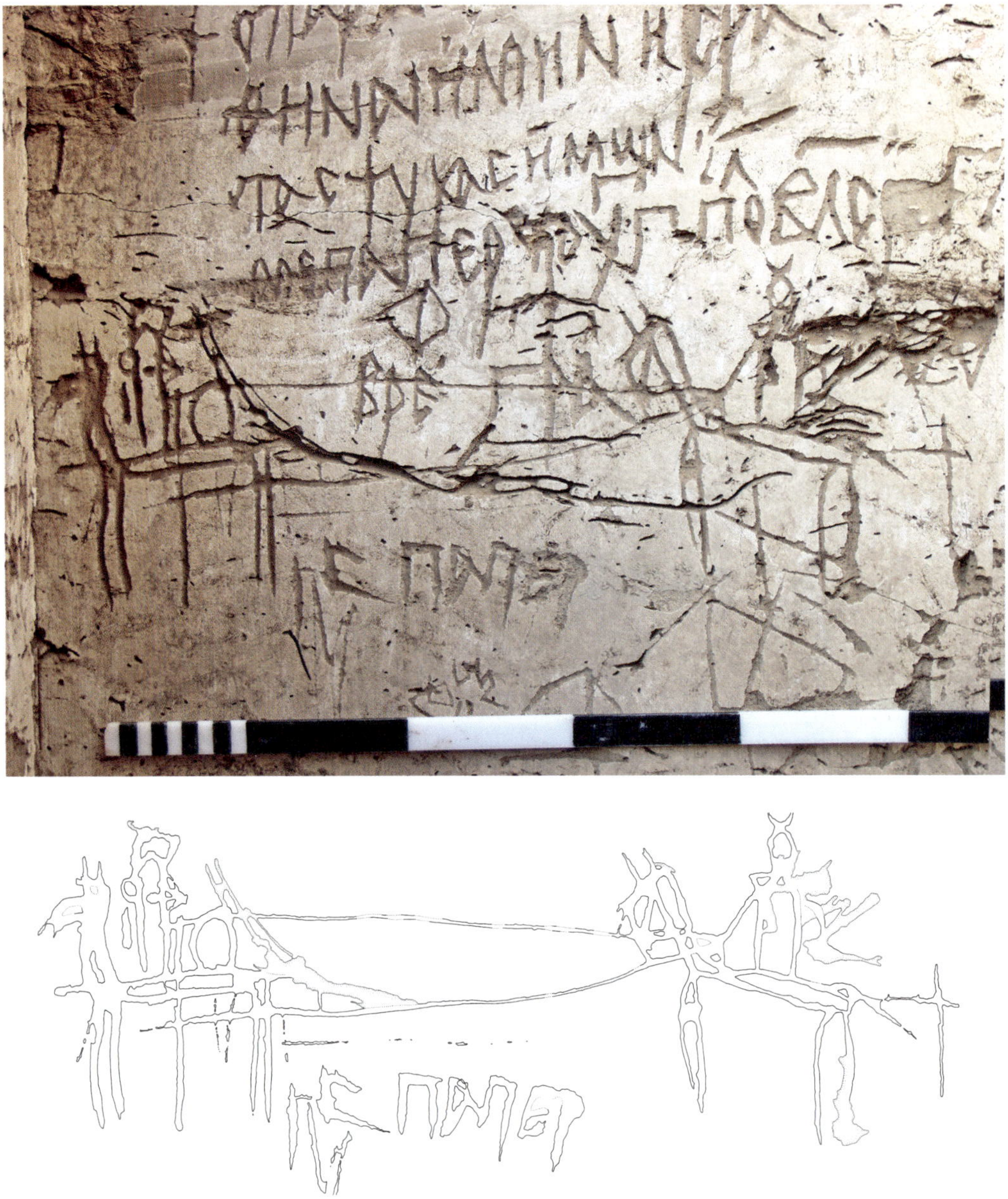

FIGURE 6.7. Text and image graffito of King Paper, in the northern entrance vestibule to the Upper Church.
Photo: Bogdan Żurawski; ink copy: Anna Błaszczyk

that he would be appointed a *naib* (king's deputy), while the kingdom remained in the hands of the Lord of Daw.[20] This is another good reason for his strange title, *basileus brephos*.[21]

Although in the eastern chapels of the Raphaelion the portraits of sacrosanct kings of Makuria occupy the most exposed places, it was the Archangel Raphael who received the main reverence and honor in the pilgrimage church. No wonder, since in popular reception

20. Al-Maqrizi in Vantini 1975, p. 699.
21. Łajtar forthcoming a, cat. no. 67.

he was acclaimed a reliable protector of human health. An unusual spelling of his name in some of the Banganarti inscriptions exemplifies Raphael's virtue as a healer of eyes. Without affecting the name's orthography, either a pair of eyes is inserted into the circle of the Greek letter Φ on both sides of the vertical stroke, or two wings are attached to the upper part of the circle (**FIGS. 6.8–9**), no doubt also making reference to Raphael's angelic nature. In one case both iconic elements are incorporated into Raphael's monogram (**FIG. 6.10**, upper left). The eyes do not seem to be apotropaic, nor do they signify the archangel's "keeping constant watch over mankind."[22] Rather, they denote the therapeutic aspects of Raphael's cult which, on the strength of the biblical precedence, acclaimed him a healer of eye diseases. In several of the Banganarti inscriptions that allude to the Old Testament book of Tobit, Raphael is denoted "as the one who was sent to Media so that the eyes of Tobit could see again." The request contained in another inscription asks Raphael to open the eyes of the supplicant, who was probably blind. In his curative duties, Raphael was helped by Saints Cosmas and Damianos, whose images were found in the vestibule of the northern staircase.[23]

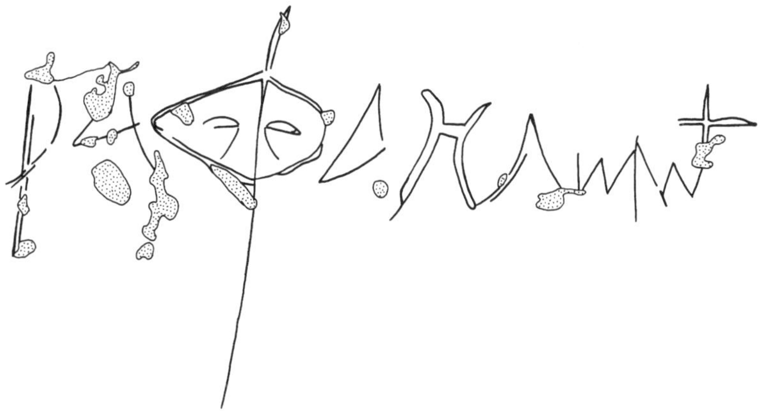

FIGURE 6.8. Raphael's name with eyes within the circle of the letter *phi*.
Ink copy: Adam Łajtar

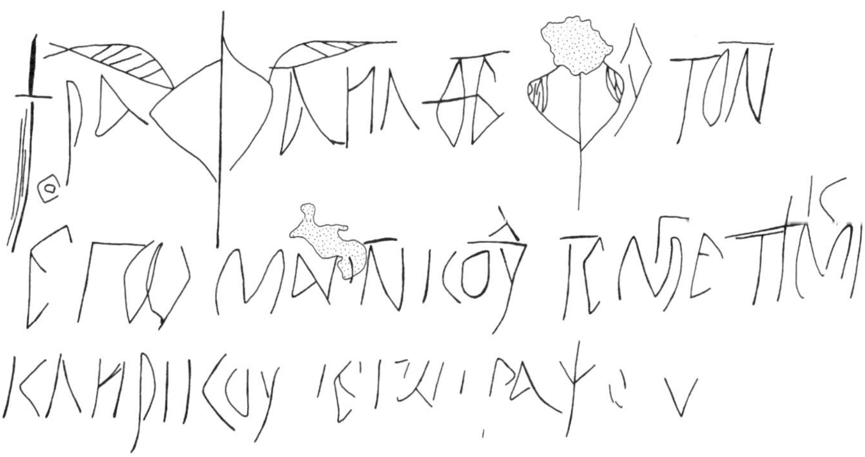

FIGURE 6.9. Raphael's name with wings on both sides of the circle of the letter *phi*.
Ink copy: Adam Łajtar

22. Łajtar 2014, p. 270.
23. Żurawski 2012, pp. 182–86.

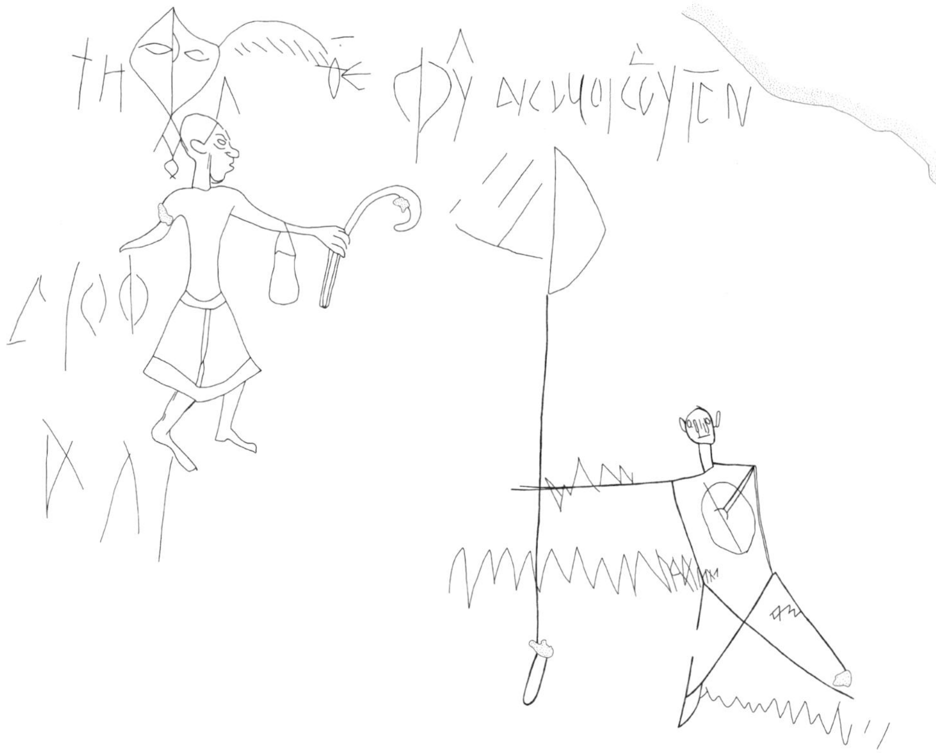

FIGURE 6.10. Text and image graffiti on the southern face of encasement of the column in the western portico.
Ink copy: Marta Momot and Adam Łajtar

Only one graffito can be labeled an image of a pilgrim (**FIG. 6.10**, upper left). The figure depicts a man wearing a knee-length skirt, recalling the Meroitic attire known from the Meroitic Chamber I in Philae.[24] In his left hand he holds a walking stick with which he feels the ground in front of him. A pilgrim bag dangles from his left wrist. The inscription scratched beneath the image transliterates two Arabic words, *diof Ali,* "Ali the guest," using the letters of the Greek alphabet.[25] No doubt Ali was a Muslim pilgrim, or *derwish*; it is hard to imagine that in the 12th century a Christian would have such a name. Ali apparently came to Banganarti attracted by the thaumaturgical esteem of the Raphaelion, where eye diseases were cured by the intercession of the Archangel Raphael.[26] The message of this image is ambiguous. On the one hand, it proves that Muslims were a part of the Middle Nile society in its heartlands near Tungul; on the other hand, its location outside the church proper, in the western portico where people would await their turn to undergo incubation, implies a sort of negligence toward the representative of the alien religion.

In the western portico, "Ali the guest" could meet other visitors to the church whose religious orientation was at least doubtful. A large number of animal drawings were applied to the walls of the Upper Church, possibly by their owners. These images plausibly serve as substitute animal offerings to the sanctuary or were placed in there with the intention of providing care, healing, success in hunting, good grazing, or other benefits. Among the

24. Griffith 1912, pp. 34–42, pls. XVIII–XXVII.
25. Łajtar 2008a, p. 398.
26. Żurawski 2008, p. 317.

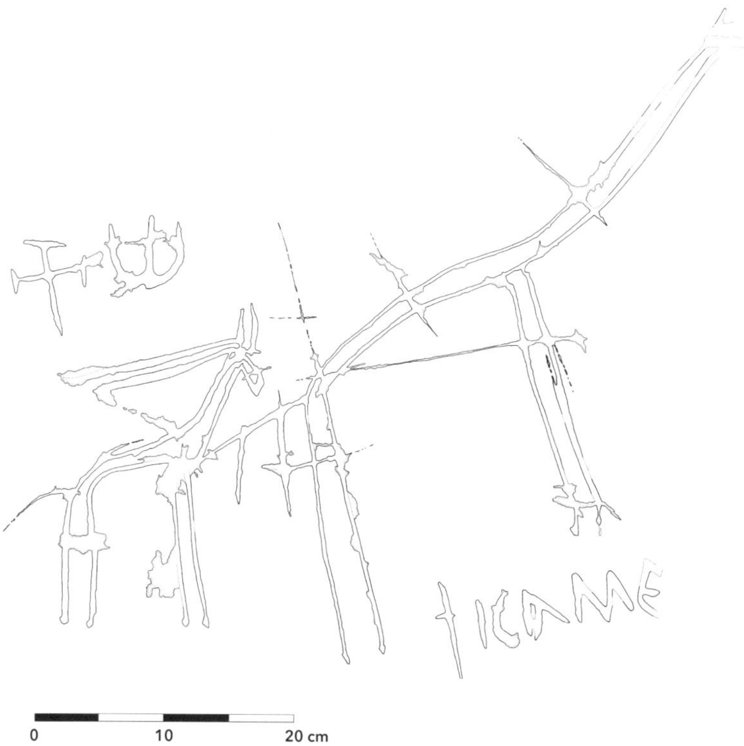

FIGURE 6.11. Graffiti representation in the Upper Church of an oryx antelope and a giraffe; the Greek word *kame* written below. *Ink copy: Marta Osypińska*

forty-four figures representing a variety of animals, dromedaries are the most numerous (27). Other figures represent donkeys (3), horses (2), antelopes (2), a giraffe (1), a gazelle (1), and a pig (1). Several cannot be identified.[27]

The twenty-seven dromedaries depicted in the graffiti of the Raphaelion are so schematically rendered that often it is only their hump that indicates their identity. The single pig drawing probably refers to the well-attested custom of bringing pigs to pilgrimage churches as offerings to the patron saint.[28]

The vital role of horses in the formation of the African states is well documented and needs no further discussion here.[29] Horses and mounted riders are favorite themes in Nubian rock art, and among the animal representations scratched on the walls of the Upper Church, only camels and giraffes outnumber equestrian motifs. In the past, higher annual rainfall supported large pastures in the Dongola Reach, between the 3rd and 4th Cataracts. At the beginning of the 19th century, however, the center of horse breeding and horse trading moved from Dar Dongola[30] upriver to Berber and Shendi.[31] The disappearance of horses from

27. Osypińska and Żurawski 2014.
28. Osypińska and Żurawski forthcoming.
29. Blench 1993, pp. 100–03.
30. On Dar Dongola, "country of Dongola" (*daar*, plural *diyar*, Arabic for "home, homeland"), see Żurawski 2012, pp. 41–58.
31. Burckhardt 1819, pp. 287–88.

the Dongola Reach due to the gradual desiccation of the region is one of the most important indicators of the climatic change within the province.[32]

Al-Idrisi (fl. before 1170) wrote of giraffes (together with elephants) living in the Dongola Kingdom in his lifetime.[33] The medieval Arab traveler al-Masudi (896–956) recounted that "the most common animal in their country is the one called 'zarafa'; it is very common only in Nubia and nowhere else in the country of the Ahabish."[34] The Ottoman Turkish traveler Evliya Çelebi (1611–1682) commented that the Re`aya (Rabi'a?) living in the environs of Old Dongola used to hunt giraffes, elephants, rhinoceroses, and gazelles.[35] Giraffes survived in the southern Dongola Reach until 1821 and probably managed to continue grazing in the wadis of the Bayuda for at least a decade or two longer.[36]

Image graffito accompanied by text can be a source of confusion. A nice drawing scratched on the eastern wall of the pilaster flanking the southern entrance is a compound text and image graffito that depicts a giraffe and an antelope (**FIG. 6.11**) accompanied by the word *kame* preceded by a cross. This is not a mistake made by a scribe who meant to write *kam* — Old Nubian for "camel" — beneath the representation of giraffe, nor is it an abbreviation for *kamelopardalis*, Greek for "giraffe." He definitely chose to use the Greek word *kame*, "and myself," instead of writing his real name. For reasons that are not perfectly clear to us,

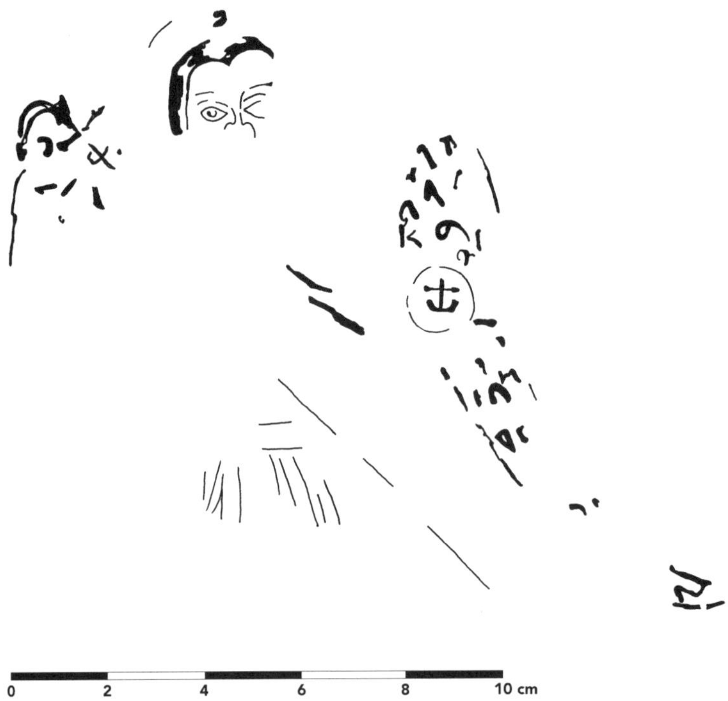

FIGURE 6.12. Graffito of an archangel holding an orb containing a cross, from the baptistery room of the Lower Church.
Ink copy: Anna Błaszczyk

32. The dwarf horse is still used in Dar Dongola, as the present writer has had the privilege to ascertain on several occasions.
33. Vantini 1975, p. 274; cf. Jackson 1957, p. 61.
34. Vantini 1975, p. 128.
35. Çelebi 1994, p. 151.
36. Stresemann 1954, p. 61.

he preferred to stay anonymous to his brethren. The author of the graffito above the horns of an image of the antelope went a step further. He contracted his apparently Nubian name beginning with ω to one letter only. Gerald Browne's dictionary of the Nubian language knows three names that start with ω.[37] The peculiar manner in which (ω) is written, with a cross inside, resembles what seems to be a monogram on the orb held by an archangel drawn on the wall of baptistery room in the Lower Church (**FIG. 6.12**). This rare image graffito from the Lower Church was anonymously drawn on the lower section of the wall near the baptismal tank.[38]

The only depiction of an animal hunt in the Upper Church is a narrative scene scratched in the western portico (**FIG. 6.13**). It shows a fragmentarily preserved figure of a possibly naked hunter with a *safarog* (plural *safdrig*), a throwing-stick still used today by the Beja, ancient "Blemmyes," a Cushitic ethnic group inhabiting the region between the Nile River and the Red Sea. A figure of a running female antelope is depicted in the center of the composition.

The graffito of the highest informative value was found in the middle room of the row of rooms arranged along the southern wall of the church. It is the only wall inscription written in the Latin alphabet known from the Christian period in Nubia. The man who scratched the text came from southern France or northern Spain since the language he used was Catalan/Provençal. His name was Beneseg (Benedict, in Provençal), and he visited the Raphaelion in the 14th century.[39] The barely visible incised text was squeezed in between the framed Greek

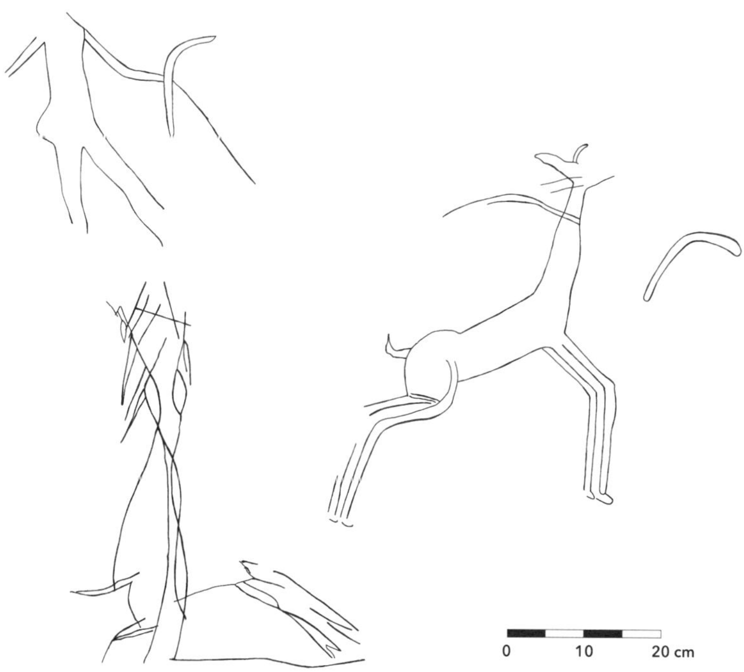

FIGURE 6.13. Depiction of a human hunting an antelope with a throwing-stick (*safarog*) and lasso, from the western portico of the Upper Church.
Ink copy: Adam Łajtar and Tomasz Płóciennik

37. Browne 1996, p. 245.
38. Żurawski 2012, p. 210.
39. Łajtar and Płóciennik 2011, pp. 95–119, esp. p. 105.

legend to the painting depicting the Apparition of Christ to Doubting Thomas and an Old Nubian inscription.[40] The reasons Beneseg came to Banganarti remain unknown. The text he left is short and unpretentious, confirming simply that "Beneseg came [to pay homage?] to Rafael." This inscription and a Catalan playing card found in Qasr Ibrim[41] confirm that European merchants continued to come to the Middle Nile in the first half of the 14th century.

The period of Beneseg's visit to Banganarti probably overlaps with the pontificate of John XXII (1316–1334), a stern and determined partisan of the Catholic Church's eastern enterprise.[42] It also coincides with the Catalan ascendancy in the Mediterranean personalized by King James II of Aragon, who possessed the most powerful fleet in the Mediterranean and knew how to use it to promote his interests. It was through James's policy that access to the *loca sancta* in Palestine was enabled to Christian pilgrims.

Pilgrims were flowing into the Raphaelion even after Beneseg's visit. An official in the court of the late 15th-century King Ioel of Makuria[43] visited the Raphaelion and left a written memento of his sojourn there. The last "visitors" to the shrine were squatters who occupied the northern portico and kept the entrance to the partly ruined church open. Their activities can be dated to the 16th century and possibly later.

In about 1670, Banganarti was visited by Evliya Çelebi, who described the site as a vibrant pilgrimage center attracting pilgrims from Egypt.[44] The last document mentioning the presence in Banganarti of a community that is aware of its Christian roots and practiced certain elements of Christian worship is a letter, written in Latin and dated 23 January 1742, from Father Giacomo Rzimarz da Cremsir, "Superiore" of the Franciscan congregation in Akhmim, in Egypt, north of Abydos, to Cardinal Belluga in Rome.[45]

Conclusions

The large number of pilgrims' graffiti in Late Christian Nubia must have their roots in the political and economic situation of the kingdom. The outburst of individual messages to the holy that appeared on the walls of Nubian churches in the 13th and 14th centuries, when pilgrimages to Nubian holy places intensified and visitors' graffiti appear en masse on the walls of pilgrimage churches, coincides with the general decline of the authority of the state, economic decline, and general impoverishment of the population. The Christian Kingdom on the Middle Nile, beleaguered by enemies and plagued by the economic crisis caused by shifts in the North African trade network, was no longer a guarantor of peace, safety, and stability. Understandably, in the face of lurking threats, people entrusted their fate to the protection of God and his messengers rather than to the ailing state and its officials. Hence the unprecedented veneration of angels, intermediaries between God and people, in the late period. Huge images of angelic creatures dominate the latest iconography at the Saint Raphael Church. In the late deposits accumulated in front of these paintings, multiple oil lamps were found.[46] The lamentable state of preservation does not allow us to say clearly whether the archangels are pictured alone or with their royal protégées.

40. Browne 2004, pp. 23–26.
41. Pamela Rose, personal communication.
42. Beazley 1906, p. 311 n. 3.
43. It is not perfectly clear which Ioel was meant here. Another king of that name was ruling at the turn of the 13th and 14th centuries.
44. Çelebi 1994, p. 160; Żurawski 2012, pp. 122–27.
45. Giamberardini 1960, p. 95; Giamberardini 1963, p. 365 n. 2; Żurawski 2012, pp. 128–29.
46. Cedro 2014, pp. 330–31 and fig. 2.

The psychological climate of the time is well characterized by the inscription dated to the late 13th century applied to the wall below the Beneseg graffito. It is addressed "to God who set up Raphael as a helper of every man who has a heart that is sick." It ends with the request: "... Make us live in this land that does not have the harshness of the evil one. Come, manifest yourself, hear us all."[47]

A sketchy drawing in black paint depicting a framed icon (**FIG. 6.14**) was probably made with a similar intention. It was found on the wall of the Lower Church next to the scene of Saint Merkurios spearing Julian the Apostate. In terms of discourse with the holy, it opens an entirely new chapter since it communicates with the heavenly being by means of a conventionalized image accompanied by an unintelligible text. It is datable to the period before the mid-11th century when the Lower Church was the main sanctuary in Banganarti and individual graffiti were extremely rare. In terms of quality and style, it is an obvious intrusion into the superb neighboring scene.

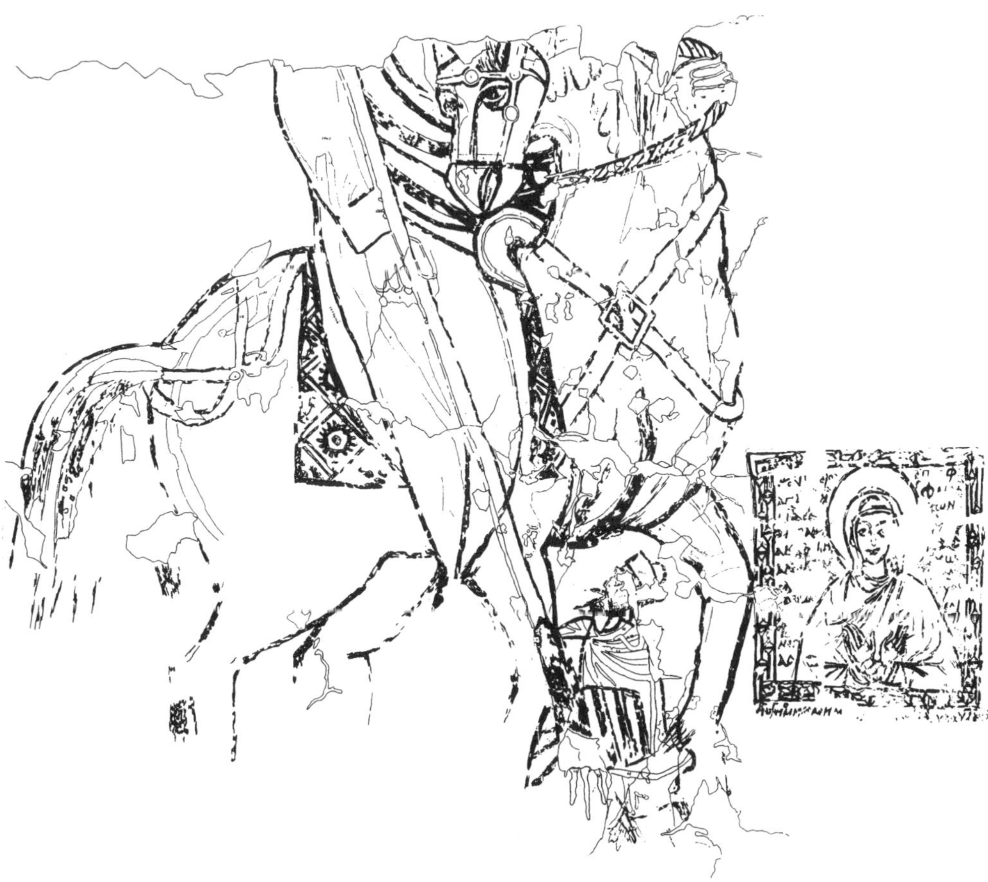

FIGURE 6.14. The *Theotokos Orans* icon (lower right) added to the scene of Saint Merkurios killing Julian the Apostate. *Ink copy: Anna Błaszczyk*

47. Browne 2004, p. 25.

The icon's iconography is unique. Within a frame, there is an image of the Virgin Mary, her hands held in front of her chest in the so-called contained praying gesture with palms turned outward (*Theotokos Orans*).[48] The space between the frame and the Theotokos bust is filled with "text" composed of Greek letters which has so far defied all attempts at any comprehensive reading. The drawing plausibly represents a wonder-working icon venerated in the Banganarti church. Theotokos is addressed here in a communal request for grace and patronage in the face of a danger that threatened the whole community of Banganarti. In times to come, this threat would become an inseparable component of everyday life in Banganarti. Paradoxically, we owe to this threat a superb collection of graffiti that conveys a realistic picture of Nubian medieval mentality and popular religion.

References

Aldsworth, Fred

2010 *Qasr Ibrim: The Cathedral Church.* Excavation Memoir 97. London: Egypt Exploration Society.

Beazley, C. Raymond

1906 *The Dawn of Modern Geography: A History of Exploration and Geographical Science,* Volume 3. London: John Murray.

Blench, Roger

1993 "Ethnographic and Linguistic Evidence for the Prehistory of African Ruminant Livestock, Horses and Ponies." In *The Archaeology of Africa: Food, Metals, and Towns,* edited by Thurstan Shaw, Paul Sinclair, Bassey Andah, and Alex Okpoko, pp. 71–103. One World Archaeology 20. London: Routledge.

Browne, Gerald M.

1996 *Old Nubian Dictionary.* Corpus Criptorum Christianorum Orientalium 556. Leuven: Peeters.

2004 "An Old Nubian Inscription from Banganarti Church." *Journal of Juristic Papyrology* 34: 23–26.

Burckhardt, John Lewis

1819 *Travels in Nubia.* 2nd ed. London: John Murray.

Cedro, Aneta

2014 "Oil Lamps in the Liturgical and Common Folk Practice." In *Kings and Pilgrims: St. Raphael Church II at Banganarti, Mid-Eleventh to Mid-Eighteenth Century,* edited by Bogdan Żurawski, pp. 327–40. Warsaw: Neriton.

Çelebi, Evliya

1994 *Ins Land der geheimnisvollen Func: des türkischen Weltenbummlers, Evliya Çelebi, Reise durch Oberägyptten und den Sudan nebst der osmanischen Provinz Habes in den Jahren 1672/73.* Translated by Erich Prokosch. Osmanische Geschichtsschreiber, n.F. 3. Graz: Styria.

Deptuła, Agata

2018 "Wall inscriptions from the Lower Church at Banganarti." Doctoral dissertation, Warsaw: University of Warsaw.

Giamberardini, Gabriele, ed.

1960 *Lettere dei prefetti apostolici dell'Alto Egitto nel secolo XVIII.* Studia Orientalia Christiana, Aegyptiaca 14. Cairo: Centro francescano di studi cristiani orientali.

1963 *I viaggiatori francescani attraverso la Nubia dal 1698 al 1710.* Studia Orientalia Christiana, Aegyptiaca. Cairo: Centro francescano di studi cristiani orientali.

48. Żurawski 2012, pp. 325–26.

Griffith, Francis Llewellyn
1912 *Meroitic Inscriptions*, Part 2: *Napata to Philae and Miscellaneous*. Archaeological Survey of Egypt, 20th Memoir. London: Egypt Exploration Society.

Jackson, J. K.
1957 "Changes in the Climate and Vegetation of the Sudan." *Sudan Notes & Records* 38: 47–66.

Łajtar, Adam
Forth. a *Late Christian Pilgrimage Centre in Banganarti: Evidence of Inscriptions*. Journal of Juristic Papyrology Supplement. Warsaw: Raphael Taubenschlag Foundation.
Forth. b "Wall Inscriptions in the Upper Church at Banganarti." In *Acts of the 14th International Conference for Nubian Studies, September 10 to 15, 2018, Paris*. Paris.
2003a "Three Greek Epitaphs from Banganarti." *Journal of Juristic Papyrology* 33: 161–75.
2003b "Wall Inscriptions in Banganarti Churches: A General Note after Three Seasons of Work." *Journal of Juristic Papyrology* 33: 137–59.
2005 "Banganarti 2004: Inscriptions." *Polish Archaeology in the Mediterranean* 16: 309–13.
2008a "Banganarti 2006: The Inscriptions." *Polish Archaeology in the Mediterranean* 18: 396–401.
2008b "Late Christian Nubia through Visitors' Inscriptions from the Upper Church at Banganarti." In *Between the Cataracts: Proceedings of the 11th Conference for Nubian Studies, Warsaw University, 27 August–2 September 2006*. Part 1: *Main Papers*, edited by Włodzimierz Godlewski and Adam Łajtar, pp. 321–31. Polish Archaeology in the Mediterranean Supplement Series, 2.1. Warsaw: University of Warsaw Press.
2009 "Varia Nubica XII–XIX." *Journal of Juristic Papyrology* 39: 93–119.
2010 "The Greek of Late Christian Inscriptions from Nubia: The Evidence from Banganarti and Other Sites." In *Between the Cataracts: Proceedings of the 11th Conference for Nubian Studies, Warsaw University, 27 August–2 September 2006*. Part 2, Fascicle 2: *Session Papers*, edited by Włodzimierz Godlewski and Adam Łajtar, pp. 759–63. Polish Archaeology in the Mediterranean Supplement Series, 2.2/2. Warsaw: University of Warsaw Press.
2014 "Archangel Raphael in Inscriptions from the Upper Church at Banganarti." In *Kings and Pilgrims: St. Raphael Church II at Banganarti, Mid-Eleventh to Mid-Eighteenth Century*, edited by Bogdan Żurawski, pp. 261–83. Warsaw: Neriton.
2015 "Wall Inscriptions in the Southwest Annex to the Monastery on Kom H at Dongola: Report on Work in the 2013 Season." *Polish Archaeology in the Mediterranean* 24: 344–51.

Łajtar, Adam, and Tomasz Płóciennik
2011 "A Man from Provence on the Middle Nile: A Graffito in the Upper Church at Banganarti." In *Nubian Voices: Studies in Christian Nubian Culture*, edited by Adam Łajtar and Jacques van der Vliet, pp. 95–120. Journal of Juristic Papyrology, Supplement 15. Warsaw: Raphael Taubenschlag Foundation.

Osypińska, Marta, and Bogdan Żurawski
Forth. *Pork for the Pilgrims: Socio-Topographic Differentiation of Livestock Breeding and Meat Consumption Models in the Medieval Pilgrimage Centre at Banganarti (Sudan, 11th–13th Centuries).*
2014 "Historic Fauna: Animal Representations and Faunal Remains from the Upper Church." In *Kings and Pilgrims: St. Raphael Church II at Banganarti, Mid-Eleventh to Mid-Eighteenth Century*, edited by Bogdan Żurawski, pp. 297–316. Warsaw: Neriton.

Raw, Barbara
2004 "Pictures: The Books of the Unlearned?" In *The Christian Tradition in Anglo-Saxon England: Approaches to Current Scholarship and Teaching*, edited by Paul Cavill, pp. 103–20. Rochester: D.S. Brewer.

Stresemann, Erwin, ed.
1954 *Hemprich und Ehrenberg: Reisen zweier naturforschender Freunde im Orient, geschildert in ihren Briefen aus den Jahren 1819–1826*. Abhandlungen der Deutschen Akademie der Wissenschaften zu Berlin. Klasse für Mathematik und Allgemeine Naturwissenschaften 1. Berlin: Akademie Verlag.

Vantini, Giovanni
1975 *Oriental Sources Concerning Nubia*. Warsaw: Society for Nubian Studies.

Żurawski, Bogdan

2005 "Peregrinatio nubiana. Kilka uwag na marginesie problematyki miejsc świetych w Nubii chrcescijańskiej." In *Sympozja kazimierskie: Poświęcone kulturze świata późnego antyku i wczesnego chrześcijaństwa*, Vol. 5: *Miejsca święcie w epoce późnego antyk* (The Kazimierz Symposia on the Culture of Late Antiquity and Early Christianity, Vol. 5: Loca Sancta in Late Antiquity), edited by Bożena Iwaszkiewicz-Wronikowska and Daniel Próchniak, pp. 300–25. Prace Wydziału Historyczno-Filologicznego 121. Lublin: Towarzystwo Naukowe Katolickiego Uniwersytetu Lubelskiego.

2008 "The Churches of Banganarti, 2002–2006." In *Between the Cataracts: Proceedings of the 11th Conference for Nubian Studies, Warsaw University, 27 August–2 September 2006*. Part 1: *Main Papers*, edited by Włodzimierz Godlewski and Adam Łajtar, pp. 303–21. Polish Archaeology in the Mediterranean Supplement Series, 2.1. Warsaw: University of Warsaw Press.

2012 *St. Raphael Church I at Banganarti: Mid-Sixth to Mid-Eleventh Century; an Introduction to the Site and the Epoch*. Gdańsk Archaeological Museum, African Reports 10. Gdańsk: Gdańsk Archaeological Museum.

2014 *Kings and Pilgrims: St. Raphael Church II at Banganarti, Mid-Eleventh to Mid-Eighteenth Century*. Warsaw: Neriton and Institute of Mediterranean and Oriental Cultures of the Polish Academy of Sciences.

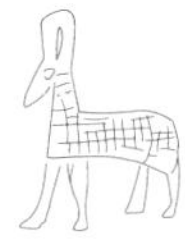

7

Fawzi Hassan Bakhiet

An Overview of Nubian Rock Art in the Region of the 4th and 5th Cataracts

The creation of rock art, or non-textual markings on natural rock surfaces, was an extremely widespread graphical practice in ancient Nubia. The rock art of Nubia consists almost entirely of petroglyphs — that is, images or patterns made by removing part of the rock surface, either by hammering or by pecking with a hard object such as a stone, or by scratching or incising with a cutting implement of stone or metal. While there are examples dating from the late Paleolithic to the Islamic era, the height of the tradition occurred during the Neolithic period (ca. 5000–3000 BCE).

Nubian rock art is known from many hundreds of sites along the margins of the Nubian Nile Valley and in the desert hinterlands to the east and west. Our knowledge of Nubian rock drawings is due to the work of many travelers and archaeologists since the 18th century. In broad terms, these researchers documented a wide range of subjects for rock art, including domestic and wild animals (cattle, dromedaries, giraffes, hippopotami, elephants, antelopes, gazelles, ostriches and other birds), boats, human representations (including riders on camels), sandals, abstract signs, Christian symbols and churches, and Islamic textual inscriptions. In some areas, "rock gongs" are found near concentrations of rock drawings. Rock gongs are clusters of cup-shaped depressions of varying diameter and depth that make a sound like a bell when struck with a pebble or a piece of metal.

Rock drawings in Nubia tend to be found on rock outcrops near the banks of the Nile and in wadis (dry riverbeds) leading to the Nile. They are also found west of the Nile and across the Sahara, where they are also found in caves and rock shelters. They are often clustered near each other, perhaps reflecting gathering points for herders or caravans. It is possible that these images were made with a ritual or magical purpose, although it is difficult to establish this with certainty.

Particularly rich areas for rock art in the Nubian Nile Valley are the cataract zones, where rock outcrops are abundant. Travel by boat is more difficult at the cataracts, perhaps providing travelers with more time to create drawings. This chapter provides a look at concentrations of rock drawings in the 4th–5th Cataract region near the heartland of ancient Napata (**FIGS. 7.1-2**). I documented the rock drawings in 2004–2008, particularly in areas known as the Khor Daghfali, Boni Island, and the site of Sihan on Mograt Island near Abu Hamed. The goal of the project was to record important rock art sites. Since completion of the Merowe Dam in 2009, it has become clear that rock engravings in Sudan are in danger due to the numerous dam and highway construction projects.

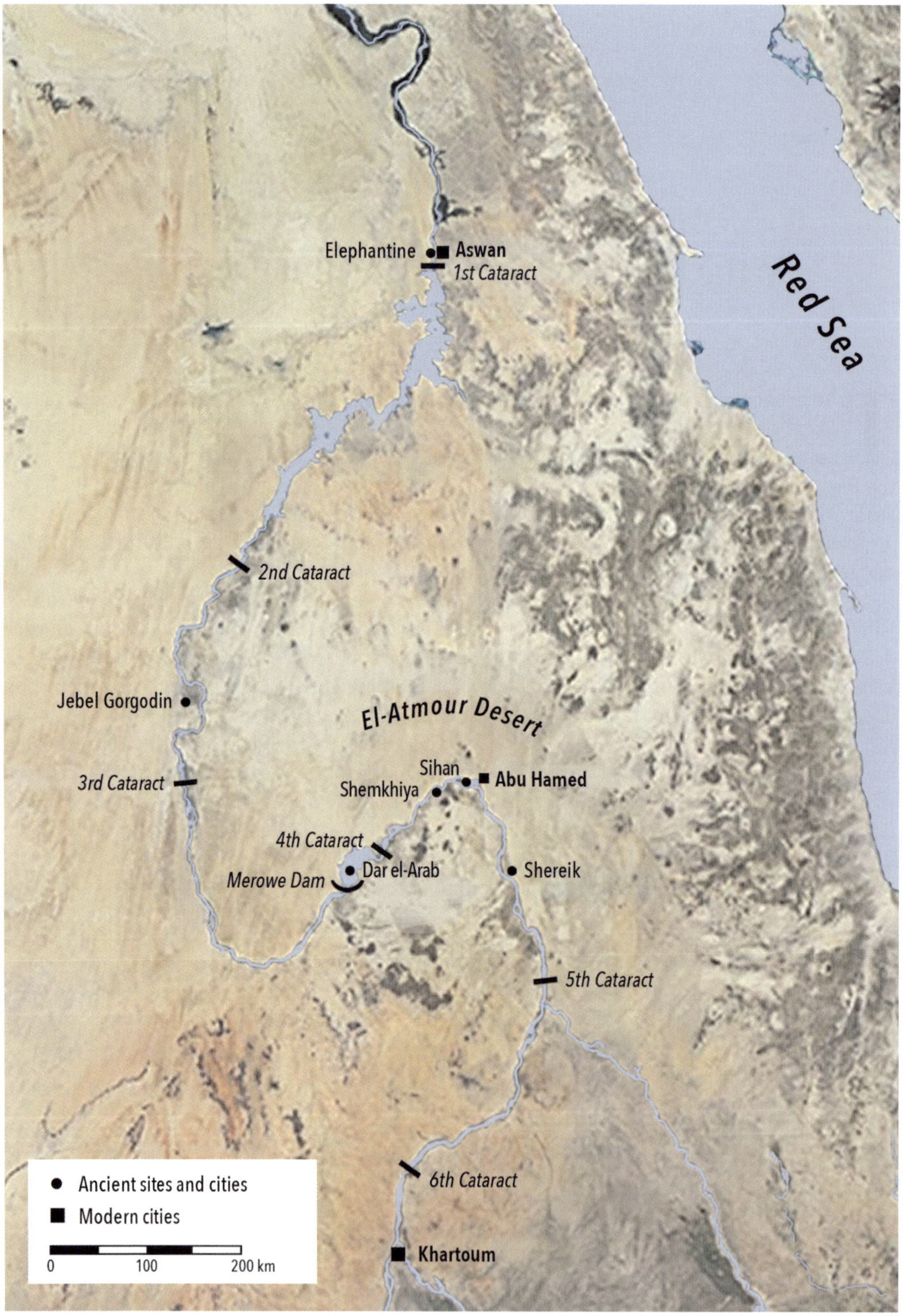

FIGURE 7.1. Map of southern Egypt and Sudan.
Map: Lorene Sterner

Geographic Areas Surveyed: 4th and 5th Cataract Regions

The 4th Cataract extends southwest from the Nile's bend at Abu Hamed. In this area, the Nile flows from northeast to southwest through an area of hard volcanic stone. The rapids here are dangerous and access to the river banks is very difficult. There was no systematic archaeological study or study of the rock drawings in this area before the Merowe Dam Archaeological Salvage Project (MDASP), from 2001 to 2009.[1]

The Khor Daghfali area of the 4th Cataract is mostly covered by sand, from which emerge clusters of granite boulders. There was no human settlement at the time of our study, nor was there any agriculture on the Nile bank. The rock drawings are situated on the right (northern) bank between the desert of El-Atmour and the Nile, and between Abu Hamed and the village of Meheisa downstream. This area is 32 kilometers long and 1.5 to 2 kilometers in width, covering approximately 300 square kilometers and including several wadis. In this area there are several rock drawing sites dated from the Neolithic to the Islamic period. Thirteen sites were identified with various motifs, including animals (camels, cattle) and geometric signs.

Boni Island, another 4th Cataract site with rock drawings, is located around 30 kilometers upstream of the 4th Cataract. It is 12 kilometers long and ranges between 1 and 3.4 kilometers wide, covering a surface of approximately 39 square kilometers. This zone

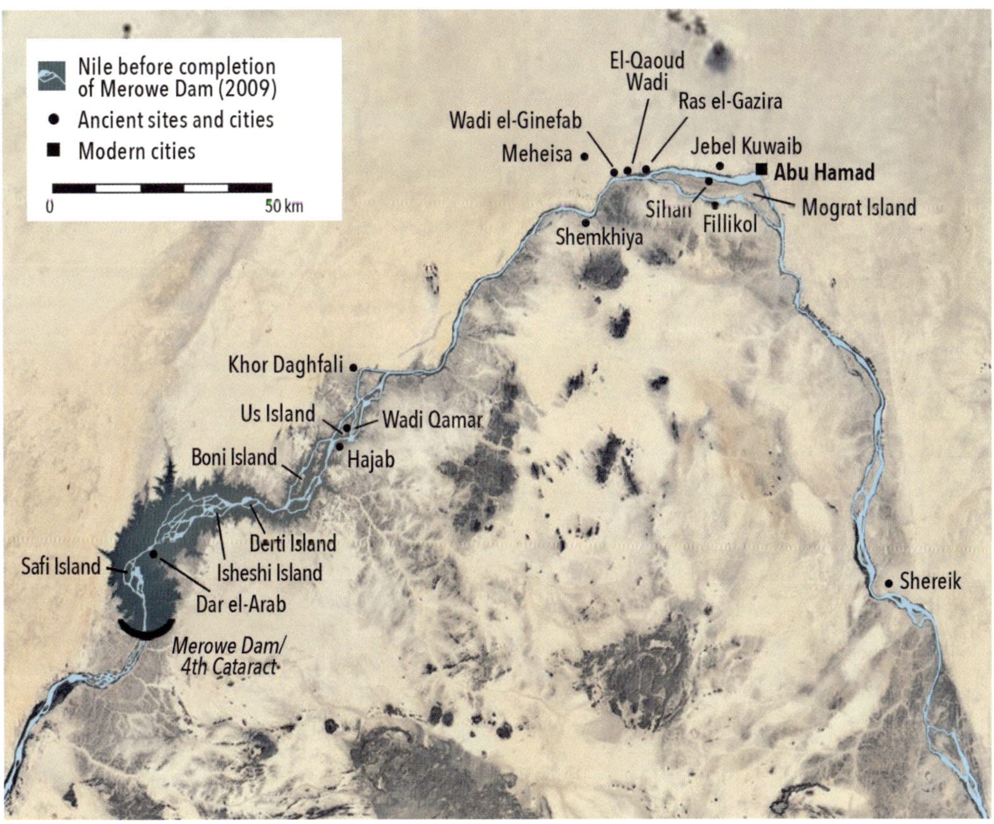

FIGURE 7.2. Map of the region of the 4th and 5th Cataracts showing the sites mentioned in the text.
Map: Lorene Sterner

1. Ahmed 2003.

is covered by numerous drawings on granite and quartz. The engravings are distributed on rocks around wadis and at the edge of the Nile. Boni Island was mentioned in print for the first time in 1865 by the German explorer Theodor von Heuglin, who described a cave in Wadi Qamar.[2] This cave opens directly on the Nile and is accessible only by swimming or by boat. It is so big that in the 18th and 19th centuries villagers and their cattle could hide inside it to avoid the Turkish soldiers who were collecting taxes.[3] The first survey of rock drawings here was made in 1989 by Sudan's National Corporation for Antiquities and Museums (NCAM),[4] the next between 2004 and 2008 by the University of Cologne. Additional sites have been found in recent years.

In the area of the 5th Cataract, rock drawings are found on Mograt Island, located near the bend of Abu Hamed. Measuring 40 kilometers long and ranging between 4 and 8 kilometers wide, Mograt Island is the largest of the numerous islands in the Nile in this region. The island's vast, uninhabited center is covered with gravel and other superficial deposits, but on its banks can be found large granitic rocks. It is on the banks that the island's residents have settled, and where three rock art sites — Sihan, Ras el-Gazira, and Fillikol — were found in 2006 during fieldwork conducted by NCAM and the mission of University of Humboldt (HUNE).[5] Sihan, called Al-Hogab, "the oldest," by the local villagers, is the largest of the three sites, covering an area of 150 × 30 meters at the base of Jebel Kuwaib on the right bank of the Nile. It consists of a granite base topped with numerous round blocks of diverse sizes

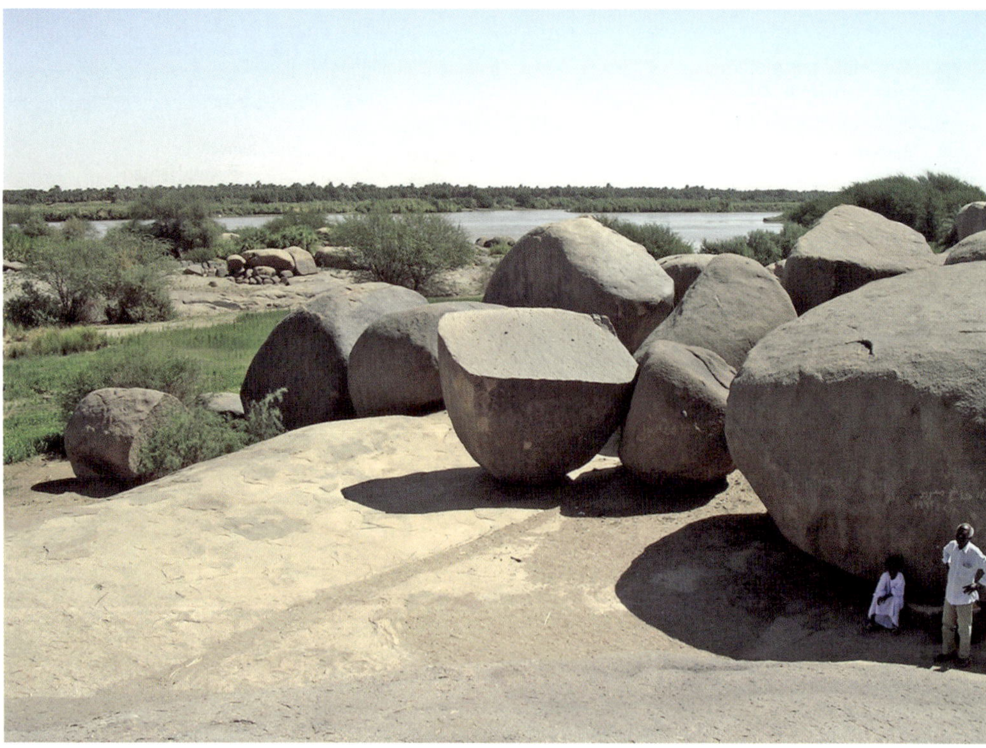

FIGURE 7.3. An overview of the site of Sihan on Mograt Island.
Photo: Fawzi Hassan Bakhiet

2. Von Heuglin 1865, pp. 22–24.
3. Ibid., p. 23.
4. Al-Hakim 1993.
5. Fawzi Hassan Bakhiet 2014. For a map of the various research areas, see Welsby 2008, fig. 1.

(FIG. 7.3); a total of sixty-seven engravings were documented on over thirty-five rocks. These include wild and domestic animals (elephant, lion, ostrich, hippopotamus, gazelle, giraffe, antelope, horse, bovid, camels), human figures, crosses, and boats. Sihan is an exceptional site, representing the complete range of the rock art of this area, including Arabic inscriptions and rock gongs.

Overall, in the study area within the region of the 4th and 5th Cataracts, we documented 1,822 engravings. The highest concentration of was found on the island of Boni (91% of all found; TABLE 7.1). Christian rock engravings are the most common in the region, accounting for about 34 percent of all engravings.

TABLE 7.1. Number of engravings found in the study area within the region of the 4th and 5th Cataracts.

	Mograt Island	*NCAM Concession*	*Boni Island*	*Sum of all Engravings*
Number of Engravings	140	175	1,507	**1,822**

The Rock Drawings

The abundant rock drawings in the region of the 4th and 5th Cataracts present scenes inspired by the environment familiar to the ancient Nubians. Before describing the drawings themselves, I present an overview of the techniques and composition styles used to create them. The study of these techniques is very important because it not only reveals the skill of ancient craftsmen, but also informs us about their deep intentions.

The ancient artists sought good-quality stone and the appropriate tools to achieve their engravings. The artists employed different techniques: deep straight-line incision, grooving with a polished finish, and pecking, which was employed for both curvilinear outlines and full figures. The state of patination (surface weathering of the engravings) ranges from a light color that is very clear and visible (typically indicating younger graffiti) to dark and invisible (typically indicating older graffiti). We found that most of the engravings of the Nile Valley were made on granite.

A study of how the drawings were composed provides essential elements for an approach to the thought systems that are at the source of this art. Most representations of wild animals are depicted using one of two techniques: depiction of several small animals over the entire surface of the rock, or a single large depiction.

Two styles of representation have also been used in the study area. The first is schematic (not realistic). This style has been noticed on rock carvings in several regions of the Nile Valley and in the Sahara. We noted several engravings in this style, the majority of which were on Boni Island. It is either a linear engraving test or an unfinished (geometric) sign. Some signs are not identifiable. The second style is naturalistic (realistic). This type is frequently found in the study area, and it is seen in three levels. The first is "stylized"; it is a suggestion of a drawing, not very clear, but we can understand the general idea. The second level is "trained"; it is a clear drawing with few details. The third style is "elaborate"; these are very detailed drawings.

The scenes represented can be classified into four main categories: animals (wild and domestic); humans, boats, and "other representations," including Christian monuments and symbols (churches, crosses); geometric symbols; and inscriptions.

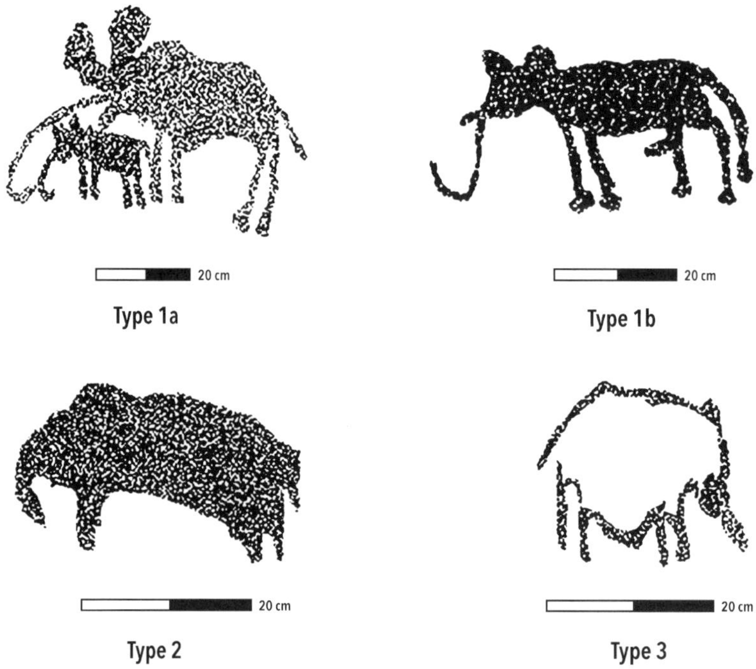

FIGURE 7.4. Different styles of elephants from Sihan.
After Fawzi Hassan Bakhiet 2009, cat. nos. 1, 2, and 3

Animals

Large wildlife is attested by only a few figures of elephants, giraffes, antelopes, and single representations of hippopotamus and gazelle. There are also representations of domestic animals: horses, bovines, and camels.

Three types of elephant representation have been classified, based on the style, body shape, ears, legs, trunk, and tusks (**FIG. 7.4**). We propose a Neolithic period date for depictions of elephants.

In our survey of Boni Island, Mograt Island, Isheshi Island, Hajab, Saffi Island, and Dar el-Arab we found only five significant representations of giraffes (**FIG. 7.5**). This rarity is surprising, because giraffes were still present in central and southern Sudan in the Neolithic period, and we therefore expect them to be more commonly represented in the engravings. Perhaps it is simply that giraffes are rare in the north that explains their under-representation in relation to rock art of the south. The giraffe would have appeared to northerners as an extraordinary animal.

We identified three different types of representations of giraffes. Static giraffes are related to the ancient art of the Nile. They are small and scratched on the entire surface. There is also a single giraffe, whose outline is incised. Finally, there is a scene where bovines are followed by giraffes, and two other scenes in which the animals are isolated. Representations of giraffes in the study area are distributed in different wadis, on the island of Boni, and at the site of Sihan. Like the elephants, we propose a Neolithic date for the giraffes.

In our area of study, there is only one representation of a hippopotamus, located at Sihan on Mograt Island (**FIG. 7.6**). It is inscribed across the whole surface of the rock, and both the ears as well as the small tail and feet are visible. Based on the patina, which is the same as that of the elephants, we propose a Neolithic date for this depiction. This figure

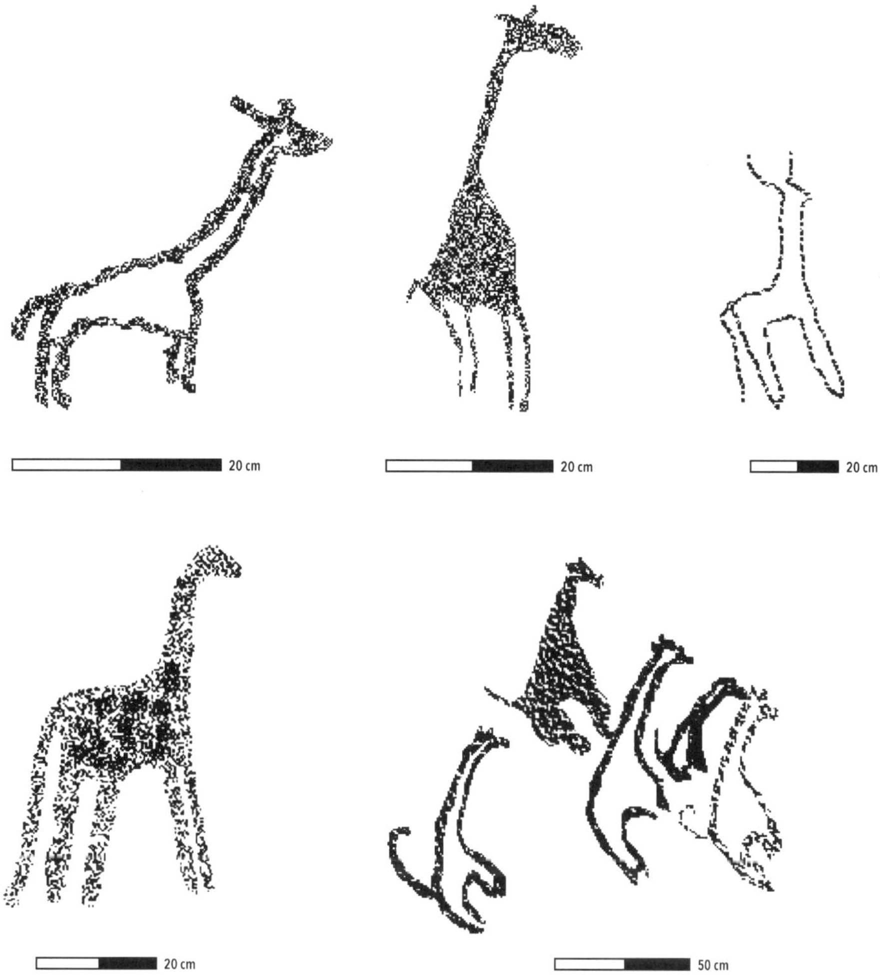

FIGURE 7.5. Representations of giraffes from the region of the 4th Cataract.
After Fawzi Hassan Bakhiet 2009, top to bottom, left to right: cat. nos. 4, 5, 292, unknown, 351

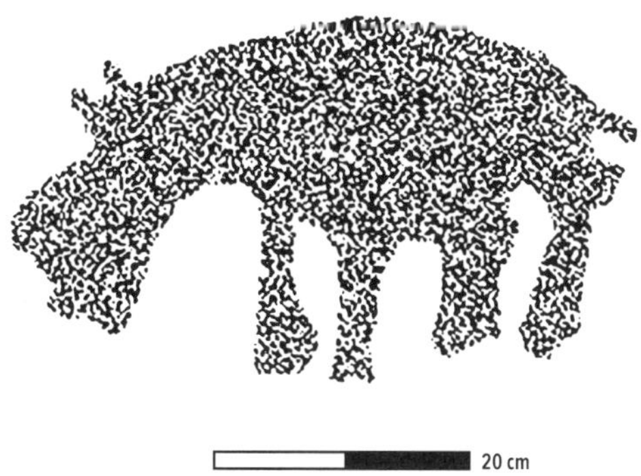

FIGURE 7.6. Hippopotamus from Sihan.
After Fawzi Hassan Bakhiet 2009, cat. no. 30

resembles in form one found at Akkad,[6] in the area of the 3rd Cataract, which dates from the beginning of Nagada I (ca. 3800–3650 BCE), and one from the Selima Oasis, 125 kilometers west of the 2nd Cataract, published by Stefan Kröpelin.[7]

There are very few representations of other wild animals, such as lions, gazelles, or antelopes. On the other hand, there are many and varied representations of ostriches. Drawings of turtles and rhinoceroses are rarely found even in the area of the 4th Cataract. Only one turtle has been recorded, on Us Island, but it is represented with many details.

Turning to domestic animals, cattle are the most popular subject of rock drawings in earlier periods, before the introduction of camels in the Neolithic period. Some are associated with a human figure, which could suggest the domestication of cattle in this region. All types of composition are used for representing cattle, and we can classify them not only by the type of horns — long and short as well as deformed — but also by the head, neck, body, dress, legs, and tail. Most of the cattle represented in the area of our research have long horns (**FIG. 7.7**). There are some representations with net decorations which could indicate the cultural influence of the C-Group culture from Lower Nubia (**FIG. 7.8**).

Camels are shown isolated or in groups or caravans, and are represented with and without riders. The rider, when present, commonly carries something in the hand, like a spear, a stick, or a sword (**FIG. 7.9**). Within the study area, the appearance of camel engravings corresponds approximately to the medieval and Islamic periods. More than 55 percent of rock representations in the Middle Nile Valley study area are camels and bovid representations.

Only a very few depictions of reptiles, horses, felines, or small birds have been found in the region.

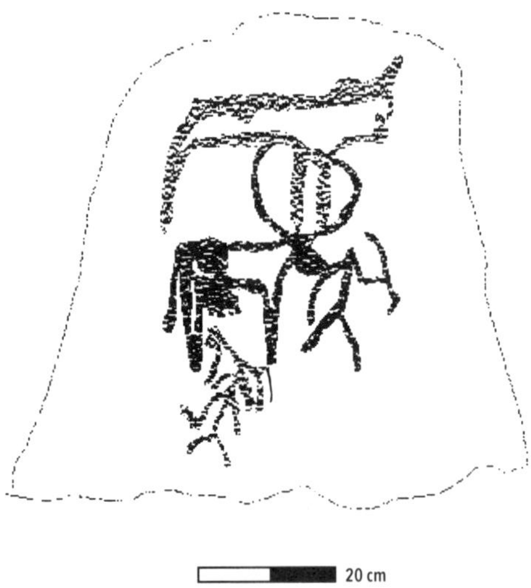

FIGURE 7.7. Depiction of cattle associated with a human figure from Boni Island.
After Fawzi Hassan Bakhiet 2009, cat. no. 315

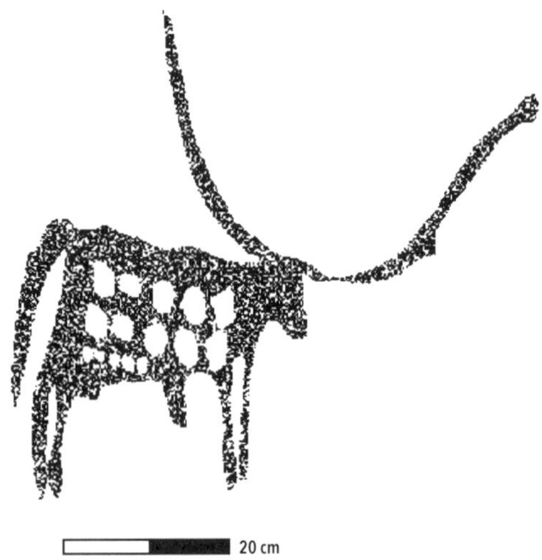

FIGURE 7.8. Depiction of a cow with net decoration from Sihan.
After Fawzi Hassan Bakhiet 2009, cat. no. 19

6. Smith 2003, p. 166, fig. 7.
7. Kröpelin 2004, p. 116, fig. 15.

Humans

Many representations of human figures have been documented in the region, representing 5 percent of the engravings. Some of them are identifiable as men, women, or children. Most representations show a figure either carrying something in the hand (a weapon or stick) or with raised hands. A few of the representations are of fighters and some are associated with animals such as camel (see **FIG. 7.9**), cattle, horses, and giraffes, or in hunting scenes (**FIG. 7.10**).

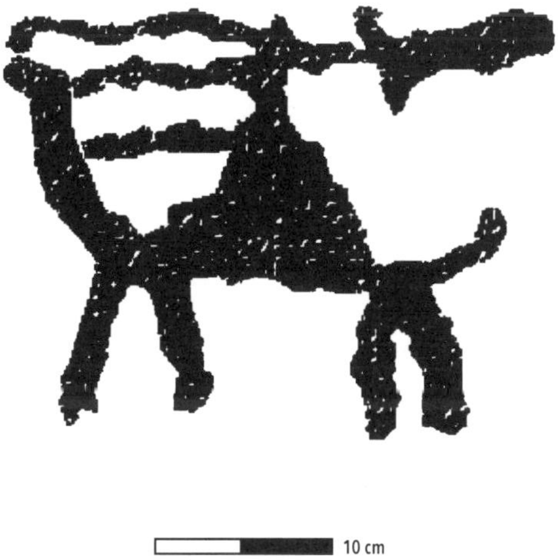

FIGURE 7.9. Depiction of a camel with rider carrying a sword from Boni Island.
After Fawzi Hassan Bakhiet 2009, cat. no. 329

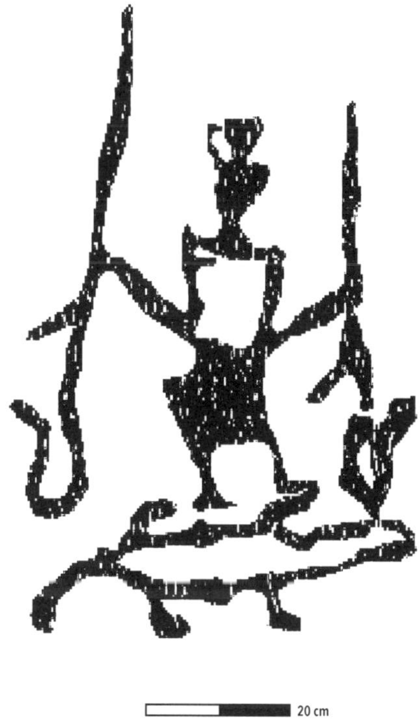

FIGURE 7.10. Crocodile hunt scene from Boni Island.
After Fawzi Hassan Bakhiet 2009, cat. no. 284

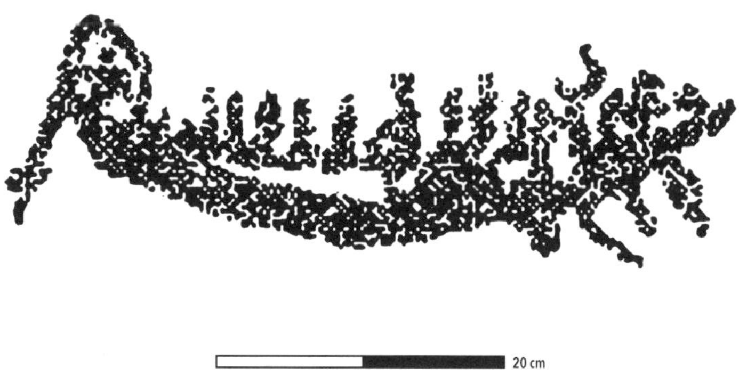

FIGURE 7.11. Depiction of trading boat from Sihan.
After Fawzi Hassan Bakhiet 2009, cat. no. 8

Boats

Three different types of boat depictions were documented in the region of the Middle Nile region, at Sihan and on Boni Island. These include trading boats (FIG. 7.11), sailing boats, and small craft for crossing the river. Some of them are similar to Egyptian boats of the Predynastic period.

Other Representations

Christian sites are common in the region, and rock drawings with Christian signs are also remarkably common. Different types of crosses have been engraved on many boulders at Sihan, Boni Island, and Daghfali. These include, for example, a cross on a circle motif, a cross attached to a circle, the Latin cross, the Jerusalem cross, the Maltese or Coptic cross, and the Greek cross. Crosses were also found at various sites accompanying animals and human figures (FIG. 7.12). There is also a single depiction of a church, found on Boni Island (FIG. 7.13).

There are many geometric shapes and signs of unknown significance documented in the region, such as squares, nets, and other shapes (FIG. 7.14).

Some Arabic text inscriptions have also been documented around the region. Some are ancient while others are from modern people who believe that their ancestors are responsible for many of the ancient engravings. There are also some isolated, holy text inscriptions that could be dated to the early Islamic period (FIG. 7.15).

Rock gongs were also found in the study area. Called *nugara* (drums) or *hagar mosiagha* (musical rocks) by the local population, these are clusters of cup-shaped depressions of varying diameter and depth that make a sound like a bell when struck with a pebble or piece of metal. Typically located in an open area, they range from single clusters to larger complexes that can be played by many people (FIG. 7.16). Rock gongs are numerous at many sites, especially on Boni Island and at Sihan. A total of nineteen rock gong sites were found in the region of the 4th and 5th Cataracts; a few of these were associated with rock drawings or archaeological sites, found on boulder surfaces in an area of pecked non-figurative rock drawings.[8]

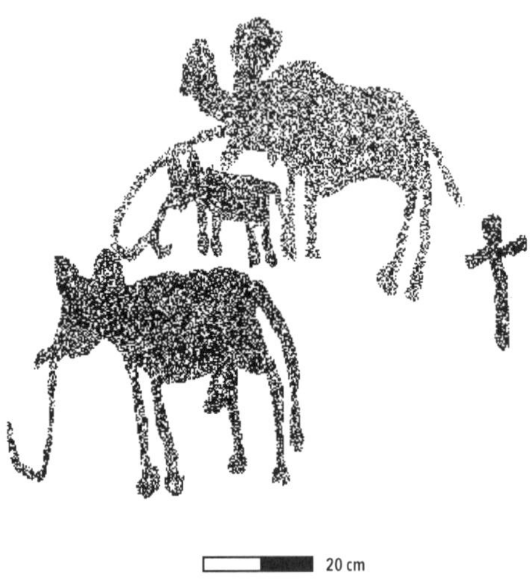

FIGURE 7.12. Elephants with a cross from Sihan.
After Fawzi Hassan Bakhiet 2009, cat. no. 1

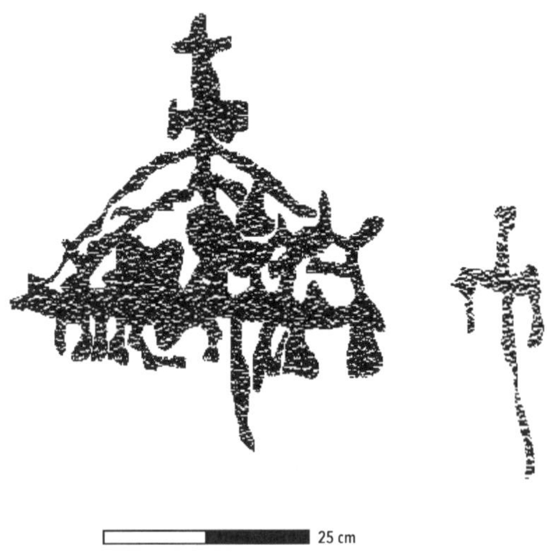

FIGURE 7.13. Representation of a church associated with a cross from Boni Island.
After Fawzi Hassan Bakhiet 2009, cat. no. 140

8. Fagg 1997, p. 6.

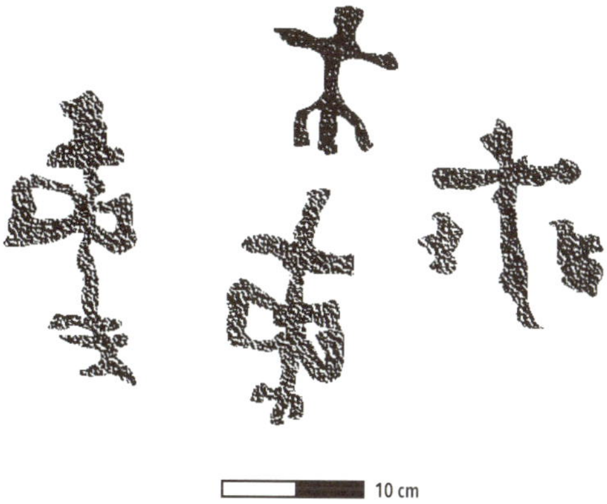

FIGURE 7.14. Examples of a geometric sign with cross from Khor Daghfali.
After Fawzi Hassan Bakhiet 2009, cat. no. 66

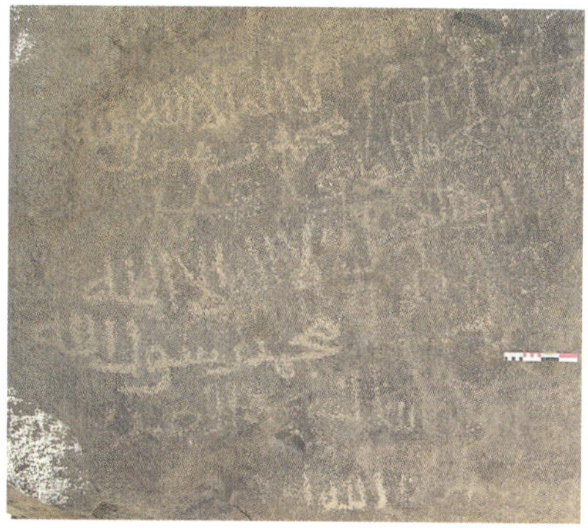

FIGURE 7.15. Arabic inscription of the *shahada* from Sihan: "There is no God but God, Mohammed is the Prophet of God."
After Fawzi Hassan Bakhiet 2009, cat. no. 37

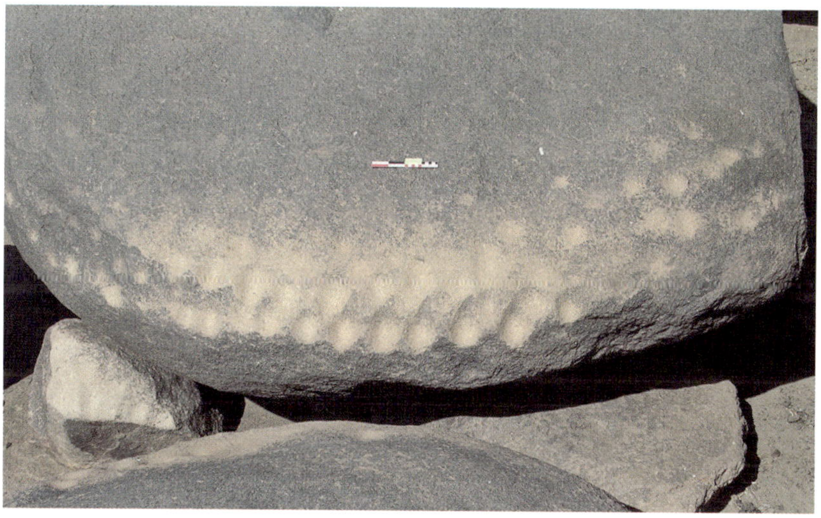

FIGURE 7.16. Rock gong complex at Sihan.
After Fawzi Hassan Bakhiet 2009, cat. no. 41

Discussion and Conclusions

The rock drawings in this study region are essentially an art engraved outdoors; there are no examples in caves. Except for the very few that are accompanied by crosses (see **FIGS. 7.12–14**) and can therefore be assigned with confidence to the Christian period, it is difficult to establish a date for these engravings. Nevertheless, we attempted to date them in relation to nearby archaeological remains. There are many rock engravings and other archaeological sites in the region of the 4th Cataract, though most are located in areas that are very difficult to access. The majority of the engravings seem to date to the Neolithic period (ca. 5000–3000 BCE), but the practice continued into the Islamic period (**TABLE 7.2**). It should be noted that the sites on the banks of the Nile are more recent, while the older sites are currently far from the river banks, especially on the island of Boni. This situation helps us to classify rock sites.

TABLE 7.2. Categories of graffiti in the region of the 4th and 5th Cataracts.

Wild Animals	*Suggested Dating*	*Remarks*
Elephants	Neolithic	–
Giraffes	Neolithic	–
Ostriches	Neolithic?	–
Hippopotami	Neolithic?	–
Crocodiles (?)	Neolithic	–
Lions (?)	Neolithic	–
Gazelles	Modern?	Unique representation in our engravings; seems recent
Antelopes	?	–
Domesticated Animals	*Suggested Dating*	*Remarks*
Horses?	?	–
Cattle	Neolithic	–
Camels	1st millennium BCE	Some examples of camel depictions associated with cross
Other Representations	*Suggested Dating*	*Remarks*
Human Figures	?	Some examples associated with animals and crosses
Boats	Pre-Kerma–Christian	Contemporaries of the Predynastic until the Christian era
Cross and Church	Medieval	–
Weapon	Post-Kerma	Metal weapons
Arabic Inscription	Early Islamic and modern	The *shahada* and modern name
Rock Gong	?	An example has been represented with a cross

After checking the patina, which can help to indicate the age of a rock drawing, we can say that we agree with J. H. Dunbar's proposal[9] that rock representations begin with the elephant, then proceed to the giraffe, the antelope, the ostrich, the boat, the bovine, the dynastic inscriptions, the Greek inscriptions, Christian graffiti, and finally the camel. But in some cases, it is difficult to determine the age of a rock drawing and to follow this theory completely.

Comparison of the rock engravings from the 4th and 5th Cataracts in the Middle Nile Valley with other nearby regions reveals similarities and differences. Examples from the 2nd and 3rd Cataracts demonstrate similarities in technique and style. In the Sahara, rock drawings tend to be naturalistic and monumental,[10] in contrast to those along the Nile, which begin with schematic figures of modest dimensions. However, archaeological remains and rock art in both the Sahara and the Middle Nile region also indicate shared cultural

9. Dunbar 1941, p. 38.
10. Leclant and Huard 1980, p. 560.

traits. For example, depictions of cattle with long horns and net decoration, attributed to the C-Group, are found in the rock drawings of both areas. Dated C-Group sites are located north of Aswan, and a C-Group rock art site has been found in the Jebel Gorgodin, in the area of the 3rd Cataract. In the area of our research, which is outside the C-Group area, we nevertheless note its influence in rock art (see **FIG. 7.8**).

We also see similarities between our study area in the Middle Nile Valley and Lower Nubia, for example, in some parallel geometric signs in the two regions. But there are also significant differences. Some patterns seem to be rare in this region compared to Lower Nubia.[11] Conversely, representations of camels as well as Christian motifs are much more common in our research area than in Lower Nubia. We also estimate that the rock gongs are more common in the 4th Cataract region.

Rock heritage is obviously abundant in the region of the 4th and 5th Cataracts, and it represents scenes inspired by the familiar environment of the ancient Nubians. The engraver represented scenes of nature, domestic and wild animals, and his own traditions. He also probably represented themes from his imagination, revealing his fears and beliefs. It was a way of perpetuating thoughts and conveying a message, a story. The rock engravings studied also summarize the evolution of the inhabitants' lives in this region, focusing especially on the use of animals. A detailed engraving of a truck (**FIG. 7.17**) marks the evolution of means of transport from the dromedary to the machine. Without excluding other possible meanings and motivations, it seems that most rock art closely reflects the religious and ideological concerns of its makers.

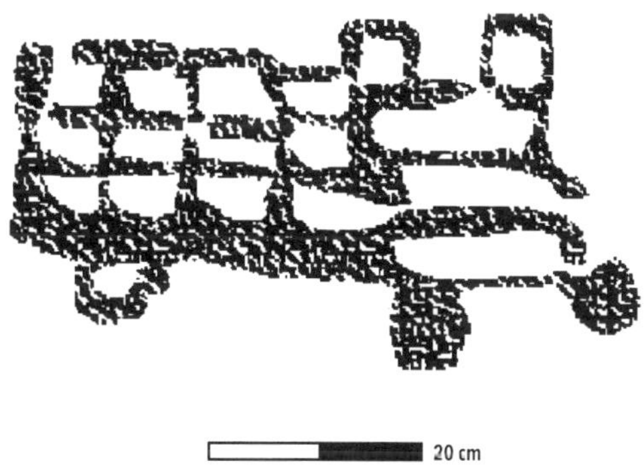

FIGURE 7.17. Detailed graffito of a truck from Boni Island.
After Fawzi Hassan Bakhiet 2009, cat. no. 164

11. Winkler 1938; Almagro Basch and Almagro-Gorbea 1968; Otto and Buschendorf-Otto 1993.

References

Ahmed, Salah Mohamed

2003 "Merowe Dam Archaeological Salvage Project (MDASP)." *Sudan & Nubia* 7: 11–14.

Al-Hakim, Ahmed M. A.

1993 "Merowe (Hamadab) High Dam and Its Impacts." *Kush* 16: 1–25.

Almagro Basch, Martín, and Martín Almagro-Gorbea

1968 *Estudios de arte rupestre nubio 1. Yacimientos situados en la orilla oriental del Nilo, entre Nag Kolorodna y Kars* [sic] *Ibrim (Nubia Egipcia).* Memorias de la Misión arqueológica española en Egipto 10. Madrid: Ministerio de Asuntos exteriores.

Dunbar, J. H.

1941 *The Rock-Pictures of Lower Nubia.* Cairo: Government Press.

Fagg, M. Catherine

1997 *Rock Music.* Occasional Papers on Technology 14. Oxford: Pitt Rivers Museum, University of Oxford.

Fawzi Hassan Bakhiet

2004 *Inventaires des gravures rupestres de la région de la quatrième cataracte.* Mémoire de maîtrise. Lille: Université Charles de Gaulle-Lille 3, Villeneuve-d'Ascq.

2009 "Étude sur les gravures rupestres du Nil moyen. Les sites de Boni, Daghfali, Mograt et Fillikol." Doctoral dissertation, Lille: Université Charles de Gaulle-Lille 3, HALMA-IPEL, UMR 8164 CNRS.

2014 "Rock Drawing Studies: Four Seasons in the Middle Nile Region." In *The Fourth Cataract and Beyond: Proceedings of the 12th International Conference for Nubian Studies,* edited by Julie R. Anderson and Derek A. Welsby, pp. 1057–68. British Museum Publications on Egypt and Sudan 1. Leuven: Peeters.

Kröpelin, Stefan

2004 "New Petroglyph Sites in the Southern Libyan Desert (Sudan-Chad)." *Sahara* 15: 111–17.

Leclant, Jean, and Paul Huard, eds.

1980 *La culture des chasseurs du Nil et du Sahara.* 2 vols. Mémoires du Centre de recherches anthropologiques, préhistoriques et ethnographiques 29. Algiers: Centre de recherches anthropologiques, préhistoriques et ethnographiques.

Otto, Karl-Heinz, and Gisela Buschendorf-Otto

1993 *Felsbilder aus dem sudanesischen Nubien.* Publikation der Nubien-Expedition 1961–1963. Berlin: Akademie Verlag.

Smith, Stuart Tyson

2003 "The University of California Dongola Reach Expedition, West Bank Reconnaissance Survey: 1997–1998." *Kush* 18: 157–72.

von Heuglin, Theodor

1865 *Die Tinne'sche Expedition im westlichen Nil-Quellgebiet 1863 und 1864. Aus dem Tagebuch von Th. von Heuglin.* Petermann's Geographische Mittheilungen, Ergänzungsheft 15. Gotha: Justus Perthes.

Welsby, Derek A.

2008 "The Merowe Dam Archaeological Salvage Project." In *Between the Cataracts: Proceedings of the 11th Conference for Nubian Studies, Warsaw University, 27 August–2 September 2006.* Part 1: *Main Papers,* edited by Włodzimierz Godlewski and Adam Łajtar, pp. 33–47. Polish Archaeology in the Mediterranean, Supplement Series, 2.1. Warsaw: University of Warsaw Press.

Winkler, Hans A.

1938 *Rock-Drawings of Southern Upper Egypt.* 2 vols. Archaeological Survey of Egypt, Memoir 26–27. London: Egypt Exploration Society.

8

Rebecca Benefiel

Graffiti at Pompeii, Italy

In the year 79 CE, the volcano of Mount Vesuvius, which had been dormant for nearly two thousand years, erupted and devastated the surrounding regions. The volcanic debris that rained down over the course of two days ended up burying the town of Pompeii to a depth of more than 10 meters. The devastation to the area was total. The Roman emperor Titus sent a commission to the area to see what could be salvaged, but the cities of Pompeii and Herculaneum were deemed a total loss, buried under too much volcanic material, and the decision was made to abandon them. The sites were effectively sealed off, and as a result the friable wall plaster that covered virtually every surface of Pompeii, both indoors and out, was preserved. That wall plaster has yielded the majority of wall painting from the ancient world; it has also revealed more than 11,000 individual pieces of writing, inscriptions committed to the surface of a wall.

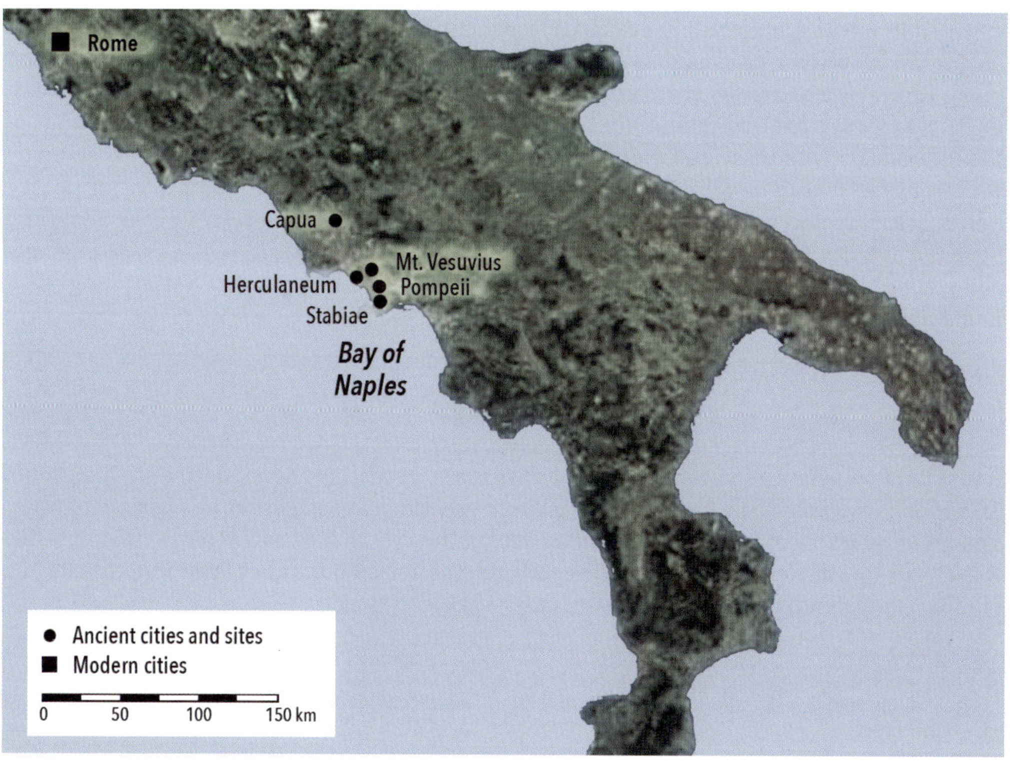

FIGURE 8.1. Map of southern Italy showing the Bay of Naples and sites mentioned in the text.
Map: Lorene Sterner

The wall inscriptions at Pompeii take two forms: painted inscriptions (dipinti) and inscriptions scratched into wall plaster (graffiti). The painted inscriptions communicate information of a public nature, similar to our billboards or posters today. They were painted by teams of workers,[1] in dark paint, large letters, and high up on the wall along busy streets, designed to reach a large audience. The dipinti contain information for public consumption; they include hundreds of endorsements for political candidates as well as announcements of gladiatorial games.[2]

The graffiti, by contrast, comprise handwritten messages and could be composed by anyone who had access to a sharp implement and the desire to write something. They occur not only in public spaces but also in workshops, taverns, shops, and even private houses. They are not concentrated in certain parts of town but appear across the entire city. The plaster that covered buildings inside and out provided a ready surface for Pompeians to write messages that could be read by others. The term "graffiti" in fact originated in the mid-19th century, as excavations of Pompeii's Roman ruins proceeded to uncover more and more of these handwritten texts, lightly scratched into the plaster of ancient buildings. The Italian noun *graffio*, "scratch," was turned into an adjective to describe these "scratched" inscriptions, *iscrizioni graffite.*[3] Only a century later did the term "graffiti" come to be more broadly applied to any informal writing on walls.[4]

Other cultures preserve graffiti scratched onto stone and hard substances that might survive centuries, but the destruction of Pompeii and the nearby region led to the preservation of fragile material that hardly ever survives in sites that do not have a dramatic end. The plaster from Pompeii reveals how much writing there might be in an ancient city. Without the Vesuvian areas, we would likely never guess as to this extent.

A wide swath of ancient society was involved in writing and reading graffiti in Pompeii. From leading citizens to slaves, male and female, inhabitants and visitors to the town all engaged in writing and reading graffiti. For example, in the House of Decimus Lucretius, a magistrate who sponsored gladiatorial spectacles for the city, a graffito applauded him and his children,[5] while over by the theater a female slave inscribed a prayer to Venus, entreating the goddess to bless her and her beloved.[6] In concert with the diverse backgrounds of the individuals who inscribed messages, the content of graffiti at Pompeii is exceedingly wide-ranging. These inscriptions comprise greetings, word games, quotations of poetry, tally marks, many types of drawings, and more. These handwritten traces evoke a vibrant, dynamic activity that filled the ancient city with people in motion, writing, reading, and going about their day. The following examples offer a window into the variety of graffiti found at Pompeii and the surrounding areas.

Greetings

Graffiti in Pompeii were not anonymous as are many graffiti of the modern era. The people of Pompeii inscribed their names and expressed greetings to each other in a variety of ways. The great quantity of inscribed greetings across the city makes clear that writing graffiti was a very social exchange. It strengthened and publicized bonds between individuals in a familiar and friendly way.

1. Franklin 1978.
2. Cf. Franklin 2001.
3. Avellino 1841.
4. Gorrell 2001, p. 77.
5. *CIL* IV 8497b.
6. *CIL* IV 2457.

Beginning Latin students often start class by pronouncing in unison: *Salve, magistra!* Pompeian graffiti contain several instances of this address: *Salve filia* ("Hello, daughter!"), *Salve Vitali* ("Hello, Vitalis!").[7] Yet this was not the only way to say hello. In addition to the imperative of the verb *salvēre* ("to be healthy"), graffiti employ the noun *salutem*. The convention may have derived from letter writing, where the writer sends greetings to the addressee, for example, *Cicero Attico salutem dat* (literally, "Cicero gives health to Atticus"). The graffiti almost always elide the verb and present simply the names of writer and addressee followed by *salutem*, for example, *Optata Secundo suo salutem* ("Optata to her Secundus, greetings").[8] One could wish the very best with a phrase like *plurimam salutem*, as occurs in an exuberant exchange between brothers at the House of Fabius Rufus: *Secundus Onesimo fratri suo p[lu]rimam perpetuamque salutem* ("Secundus, lots of greetings forever and ever, to his brother Onesimus"); *Onesimus ... Secundo plurimam amabiliter salutem* ("Onesimus ... to Secundus, lots of greetings, with love").[9]

Even more popular was the variation on this address: *sal*, an abbreviation of *salutem*. This very common expression, which appears about 100 times on the walls of Pompeii, was the equivalent of our "hi." Here too we find greetings written back and forth. Pyrrichus wrote elegantly inscribed greetings to Alcimus (**FIG. 8.2**). Alcimus then wrote back with the help of a friend, who added his own name: *Alchimus Pyrrho sal • scribit Samannara* ("Alcimus says hi to Pyrrhus. Samanarra wrote this").[10]

The imperative of *valēre* ("to be strong") was also used to tell a friend to "take care" or "fare well." These sentiments were written to both men and women and seem to have been addressed exclusively to individuals rather than to groups. The greeting *vale* was also frequently abbreviated, most often to just two letters: *va(le)*. These were usually short messages, for example, *Niobida va(le)*, *Mnester va(le)*, *Gloriose va(le)*.[11] The main difference between the two types of greetings was that, while *salutem* greetings named both writer and addressee, *vale* greetings named only the addressee. Greetings among the graffiti are frequently found in clusters, where it seems that a group of friends engaged in writing back and forth.[12]

One further way to send warm greetings to a friend in Pompeii uses an acclamation that has no modern-day complement: *feliciter*, or "be happy!" A literal translation is: "may

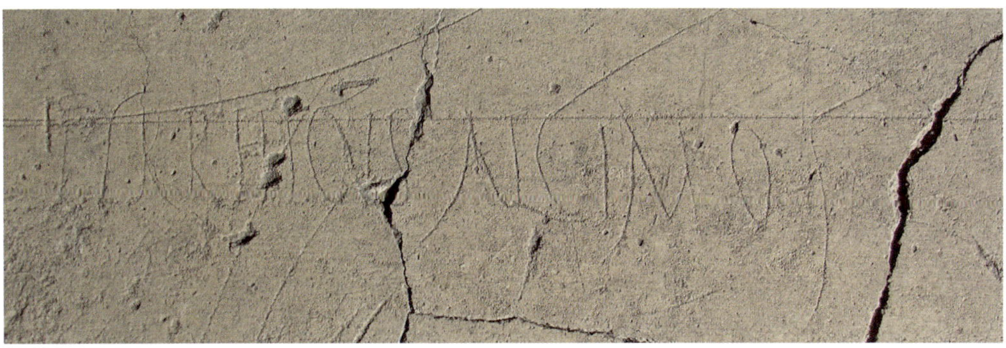

FIGURE 8.2. *Pyrrhicus Alcimo sal.* Greetings between friends, from the basilica of Pompeii. *CIL* IV 1944.
Photo: Rebecca Benefiel. Reproduced courtesy of the Soprintendenza Archeologica di Napoli. Reproduction prohibited

7. *CIL* IV 2173, 8072.
8. *CIL* IV 6755.
9. Giordano 1966, nos. 9–10, 13.
10. *CIL* IV 1934.
11. *CIL* IV 1800, 1862, 2012.
12. Cf. Benefiel 2011, a group of greetings to women in the House of the Four Styles.

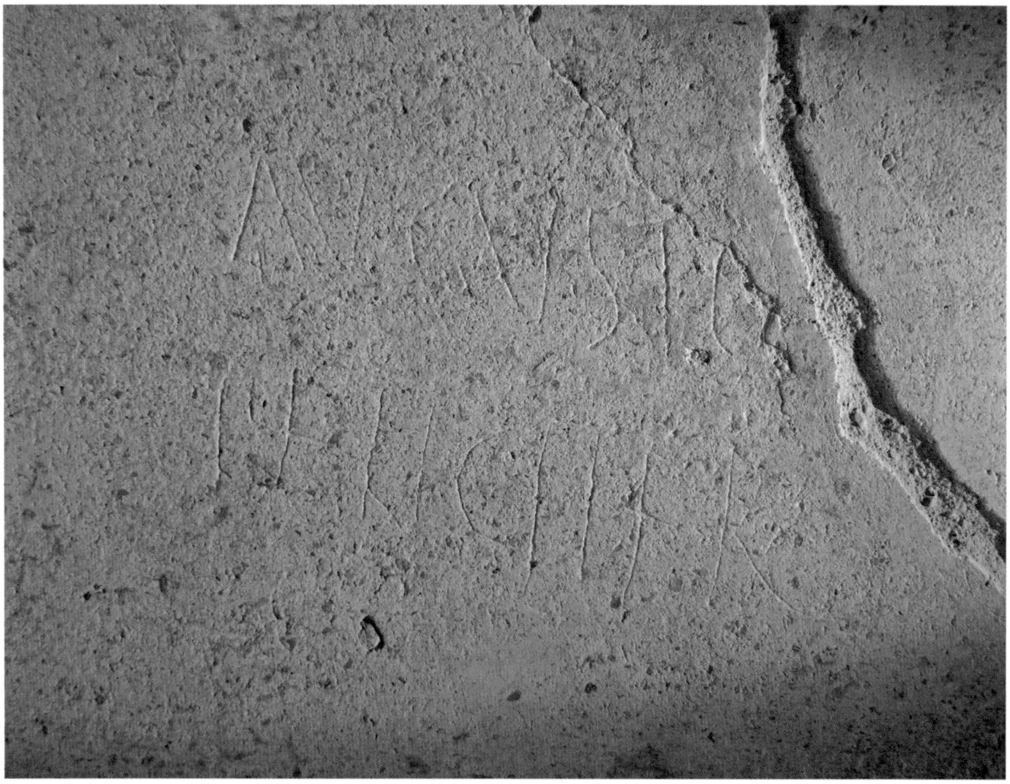

FIGURE 8.3. *Augusto feliciter,* "Long live the emperor!" from the House of Maius Castricius.
Photo: Rebecca Benefiel. Reproduced courtesy of the Soprintendenza Archeologica di Pompei. Reproduction prohibited

things go happily for so-and-so." We might translate *Augusto feliciter* (**FIG. 8.3**) as, "Long live the emperor!"[13] or *Iustae feliciter* as, "Good wishes for Iusta!" But the root of *feliciter* is the adjective *felix,* meaning "happy" or "lucky," which a general sentiment of good wishes does not capture. This expression of *feliciter* is found throughout Pompeii and likely reflected spoken communication.[14] It might be addressed to individuals, groups of people, or even entire towns: *Coloniae Puteolanae feliciter,* "Happy things for the colony of Puteoli!"; *omnibus Pompeianis feliciter,* "Hooray for all the Pompeians!"[15] One graffito wishes happiness for those of good will: *Ben{i}volentibus felic{e}ter!*[16] A number of painted inscriptions also applaud the emperor and his "decisions" with the acclamation *feliciter:*[17]

Iudiciis Augusti Augustae feliciter! Vobis salvis felices sumus perpetuo

"Hooray for the decisions of the emperor and empress!
With you both safe and sound, we are happy forever."[18]

13. See Benefiel 2010, cat. no. 13.
14. Cf. Benefiel 2018.
15. *CIL* IV 4262, 7343.
16. *CIL* IV 1326.
17. Benefiel 2004; Mouritsen and Gradel 1991.
18. *CIL* IV 1074, Add. pp. 199, 461.

Love

Love finds its way into the graffiti of many cultures. At Pompeii, however, graffiti expressing love between friends far outnumber graffiti expressing love between couples. There are a few outright declarations: *Auge amat Amotenum* ("Auge loves Amotenus"),[19] *Figulus amat Idaia(m)* ("Figulus loves Idaia"),[20] *Caesius Fidelis amat Mecone(m) Nucerin(um)* ("Caesius Fidelis loves Meco from Nuceria").[21] More often, the idea of love appears in other forms among the graffiti.[22] It might be a driving force, for example, as a writer composes:

Scribenti • mi • dictat • amor • mostratque • cupido
... peream • sine • te • si • deus esse velim

"Love dictates to me as I am writing and desire shows me the way.
May I perish without you if I should wish to be a god."[23]

Love also appears as the motivation for personal prayers. One of the most evocative of these was written by a female slave and presents a prayer to Venus:

Methe Cominiaes Atellana amat Chrestum. Corde [si]t utreis que Venus Pompeiana propitia [e]t sem[per] concordes veivant

"Methe from Atella, the slave of Cominia, loves Chrestus. May Pompeian Venus be propitious in her heart to both, and may they always live harmoniously."[24]

Venus was the principal deity of Pompeii and this local version of the deity, Venus Pompeiana, was depicted in art and was called on by others, both in her role as protectress of love and as a potent, ruling goddess. Another Pompeian publicly called on Venus's protection with a warning below a large painting of gladiators:

(H)abiat Venere(m) {B}ompe{i}iana(m) iratam qui hoc laeserit

"May he who shall have harmed this have Pompeian Venus angry at him."[25]

Poetry

The topic of love also appears among the many poetic expressions inscribed on the walls of Pompeii. One sentiment found repeatedly through Pompeii presents an elegiac couplet that is not identified with any known work of literature. Rather, this is one of several poems that circulated widely among Roman towns, poetic epigrams which Marcello Gigante termed

19. *CIL* IV 1808.
20. *CIL* IV 3131.
21. *CIL* IV 1812.
22. Varone 1994.
23. *CIL* IV 1928.
24. *CIL* IV 2457.
25. *CIL* IV 538.

"voices of the city."[26] The (nearly) full version of the poem appears in the House of Caecilius Iucundus:

(quis)quis amat valeat, pereat qui
nescit amare bis tanto pereat
quisquis amare vetat

"Whoever loves, may he fare well.
May he who knows not how to love perish.
May he perish twice over, whoever forbids love."[27]

Elsewhere, people wrote out just the beginning of the verse, either the first line or even just the first few words. Including variations on the theme, this poem appears fifteen times at Pompeii. Some writers inverted the sentiment to be: "Whoever loves, may he perish." The most elaborate version was written as a graffito in the basilica of the town. It clearly takes *quisquis amat* as its inspiration, only to change the message completely:

"Whoever loves, let him come (*quisquis amat veniat*). I want to break Venus's
ribs with clubs and incapacitate the loins of the goddess.
If she can pierce a hole through my tender heart,
why can't I break her head with a club?"[28]

The "whoever loves" epigram seems to have inspired Pompeians; several adapted the poem and made it their own. The sentiment was used as a flourish to conclude another epigram in the House of Maius Castricius.[29] It was slightly modified in a message about love for a certain Leda.[30] And it was personalized to serve as a message of welcome in the House of the Four Styles, where a message inscribed in elegant lettering greeted visitors: *Quos LVP amat valeant,* "Welcome to those whom L(ucius) V. P. loves" (**FIG. 8.4**).[31] The epigram even appeared in a wall painting, written in infinitesimally small letters on a scroll depicted in a still life of writing implements.[32] The author remains unknown, but this elegiac couplet was clearly popular throughout town and beyond.

Quotations of literature also appeared on the walls of the town. The most frequently cited poet is Virgil, author of the *Aeneid.* As one might expect, the opening words of his epic poem (*arma virumque cano ...,* "I sing of arms and the man ...") are frequently inscribed,[33] but the opening of the second book of the *Aeneid* is just as popular: *conticuere,* "they fell silent." Virgil's other works are quoted at Pompeii too, as are the works of the poets Propertius and Ovid and the philosopher Lucretius.[34]

Verses of poetry also appear in clusters, where it seems that a reference to a well-known verse might inspire others to add their own additions. Examples of this tendency for poetry

26. Gigante 1979, pp. 223–36.
27. *CIL* IV 4091.
28. *CIL* IV 1824.
29. Benefiel 2010, p. 68, fig. 9.
30. *CIL* IV 9202.
31. Benefiel 2011, pp. 33–39.
32. *CIL* IV 1173.
33. Cf. Milnor 2009.
34. Cooley and Cooley 2014, pp. 292–93.

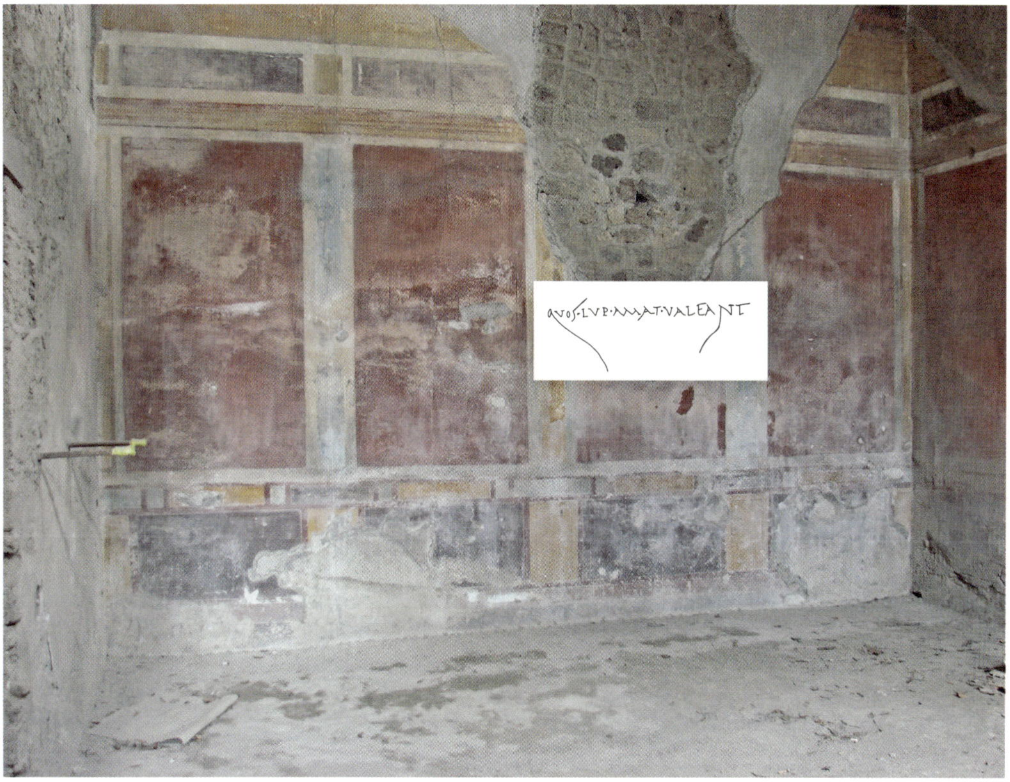

FIGURE 8.4. *Quos LVP amat valeat.* Adaptation of a popular poem, graffito in the House of the Four Styles. *CIL* IV 8215.
Photo: Rebecca Benefiel. Reproduced courtesy of the Soprintendenza Archeologica di Pompei. Reproduction prohibited

to cluster can be found in several locations, including the tavern of Euxinus,[35] the House of Maius Castricius,[36] and the basilica of the town.[37]

Figural Graffiti

Pompeii is better known for its textual graffiti but, in addition to written messages like these, the walls of Pompeii also featured a variety of hand-sketched drawings. These figural graffiti were initially treated as secondary and very few were documented with illustrations or anything more than a brief summary, but following Martin Langner's collection of figural graffiti across the ancient Mediterranean,[38] recent work has begun to consider Pompeian textual and figural graffiti together. The Ancient Graffiti Project[39] now provides an online database and scholarly resource where figural and textual graffiti from Pompeii and Herculaneum can be researched and studied together.

Certain subject matters recur frequently on the walls of the town. The most popular motifs to draw in Pompeii included faces in profile, gladiators, boats, animals, and geomet-

35. Jashemski 1967.
36. Benefiel 2010.
37. Benefiel 2018.
38. Langner 2001.
39. http://ancientgraffiti.org.

rical images.[40] Some of the largest houses in Pompeii featured all these types of drawings. In the House of Maius Castricius in Pompeii, for example, figural graffiti included a boat, a palm frond, a bird, and a deer.[41] Another large house at Pompeii, the House of Paquius Proculus, featured drawings of birds, boats, a gladiator, and a face in profile. The boats, faces, and animals found on the walls of Pompeii are common motifs that are also found drawn throughout the ancient world.[42] Not far from Pompeii, the large Villa San Marco at Stabiae featured these same motifs: a bird, two drawings of gladiators and gladiatorial helmets, and a figure in profile.[43]

Boats

Boats were a popular image across the Mediterranean for people to draw. More than 400 ancient graffiti depicting boats have been collected.[44] The importance of boats for travel and commerce is likely responsible for their ubiquity. Numerous graffiti depicting boats appeared on the island of Delos, a busy trading center in the Mediterranean.[45] The graffiti at El-Kurru likewise feature boats prominently.[46] Pompeii had its own harbor and served as the port for cities in the hinterland, and thus many boats appear among the graffiti of Pompeii as well. The boat drawings at Pompeii include a variety of forms, from simple rowboats to fishing vessels to elaborate sailboats.

A boat drawn in the House of Maius Castricius, a house at the edge of town and overlooking the bay, presents the outline of a seagoing vessel, with attention given to depicting the stern and prow (FIG. 8.5). Scratched onto a background of red plaster, the white lines of

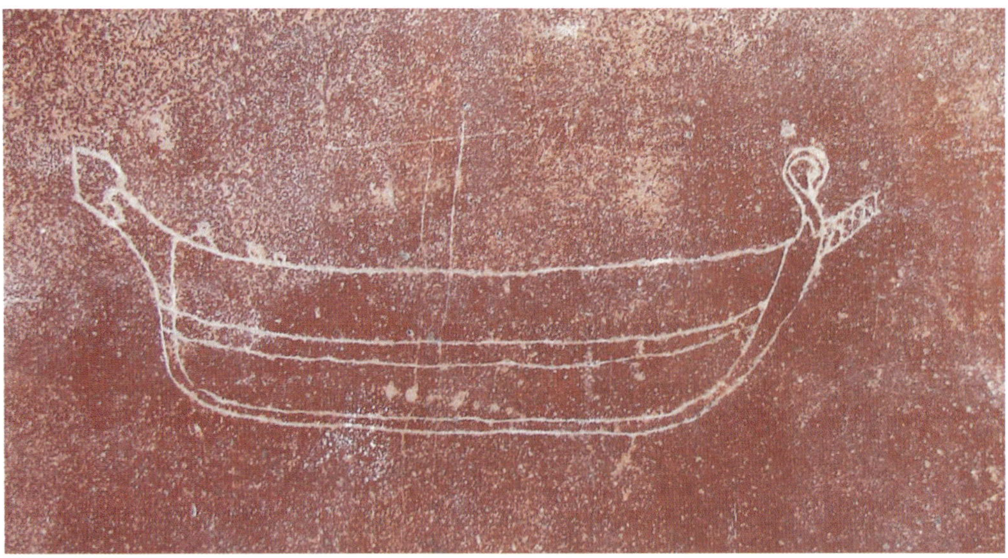

FIGURE 8.5. Graffito of a boat in the House of Maius Castricius.
Photo: Rebecca Benefiel. Reproduced courtesy of the Soprintendenza Archeologica di Pompei. Reproduction prohibited

40. Langner 2001, p. 84, fig. 40.
41. Benefiel 2010.
42. Langner 2001.
43. Varone 1999.
44. Langner 2001, cat. nos. 1844–2265.
45. Zarmakoupi 2016.
46. See Williams, this volume.

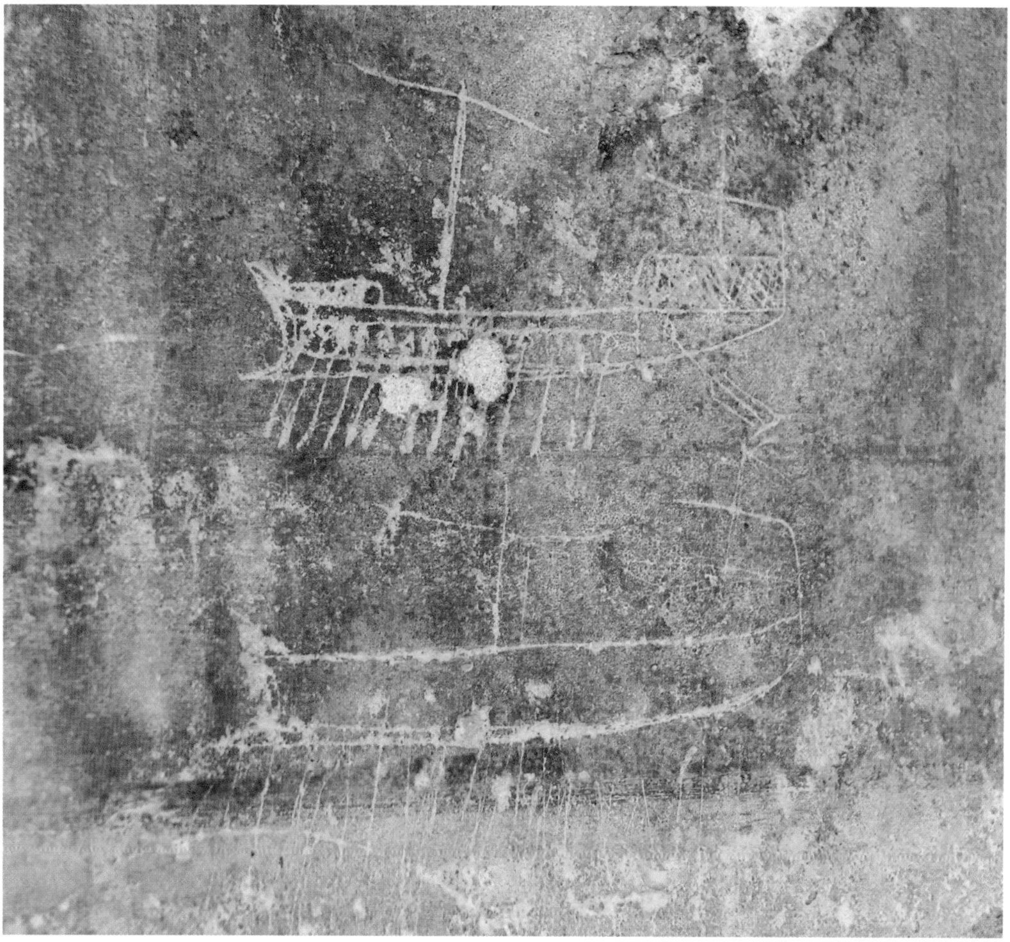

FIGURE 8.6. Figural graffiti in the House of the Four Styles presenting two boats.
Photo: Rebecca Benefiel. Reproduced courtesy of the Soprintendenza Archeologica di Pompei. Reproduction prohibited

the boat (7.5 × 22.0 cm) stand out and make the drawing easily legible.[47] Across town, in the House of the Four Styles, two boat drawings appear in the atrium (FIG. 8.6). These graffiti presented long boats with banks of oars. They are situated one above the other and, from the similar layout of the two drawings but a difference in the certainty of the hand, it would appear that someone was teaching another person how to draw a boat.[48]

Many boat graffiti at Pompeii consist of a hull, a mast, and a stern, but the largest and most detailed boat among Pompeian graffiti is a large sailing vessel with mast and intricately detailed depictions of the numerous ropes used to direct and sail it. Below the drawing, the shape of a *tabula ansata* (tablet with dovetail handles) was inscribed and inside was written the name Europa. This elaborate drawing on the wall was the most conspicuous feature of the house located at I.15.3,[49] and so the residence was named *la casa della nave*

47. Benefiel 2010, no. 49.
48. Benefiel 2011.
49. Pompeii is divided into nine regions, numbered I–IX; the insulae (blocks of houses and shops bounded by roads) in each region are numbered with arabic numerals, and within each insula, every entryway is also assigned an arabic number. In this way, each dwelling or shop can be identified by an "address" of three numbers.

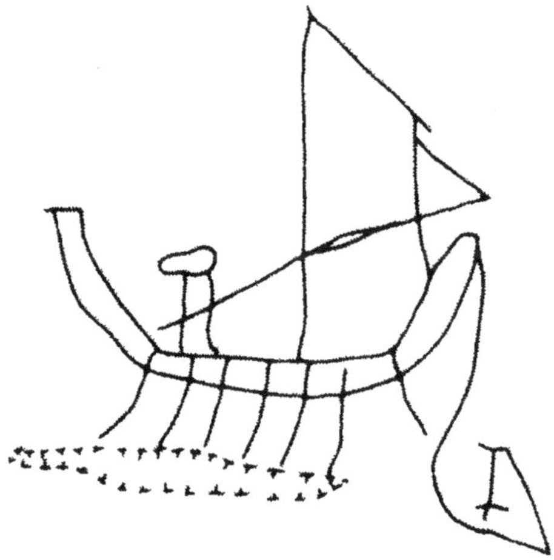

FIGURE 8.7. Graffito of a fishing boat, from the Villa San Marco at Stabiae.
After Varone 1999, cat. no. 23

Europa (the House of the Ship Europa). In all three of these houses, the boat graffiti appear in the central living space where conversations and socialization would take place, suggesting that they were an addition to the built environment that may have inspired discussion.

Just beyond Pompeii, at the seaside community of Stabiae, the Villa San Marco likewise communicated an overwhelming interest in boats. Most locations in Pompeii contain one or perhaps two boat graffiti, but the Villa San Marco holds more than fifteen examples.[50] Boats were drawn here individually and in pairs. Some have oars, some are fishing vessels (**FIG. 8.7**), some are simple skiffs. The Villa San Marco was perched atop a bluff and, with its large windows and open plan, its design was calculated to highlight its setting and its expansive view over the Bay of Naples. That view would have certainly encompassed any number of boats on a daily basis, as the bay was traversed by numerous vessels being used to fish the day's catch, as well as for transport around the region. Remarkably, several of the boats drawn in the Villa San Marco are sketched with people on board. At Pompeii, among the boat graffiti, the artist's interest is squarely on the vessel. The boat is hardly ever populated.

The figures in these drawings nudge us toward thinking about the individuals who may have drawn them. The location of these many boat drawings in the service quarters suggests that they were not the work of visitors or clients, but perhaps the work of the villa staff, whose duties may have included fishing to stock the villa with provisions. These examples thereby suggest that a strong motivation for writing on the wall may have been the influence of one's surroundings.

Gladiators

Hand-sketched graffiti also illustrate the fascination that Romans held for gladiators and how closely Pompeians might follow the successes of individual athletes. Sketches of gladiators appeared across Pompeii, sometimes with labels to identify the figures; other graffiti presented the images of gladiators alone or even sketches of gladiatorial equipment. Altogether, these drawings offer a glimpse into how Pompeians might use graffiti to communicate and share an interest in the major sport of their time.

A collection of graffiti featuring multiple drawings and texts was drawn on a funerary monument outside the city walls south of town. The roads that led into any Roman town were lined with funerary monuments, a place outside the city to bury the dead and to represent one's achievements. Shade, seats, and shelter among these monuments provided a place for travelers to pause and rest before entering town. The monument featuring the gladiator graffiti stood outside the Nocera Gate, an artery connecting Pompeii and points south.

50. Varone 1999.

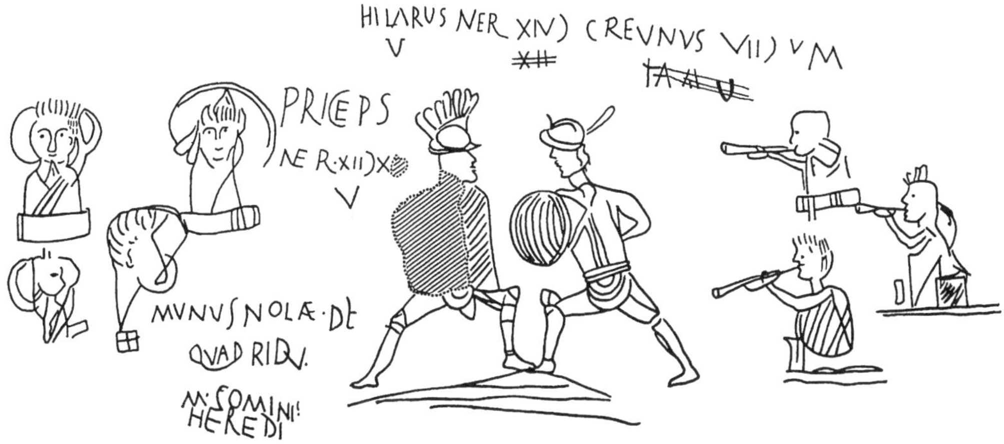

FIGURE 8.8. Gladiator graffiti, from a tomb outside the Nocera Gate.
CIL IV 10237

The graffiti sketched here commemorate a series of gladiatorial matches.[51] A central scene (**FIG. 8.8**) includes text that describes the event: four days of gladiatorial games sponsored by a Marcus Cominius and held in the city of Nola.[52] Three pairs of gladiators are represented, and labels above the figures allow us to reconstruct the order of events. Hilarus first fought against Creunus and won; that match was Hilarus' fourteenth victory. Next, he fought Marcus Attilius and lost. Then Marcus Attilius fought against Lucius Raecius Felix and himself notched another victory.

The brief texts shed light on why this would have been such an exciting spectacle to watch. Hilarus, a Neronianus, was trained at the imperial gladiatorial training school in Capua. Even though most gladiators were slaves, they received extensive training since matches involved not only a show of strength but also tactical prowess. Gladiators were trained in a particular fighting style and would be matched against an opponent outfitted with different equipment. As a gladiator from the imperial training school, Hilarus would have had more and better training than his opponents, and he was accomplished, with fourteen victories to his name. Yet in his next match he loses to Marcus Attilius, who is labeled a *t(iro)*, or novice, meaning this was his first appearance in the arena. What an upset this must have been, for a brand-new gladiator in his first match to defeat a premier, imperially trained athlete!

Another set of gladiator graffiti appears inside a well-appointed house, the House of the Ceii. In a hallway facing the garden, four figures of gladiators are depicted (**FIG. 8.9**).[53] Each figure is labeled with his name — Oceanus, Aracintus, Severus, and Albanus — and his record of wins. Here, the graffito communicates the outcome of the match visually; the defeated gladiator still stands but his shield lies on the ground. Albanus, the victor of the second vignette, is labeled with "SC" for *sc(aevus)*, or "left-handed" and is depicted holding his sword in his left hand.[54] Since the majority of gladiators were right-handed and trained against right-handed athletes, Albanus would have had the advantage in a match; his dexterity required opponents to alter their strategy. This uncommon characteristic may

51. *CIL* IV 10236–10238.
52. Coleman 1999.
53. *CIL* IV 8055–8056.
54. Coleman 1996.

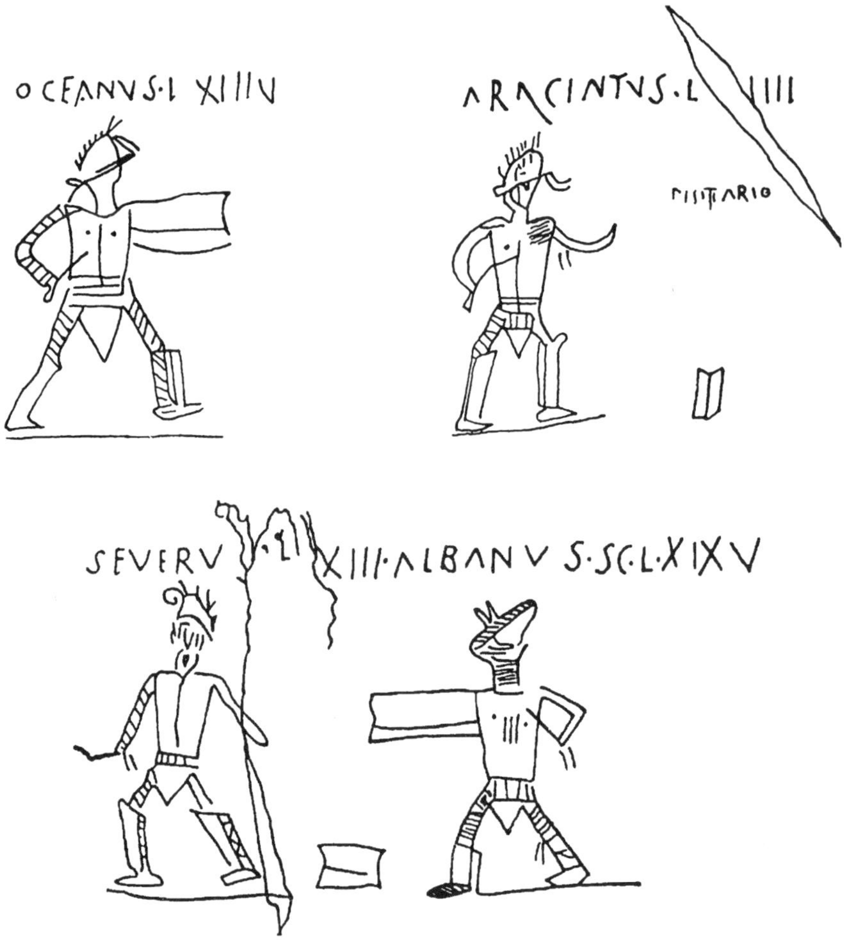

FIGURE 8.9. Gladiator graffiti, from the House of the Ceii.
CIL IV 8055 (top) and 8056 (bottom)

have heightened the tension at the spectacle. Albanus is the only left-handed athlete among all the graffiti depicting gladiators in Pompeii.

Among graffiti depicting gladiators, care is given to depict accurately the type of equipment each is carrying. Hilarus, for example, wears a crested helmet in both of his depictions and carries a mid-length rectangular shield. His two opponents each wear a helmet with a single feather but carry different gear; Creunus fought with a small circular shield, while Marcus Attilius held a full-length shield. In the House of the Ceii, crosshatching represents the protective gear of the arm guard and shin guards worn by the gladiators. These sketches reveal a close familiarity with individual athletes. Not only does the writer know the names and records of each, he knows the gladiator's fighting style and how it differs from that of his opponent. Audience members were not sitting in the amphitheater watching just any sport; they were watching and likely cheering for individual athletes.

Gladiatorial spectacles were not held very often, and when they did occur, it was big news. Gladiatorial games were advertised with posters and spectators might travel some distance to attend.[55] These graffiti can show us from the view of the spectator how exciting it was to watch the games. There was clearly a shared visual language, with a focus on the type of equipment gladiators carried. There was also a close familiarity with the athletes themselves and knowledge of their records. When a brand-new gladiator defeated the imperially trained Neronianus, a Pompeian may have sketched out the scene to share the exciting news with others. The example in the House of the Ceii shows that this was not something just for public spaces. The scratched designs here were only a few centimeters high, not obtrusive but certainly a conversation starter that illustrated one's knowledge of the famous athletes of the day and maybe attendance at a particularly thrilling match. These graffiti reveal how Pompeians might communicate by means of graffiti about a major social event of their world.

Other Figural Graffiti

The walls of Pompeii and nearby Herculaneum contain numerous other figural graffiti, from a camel to a drawing of the labyrinth (with the caption, "the Minotaur lives here"; **FIG. 8.10**). In Herculaneum, the House of the Stags contained many statues of deer in its garden and an upstairs room featured a series of sketched stags as well.[56] Geometric shapes appeared on walls as well. A favorite design at Pompeii and Herculaneum was to take a compass and create a series of circles.

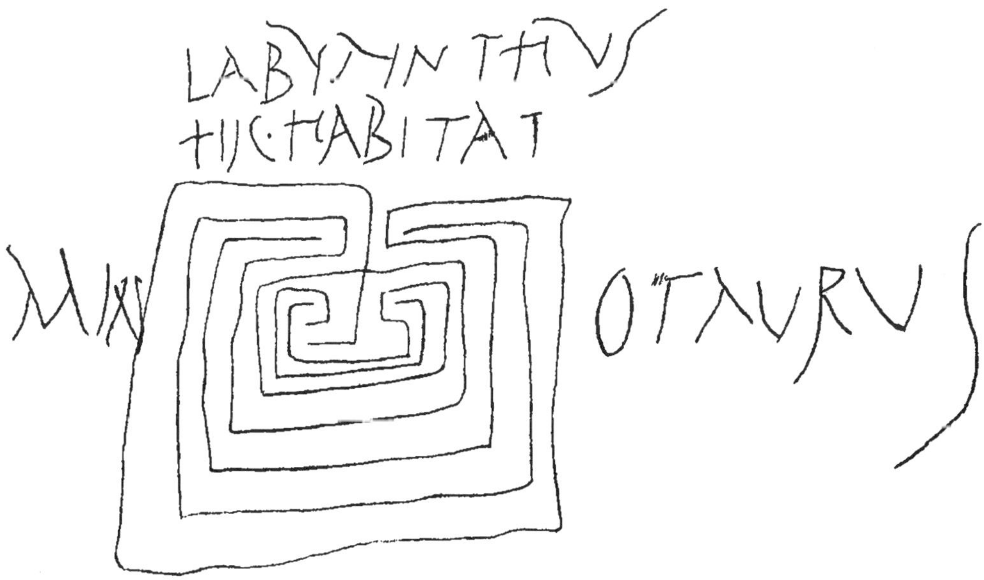

FIGURE 8.10. Graffito of the labyrinth, from the House of the Labyrinth.
CIL IV 2331

55. Sabbatini Tumolesi 1980.
56. *CIL* IV 10561; cf. ancientgraffiti.org.

Conclusion

Altogether the graffiti of Pompeii communicate the interests of those writing and their engagement in the world around them. Graffiti in this small town of the early Roman empire neither focus on the political realm nor confront those in power. Rather, it was the local environment that inspired these messages: what people were watching, reading, or hearing, as well as those friends, family members, and visitors with whom they came into repeated contact.

The graffiti of Pompeii are almost never antagonistic; in fact, it is remarkable to see how positive this mode of communication was. The clustering and the responsive nature of graffiti underscore the social behavior of those writing these messages. One can imagine Pompeians discussing an exciting gladiator match, leaving a message for a friend to read, or inspiring others to quote a favorite verse. The destruction of Pompeii has left us a town full of personal communications. Messages featuring friendly greetings, poetic quotation, and interest in gladiators speak to the culture and the time, local conditions, and the motivation for scratching graffiti in this town of the 1st century CE.

Abbreviations

CIL IV — *Corpus Inscriptionum Latinarum*, Volume 4: *Inscriptiones parietariae Pompeianae, Herculanenses, Stabianae.* Edited by Richard Schöne and Karl Friedrich Wilhelm Zangemeister. Berolini: G. Reimerum, 1871. Supplementi pars II: *Inscriptiones parietariae et vasorum fictilium,* edited by August Mau, 1909. Supplementi pars III, Lieferung 1–4: *Inscriptiones Pompeianae Herculanenses parietaraiae et vasorum fictilium,* edited by Matthaeus Della Corte and Pius Ciprotti, 1952–1970.

In transliterations

a(bc) — An abbreviation expanded by the editor
[abc] — Damaged text supplied by the editor
{abc} — Text included by mistake and expunged by the editor

References

Avellino, Francesco Maria

1841 *Osservazioni sopra alcune iscrizioni e disegni graffiti sulle mura di Pompei.* Naples: Stamperia reale.

Benefiel, Rebecca R.

2004 "Pompeii, Puteoli, and the Status of a Colonia in the Mid-First Century AD." In *Pompei, Capri e La Penisola Sorrentina,* edited by Felice Senatore, pp. 349–68. Capri: Oebalus.

2010 "Dialogues of Ancient Graffiti in the House of Maius Castricius in Pompeii." *American Journal of Archaeology* 114 (1): 59–101.

2011 "Dialogues of Graffiti in the House of the Four Styles at Pompeii (Casa Dei Quattro Stili, 1.8.17, 11)." In *Ancient Graffiti in Context,* edited by Jennifer A. Baird and Claire Taylor, pp. 20–48. Routledge Studies in Ancient History 2. New York: Routledge.

2018 "Gladiators, Greetings, and Poetry: Graffiti in First Century Pompeii." In *Scribbling through History: Graffiti, Places and People from Antiquity to Modernity,* edited by Chloé

Ragazzoli, Ömür Harmansah, Chiara Salvador, and Elizabeth Frood, pp. 101–16. London: Bloomsbury Academic.

Coleman, Kathleen M.

1996 "A Left-Handed Gladiator at Pompeii." *Zeitschrift für Papyrologie und Epigraphik* 114: 194–96.

1999 "Graffiti for Beginners." *Classical Outlook* 76 (2): 41–47.

Cooley, Alison E., and M. G. L. Cooley

2014 *Pompeii and Herculaneum: A Sourcebook.* 2nd ed. Routledge Sourcebooks for the Ancient World. London and New York: Routledge.

Franklin, James L., Jr.

1978 "Notes on Pompeian Prosopography: Programmatum Scriptores." *Cronache Pompeiane* 4: 54–74.

2001 *Pompeis Difficile Est: Studies in the Political Life of Imperial Pompeii.* Ann Arbor: University of Michigan Press.

Gigante, Marcello

1979 *Civiltà delle forme letterarie nell'antica Pompei.* Naples: Bibliopolis.

Giordano, Carlo

1966 "Le iscrizioni della Casa di M. Fabio Rufo." *Rendiconti della Accademia di Archeologia Lettere e Belle Arti (Napoli)* n.s. 41: 73–89.

Gorrell, Robert M.

2001 *What's in a Word? Etymological Gossip about Some Interesting English Words.* Reno: University of Nevada Press.

Jashemski, Wilhelmina F.

1967 "The Caupona of Euxinus at Pompeii." *Archaeology* 20 (1): 36–44.

Langner, Martin

2001 *Antike Graffitizeichnungen: Motive, Gestaltung und Bedeutung.* Palilia 11. Wiesbaden: Ludwig Reichert.

Milnor, Kristina

2009 "Literary Literacy in Roman Pompeii: The Case of Vergil's Aeneid." In *Ancient Literacies: The Culture of Reading in Greece and Rome,* edited by William A. Johnson and Holt N. Parker, pp. 288–319. Oxford: Oxford University Press.

Mouritsen, Henrik, and Ittai Gradel

1991 "Nero in Pompeian Politics: *edicta Munerum* and Imperial Flaminates in Late Pompeii." *Zeitschrift für Papyrologie und Epigraphik* 87: 145–55.

Sabbatini Tumolesi, Patrizia

1980 *Gladiatorum paria: annunci di spettacoli gladiatorii a Pompei.* Tituli 1. Rome: Storia e Letteratura.

Varone, Antonio

1994 *Erotica pompeiana: iscrizioni d'amore sui muri di Pompei.* Studia archeologica 71. Rome: "L'Erma" di Bretschneider.

1999 "I graffiti." In *La Villa San Marco a Stabia,* edited by Alix Barbet and Paola Miniero Forte, pp. 345–62. Naples, Rome, Pompeii: Centre Jean Bérard, École Française de Rome, Soprintendenza archeologica di Pompei.

Zarmakoupi, Mantha

2016 "The Spatial Environment of Inscriptions and Graffiti in Domestic Spaces: The Case of Delos." In *Inscriptions in the Private Sphere in the Greco-Roman World,* edited by Rebecca R. Benefiel and Peter Keegan, pp. 50–79. Brill Studies in Greek and Roman Epigraphy 7. Leiden and Boston: Brill.

Epilogue

Hajj Paintings in El-Araba and El-Ghabat, Egypt: A Photo Essay

Photographs by Ayman Damarany

Multiple essays in this book focus on ancient devotional graffiti at the site of El-Kurru, Sudan. Associated with pilgrimage, the graffiti from El-Kurru depict a variety of subjects. Although the idea of a pilgrim making graffiti as an act of devotion might seem strange today, a modern tradition of making pilgrimage images exists in some parts of the Nile Valley.

This photo essay explores graffiti-like images painted onto the sides of houses in the small towns of El-Araba and El-Ghabat near Abydos, Egypt. These paintings are commemorative in nature, recording and celebrating the hajj, or a Muslim's pilgrimage to Mecca. They often include the pilgrims' names, information about which family members made the trip, the year of travel, and the mode of travel — whether the pilgrimage was made by airplane, boat, or camel. Personal, devotional, and detailed, these paintings are a colorful and attractive form of social communication.

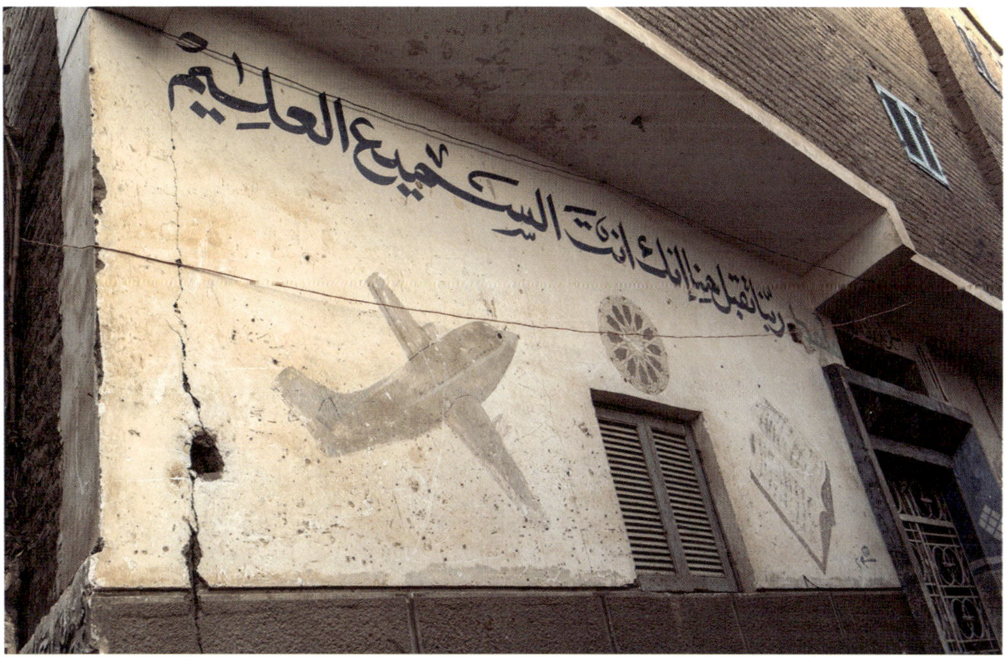

EL-ARABA 1

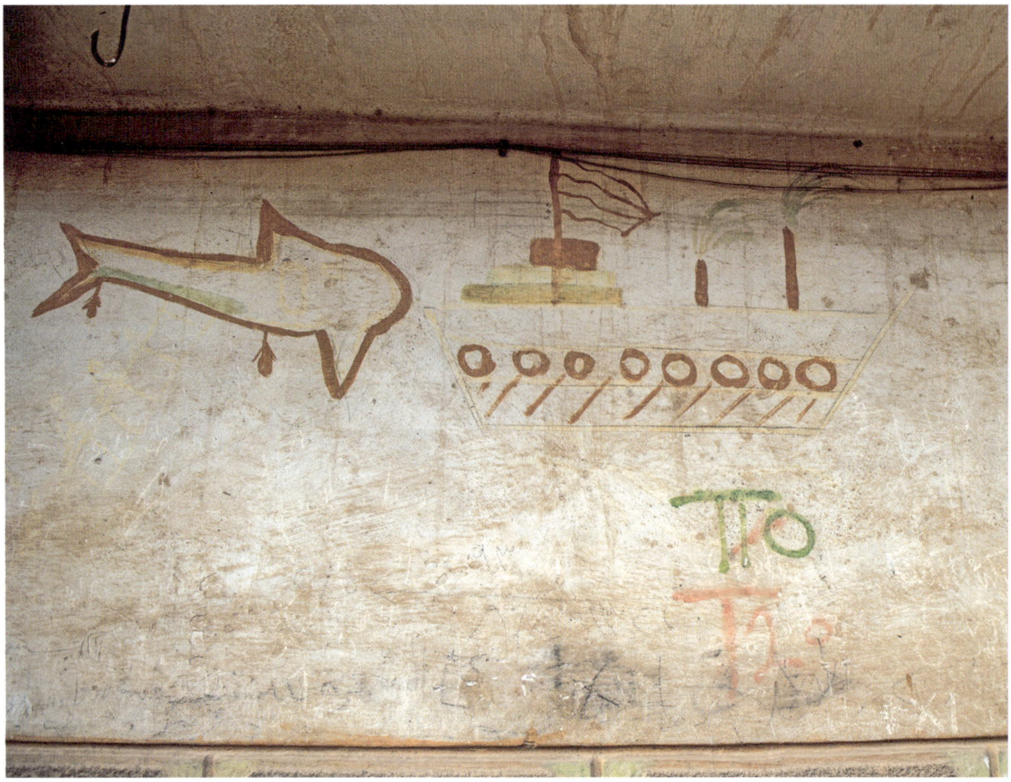

EL-ARABA 2

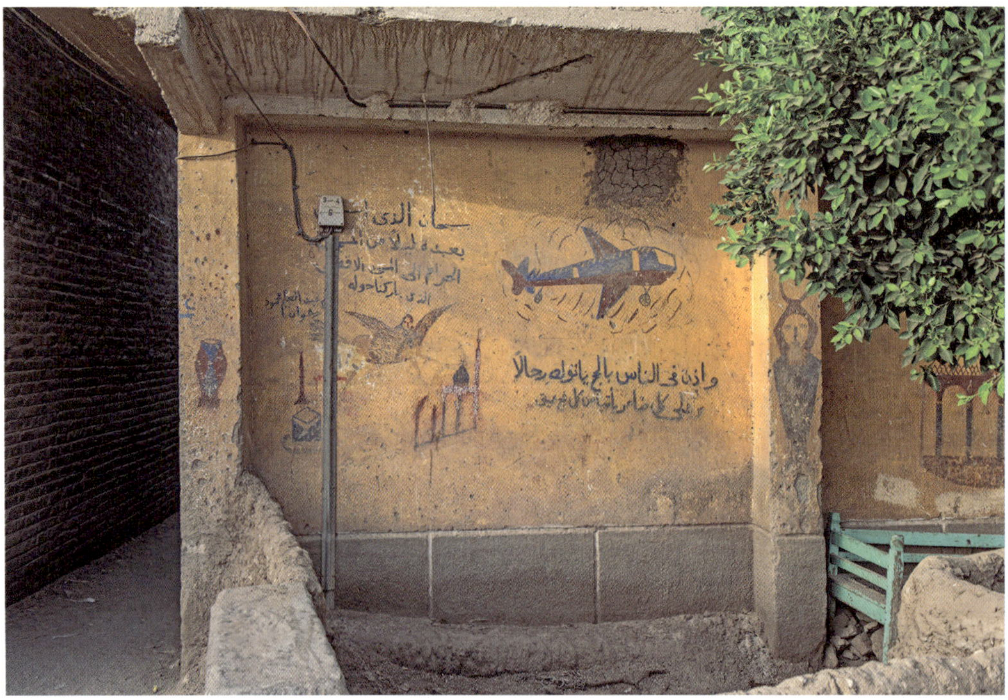

EL-ARABA 3

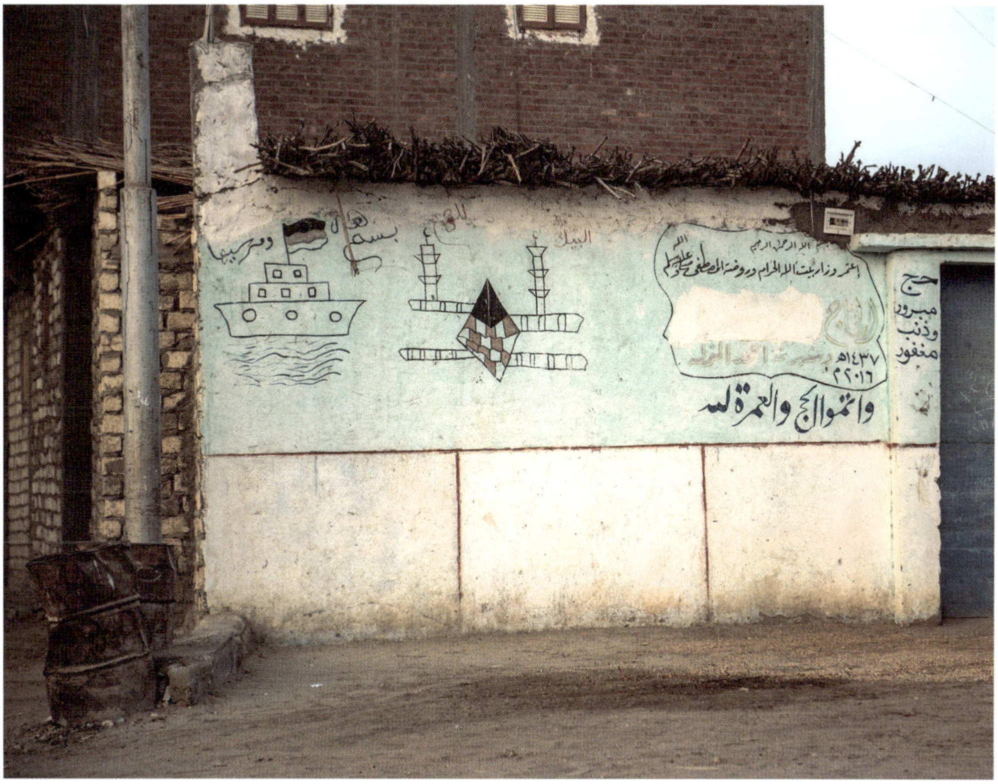

EL-GHABAT 1

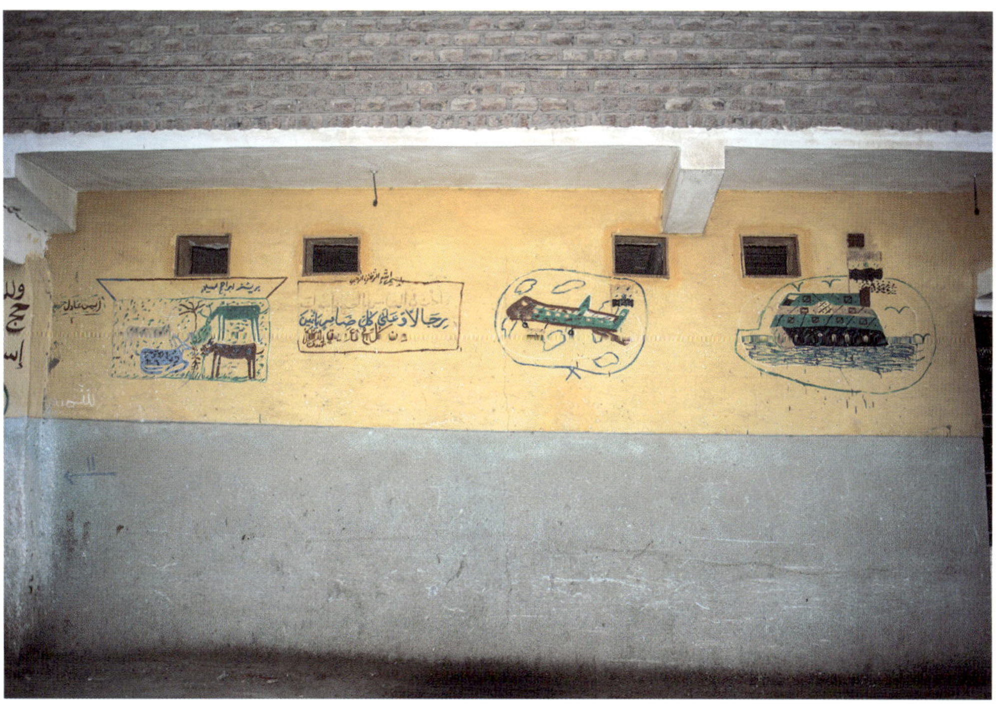

EL-GHABAT 2

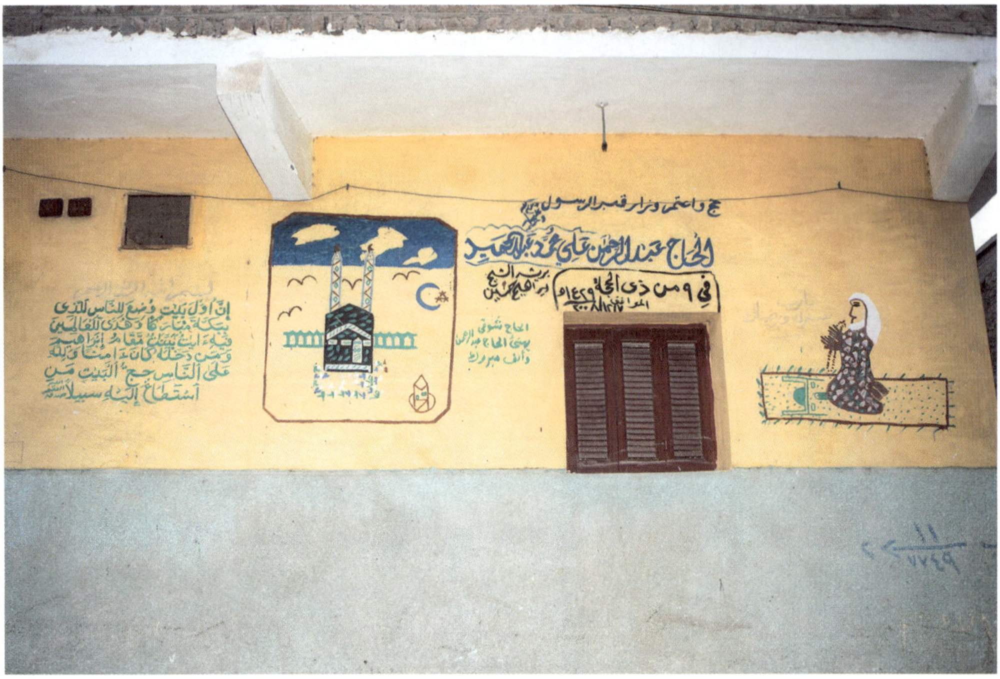

EL-GHABAT 3

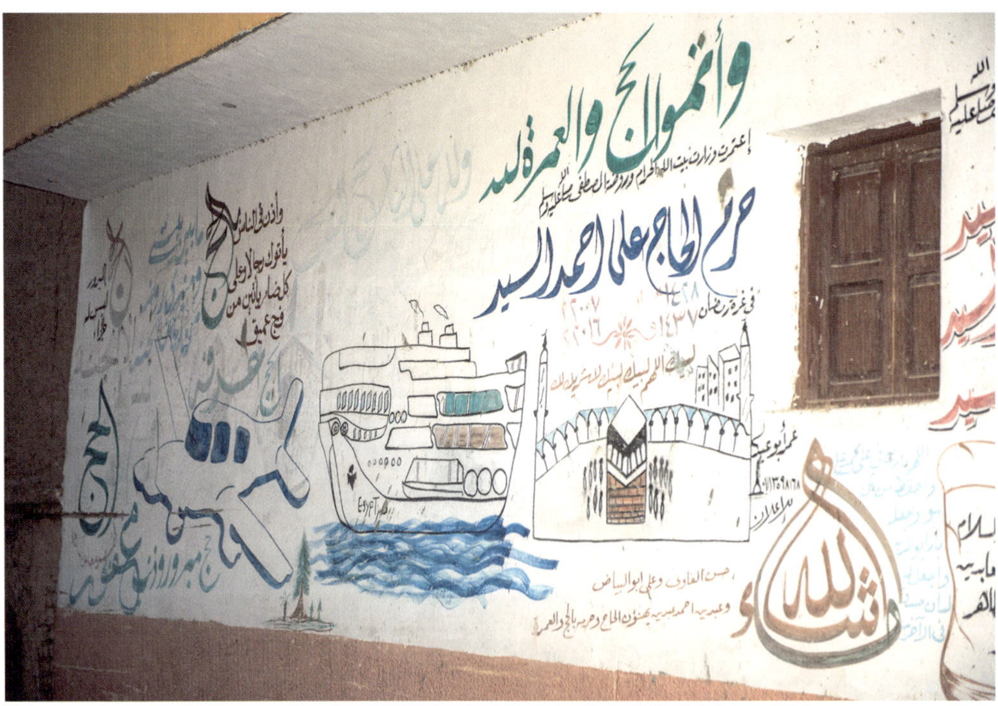

EL-GHABAT 4

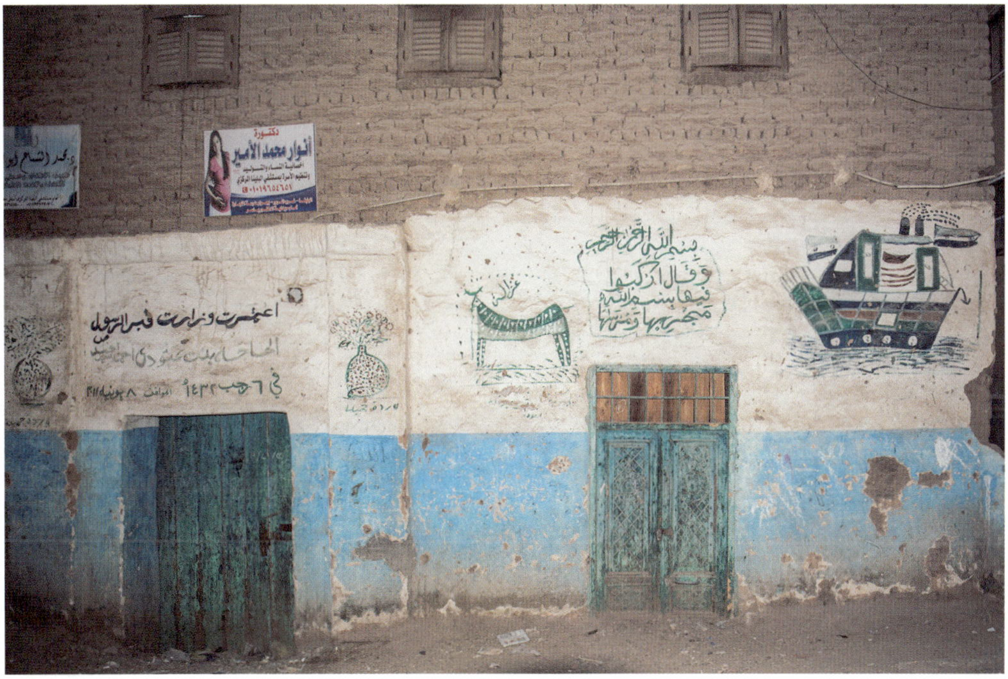

EL-GHABAT 5

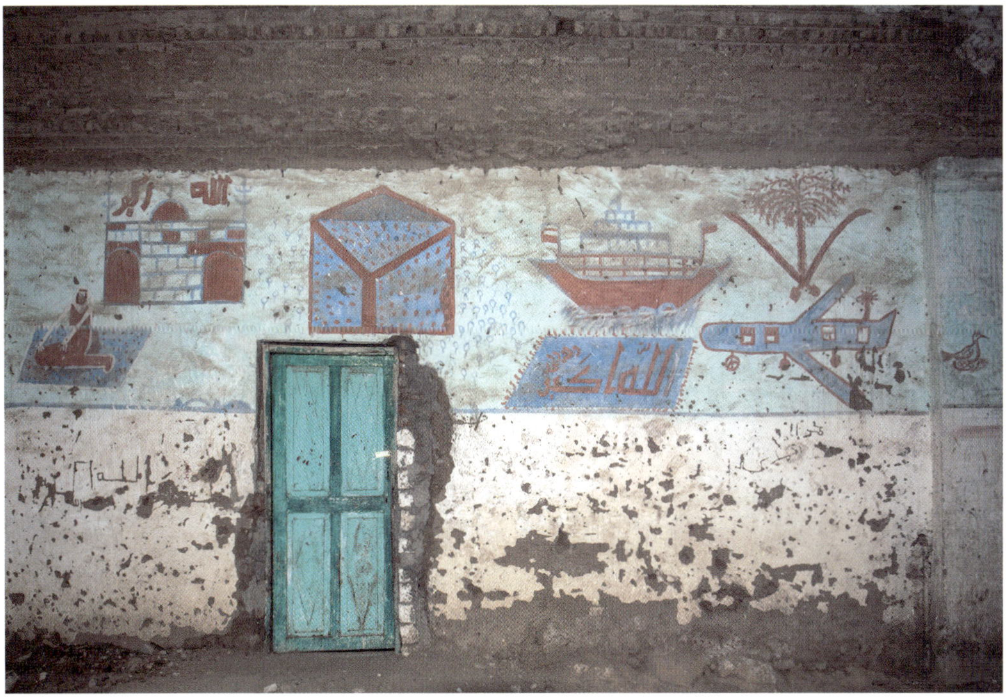

EL-GHABAT 6

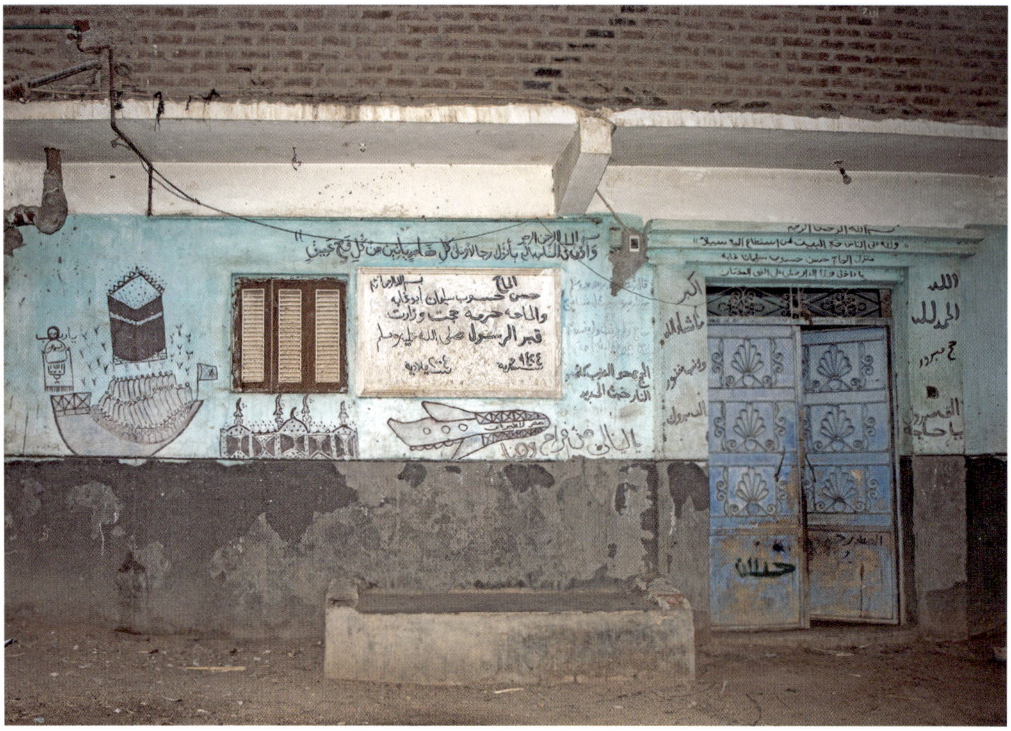

EL-GHABAT 7

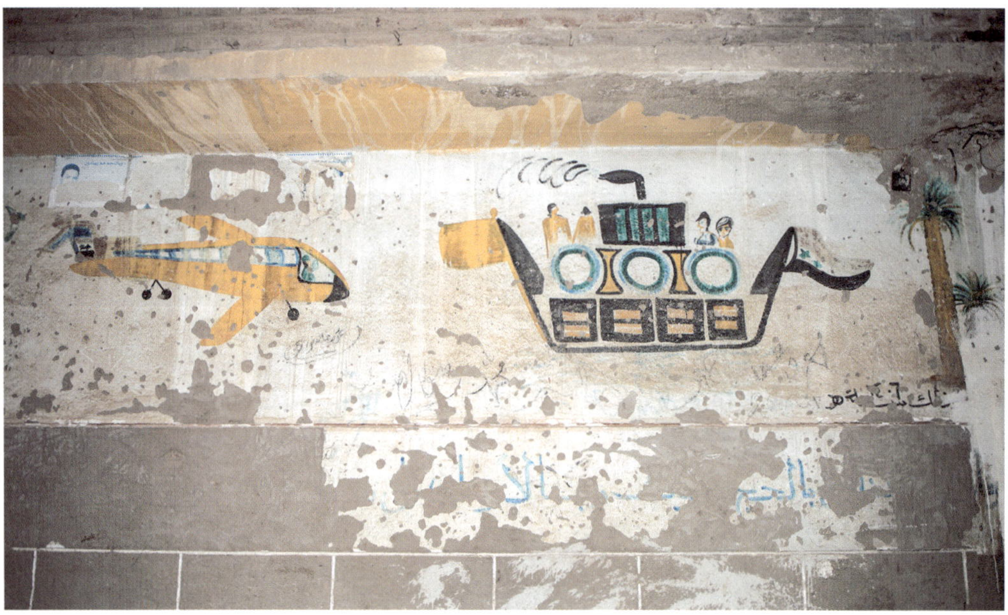

EL-GHABAT 8

Catalog of Selected Graffiti at El-Kurru

Funerary Temple Ku. 1500

Descriptions by Suzanne Davis & Geoff Emberling

Pyramid Ku. 1

Descriptions by Bruce Beyer Williams

Introduction

The following catalog presents a representative selection of Meroitic and medieval graffiti from the funerary temple (Ku. 1500) and pyramid (Ku. 1) at El-Kurru. All the graffiti will be published in the forthcoming final report on the El-Kurru excavations. A concordance at the end of the catalog links these catalog numbers with their entries in the El-Kurru research database, where they are listed by their graffito ID number. Note also that these graffiti can be explored via the website for the exhibition *Graffiti as Devotion along the Nile: El-Kurru Sudan* (http://exhibitions.kelsey.lsa.umich.edu/graffiti-el-kurru), and most catalog entries on the website include an interactive viewer for the reflectance transformation imaging (RTI) files.

Incised graffiti are surprisingly difficult to photograph. Photography with strong side-lighting will make some lines very clear while minimizing others. It can also give the impression of lines that do not actually exist — lines that seem to be part of the graffito but which are, instead, just natural contours or weathering of the rock. Photography in the temple at El-Kurru is further complicated by the difficulty posed by graffiti on curved surfaces, such as the columns, and in the tight spaces that occur between columns and between columns and the surrounding wall. To address these challenges, graffiti projects often use multiple documentation strategies. At El-Kurru, graffiti have been documented with various techniques including 3D photo-modeling, reflectance transformation imaging, and strong side-light from the sun. In the following catalog, we have tried to choose the image that shows the graffito best, and readers will see images generated by each of the above techniques. For very worn graffiti, the image often comes from the RTI file. RTI images can appear dark, but they often show eroded graffiti well.

The color of the images in this catalog also varies. Sandstone at El-Kurru can be pale buff, gold, or rose-gold in color, and the appearance of the stone also varies based on the time of day, appearing rosier in the early morning and more golden in the late afternoon.

Another challenge at El-Kurru is that many graffiti can occupy the same surface, with some carved into and over others, resulting in a confusing jumble of images. As with photography of graffiti, archaeological projects deal with this difficulty in different ways, sometimes recording single graffiti and sometimes recording instead by masonry unit, such as a block or column drum. In the following catalog, our descriptions focus on single graffiti and we attempt to disentangle and distinguish them from their neighbors. When it is especially difficult to discern a graffito from surrounding images, we have placed a marker around it.

Location information is included for each graffito. A P prefix is given to graffiti on the pyramid, and T to those on the temple. Within the temple, alphanumeric codes are used to indicate the specific masonry unit that contains the graffito. For example, "A" indicates a column surface, a number indicates which column, and another number indicates the drum. So A03-3 means a graffito is on column three, third drum. H03-1, on the other hand, indicates a location on wall face H, course 3, block 1. Please see the plan of the temple with walls and columns labeled (FIG. C.1). For each graffito, we have also indicated the direction it faces — a key piece of information for finding the graffiti on site, especially when they appear on columns.[1]

1. Pyramid Ku. 1 and funerary temple Ku. 1500 are not perfectly aligned with the cardinal points. Therefore what in this catalog is called "north" in relation to these structures is actually north-northeast, "south" is south-southwest, "east" is east-southeast, and "west" is west-northwest.

Funerary Temple Ku. 1500

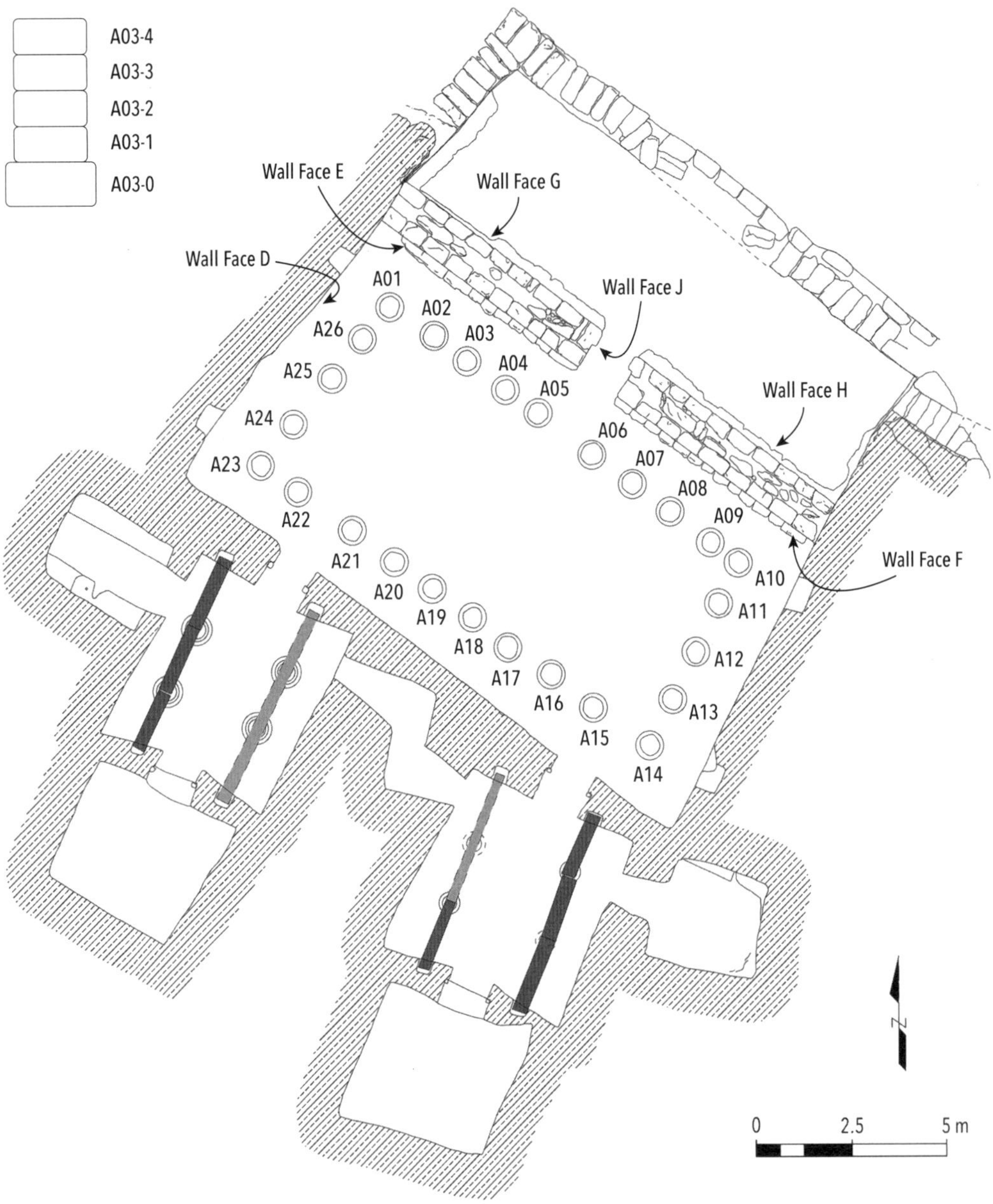

FIGURE C.1. Plan of funerary temple Ku. 1500 with walls and columns labeled. Note that only those walls that bear graffiti featured in this catalog are labeled. At upper left is a diagram of a column (not to scale) showing how the drums are numbered.
Base plan: Jack Cheng and Martin Uildriks / IKAP, 2015

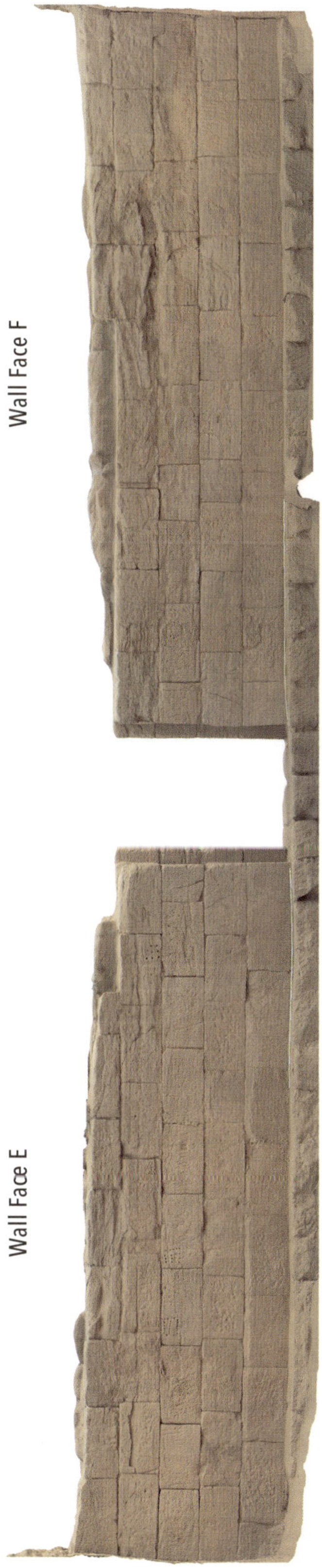

FIGURE C.2. Wall faces E and F.
Photo model: Nadejda Reshetnikova / IKAP, 2019

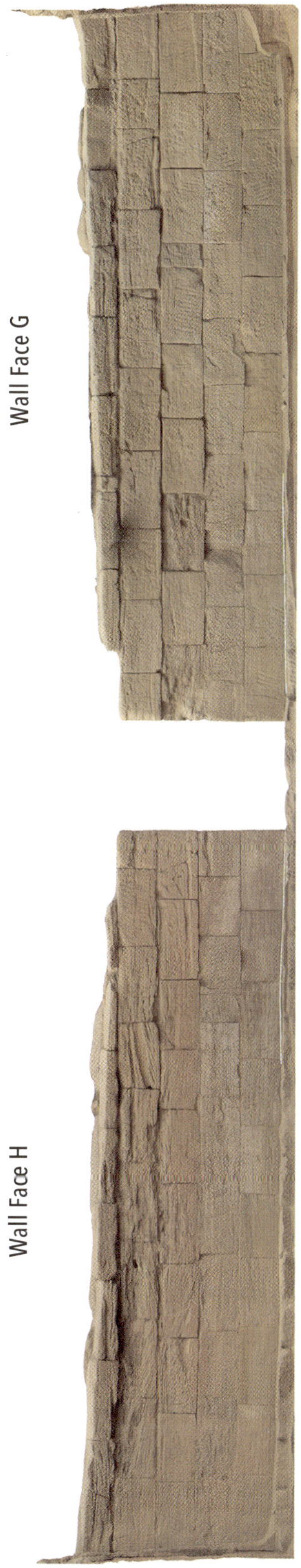

FIGURE C.3. Wall faces H and G.
Photo model: Nadejda Reshetnikova / IKAP, 2019

HUMAN FIGURES

Graffito T1
Human – Figure with Bow

Location: Column A07-3:3, northeast face

Dimensions (H × W): 40 × 23 cm

The large, elongated figure of an archer is shown in the foreground. Striding to the right, the figure holds a bow out in front of his body. The outline of a smaller, similar figure can be seen between the archer's body and the bow. Although the surface is worn, details of the main figure's kilt are still visible. The top surface of this column is very eroded, and the archer's head has been lost.

Archers are commonly represented in rock art, sometimes singly, but often in scenes of hunting (e.g., Červíček 1974, figs. 23, 69, 151, 161) or warfare (e.g., Červíček 1974, figs. 153, 219, 220), the latter sometimes wearing a single feather on their head, as is common in representations of Kushite warriors.

See Also: Hellström 1970 v. 1:2, corpus A210–269.

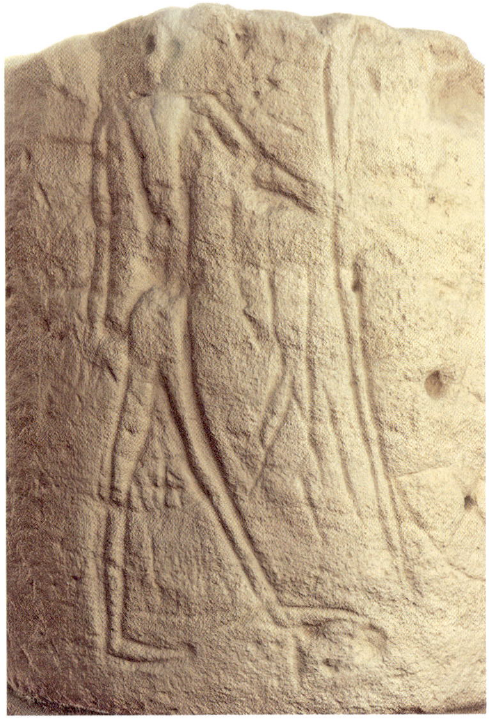

Graffito T2
Humans

Location: Column A03-3:1, west face

Dimensions (H × W): 12.0 × 9.5 cm (lower human)

This image shows a scene with at least two humans carved in outline: one at the upper left (head now worn away) and one at the lower center. Both are indicated with legs striding, or perhaps in an archer's stance. Geometric shapes appear to the lower left and upper right.

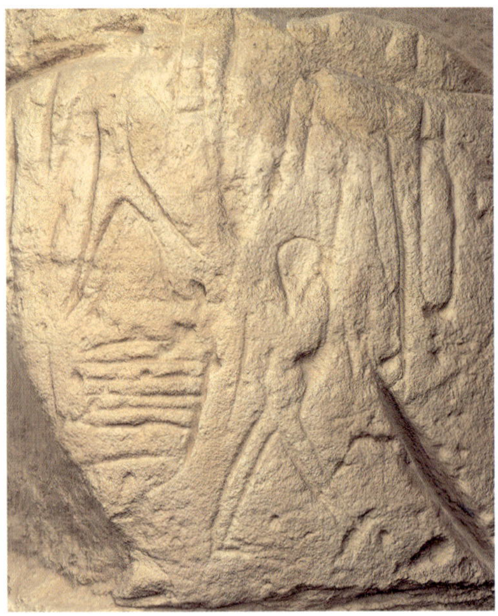

Graffito T3
Human

Location: Column A26-3:1, southeast face

Dimensions (H × W): 28 × 9 cm

This tall, thin human figure is shown facing right. It is carved with simple vertical lines indicating the legs, torso, arms, and neck. Short horizontal lines indicate the shoulders and feet. The head is a shallow circular depression. A short diagonal line at the figure's waist may indicate a weapon held in the proper right hand.

See Also: Hellström 1970 v. 1:2, corpus A282–300.

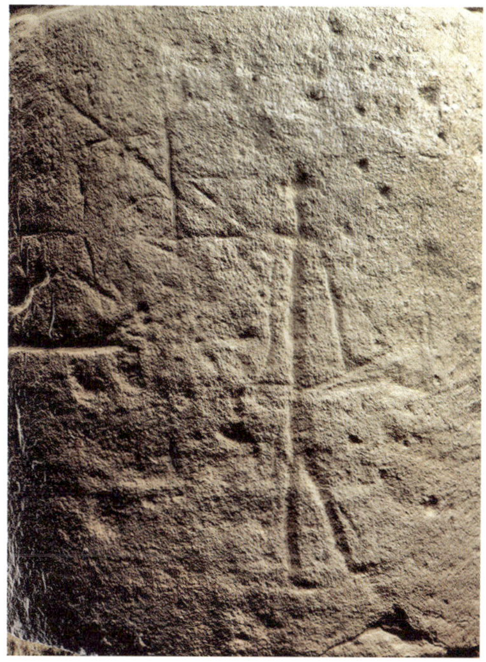

Graffito T4
Human

Location: Column A18-3:1, northeast face

Dimensions (H × W): 25.5 × 12.0 cm

Although very worn, this graffito has a human shape, with a long neck, broad shoulders and torso, and long legs extending to feet that point to the right. The large, butterfly-shaped design over the torso is similar to graffito T50 and might indicate a shield or some other equipment or special clothing worn over the front of the body.

See Also: Hellström 1970 v. 1:2, corpus A1–10.

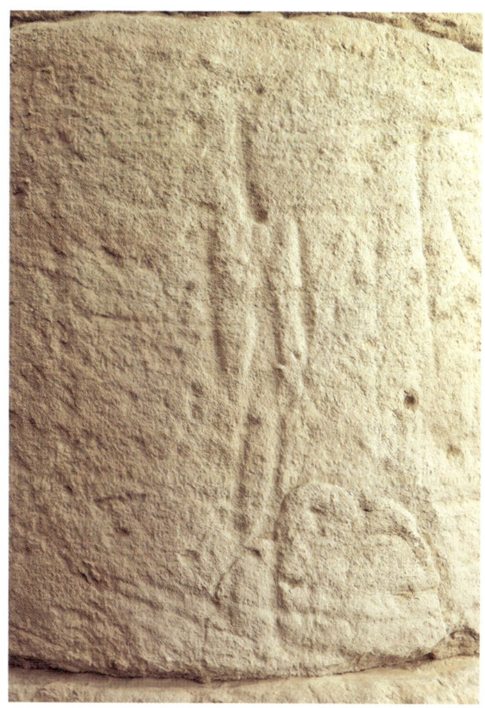

Graffito T5
Human

Location: Column A17-3:2, northwest face

Dimensions (H × W): 12 × 7 cm

This extremely stylized design has clear similarities to human figures in rock art from the area of the 2nd Cataract.

See Also: Hellström 1970 v. 1:2, corpus A16–19 and A152–153.

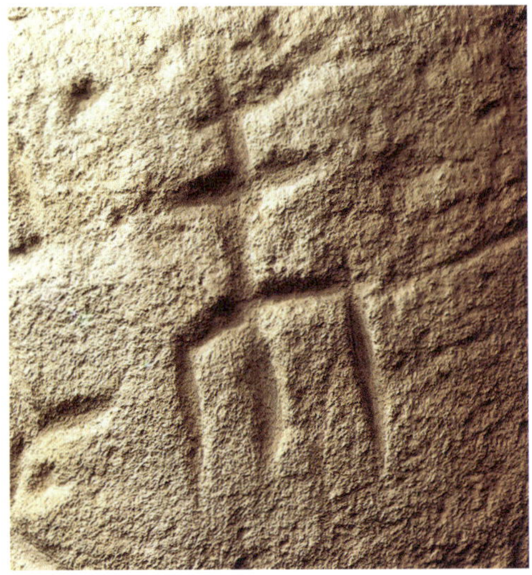

Graffito T6
Human – In Worshiping Posture

Location: Wall face E03-1:2

Dimensions (H × W): 15 × 9 cm

In the top center of this block a faint graffito shows a human figure standing in a worshiping pose with arms outstretched. To the left, an even fainter, blocky figure can be seen. Facing left on the block, this figure holds one arm outward, bent at the elbow. A sash or other design crosses the body diagonally from proper left hip to proper right shoulder. A collection of linear designs to the right of the worshiping figures may also represent humans, since there are similarities with rock art from farther north in Nubia (see Hellström 1970 v. 1:2, corpus A17–19).

See Also: Hellström 1970 v. 1:2, corpus A157–160.

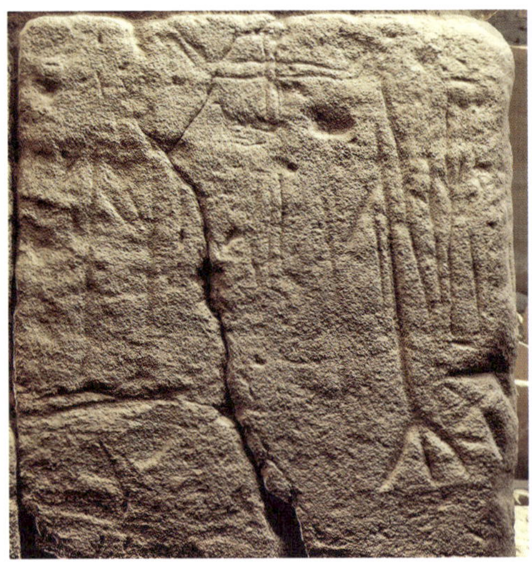

Graffito T7
Human

Location: Column A03-3:7, southeast face

Dimensions (H × W): 20 × 10 cm

To the left, a blocky design of stacked Xs in boxes appears to have a curved arm, suggesting that this might represent a human figure. It is shown next to a horned altar (T27) and seems to be part of a scene that includes a third geometric graffito to the right (T49).

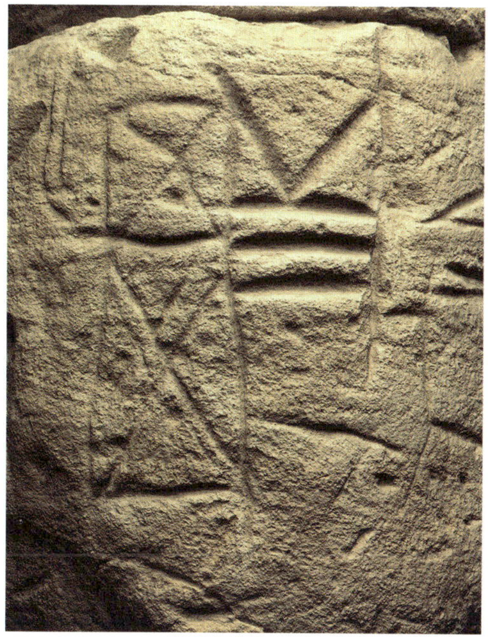

Graffito T8
Human — Seated, Possibly with Staff or Scepter

Location: Wall face G04-10:1

Dimensions (H × W): 32 × 14 cm

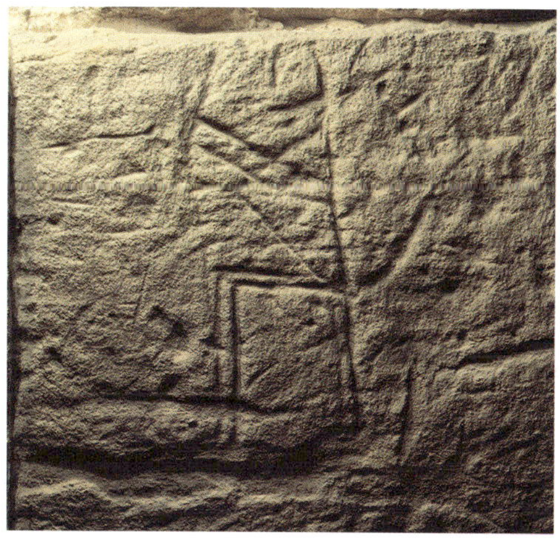

This graffito shows a human, facing left, seated on a bench or stool. The head is outlined, and the arms and legs are described with simple lines. The figure holds a staff or scepter in both hands.

Seated figures are rare in rock art and graffiti, and it is not clear whether this figure would be more likely to represent a ruler or a deity. If a deity, then the god Ptah is the most likely candidate, as he is often depicted holding a staff or scepter in each hand. Ptah, as the patron deity of the Egyptian city of Memphis, was not worshiped in temples in Kush. However, during Kushite control over Egypt as Egypt's 25th Dynasty (744–656 BCE), the Kushite king Shabaqo installed a stone in the temple of Ptah in Memphis. The inscription, known as the Shabaqo stone, describes Ptah as the creator god (see Morkot 2000, pp. 217–18).

Graffito T9
Human – Rider on Horse

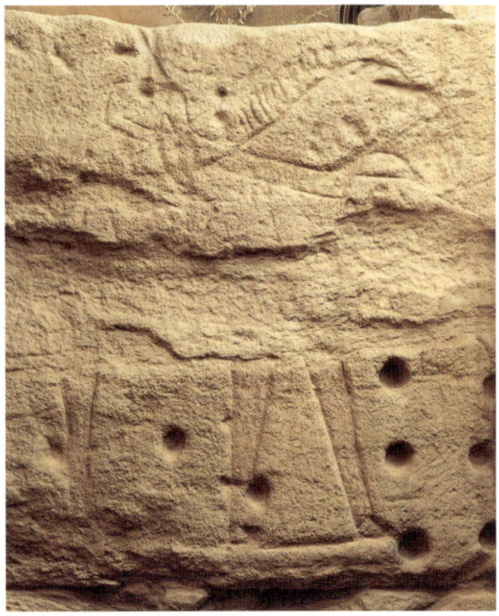

Location: Wall face E04-2:5

Dimensions (H × W): 30 × 22 cm

This was once one of the most elaborate and carefully carved graffiti in the funerary temple. It is now unfortunately damaged by a horizontal band of erosion, undoubtedly from repeated flooding from the nearby wadi. The image is difficult to read at first glance, but it depicts a rider on a horse.

The rider is at top center, with head damaged, but twisted shoulders and the right elbow are clearly visible. A row of short, vertical lines extending up and to the right indicates the horse's mane, and the horse's muzzle is at the upper right. A broad bridle with geometric decoration extends from the muzzle back to the rider. Two of the horse's forelegs and one back leg can be seen extending down. The horse's head and legs are stylized, with the proportions not quite realistic, and the knee or ankle joints are not indicated in the legs. The legs are carved in bas relief and appear to have reddish pigment in them. The upper part of the graffito is incised.

Horses, both with and without riders, are represented in rock art and at other sites with graffiti. In the context of the temple at El-Kurru, we might assume that this image represents a pilgrim and his means of transportation.

Graffito T10
Human – Rider on Quadruped

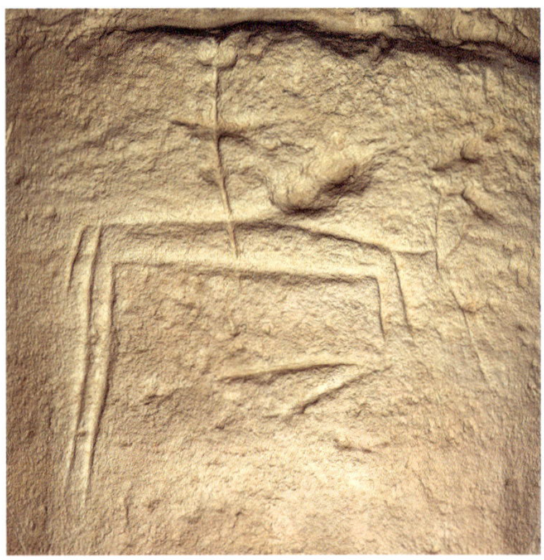

Location: Column A15-3:2, south face

Dimensions (H × W): 26 × 27 cm

This stylized quadruped is shown leaping, a human rider on its back. The human figure has a circular depression or gouge for the head, and a vertical line indicating the neck and torso. The bent, right arm extends behind the figure. The left arm has been lost due to erosion in the rock, and only the faintest trace of the legs is visible. The animal's oval head is outlined, and the body is indicated by two horizontal lines, each of which extends to form the front and back legs. A short vertical line indicates the tail. Although this graffito could be intended to represent a horse, the animal's long body and short tail might also indicate a donkey. Donkeys or asses were domesticated 6,000 years ago and were important in ancient Kush and Egypt (royal donkeys were even buried with one of the early kings of Egypt at Abydos; see Rossel et al. 2008), and they continue to be valuable commodities in Sudanese farming communities like El-Kurru.

See Also: Winkler 1939, pl. II, 2.; Hellström 1970 v. 1:2, corpus B9–15.

ANIMALS AND PLANTS

Graffito T11
Animal - Ram of Amun

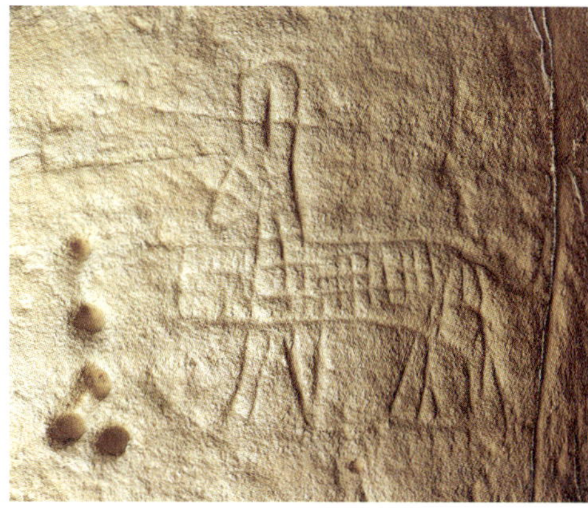

Location: Column A09-3:1, east face

Dimensions (H × W): 15 × 17 cm

A ram, highly significant in ancient Kush as the animal of the Kushite form of the god Amun, whose temple was in nearby Napata (modern Jebel Barkal). Amun of Napata was ram-headed and the processional entrance to his temple was lined with pairs of carved stone rams. By contrast, Amun of Karnak (in Egypt) was human-headed. The ram depicted above wears the double crown of Amun.

The body of this ram is decorated with hatch marks, probably meant to indicate fleece. The forelegs are outlined and the back legs indicated with multiple vertical lines. The chest extends past the head; the lines here are fainter and may indicate a proportional mistake by the carver, which was "fixed" by carving the rest of the body more deeply once the head was added. Alternatively, this extended area of carving could be meant to indicate an object in proximity to the ram.

Graffito T12
Animal - Bull Heads with Hooves

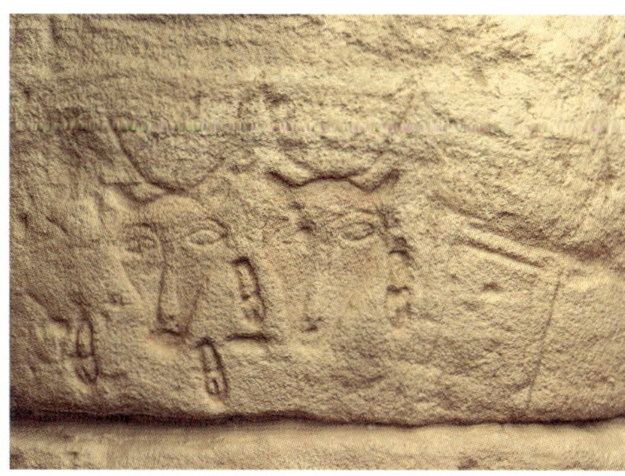

Location: Column A04-3:1, northeast face

Dimensions (H × W): 13.5 × 23.5 cm

Two small, horned cattle heads with narrow, elongated noses and human eyes. The heads are surrounded by four tiny, hoofed feet. A small square shape to the right may represent an altar or an offering table, albeit without a spout. It may also represent an enclosure.

The supernatural character of these beings comes from their combination of human and animal characteristics and from the frontal representation of their faces. Slightly demonic frontal faces also appear in Meroitic painted pottery (Adams 1986, p. 283; for date of "Style N.IA," see p. 239). For a frontal image of a bovine in rock art, see Winkler 1938, pl. VI.

Graffito T13
Animal – Horse

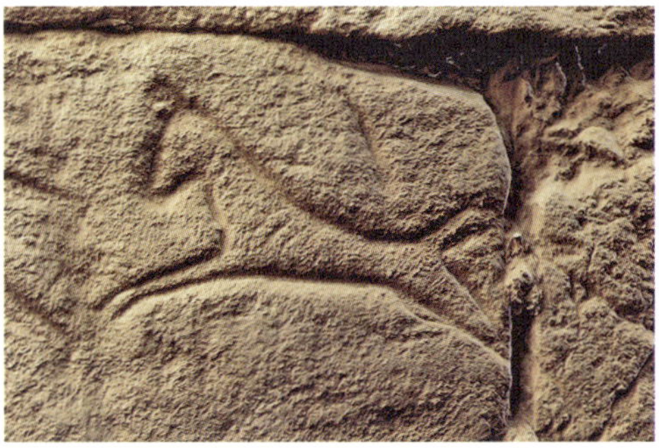

Location: Wall face E03-5:1

Dimensions (H × W): 9.0 × 14.5 cm

This horse is depicted in mid-gallop with deeply incised lines. It is outlined with careful attention to detail, and three small, curved lines on the upper body may indicate a rider, although this figure would have been carved very shallowly since no other traces remain. This horse is the rightmost in a group of three animals that includes another horse (T14) and a bird (T22) (see **FIGS. 2.13, 4.7**).

See Also: Hellström 1970 v. 1:2, corpus B5.

Graffito T14
Animal – Horse

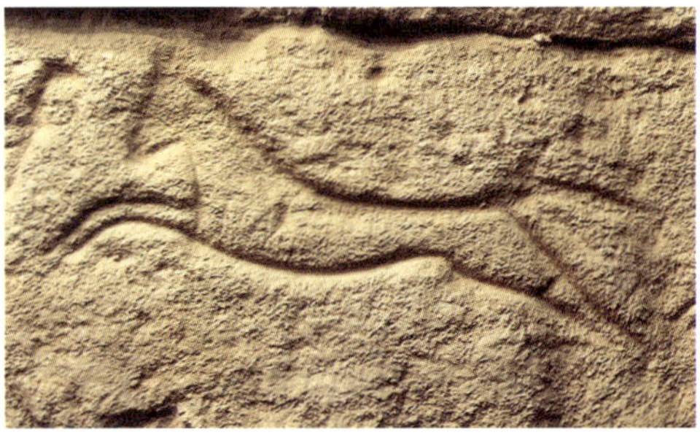

Location: Wall face E03-5:2

Dimensions (H × W): 10 × 23 cm

This horse forms a pair with the previous entry (T13). Like its partner, it is carefully carved and is shown mid-gallop, with its tail flying behind. Although not shown in this photo, a bird (T22) — depicted at a much larger scale than the horses — appears to the left (see **FIGS. 2.13, 4.7**).

See Also: Hellström 1970 v. 1:2, corpus B1–8.

Graffito T15
Animal – Giraffe

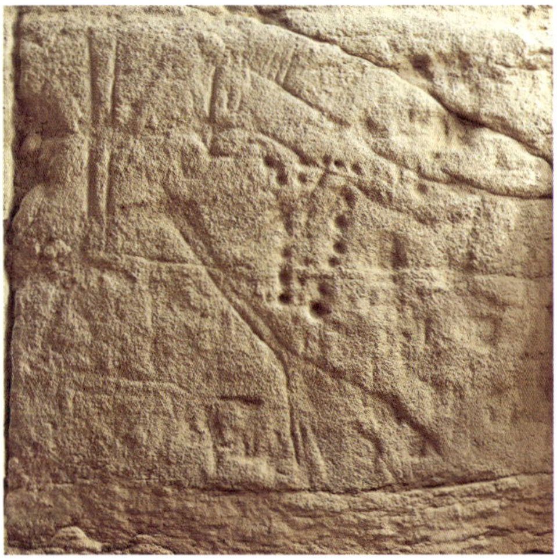

Location: Wall face E04-3:1

Dimensions (H × W): 18.5 × 20.5 cm

This giraffe graffito, likely Meroitic in date, occupies the left central area of the block on which it is carved. Facing left, it is carved in simple outline, with a long neck extending upward. Faint lines for the legs and tail are worn, but can still be seen extending down from the body. The head is indicated with a shallow depression, but the rock is eroded in this area and any finer details have been lost. Marks to the lower left may indicate other, smaller animals accompanying the giraffe. Above the giraffe, the head and neck of another creature can be seen. This animal is carved at a much larger scale, but could be another giraffe, with a long neck, short face and muzzle (as compared to a horse), and short hatch marks at the back of the head, which could indicate the giraffe's ears and horns. The rest of this other animal's body has been lost.

Giraffes are common in rock art of the Middle Nile, but their significance is elusive. It is not clear, for example, that graffiti or rock art representations of giraffes can be taken as evidence that giraffes lived near the place of representation when the image was made. Images of giraffes might instead reference folktales or be meant to represent what Kleinitz termed "the symbolic universe of the Meroitic world" when discussing such graffiti at Musawwarat es-Sufra (Kleinitz 2014, p. 100).

See Also: Hellström 1970 v. 1:2, corpus K1–113; Otto and Buschendorf-Otto 1993, pp. 258–69, 347–57.

Graffito T16
Animal - Giraffes

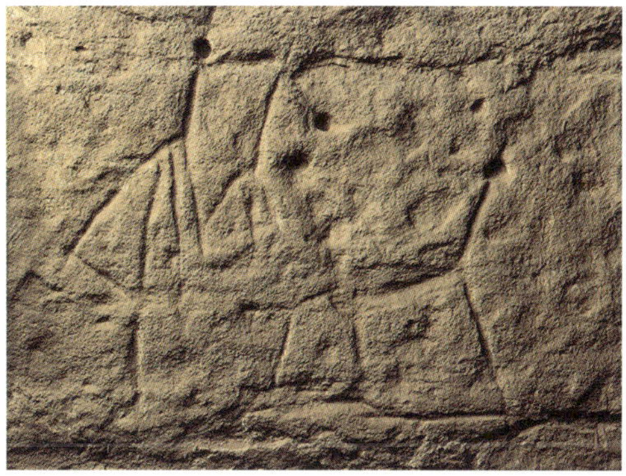

Location: Wall face F03-2:1

Dimensions (H × W): 26 × 31 cm

Another example of giraffes, showing three animals together. This group is carved more simply than the previous examples, with angled lines for neck, body, and legs. The heads are indicated with small, drilled depressions.

Graffito T17
Animal - Gazelle

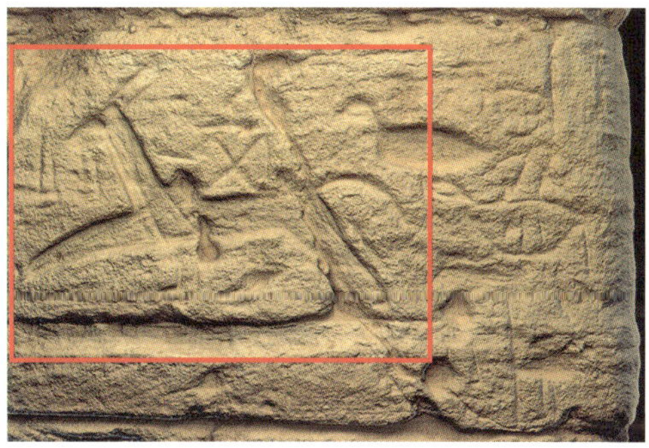

Location: Wall face H03-1:2

Dimensions (H × W): 21 × 39 cm

This running gazelle, carved in bas-relief, is depicted with straight horns and a long curved tail. An X-in-box is immediately above its back (T44), and two birds are shown to the right.

See Also: For a very wide variety of antelopes, see Hellström 1970 v. 1:2, corpus L1–227; although categorized as a "dog chasing hare" motif, graffito 304_301W.144 in the Musawwarat Graffiti Archive looks very similar to the gazelle shown here.

Graffito T18
Animal - Dog Chasing a Hare

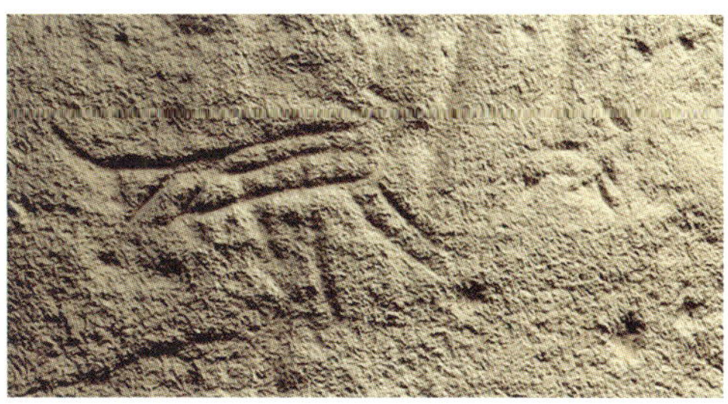

Location: Column A07-3:6, northwest face

Dimensions (H × W): 6.0 × 8.5 cm

This graffito and T19 are difficult to read, but they are intended to represent a dog chasing a hare. The larger animal — the dog — is at left, chasing the hare which races to escape at right. This is perhaps a strange scene to find in a temple setting, but the fact that it is represented at least twice here (and seven times at Musawwarat es-Sufra) suggests that it had some broader significance. It has been proposed that images of this kind may represent scenes from the myths or folk tales of ancient Kush (Hofmann 1988).

See Also: Musawwarat Graffiti Archive.

Graffito T19
Animal – Dog Chasing a Hare

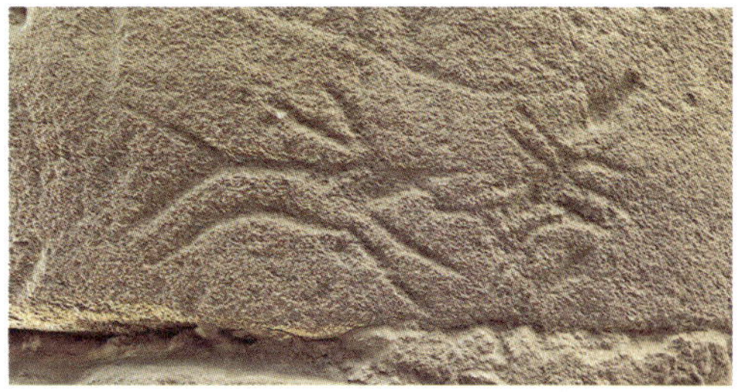

Location: Column A01-3:4, northeast face

Dimensions (H × W): 5.5 × 14.0 cm

In this version of the dog-chasing-hare scene, the lines describing the dog are much clearer, although the small hare — at right — remains difficult to distinguish.

See Also: For dogs, see Hellström 1970 v. 1:2, corpus E1–59.

Graffito T20
Animal – Quadruped

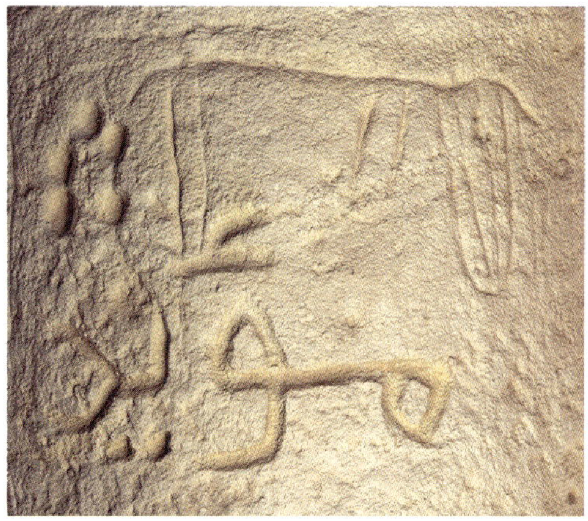

Location: Column A12-3:3, northwest face

Dimensions (H × W): 12 × 22 cm

An unknown quadruped facing right. This animal has an unusually long head decorated with vertical lines. With short legs, a long body, and short tail, it may be meant to represent a donkey, but this animal also resembles rock art depictions of hippopotami and pigs (see Hellström 1970 v. 1:2, corpus H1–I4). Below the ancient graffito, a recent Arabic inscription spells the name Muwayyid.

Graffito T21
Animal – Quadrupeds

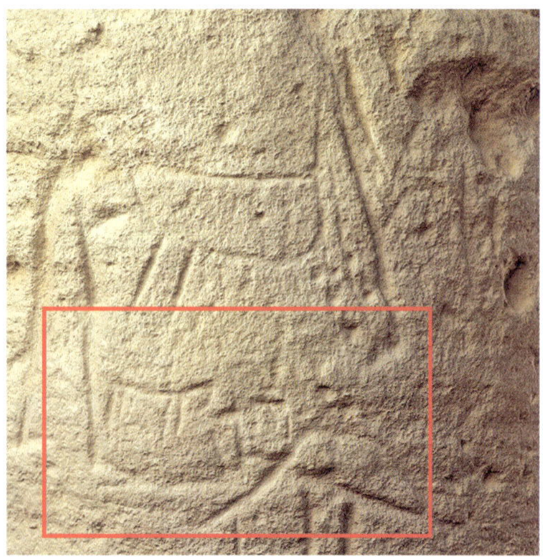

Location: Column A17-3:1, northeast face

Dimensions (H × W): 10 × 15 cm

This scene shows a few small animals — perhaps dogs (see Hellström 1970 v. 1:2, corpus E1–59) — below a larger boat graffito of a boat (T35).

Graffito T22
Animal - Bird

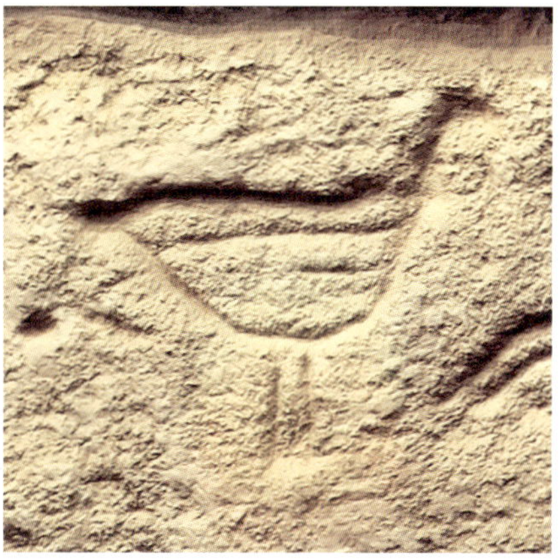

Location: Wall face E03-5:3

Dimensions (H × W): 8.5 × 9.0 cm

Birds are one of the more common images among the graffiti at El-Kurru, with at least thirteen bird graffiti in the temple, but it is not entirely clear which species is intended. They are certainly not ostriches or birds of prey and they do not appear to be ducks or geese. Rather, with legs that are sometimes short and sometimes long when extended, their plump bodies, narrow heads, and down-turned tail feathers, they seem most likely to be guinea fowl, which are more clearly represented on Meroitic ceramic decoration (see, e.g., Adams 1986, fig. 105). Like the images of dogs chasing hares (T18–T19), the ubiquity of this likely domesticated bird in graffiti has led some scholars to think that they must have figured in the folk tales of ancient Kush (Hofmann 1988).

See Also: Hellström 1970 v. 1:2, corpus Q101–109.

Graffito T23
Animal - Birds

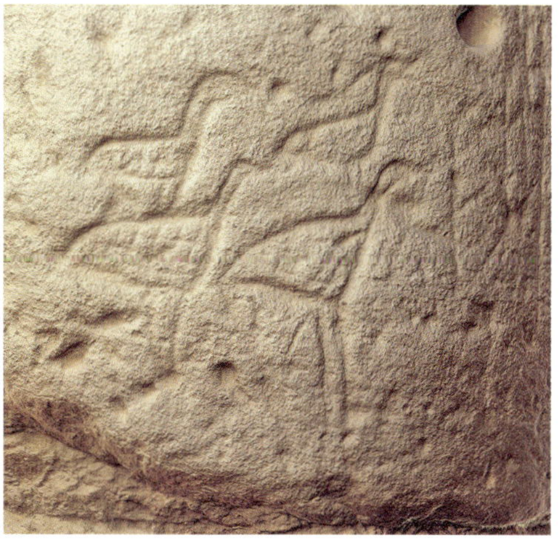

Location: Column A21-3:2, northwest face

Dimensions (H × W): 20 × 20 cm

Here, four birds are represented together as a group. A delicate crosshatch pattern on their bodies indicates their feathered texture.

Graffito T24
Animal - Birds

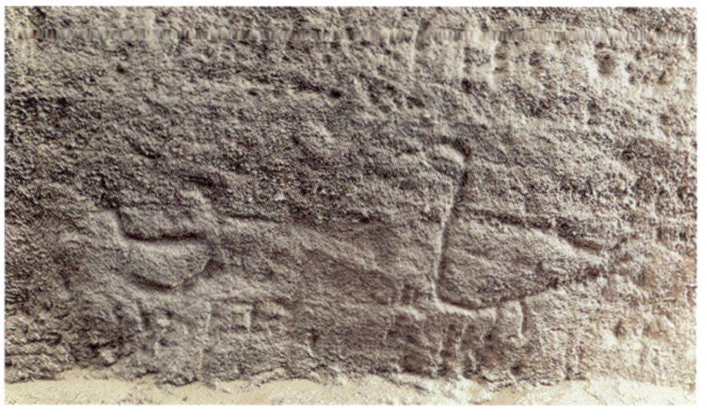

Location: Wall face D:1

Dimensions (H × W): 28 × 72 cm

Difficult to make out, these three birds are the only graffiti in the temple that are carved on the rough rock-cut walls of what was originally the quarry, rather than being on the shaped and smoothed columns or the built stone wall dividing the two outer rooms. They are also significantly larger than the other examples of bird graffiti in the temple.

Graffito T25
Animal – Horned Viper

Location: Wall face F03-2:2

Dimensions (H × W): 9 × 9 cm

The horned viper is a poisonous snake that lives in northern Sudan and Egypt. It is a hieroglyphic sign for the sound "f" in Egyptian writing and because of its deadly nature, the sign was sometimes "killed" in monumental writing by showing the body separated into two parts.

See Also: Hellström 1970 v. 1:2, corpus S1–10.

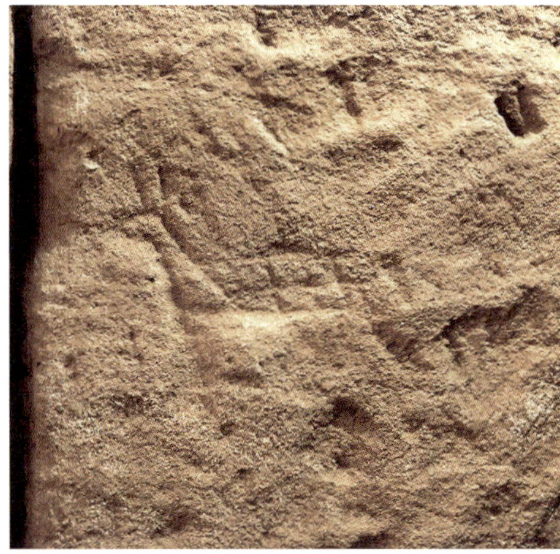

Graffito T26
Plant – Papyrus Frond or Lotus Bud

Location: Wall face E04-2:3

Dimensions (H × W): 12 × 12 cm

This worn graffito shows a papyrus frond or lotus bud. It is one of only three identifiable plant graffiti in the temple. The other two — both palm fronds — are carved alongside depictions of offering tables (T28 and T29).

See Also: Hellström 1970 v. 1:2, corpus U6 and U8.

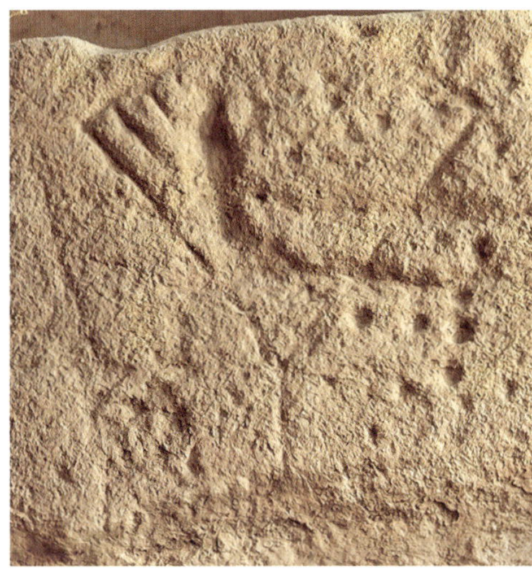

OBJECTS AND ARCHITECTURE

Altars and Offering Tables

Graffito T27
Object – Horned Altar

Location: Column A03-3:8, southeast face

Dimensions (H × W): 22 × 9 cm

Slightly to the right of center is a horned altar, a type of altar common in Ptolemaic Egypt (both as images and as physical altars) and also in the eastern Mediterranean. They were used to burn offerings to the gods, and their presence here shows the ritual nature of the temple graffiti. To the left, a blocky design of stacked Xs in boxes (T7) may represent a human figure. To the right, an enigmatic geometric graffito (T49) also seems to be part of this scene.

See Also: Winkler 1938, pl. IV, 2; Váhala and Červíček 1999, pl. 2; Rose 2007, fig. 18.3.

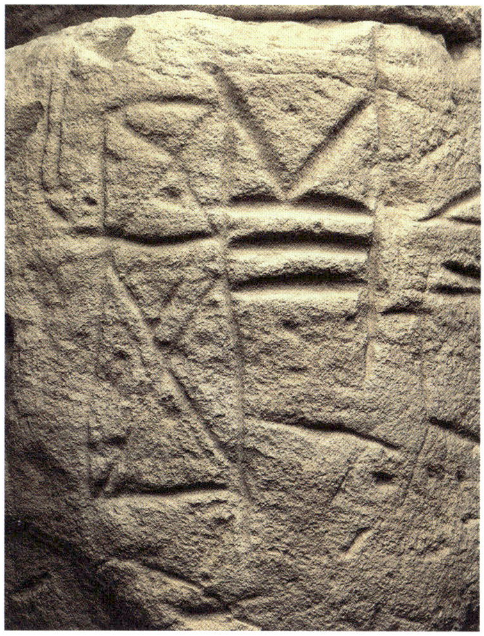

Graffito T28
Object – Offering Table with Palm Frond

Location: Column A05-2:7 (fallen drum)

Dimensions (H × W): 7.5 × 10.0 cm (offering table only)

This column shows two juxtaposed images that also occur together elsewhere in the temple (see T29): a palm frond to the left and, to the right, a square offering table, with a spout facing down. Offering tables were commonly placed outside tombs for visitors to pour liquid offerings to sustain the spirits of the deceased (see **FIG. 1.7**).

See Also: Váhala and Červíček 1999, pl. 2:6.

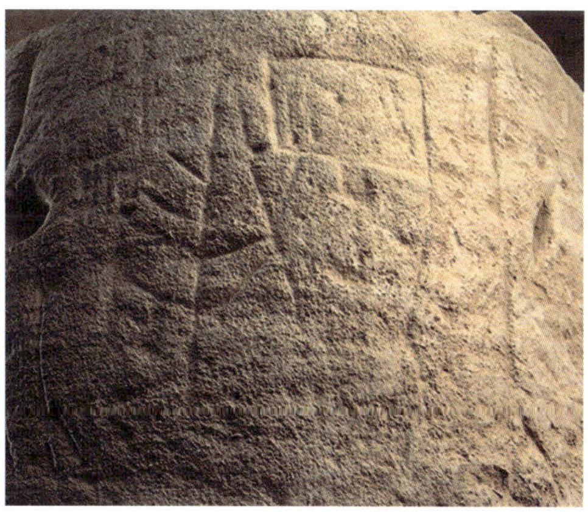

Graffito T29
Object – Offering Table with Palm Frond

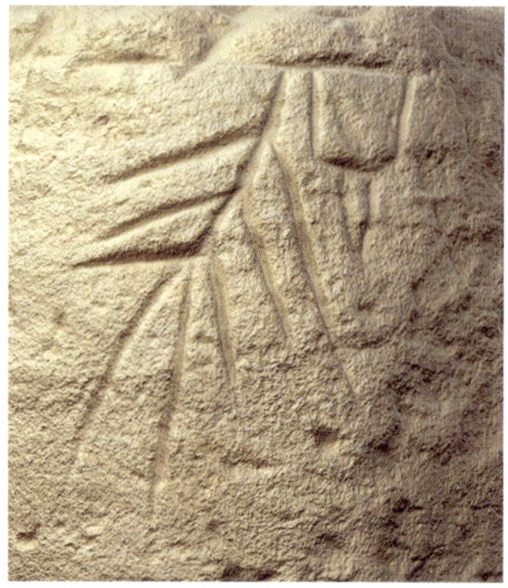

Location: Column A20-3:2, southeast face

Dimensions (H × W): 22.5 × 19.0 cm

This second example of a juxtaposed palm frond and offering table is less skillfully carved, but the imagery is clear. Unlike in graffito T28, the frond points downward.

Graffito T30
Object – Offering Table

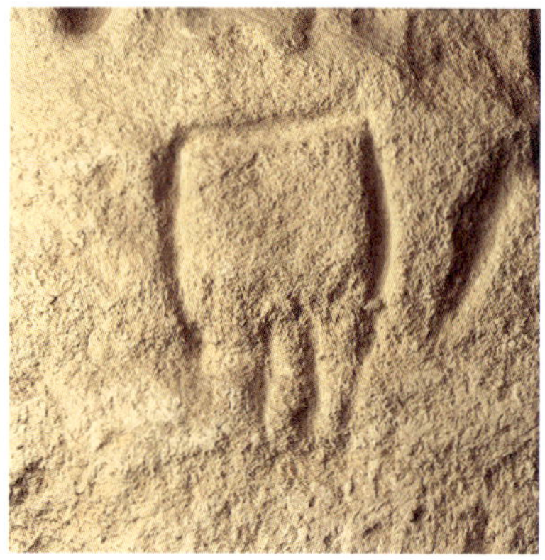

Location: Column A04-3:9, south face

Dimensions (H × W): 13 × 16 cm

This simple version of an offering table is the third example in the temple, and the only one to appear without an accompanying palm frond.

Boats

Graffito T31
Object – Boat

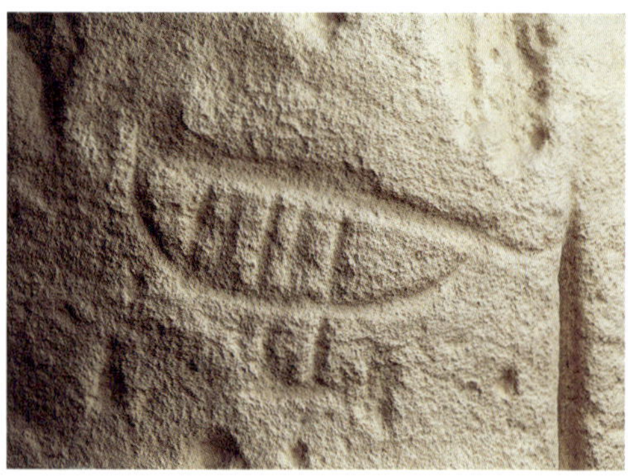

Location: Column A16-3:1, north face

Dimensions (H × W): 10.0 × 14.5 cm

Boats are common in rock art, less common in Meroitic graffiti but more common in medieval Christian graffiti, with later boats often being more elaborate. This image seems to depict a small boat with a rounded hull and five oars per side.

See Also: Hellström 1970 v. 1:2, corpus V1–69.

Graffito T32
Object – Boats

Location: Column A24-3:1, north face

Dimensions (H × W): 16 × 22 cm

These graffiti appear to depict two sailing boats with tall masts, indicated simply with a few faint lines.

See Also: Hellström 1970 v. 1:2, corpus V1–69.

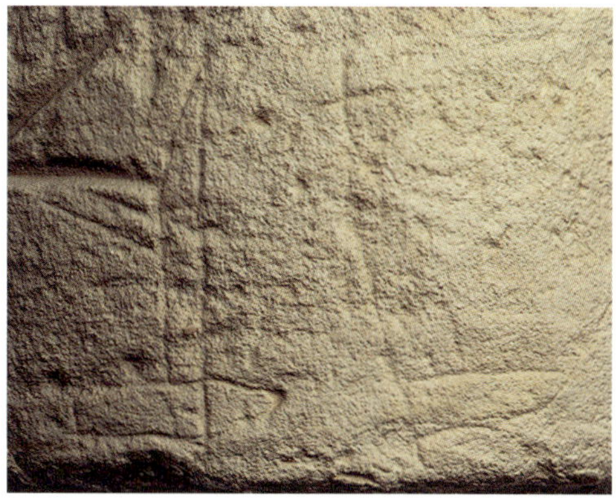

Graffito T33
Object – Boat

Location: Column A24-3:6, east face

Dimensions (H × W): 16 × 23 cm

This is a common type of boat depicted with a curved hull, a mast and sail in the center, and a cabin (indicated with vertical lines) and a steering oar at the stern (left side).

See Also: Hellström 1970 v. 1:2, corpus V1–10.

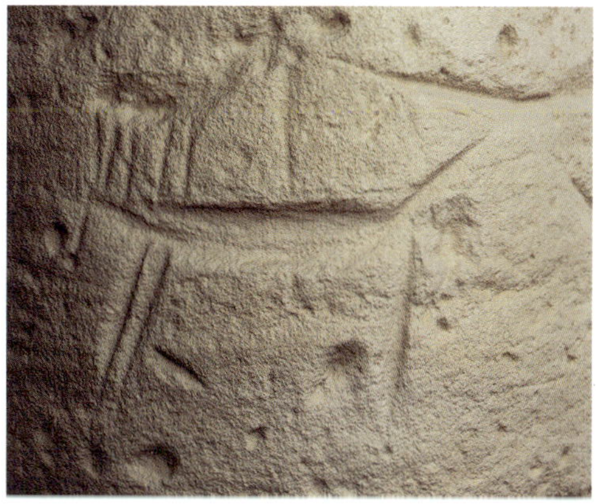

Graffito T34
Object – Boat

Location: Column A06-2:3, north face

Dimensions (H × W): 5.0 × 5.5 cm

This is a flat boat with a high bow (at right). It likely would have had a high stern but the abrasion of the stone has effaced it. In the center of the boat is a cabin; two oars are indicated at the stern (at left).

See Also: Hellström 1970 v. 1:2, corpus V32–39.

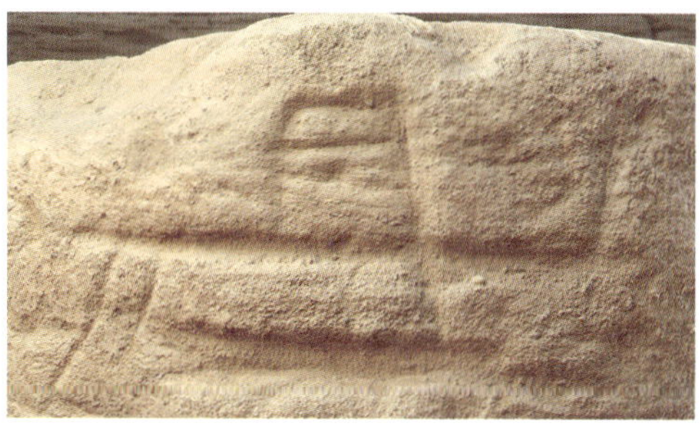

Graffito T35
Object – Boat

Location: Column A17-3:1, northeast face

Dimensions (H × W): 15 × 20 cm

A boat with a high bow at right and two oars near the stern (left side). A few small animals (T22) are depicted beneath the boat.

See Also: Hellström 1970 v. 1:2, corpus V30–42.

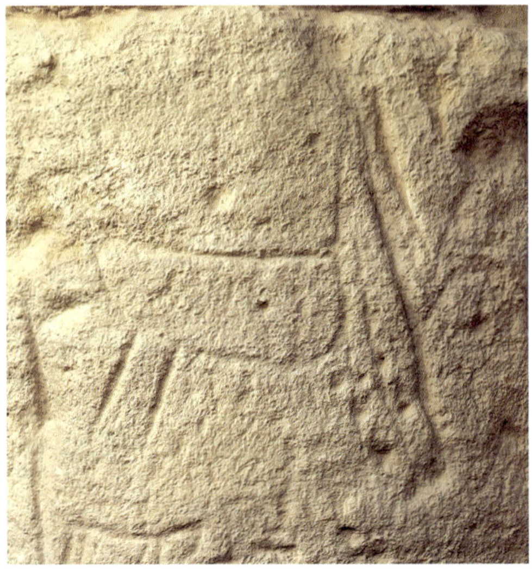

Textiles

Graffito T36
Object – Textile

Location: Column A07-3:1, west face

Dimensions (H × W): 31 × 15 cm (each "face" of the textile)

There are seven images of what appear to be textiles or mats in the temple. Three of these are elaborate, with woven interiors and fringes at top and bottom. One attractive suggestion is that these might represent prayer mats, whether Islamic or otherwise. This example seems to show two textiles side by side and joined along the center edge. These are depicted with a three-dimensional perspective as if they formed the front and side of a box or palanquin.

See Also: Winkler 1939, pls. XXXIX–XL, which depict seated women wearing dresses with fringes. Also Váhala and Červíček 1999, pl. 69:268, 9. Pope (this volume) compares T36, T37, and T38 to graffiti of flags at Philae (**FIGS. 5.4–5**).

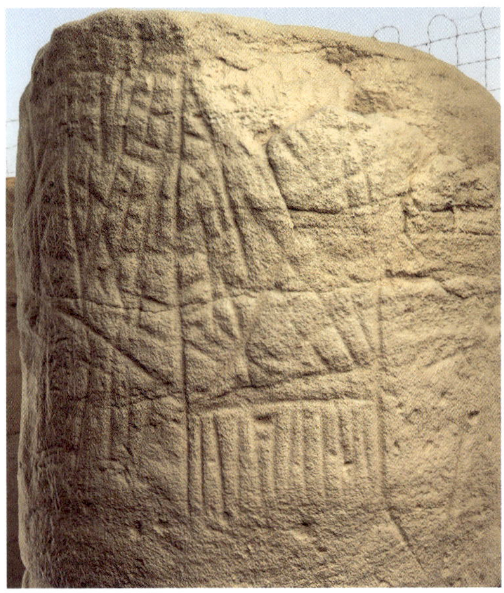

Graffito T37
Object – Textile

Location: Column A14-3:1, south face

Dimensions (H × W): 25.0 × 16.5 cm

This textile or mat has an intricate design in the central field, a patterned top border, fringe at the top and bottom, and tassels at the corner edges of the top.

See Also: Pope (this volume) compares T36, T37, and T38 to graffiti of flags at Philae (**FIGS. 5.4–5**).

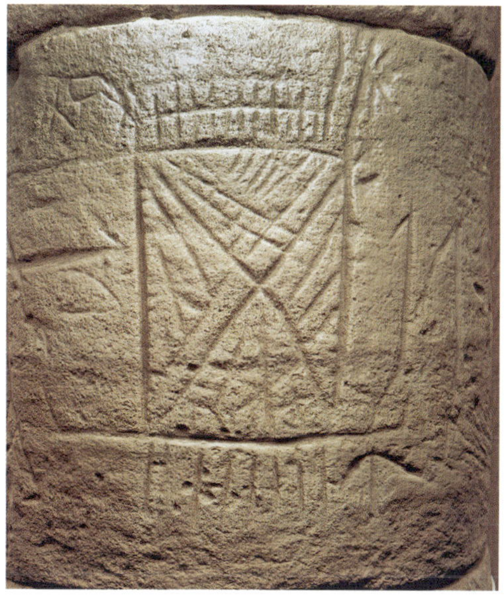

Graffito T38
Object – Textile

Location: Column A14-3:2, northwest face

Dimensions (H × W): 30 × 18

This large example is worn, but very similar in design to T37.

See Also: Pope (this volume) compares T36, T37, and T38 to graffiti of flags at Philae (**FIGS. 5.4–5**).

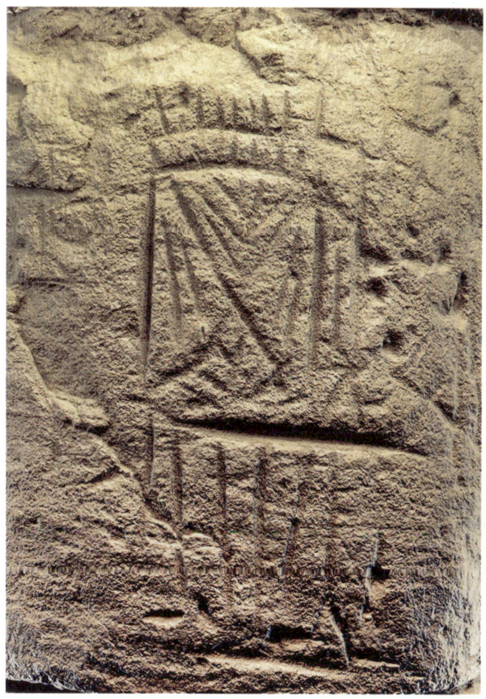

Graffito T39
Object – Textile

Location: Column A14-3:3, north face

Dimensions (H × W): 20.0 × 25.5 cm

Located on the same column as the two previous entries, this shows an example of a far less elaborate textile. Although the center is a plain, unpatterned square, fringes are indicated at the top and bottom edges. The deeply incised cross at the lower left of the textile design appears to be a later addition.

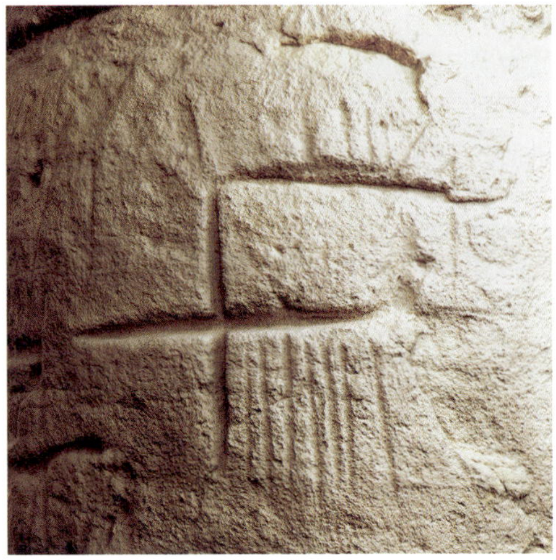

Other Images

Graffito T40
Object – Sandal

Location: Column A24-3:4, southwest face

Dimensions (H × W): 23.5 × 7.0 cm

This image may represent a sandal woven from palm leaves. Representations of sandals and feet are common in graffiti of the Meroitic period and also in rock art, and they likely represent the journey and presence of pilgrims. This form of diagonal hatching is unusual, however, and it is possible that this image is intended to represent something else. A somewhat similar motif in rock art has been interpreted as the body of a goose (Otto and Buschendorf-Otto 1993, p. 36, fig. 15), although that scarcely seems possible for this image. This is the only image in the temple that could represent a sandal.

See Also: Hellström 1970 v. 1:2, corpus Aa7–33; Váhala and Červíček 1999, pl. 71:276, 3.

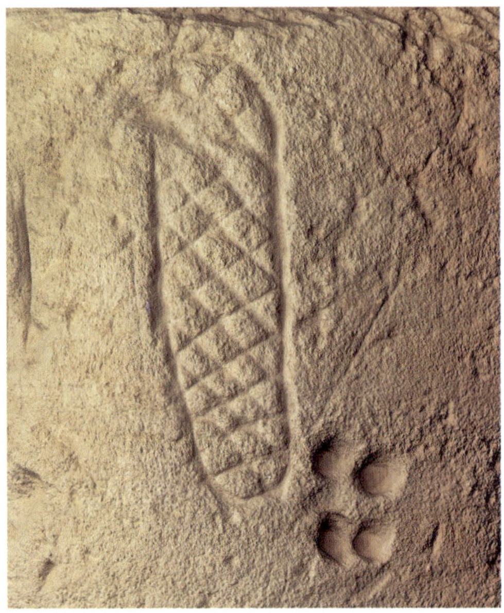

Graffito T41
Architecture – Church

Location: Wall face E04-4:1

Dimensions (H × W): 9 × 5 cm

This is the only identifiable representation of architecture in the temple. The building has a rounded pentagonal shape and is topped with a cross. A row of drilled holes appears above it.

See Also: Although not categorized as a church, graffito 304_301W.134 from the Musawwarat Graffiti Archive is similar.

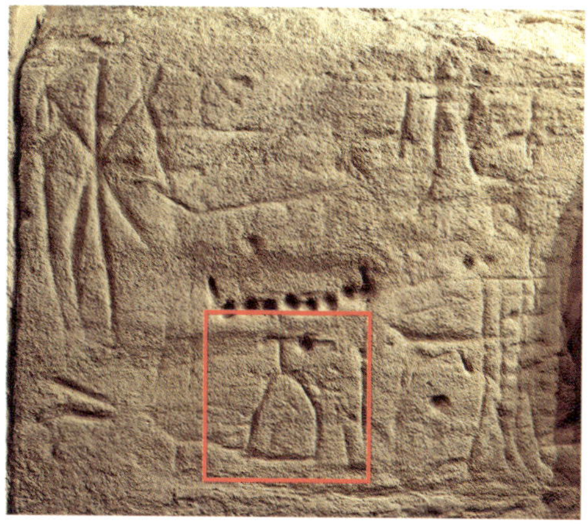

SYMBOLS

Xs in Boxes

Graffito T42
Symbol – X in a Box

Location: Column A02-3:2, northwest face

Dimensions (H × W): 17.5 × 27.0 cm

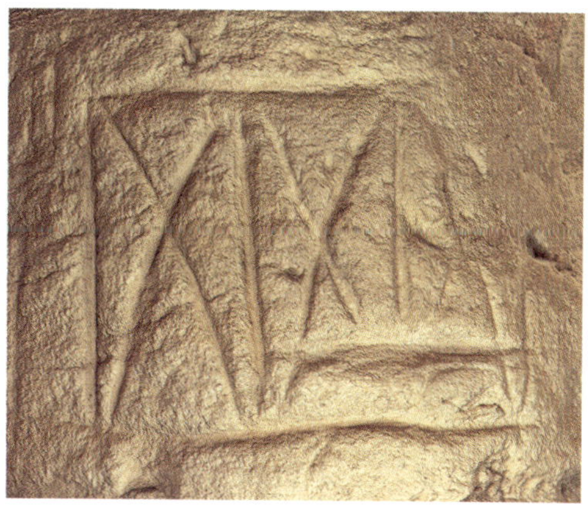

The X in a box design appears throughout the temple. Its meaning is not clear. Pope (this volume) has argued that the image has a votive character and is similar to depictions of altars and offering tables at other Egyptian and Nubian sites. The design is also similar to flag designs at Philae (and to decoration on Roman Egyptian fans in the archaeological record; T. G. Wilfong, personal communication). The most elaborate textile designs in the temple are also patterned with a central X. Here two Xs enclosed by boxes appear side by side.

Graffito T43
Symbol – X in a Box

Location: Column A04-3:10, southeast face

Dimensions (H × W): 14 × 7 cm

This X is bounded by a triangular design with the point at the top, perhaps suggesting a votive altar.

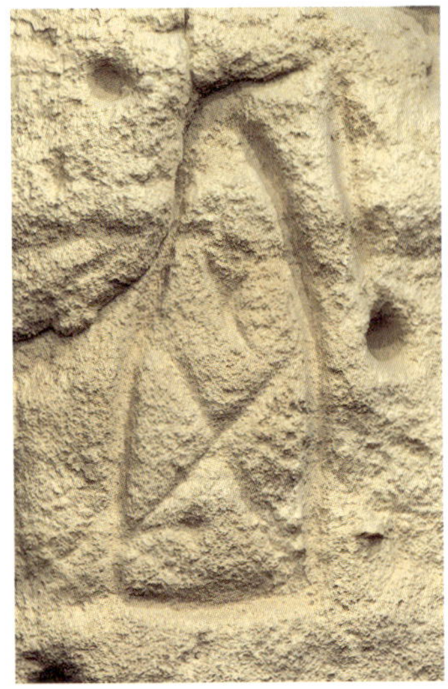

Graffito T44
Symbol – X in a Box

Location: Wall face H03-1:4

Dimensions (H × W): 7.0 × 7.5 cm

Here the X in a box appears on the back of a gazelle, T17.

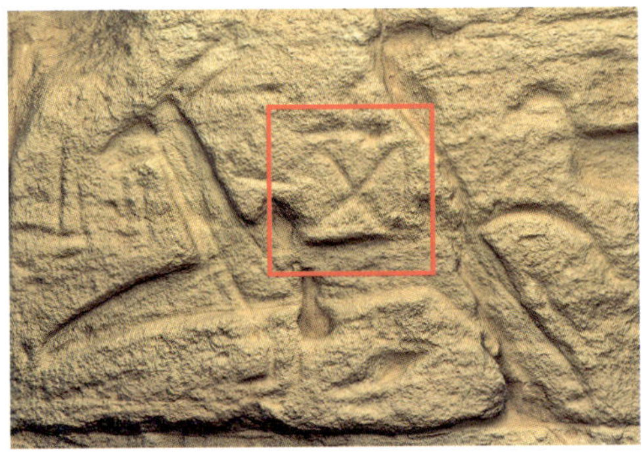

Graffito T45
Symbol – X in a Box

Location: Column A06-3:1 (fallen drum)

Dimensions (H × W): 34 × 17.5 cm

This large and elaborate grid design incorporates an X in a box at the top right.

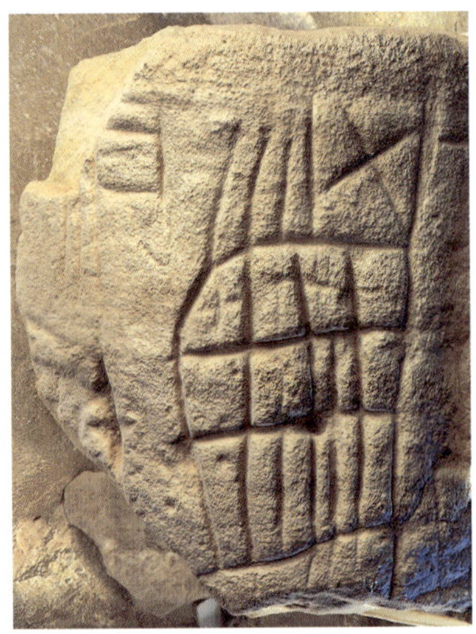

Graffito T46
Symbol – X in a Box

Location: Column A06-2:4, east face

Dimensions (H × W): 10 × 11 cm

A horizontal line crosses through the center of the X, turning it into a starburst shape. Although difficult to see, two short parallel lines extend from the top right corner of the box. These terminate in a diagonal line that slants upward to the left.

See Also: Hellström 1970 v. 1:2, corpus X6–8.

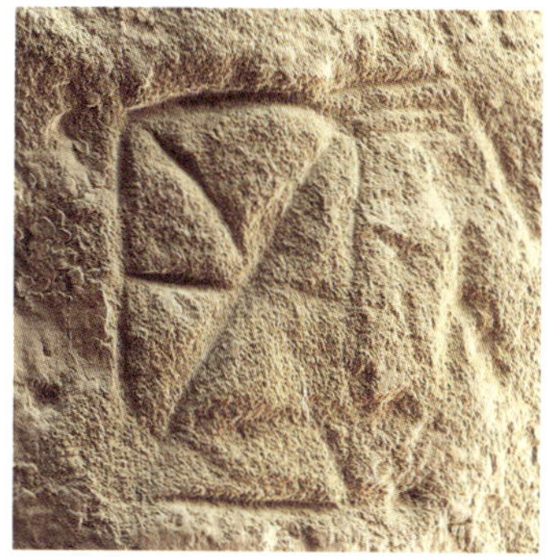

Other Symbols

Graffito T47
Symbol – Ankh

Location: Wall face F03-1:3

Dimensions (H × W): 17.0 × 7.5 cm

The ankh is the Egyptian hieroglyph (and symbol) meaning "life." It is visible on the top left of this block, which also contains a number of other motifs including three guinea fowl.

See Also: Hellström 1970 v. 1:2, corpus X12.

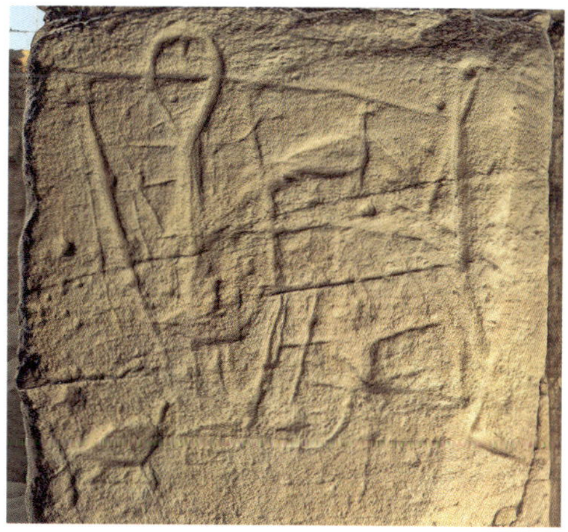

Graffito T48
Symbol – Linear Designs, with Ankh

Location: Wall face J03-2:1

Dimensions (H × W): 29 × 36 cm

This view of a block shows a complicated arrangement of many linear graffiti, including an ankh in the upper center. It is typical of many blocks at El-Kurru, which appear to have a complex, but now indecipherable, collection of geometric designs.

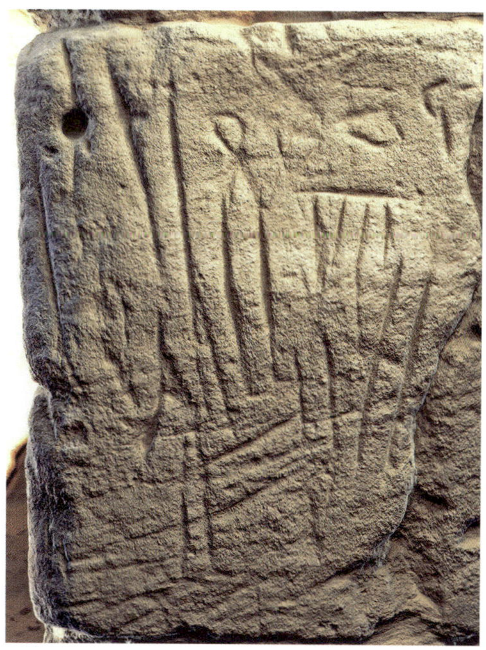

Graffito T49
Symbol

Location: Column A03-3:9, east face

Dimensions (H × W): 18 × 16 cm

This symbol appears immediately to the right of the image of a horned altar (T27), which is in turn associated with a possible human figure (T7) to the left. The base of the graffito is a square shape, possibly with legs — as if it were furniture — and it is topped by a triangle. Its meaning is unclear, but it appears to be deliberately grouped with the altar.

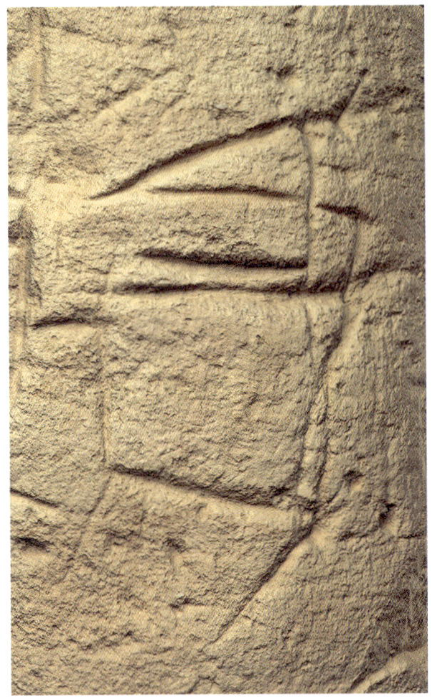

Graffito T50
Symbol

Location: Column A12-3:4, northeast face

Dimensions (H × W): 20.0 × 20.5 cm

This graffito, located just to the left of center at the top of the image, is similar in shape to the elongated butterfly design seen over the center of the figure's torso in T4. It is located among a confusing assortment of other faint marks, including what might remain of the fringe from a textile design at lower right, and it is not unlike the patterning seen inside larger textile graffiti like T37 and T38. The letter E, at center right, is a modern addition.

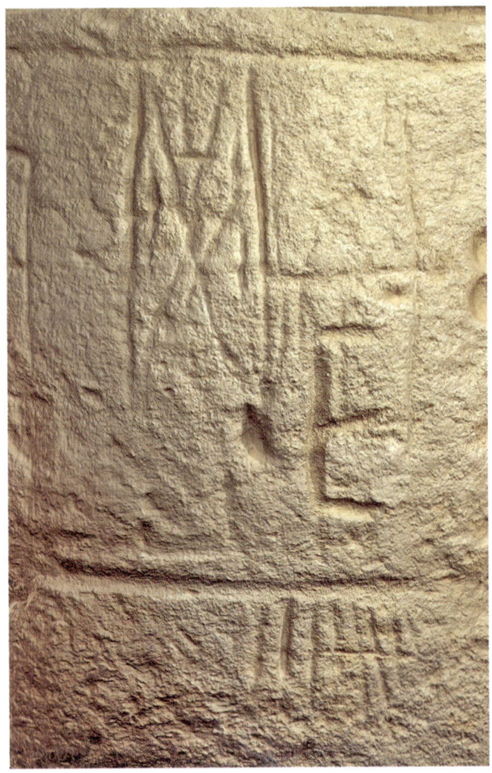

Graffito T51
Symbol

Location: Column A16-3:4, east face

Dimensions (H × W): 18 × 21 cm

The meaning of this design — and of many geometric graffiti at El-Kurru — is not clear. It shows two rounded, intersecting triangles, with interior linear demarcations. Nearby are two deep, drilled holes.

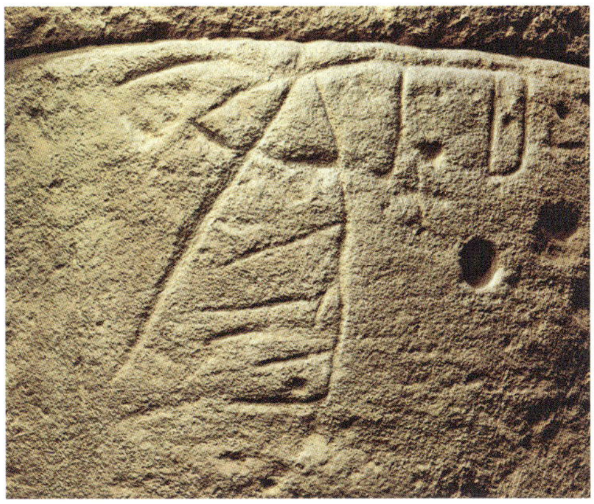

HOLES OR CUPULES

Graffito T52
Holes - Group

Location: Wall face E04-2:4

Dimensions (H × W): 13.5 × 14.0 cm

Finger-sized holes are the most common marking in the temple. Based on parallels from medieval Nubia and Coptic Egypt, it seems that this practice was connected with ingestion of the powder by pilgrims, presumably for its magical healing or fertility-enhancing properties. These marks also serve to mark the pilgrims' presence. Most of the holes are perfectly circular, indicating they were produced by drilling. The El-Kurru sandstone is so soft that they could have been hand-drilled with almost any tool, including a stick. Most of the marks are single or in smaller groups — this is one of the larger groupings.

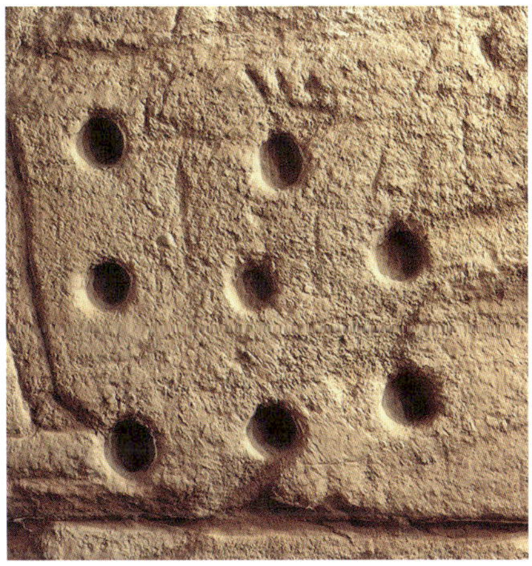

Graffito T53
Holes - Group

Location: Column A08-3:2, south face

Dimensions (H × W): 11.5 × 4.0 cm

Many groups of holes are arranged in deliberate patterns. This group is in two parallel, vertical lines. To the right is an example of a large, single hole.

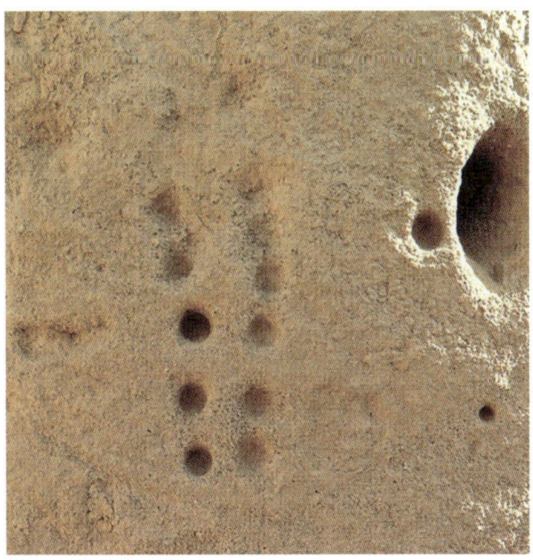

Graffito T54
Holes – Group

Location: Column A03-3:5, north face

Dimensions (H × W): 26.5 × 13.0 cm (measurements include the box at bottom and the lines at top)

Here, fourteen small holes have been added over top of an existing design.

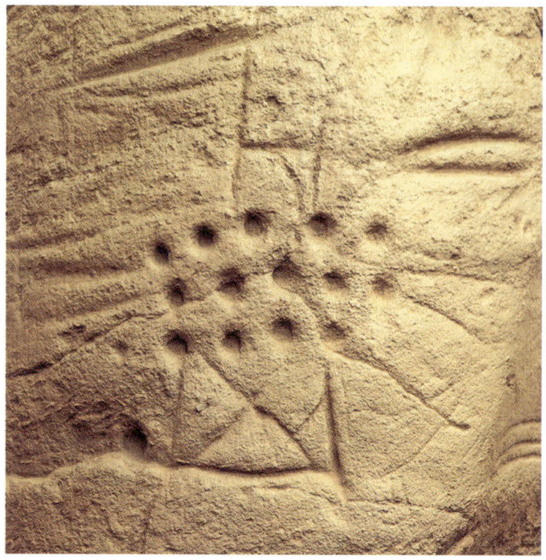

Graffito T55
Holes – Group

Location: Column E03-6:1, south face

Dimensions (H × W): 15.5 × 14.0 cm

These seventeen finger-sized holes have been arranged along incised grooves to form a square.

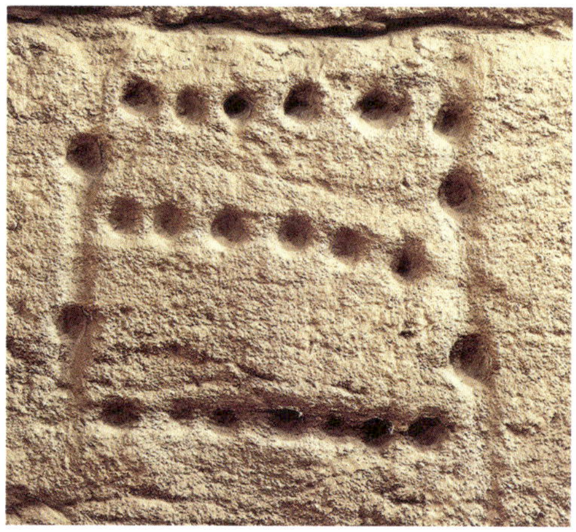

Pyramid Ku. 1

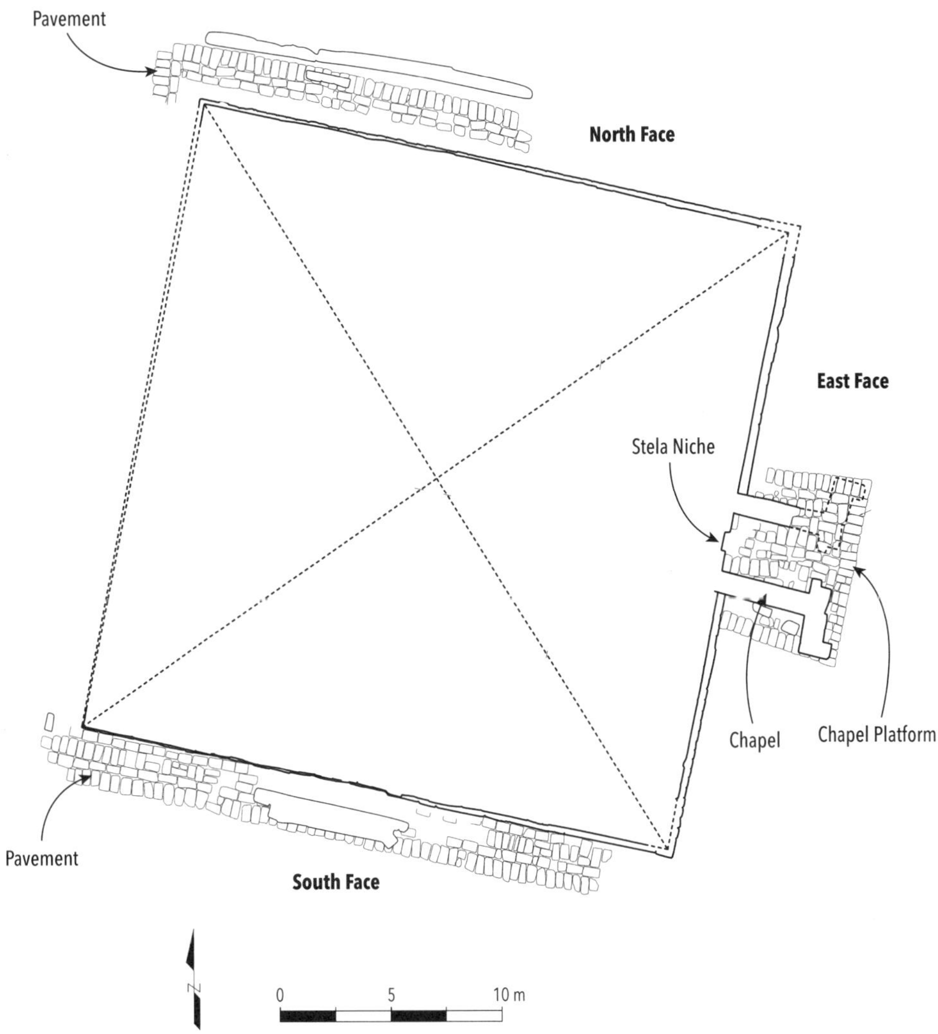

FIGURE C.4. Labeled plan of pyramid Ku. 1. Note that the descendary that extends east of the pyramid is not shown.
Base plan: Nadejda Reshetnikova / IKAP

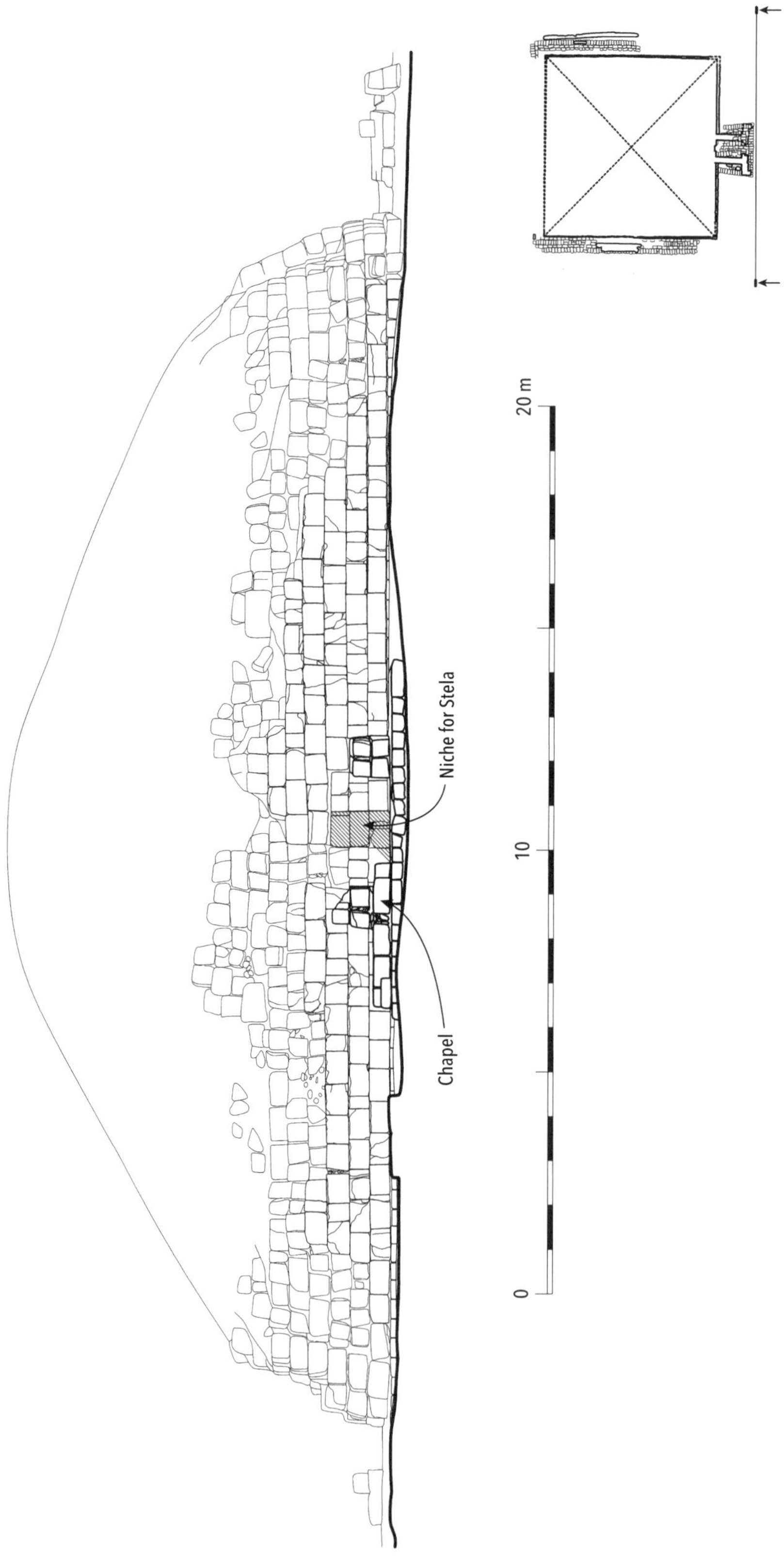

FIGURE C.5. East face of pyramid Ku. 1.
Drawing: Nadejda Reshetnikova / IKAP

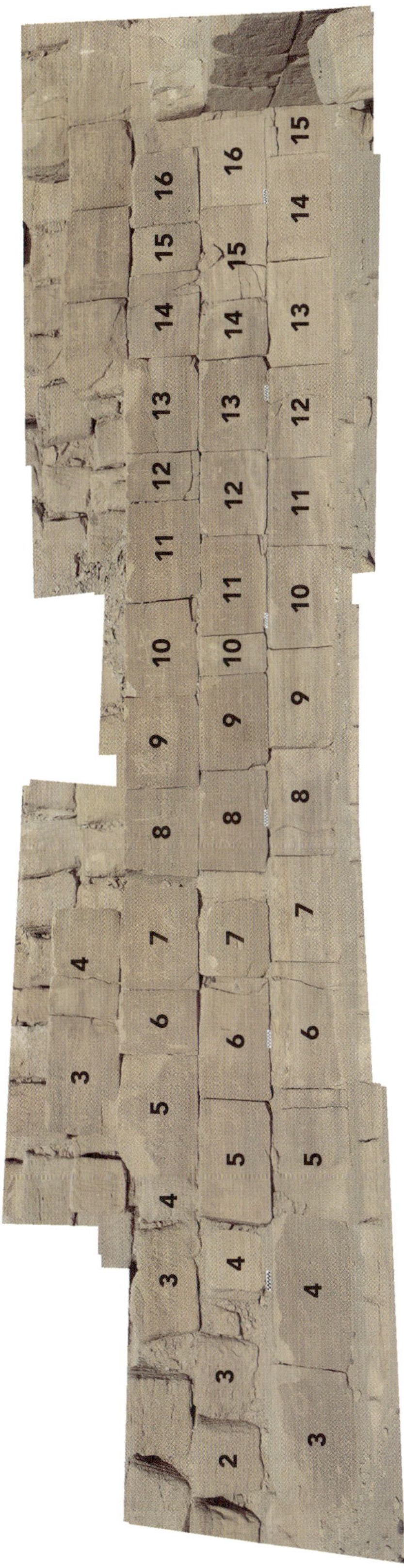

FIGURE C.6. Numbered blocks of the east face of pyramid Ku. 1, south of chapel.
Photo model: Bruce Beyer Williams / IKAP, 2019

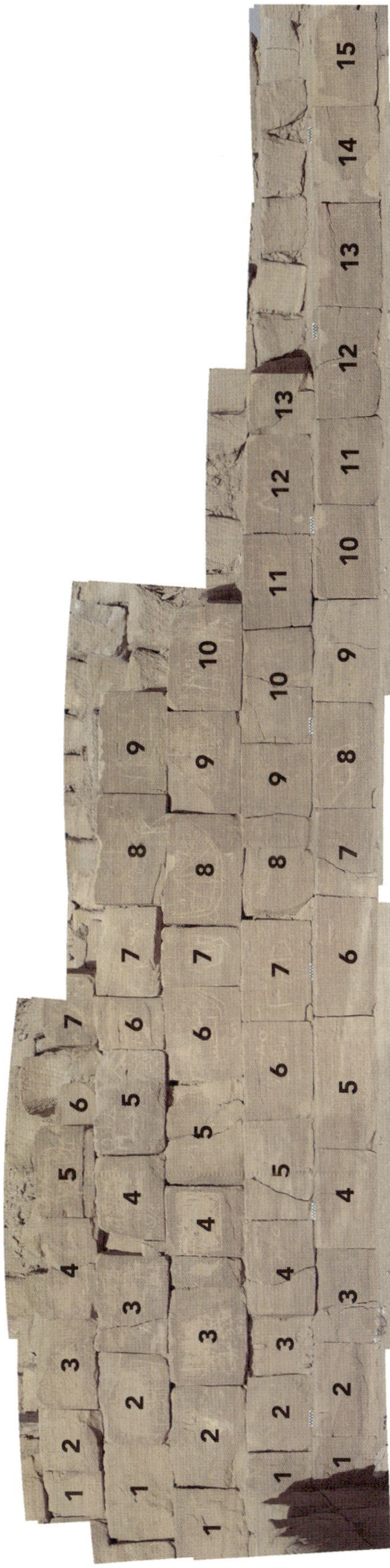

FIGURE C.7. Numbered blocks of the east face of pyramid Ku. 1, north of chapel.
Photo model: Bruce Beyer Williams / IKAP, 2019

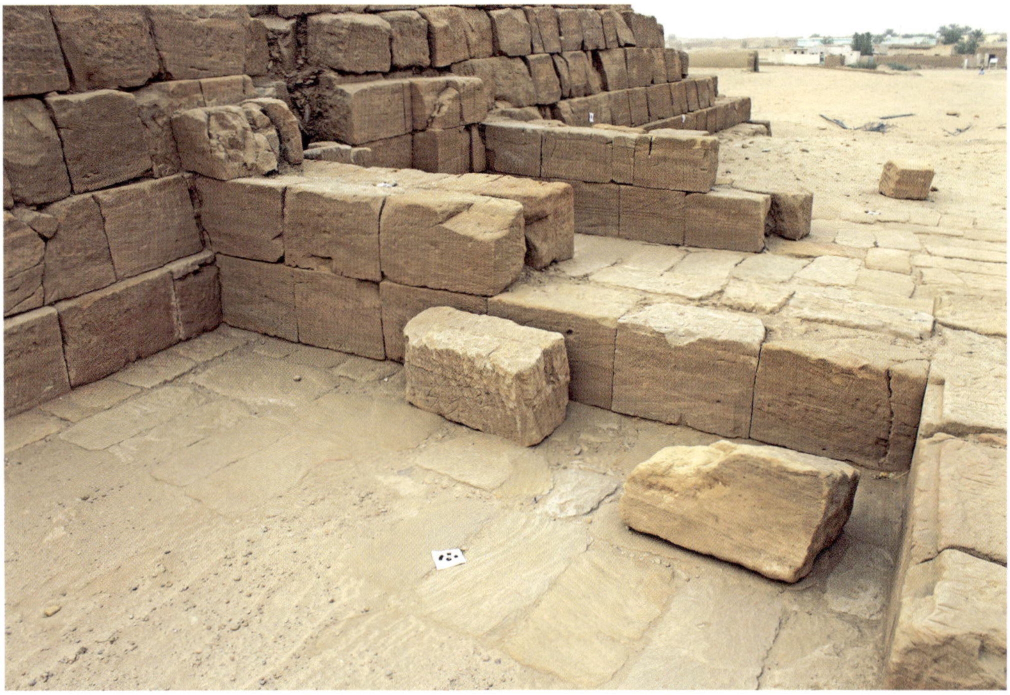

FIGURE C.8. East face, exterior of south chapel wall.
Photo: IKAP

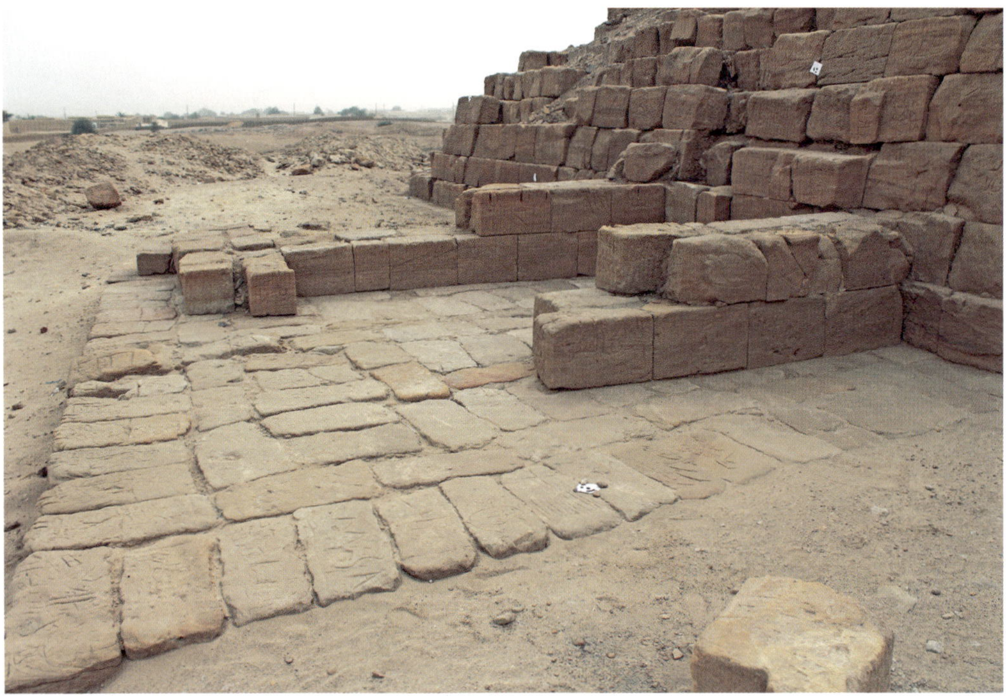

FIGURE C.9. East face, exterior of north chapel wall.
Photo: IKAP

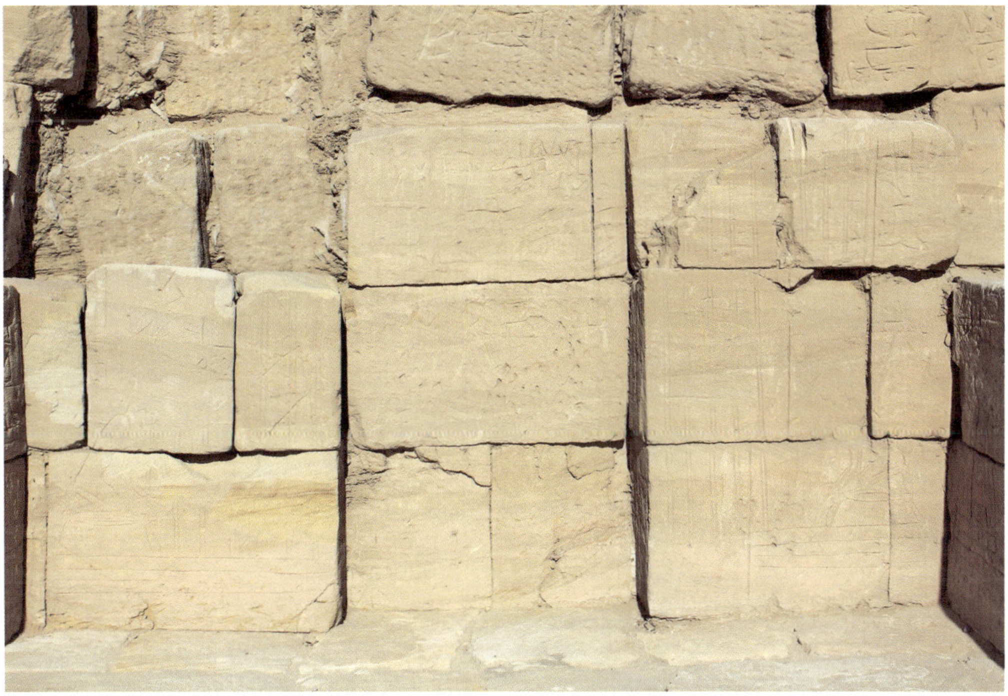

FIGURE C.10. East face, chapel interior.
Photo: IKAP

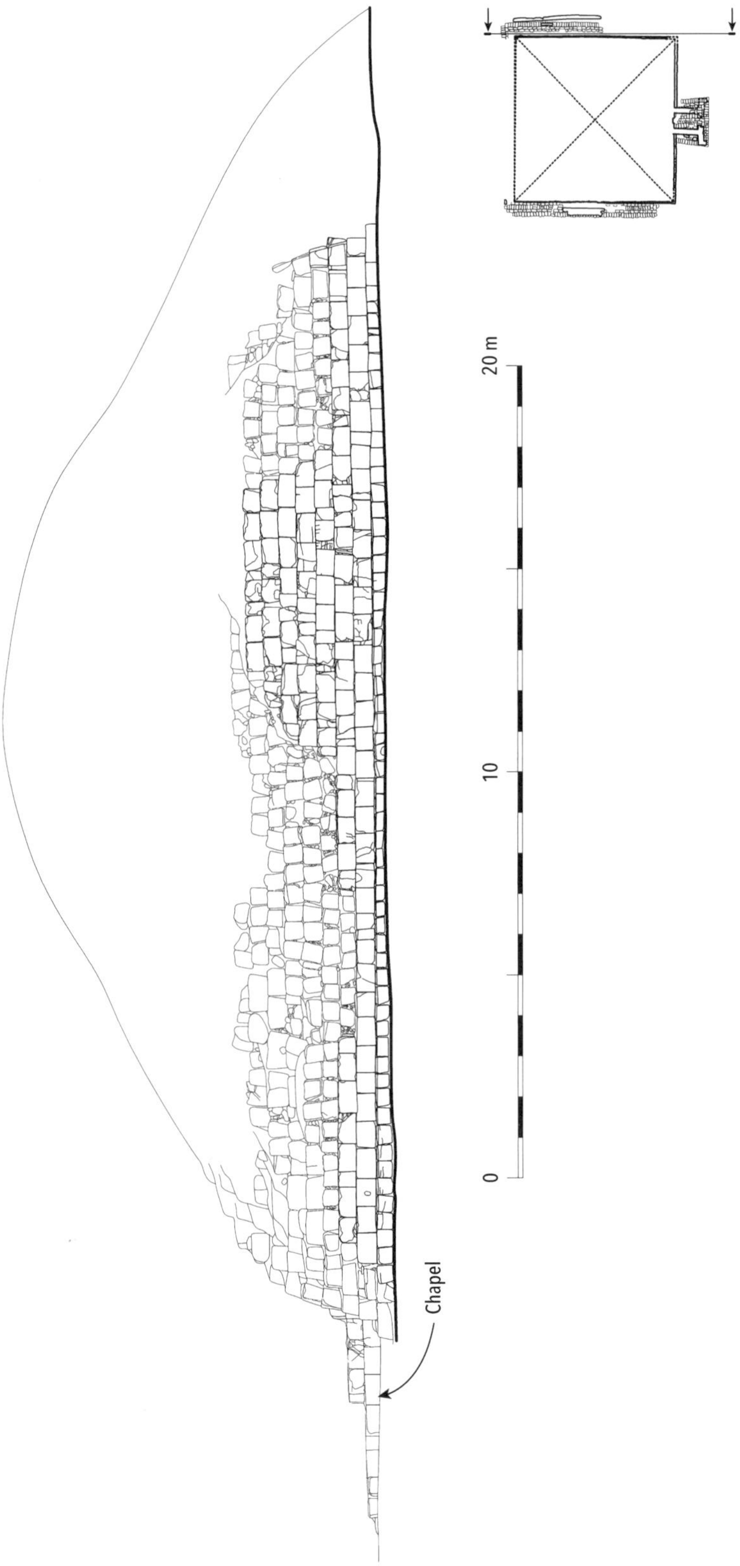

FIGURE C.11. North face of pyramid Ku. 1.
Drawing: Nadejda Reshetnikova / IKAP

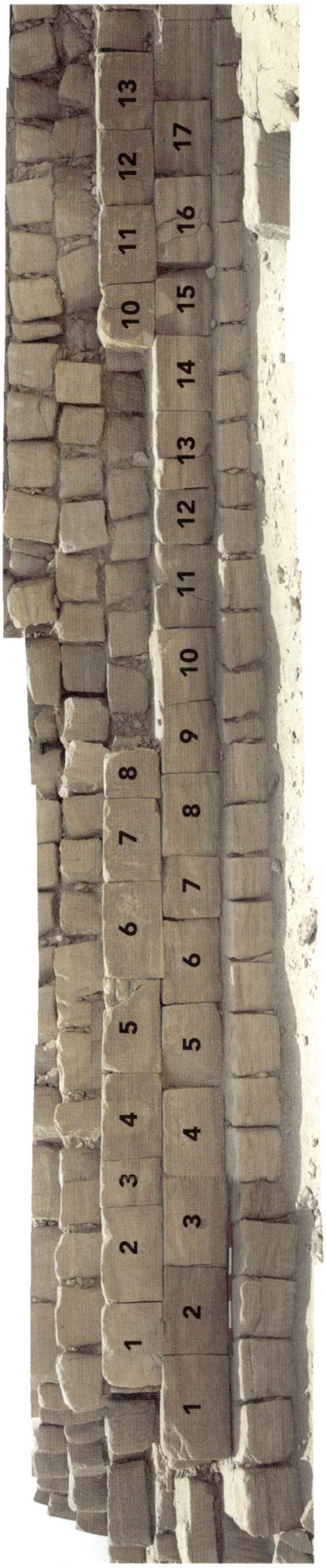

FIGURE C.12. Numbered blocks of the north face of pyramid Ku. 1, eastern half.
Photo model: Bruce Beyer Williams / IKAP, 2019

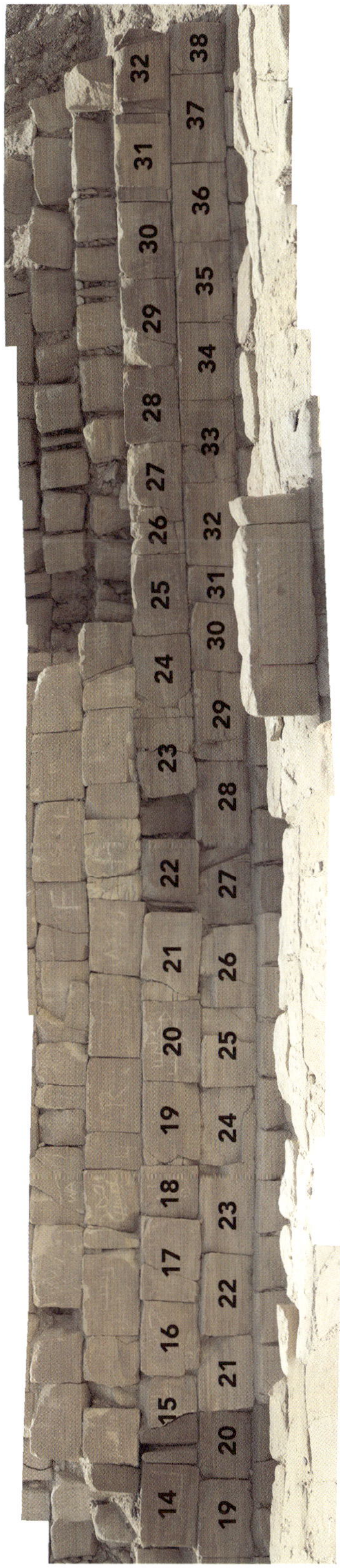

FIGURE C.13. Numbered blocks of the north face of pyramid Ku. 1, western half.
Photo model: Bruce Beyer Williams / IKAP, 2019

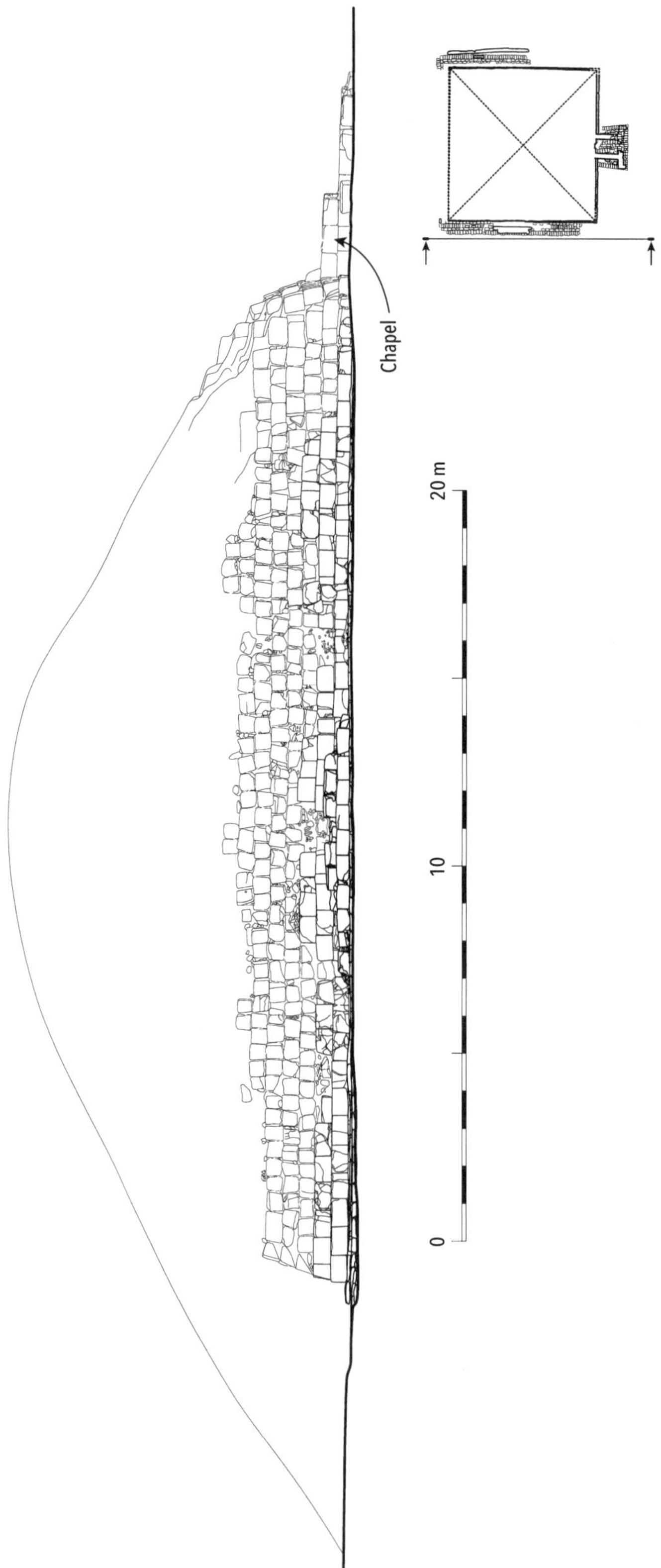

FIGURE C.14. South face of pyramid Ku. 1.
Drawing: Nadejda Reshetnikova / IKAP

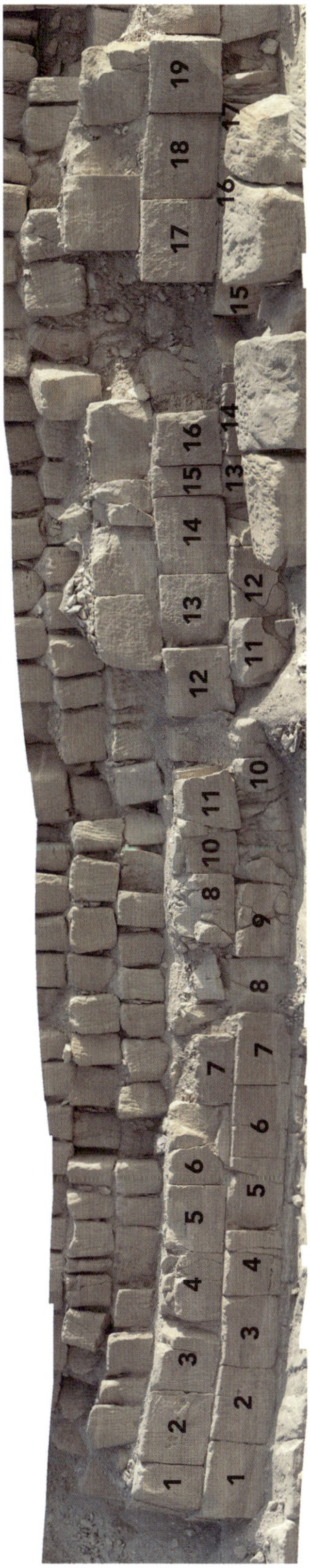

FIGURE C.15. Numbered blocks of the south face of pyramid Ku. 1, western half.
Photo model: Bruce Beyer Williams / IKAP, 2019

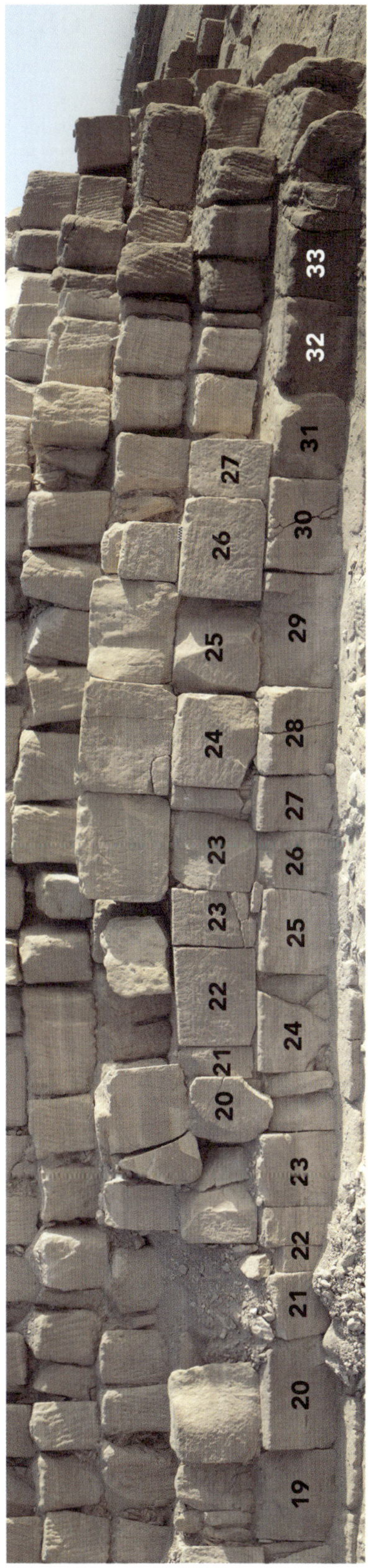

FIGURE C.16. Numbered blocks of the south face of pyramid Ku. 1, eastern half.
Photo model: Bruce Beyer Williams / IKAP, 2019

OBJECTS — BOATS

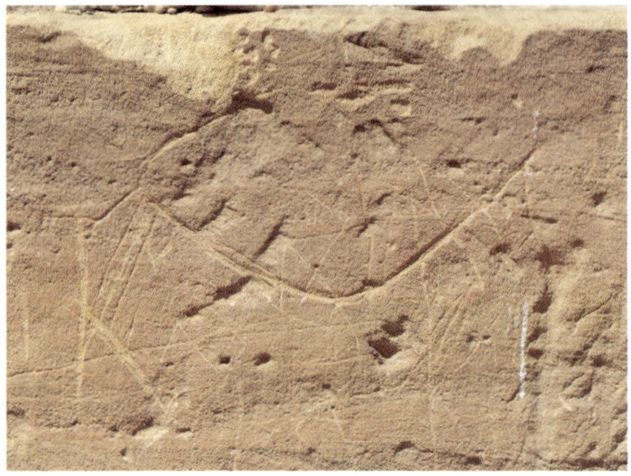

Graffito P1
Object — Boat, Type 1

Location: East face, south of chapel, course 3, block 11

Dimensions (H × W): 12 × 18 cm

The only type 1 boat at Ku. 1 has a bent hull made with a curve in the middle. To the left, there is a sharp upward bend for the stern, which curves near the tip. A line angles down from the stern ending in two splayed lines that may define the blade of a rudder. There may be two more lines slightly forward to indicate oars. In the center, a vertical line may be a mast and a horizontal one may indicate a cabin. At the bow, a vertical line ends in an inverted V that may be an anchor. While the basic shape fits with the others on this face of the pyramid as a boat with a rudder, the other lines noted here are only conjecturally identified, based on the clearer figures on other blocks.

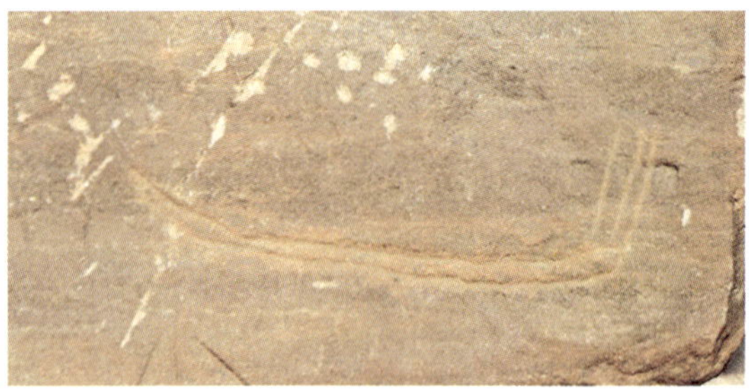

Graffito P2
Object — Boat, Type 2

Location: East face, south of chapel, course 4, block 4

Dimensions (H × W): 9 × 30 cm

In the lower right corner of the block is a type 2 boat with a shallow-curved hull that tapers to a pointed prow. The stern is indicated by three lines that end at the hull.

Graffito P3
Object – Boat, Type 2

Location: East face, south of chapel, course 3, block 7

Dimensions (H × W): 37 × 33 cm

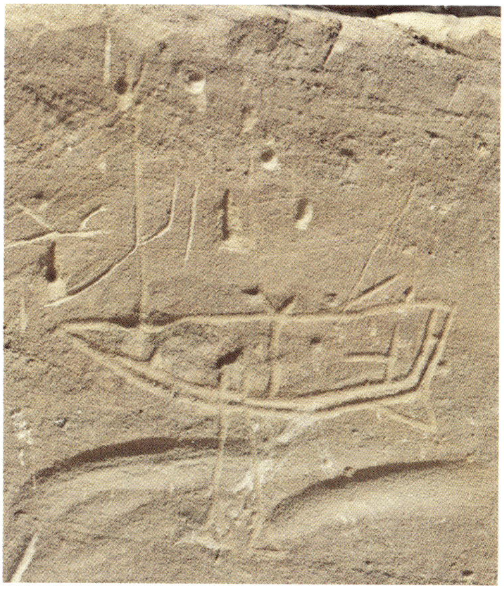

Incised toward the right side of its block, this type 2 boat does not occupy the surface completely. The outlined hull curves and tapers to a pointed bow. The stern is bent upward and is broader toward the top. The triangular rudder is attached to the hull tip-down and the tiller is a horizontal bar attached to an angled line extending up from the hull. The mast is far forward and has a crutch near the top, made by a line behind it that curves upward. The yard extends from bow to stern, resting in a forked crutch amidships. Just forward of the crutch, two long oars extend across the hull to triangular blades, base downward. A badly worn line curves from aft of the mast toward the forward oar, apparently a structure or load. This graffito appears to show a vessel going downstream, using oars, not for propulsion but to maintain steerage.

Graffito P4
Object – Boat, Type 2

Location: East face, south of chapel, course 3, block 9

Dimensions (H × W): 26 × 24 cm

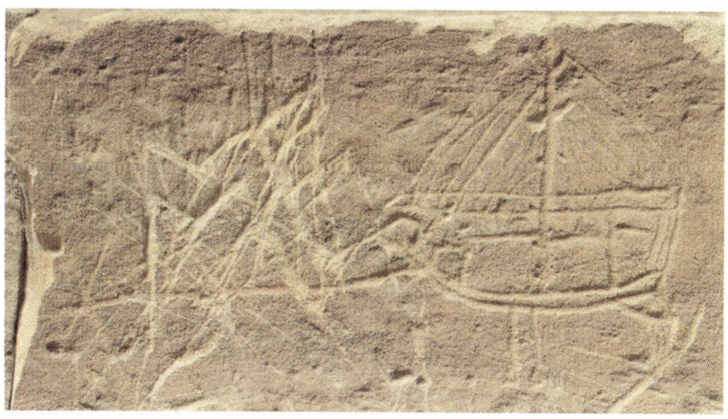

Incised near the top of the right side of the block, the hull, rudder, helm, and oars of this type 2 boat resemble those of graffito P3. The hull curves almost evenly, tapering from stern to bow. The stern is shown as a separate upward protrusion from the hull. The raked triangle of the rudder is rounded at the tip, and the tiller is a shaft with an almost horizontal handle. Two long oars with triangular blades project below the hull.

The stout mast amidships has a V-shaped crutch near the tip. Two horizontal spars are held by approximately 12–14 lines that probably represent lashings for the furled sails.

A number of large structures fill the entire deck. Two rectangles before and aft of the mast are probably cabins, while two sub-rectangles farther in front, one in the bow, are uncertain. A long line extends forward from the bow; it may not be part of the composition although the patination seems to be similar.

See Also: For cabins, cf. Musawwarat es-Sufra Graffiti Archive database 304_301E-5-13, 304_301W-5-15, etc. For the boat, cf. Hornell 1942, pl. II.

Graffito P5
Object – Boat, Type 2

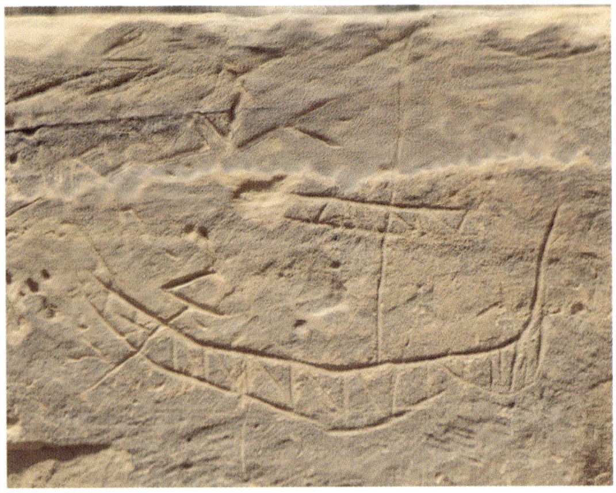

Location: East face, south of chapel, course 4, block 3

Dimensions (H × W): 40 × 48 cm

Wear above and on the left side of this block has made this otherwise rather boldly incised type 2 vessel somewhat difficult to see. The curved hull is higher at the stern than the bow, which is marked by a rounded structure below curves up and tapers sharply to a point. The hull is broadest amidships, narrowing toward the stern as it curves upward and then angles sharply inward after almost disappearing in a worn area. Above the hull, the stern angles forward sharply and ends in some angled lines that may represent a structure of the sort found on graffiti P6 and P7. The stern and hull are marked by a series of transverse and angled lines that appear like bindings, something unlikely on this kind of river craft.

In front of the stern, a line angles backward and is met by one perpendicular to it, probably indicating two sides of a triangular rudder, the third side lost to damage. The shape above may be a tiller or a later mark. The mast is somewhat forward. Roughly level with the tip of the prow and the bend of the stern are two horizontal yards with zigzag lines between indicating a furled sail. The mast continues upward and ends in the V of a crutch.

Graffito P6
Object – Boat, Type 2

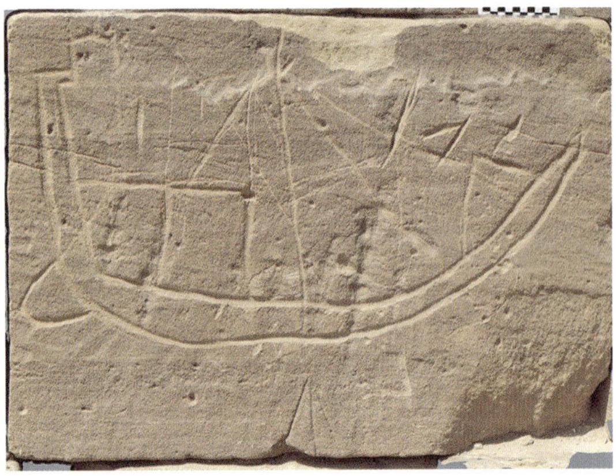

Location: East face, north of chapel, course 3, block 8

Dimensions (H × W): 38 × 68 cm

An outlined type 2 boat with a hull that broadens near the stern and tapers to a pointed bow. The stern bends sharply forward near the tip, then a single line projects up and forward again in a curve. The triangular rudder is curved at the tip and a simple line indicates the helm. Large, rectangular structures occupy the deck between the stern and the mast, which is set amidships. The mast has no spar, but one angled line near the top indicates a crutch. Three lines angle down from the top of the mast, one extending to a triangular structure in the bow. The three lines and the triangular shape are probably later additions to the graffito.

Graffito P7
Object – Boat, Type 2–3

Location: East face, north of chapel, course 3, block 10

Dimensions (H × W): 45 × 42 cm

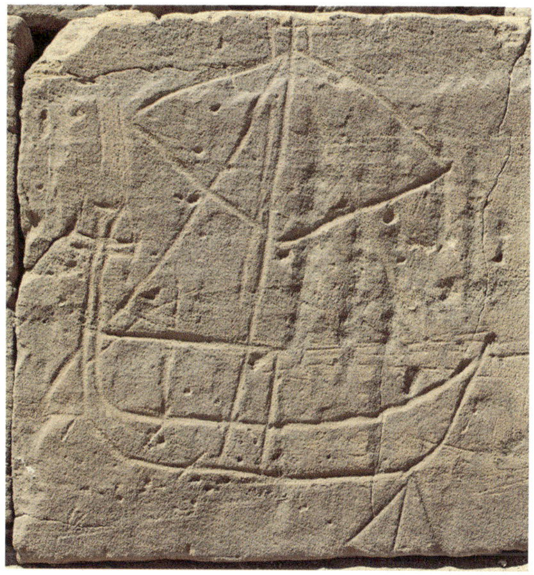

This boat fills the left half of the block and a little more. The low, pointed prow expands to a rather thick hull that narrows and curves sharply but smoothly to form the stern. The stern is high and narrow and terminates in a cruciform tip with arms splayed as the cross pattée. The triangular rudder is shown as though attached to the stern by its long side. On the deck a rectangular structure extends from the stern to forward of the mast, which stands within it. At the top of the mast is a small, nearly rectangular structure, below which four lines descend: two extend to the tips of a broad V-shaped yard, and two support a lower yard extending from bow to stern. The mast is shown extending to the bottom of the hull.

Graffito P8
Object – Boat, Type 2–3

Location: North face, course 2, block 2

Dimensions (H × W): 44 × 71 cm

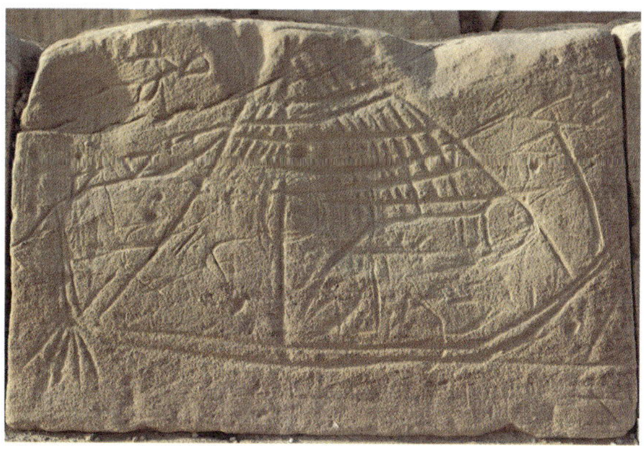

Gouges, scratches, and even some Arabic confuse this block somewhat, but a type 2–3 boat under sail is quite clearly shown. The hull, outlined from stern to prow, is slightly curved to the angled prow and still more to the sharply angled stern. Below the stern, five splayed lines indicate a rudder; an additional line angled up from the rudder apparently indicates a tiller. The mast is amidships; two lines extend forward and aft from the top of the mast to the deck near the prow and the stern. The yard is not completely clear, but a series of transverse lines crossed by longitudinals make up a triangular sail, shown reinforced by ropes as in the Nile Mosaic (see **FIG. 3.10**). (Although the longitudinals could be brails, this is not clear; see Vinson 1993.)

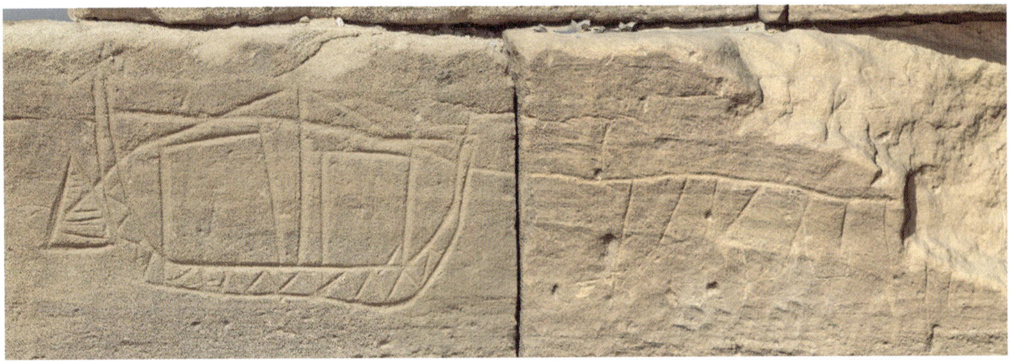

Graffito P9
Object – Boat, Type 3

Location: East face, south of chapel, course 2, blocks 5–6

Dimensions (H × W): 25 × 48 cm

A single composition spreads across two blocks in the second course. It consists of a type 3 boat with a type of mooring represented by a long horizontal line with vertical lines extending downward.

The boldly incised boat is one of the clearest of its type. From stern to bow, the hull is filled by a zigzag. The gunwale is flat, while the bottom of the hull tapers slightly toward the stern and reaches its maximum width near the bow. Both bow and stern curve sharply upward, the stern rising taller than the bow. The upper three centimeters of the stone are damaged, removing the mast, stays, and the tip of the stern, but very worn lines at the top of the stern indicate that it was cruciform, with splayed arms as the footed cross.

The rudder is triangular and separated from the hull, planks indicated by horizontal lines. The tiller is indicated by an angled line that crosses the hull. A single line amidships indicates the mast; the yard is not supported by lines and is probably not deployed. Instead, angled lines from the mast extend to the stern and bow, a feature Hornell indicates was used to support the frameless hull (Hornell 1942).

Two large, almost square shapes before and aft of the mast indicate cabins of the type used for the floating shops (*kantin*) of Dongola in the last century.

Graffito P10
Object – Boat, Type 3

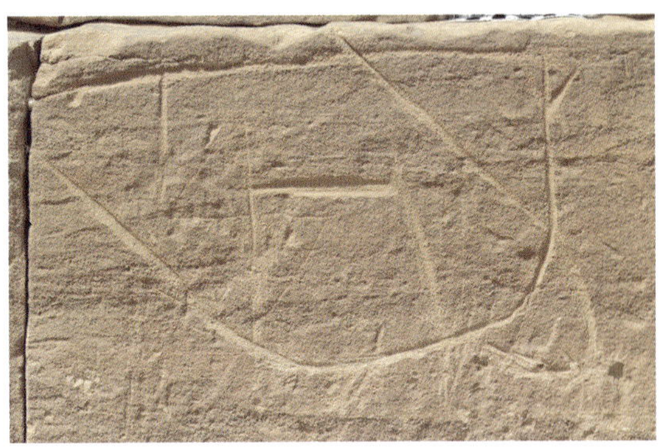

Location: East face, north of chapel, course 1, block 8

Dimensions (H × W): 25 × 40 cm

On the lowest course, north of the chapel, is a completely linear boat of type 3. The hull is almost flat and bends up at the long, angled prow and at the stern. Both the prow and stern are straight. A single short line extends backward from the stern, making a crutch. The rudder is curved but clearly related to the triangular rudders seen elsewhere, and the line defining it continues across the hull as an exaggerated tiller. There is a simple square cabin amidships. An incomplete vertical forward of the cabin is possibly a mast and the long horizontal above it probably a yard.

Graffito P11
Object – Boat, Type 3 and Rowboat

Location: East face, north of chapel, course 4, block 8

Dimensions (H × W): 34.0 × 56.5 cm

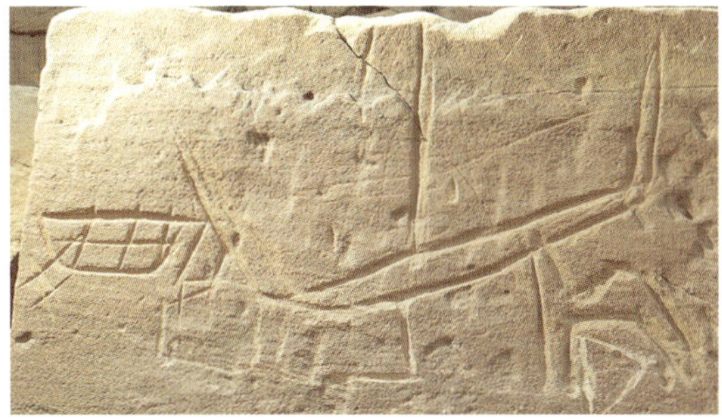

A type 3 boat with outlined hull is depicted at an angle on the upper part of the block. Bow and stern are both angled sharply upward and pointed. A nearly triangular structure attached to the stern is the rudder, either corrected slightly or shown with a plank. Amidships is a vertical mast.

Behind the stern is a small, basket-shaped boat attached to the larger boat by a line. The one horizontal and three vertical lines on this vessel seem to indicate planks. Angling backward from the hull are lines with crossed lines that may indicate oars or some kind of rudder.

See graffito P18 for the figure of a camel in the lower right corner.

Graffito P12
Object – Boat, Type 3

Location: Chapel, exterior of north wall, course 2, block 1

Dimensions (H × W): 15.0 × 33.5 cm

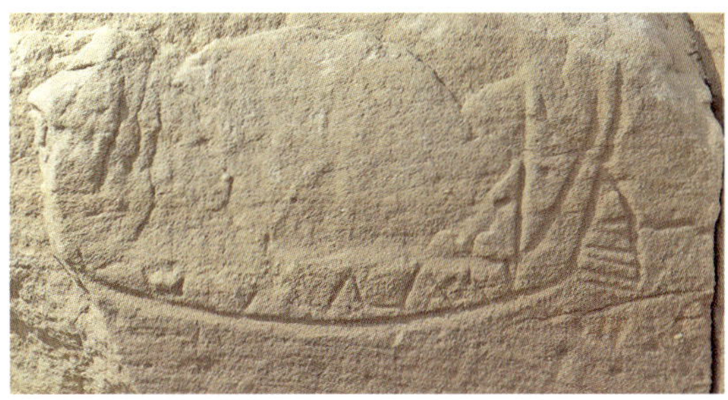

Only the lower part of the hull and the stern of this type 3 boat are preserved. The hull is slightly curved and filled with a zigzag pattern. The stern bends up sharply and is also slightly curved. Attached to the rear is a roughly triangular rudder filled with horizontal lines. The side of the rudder continues into the boat as the tiller. At the end of the tiller is a vertical line that probably indicates a cabin, now lost to erosion.

Graffito P13
Object – Boat, Type 3

Location: East face, north of chapel, course 3, block 6

Dimensions (H × W): 44.0 × 61.5 cm

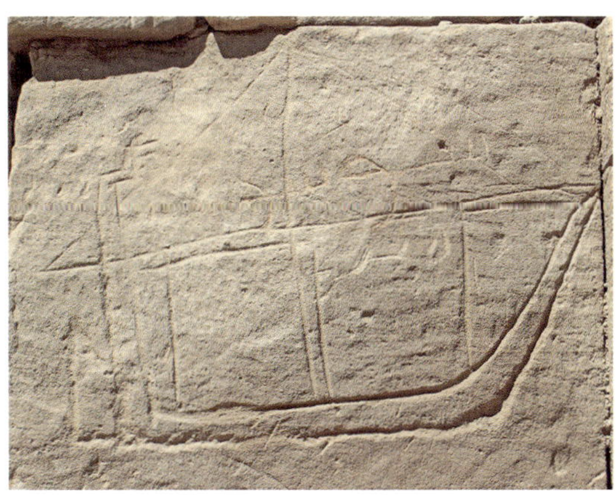

This type 3 vessel has a flat, outlined hull that curves to a straight, pointed prow and bends sharply to a vertical stern. The top of the stern bends forward, up, and forward again. The triangular rudder is partly behind the hull and has a vertical side. The mast is amidships and an unclear number of lines lead from its tip to a yard; the yard extends from the prow beyond the stern. There are cabins fore and aft, the latter using the mast as its forward side. A second line below the yard before the forward cabin is of uncertain significance.

Graffito P14
Object – Boat, Type 3

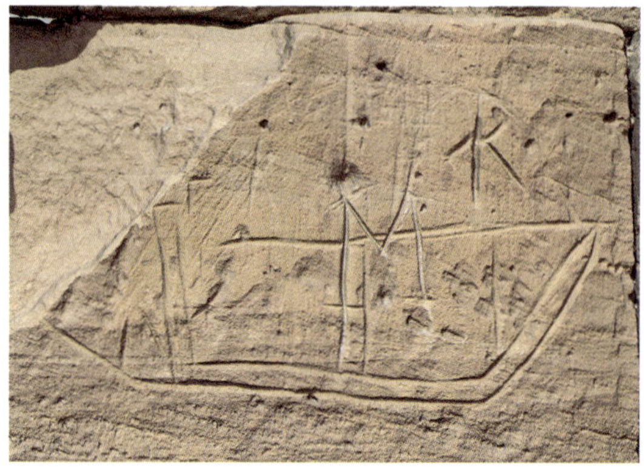

Location: East face, north of chapel, course 3, block 9

Dimensions (H × W): 43 × 55 cm

A type 3 vessel with an outlined hull, this example is quite simple. From the pointed prow to the square stern, the hull is almost uniform, with no fill, the prow angled upward, the stern bent almost vertical. At the tip of the stern is a horizontal line that projects forward, up, and forward again. The rudder is triangular, with one vertical side, a point at the stern, with no tiller indicated. A line angled back from the stern may be a tow line to a small boat (see graffito P11). A line amidships is the mast, and there is a yard that extends from near the stern to the prow. Vertical before the mast and a vestige aft may indicate one or two square cabins.

Graffito P15
Object – Boat, Type 3

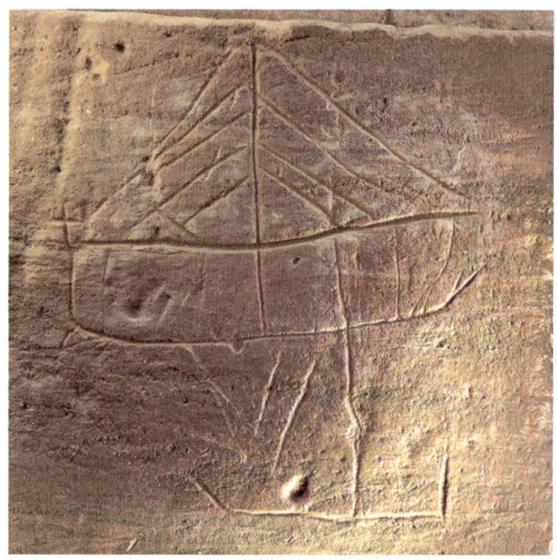

Location: East face, north of chapel, course 2, block 9

Dimensions (H × W): 27.0 × 37.5 cm

A linear type 3 boat proceeds toward the right. The hull is long and the short prow and stern angle or curve very sharply upward. The stern is cruciform; a fork at the bow probably indicates horns, which would connect it with more elaborate boats at Sahaba, Qasr el-Wizz, and in the Aswan area (see **FIGS. 3.11-13**). Below the hull at the stern is a triangular rudder. A long pendant line forward probably indicates an oar, although no blade is clear. The mast is amidships and nine angled lines support a yard that extends from bow to stern. Two rectangles before and aft of the mast indicate cabins.

Graffito P16
Object – Boat, Type 3

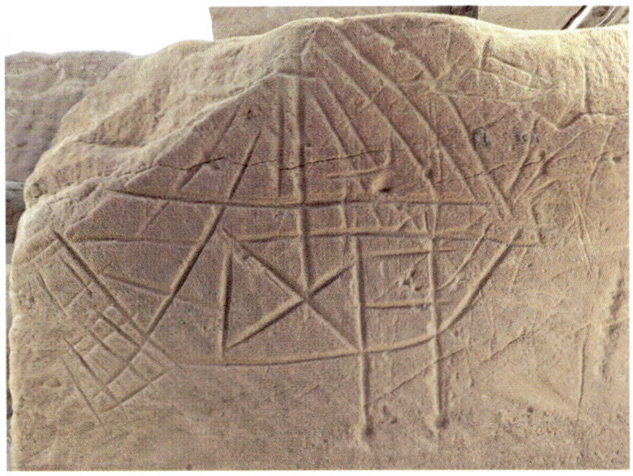

Location: North face, course 1, block 1

Dimensions (H × W): 43 × 56 cm

While this boat is boldly incised, its structures are confused such that it is difficult to interpret. The hull is partly outlined from the side, and apparently shown partly from above. In any case, some details are conjectural. The angled bow structure is outlined, as is the hull toward the stern. A structure seems to be attached to the hull at the stern; it is neither broad nor narrow, with a rectangular flag(?) attached to it. A rectangular rudder is embellished with crossed lines indicating planks.

The mast, with a crutch near the top, is shown amidships, supported by a structure that appears to be beams in a frame(?) that make an X configuration. Since this structure begins at the bottom of the hull, the view is enigmatic and conceptual rather than actual. Before this structure, two verticals extend below the hull to drill holes attached to each other by horizontals. From their position and configuration, these verticals should represent oars with blades, but the other lines are problematical.

The area above the stern is destroyed, but there appear to be two yards that extend from stern to the prow or beyond. Before the mast, five lines support the upper yard, only one from the top, while behind, three lines extend from the bottom of the hull and rudder to the mast. To add to the confusion, some lines appear attached to the bow, but that is questionable.

ANIMALS

Graffito P17
Animal – Camel

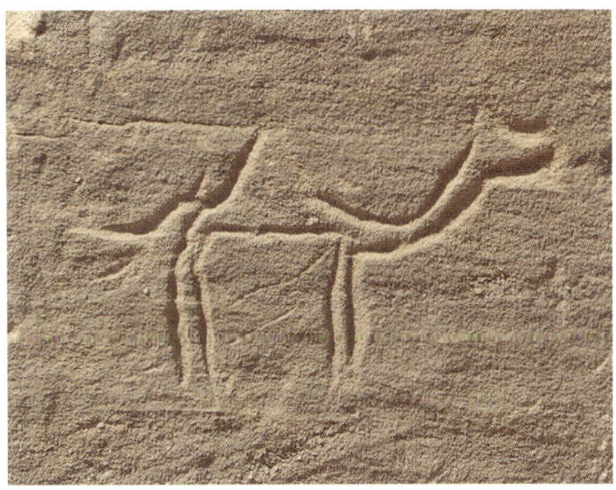

Location: East face, south of chapel, course 1, block 4

Dimensions (H × W): 13 × 22 cm

Toward the left of the block is an easily recognizable camel. The nose is snubbed and the lines of the head curve to the tip. The neck is arched to the shoulder, the upper curve ending at the peak of a hump, which tapers down again to a sinuous tail. The belly is straight, as are the forelegs, the hind legs kinked above. Although summary, this animal is clearly and confidently drawn, with parallels in rock art elsewhere.

Graffito P18
Animal – Camel

Location: East face, north of chapel, course 4, block 8

Dimensions (H × W): 16 × 18 cm

After graffito P11 was cut, a very simplified camel was carved with the head intersecting the hull. The neck and forelegs are straight, while the hind legs curve to the belly and hump.

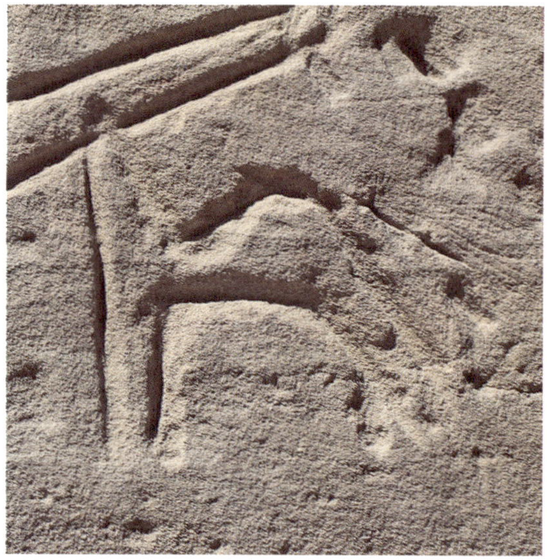

Graffito P19
Animal – Camel

Location: East face, south of chapel, course 4, block 4

Dimensions (H × W): 16 × 25 cm

Above graffito P2 is a very simple quadruped. Four vertical lines indicate the legs with a curve for the belly and a single line for the tail. To the left, a curved line seems to indicate the neck. The rest is unclear, but this is almost certainly a camel, the hump being lost in the scaling in the stone above.

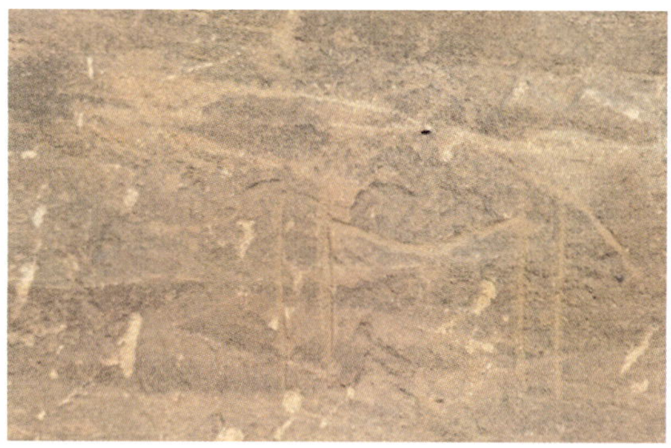

Graffito P20
Animal – Camel

Location: East face, north of chapel, course 3, block 10

Dimensions (H × W): 10 × 10 cm

In the upper right-hand corner of the block, above and to the right of graffito P7, is a simple pecked depiction of a camel, summarized almost to a geometric shape.

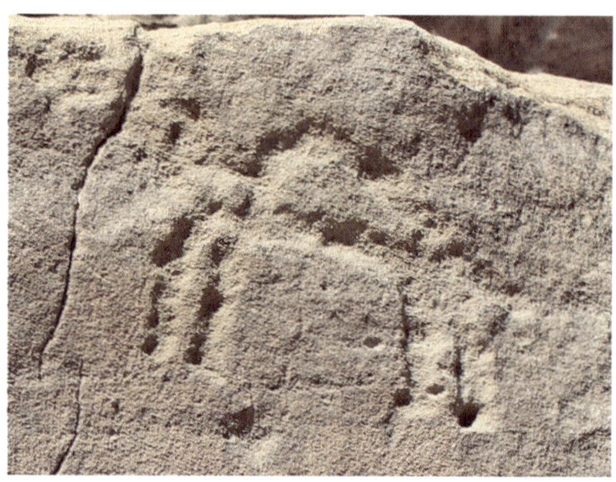

Graffito P21
Animal – Quadruped

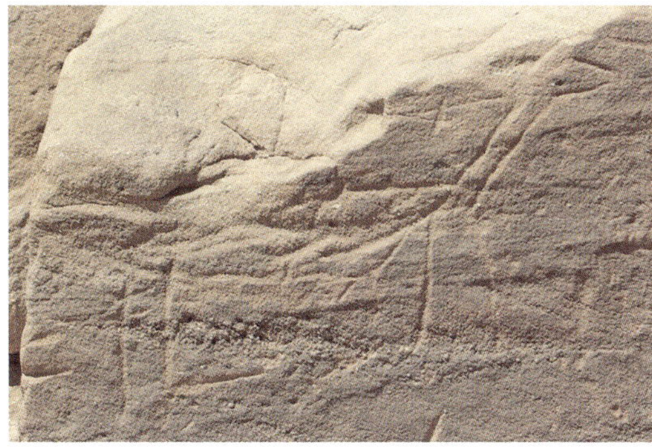

Location: East face, south of chapel, course 1, block 3

Dimensions (H × W): 17 × 26 cm

This figure, on the left side of the block, is key to the decipherment of two others on the same block (P22 and P23). Unfortunately, damage to the entire upper left portion of the block renders the graffiti difficult to interpret.

Two pairs of roughly vertical lines are connected by a series of incised lines to make a rather elongate body, a straight back and a somewhat bulged lower body. A long neck angles upward from the forelegs, topped by a forward-pointed V-shaped head. The crudity of this figure precludes a positive identification, but long-necked animals such as the gerenuk (not in this range) or even a very crude camel are as plausible as the body is long.

Graffito P22
Animal – Quadruped?

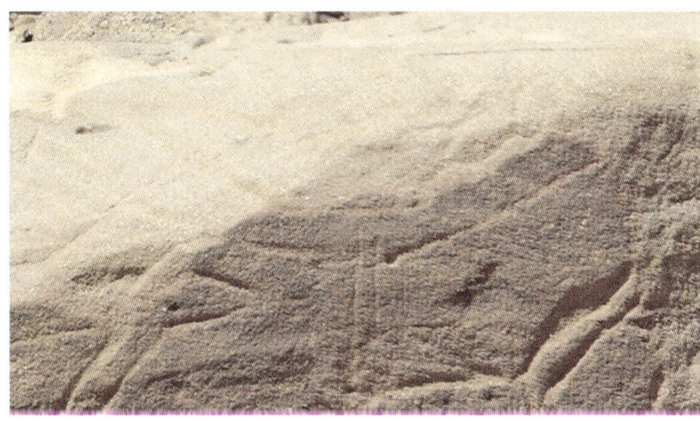

Location: East face, south of chapel, course 1, block 3

Dimensions (H × W): 3 × 16 cm

Above graffiti P21 and P23 is a curved, roughly horizontal line with two verticals midway. This is likely a figure similar to P21, but the entire upper part is destroyed.

Graffito P23
Animal – Ostrich?

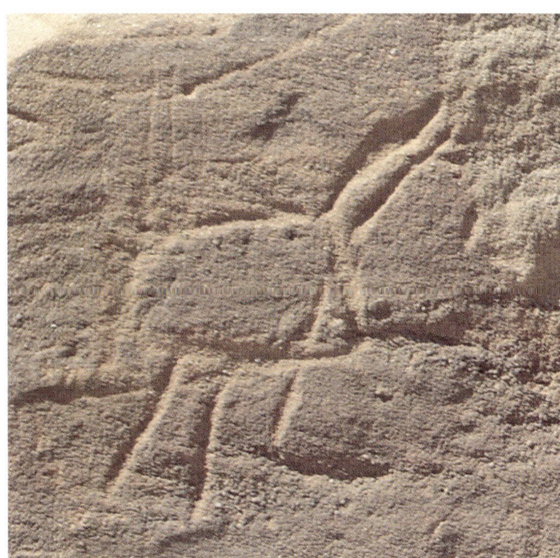

Location: East face, south of chapel, course 1, block 3

Dimensions (H × W): 16 × 16 cm

Just to the right of P21 is a crude graffito that could be an ostrich, with a short body widest at the shoulder and two boldly cut angled lines for legs toward the rear. However, there is a line in an inverted V near the shoulder.

SYMBOLS AND MONOGRAMS

Graffito P24
Symbol – Octagon

Location: North face, course 2, block 7

Dimensions (H × W): 16 × 16 cm

At the upper right of the block is an octagon of four intersecting triangles such that a square is formed in the center. This filled by an X. The symbol appears elsewhere in Christian Nubia.

Graffiti P24–P26 and P28 seem to be a group rather like one that occurs on Mis Island in the 4th Cataract (Kleinitz 2007, fig. 3).

See Also: Dinkler 1970, fig. 259, impressed pottery; Kleinitz 2007, fig. 3, without the central X on Mis Island in the 4th Cataract; Welsby and Daniels 1991, figs. 168, 283, and 286, for example, from Soba.

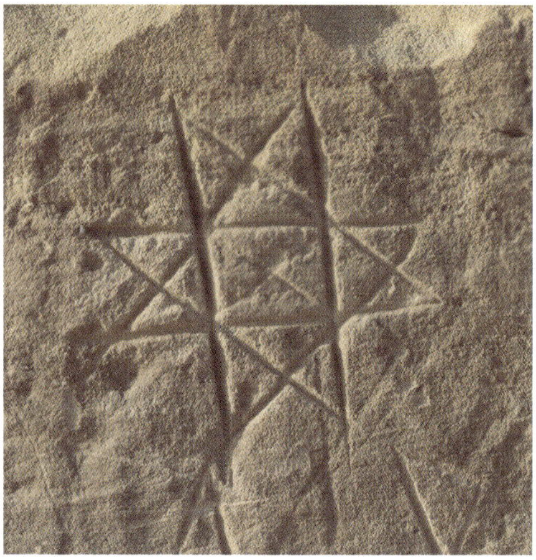

Graffito P25
Symbol – Triangles

Location: North face, course 2, block 7

Dimensions (H × W): 10 × 6 cm

Below the P24 and on either side of its lower points are two opposed shapes, each made up of two triangles arranged with their bases making a single line.

Graffiti P24–P26 and P28 seem to be a group rather like one that occurs on Mis Island in the 4th Cataract (Kleinitz 2007, fig. 3).

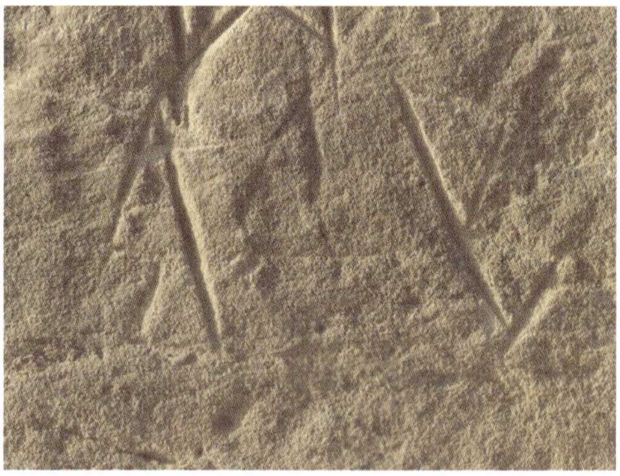

Graffito P26
Symbol – Cross Potent

Location: North face, course 2, block 8

Dimensions (H × W): 11 × 7 cm

At the upper edge of the block is a cross potent. Also at an angle to the stone.

Graffiti P24–P26 and P28 seem to be a group rather like one that occurs on Mis Island in the 4th Cataract (Kleinitz 2007, fig. 3).

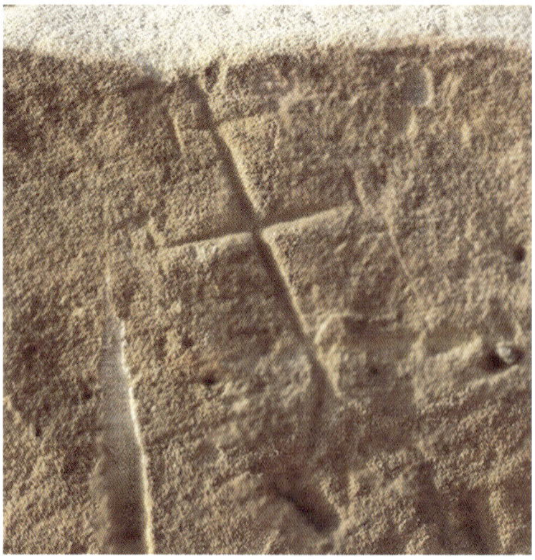

Graffito P27
Symbol – Cruciform

Location: South face, course 2, block 22

Dimensions (H × W): 18 × 25 cm

Four triangles are arranged angle to angle with a lozenge to form a cruciform shape.

See Also: For roughly similar symbols, see Welsby and Daniels 1991, figs. 158, 276, 278; Musawwarat es-Sufra Graffiti Archive database 304 301E.050.

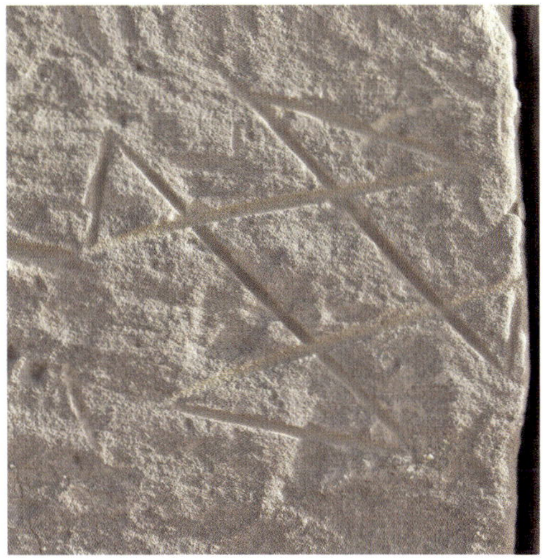

Graffito P28
Monogram

Location: North face, course 2, block 7

Dimensions (H × W): 15 × 8 cm

In the upper left corner of the block could be the Old Nubian/Greek/Coptic letter A, but the crossbar is not slanted in a manner normally found in medieval lapidary inscriptions.

Graffiti P24–P26 and P28 seem to be a group rather like one that occurs on Mis Island in the 4th Cataract (Kleinitz 2007, fig. 3).

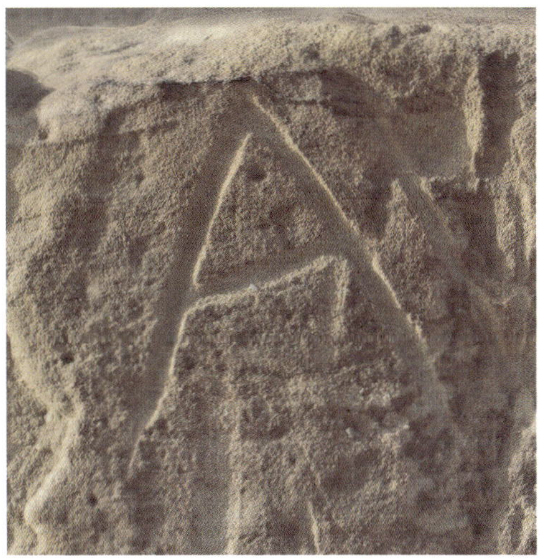

Graffito P29
Monogram

Location: East face, south of chapel, course 3, block 6

Dimensions (H × W): 8 × 10 cm

Incised on the upper part of a half-block in the third course, this monogram has an M with a bar across the top resting on a W shape.

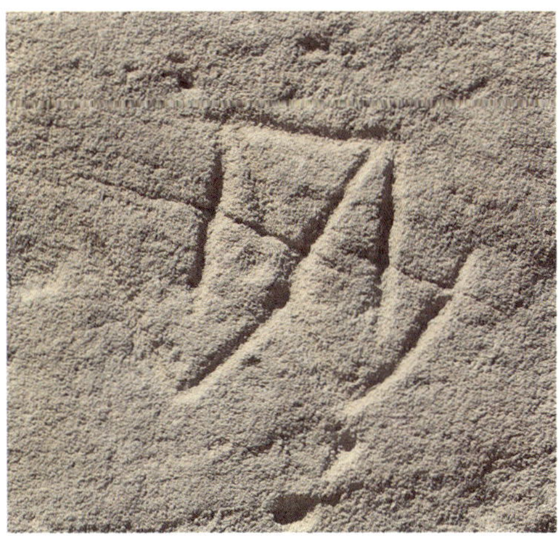

References

Adams, William Y.

1986 *Ceramic Industries of Medieval Nubia.* Memoirs of the UNESCO Archaeological Survey of Sudanese Nubia 1. Lexington: University Press of Kentucky.

Červíček, Pavel

1974 *Felsbilder des Nord-Etbai, Oberägyptens und Unternubiens.* Ergebnisse der Frobenius-Expeditionen 16. Wiesbaden: Steiner.

Dinkler, Erich

1970 "Die deutschen Ausgrabungen auf den Inseln Sunnarti, Tangur und in Kulb, 1968–69." In *Kunst und Geschichte Nubiens in christlicher Zeit: Ergebnisse und Probleme auf Grund der jüngsten Ausgrabungen,* edited by Erich Dinkler, pp. 259–80. Recklinghausen: A. Bongers.

Hellström, Pontus

1970 *The Rock Drawings.* 2 vols. The Scandinavian Joint Expedition to Sudanese Nubia 1. Copenhagen: Scandinavian University Books.

Hofmann, Inge

1988 *Hase, Perlhuhn und Hyäne — Spuren meroitischer Oralliteratur: ein Beitrag zur afrikanischen Komponente der meroitischen Kultur.* Beiträge zur Sudanforschung, Beiheft 4. Vienna: Mödling.

Hornell, James

1942 "The Frameless Boats of the Middle Nile." *Sudan Notes & Records* 25 (1): 1–36.

Kleinitz, Cornelia

2007 "Rock Art Landscapes of the Fourth Nile Cataract: Characterisations and First Comparisons." In *Proceedings of the Second International Conference on the Archaeology of the Fourth Nile Cataract,* edited by Claudia Näser and Mathias Lange, pp. 213–34. Meroitica 23. Wiesbaden: Harrassowitz.

2014 "The Graffiti of Musawwarat Es-Sufra: Current Research on Historic Inscriptions, Images and Markings at the Great Enclosure." *Sudan & Nubia* 18: 93–103.

Morkot, Robert G.

2000 *The Black Pharaohs: Egypt's Nubian Rulers.* London: Rubicon.

Otto, Karl-Heinz, and Gisela Buschendorf-Otto

1993 *Felsbilder aus dem sudanesischen Nubien.* Publikation der Nubien-Expedition, 1961–1963, 2. Berlin: Akademie Verlag.

Rose, Pamela J.

2007 *The Meroitic Temple Complex at Qasr Ibrim.* Egypt Exploration Society, Excavation Memoir 84. London: Egypt Exploration Society.

Rossel, Stine, Fiona Marshall, Joris Peters, Tom Pilgram, Matthew D. Adams, and David B. O'Connor

2008 "Domestication of the Donkey: Timing, Processes, and Indicators." *Proceedings of the National Academy of Sciences* 105 (10): 3715–20.

Váhala, František, and Pavel Červíček

1999 *Katalog der Felsbilder aus der Tschechoslowakischen Konzession in Nubien.* 2 vols. Prague: Tschechisches Ägyptologisches Institut, Philosophische Fakultät der Karls-Universität.

Vinson, Steve

1993 "The Earliest Representations of Brailed Sails." *Journal of the American Research Center in Egypt* 30: 133–50.

Welsby, Derek A., and Charles M. Daniels

1991 *Soba: Archaeological Research at a Medieval Capital on the Blue Nile.* Memoirs of the British Institute in Eastern Africa 12. London: British Institute in Eastern Africa.

Winkler, Hans A.

1938 *Rock-Drawings of Southern Upper Egypt I: Sir Robert Mond Desert Expedition Season 1936–1937 Preliminary Report.* London: Egypt Exploration Society.

1939 *Rock-Drawings of Southern Upper Egypt II (Including 'Uwēnât): Sir Robert Mond Desert Expedition Season 1937–1938 Preliminary Report.* London: Egypt Exploration Society.

Concordances

By Catalog Graffito Number

Catalog Graffito No.	*Kurru Graffito ID No.*	*Description*
T1	074	Human – Figure with Bow
T2	049, 050	Humans
T3	048	Human
T4	028	Human
T5	024	Human
T6	080	Human – In Worshiping Posture
T7	055	Human
T8	103	Human – Seated, Possibly with Staff or Scepter
T9	599, 602	Human – Rider on Horse
T10	020	Human – Rider on Quadruped
T11	078	Animal – Ram of Amun
T12	057	Animal – Bull Heads with Hooves
T13	082	Animal – Horse
T14	083	Animal – Horse
T15	604	Animal – Giraffe
T16	093	Animal – Giraffes
T17	112	Animal – Gazelle
T18	579	Animal – Dog Chasing a Hare
T19	630	Animal – Dog Chasing a Hare
T20	004	Animal – Quadruped
T21	646	Animal – Quadrupeds
T22	084	Animal – Bird
T23	035-038	Animal – Birds
T24	079	Animal – Birds
T25	648	Animal – Horned Viper
T26	600	Plant – Papyrus Frond or Lotus Bud
T27	056	Object – Horned Altar
T28	627, 628	Object – Offering Table (627) with Palm Frond (628)
T29	647, 033	Object – Offering Table (647) with Palm Frond (033)
T30	576	Object – Offering Table
T31	021	Object – Boat
T32	042, 043	Object – Boats
T33	567	Object – Boat
T34	066	Object – Boat

Catalog Graffito No.	*Kurru Graffito ID No.*	*Description*
T35	023	Object – Boat
T36	073, 168	Object – Textile
T37	012	Object – Textile
T38	013	Object – Textile
T39	014	Object – Textile
T40	498	Object – Sandal
T41	592	Architecture – Church
T42	183, 184	Symbol – X in a Box
T43	577	Symbol – X in a Box
T44	638	Symbol – X in a Box
T45	296	Symbol – X in a Box
T46	578	Symbol – X in a Box
T47	092	Symbol – Ankh
T48	126	Symbol – Linear Designs, with Ankh
T49	572	Symbol
T50	005	Symbol
T51	560	Symbol
T52	601	Holes – Group
T53	318	Holes – Group
T54	054	Holes – Group
T55	614	Holes – Group
P1	P_027	Object – Boat, Type 1
P2	P_019	Object – Boat, Type 2
P3	P_016	Object – Boat, Type 2
P4	P_017	Object – Boat, Type 2
P5	P 018	Object – Boat, Type 2
P6	P_009	Object – Boat, Type 2
P7	P_011	Object – Boat, Type 2-3
P8	P_002	Object – Boat, Type 2-3
P9	P_015	Object – Boat, Type 3
P10	P_034	Object – Boat, Type 3
P11	P_012	Object – Boat, Type 3 and Rowboat
P12	P_004	Object –Boat, Type 3
P13	P_008	Object –Boat, Type 3
P14	P_010	Object – Boat, Type 3
P15	P_006	Object – Boat, Type 3

By Catalog Graffito Number (cont.)

Catalog Graffito No.	Kurru Graffito ID No.	Description
P16	P_001	Object – Boat, Type 3
P17	P_014	Animal – Camel
P18	P_030	Animal – Camel
P19	P_028	Animal – Camel
P20	P_031	Animal – Camel
P21	P_020	Animal – Quadruped
P22	P_032	Animal – Quadruped?
P23	P_021	Animal – Ostrich?
P24	P_022	Symbol – Octagon
P25	P_023	Symbol – Triangles
P26	P_024	Symbol – Cross Potent
P27	P_025	Symbol – Cruciform
P28	P_029	Monogram
P29	P_033	Monogram

By Kurru Graffito ID Number

Kurru Graffito ID No.	Catalog Graffito No.	Description
004	T20	Animal – Quadruped
005	T50	Symbol
012	T37	Object – Textile
013	T38	Object – Textile
014	T39	Object – Textile
020	T10	Human – Rider on Quadruped
021	T31	Object – Boat
023	T35	Object – Boat
024	T5	Human
028	T4	Human
033	T29	Object – Palm Frond (with 647, Offering Table)
035	T23	Animal – Bird
036	T23	Animal – Bird
037	T23	Animal – Bird
038	T23	Animal – Bird
042	T32	Object – Boat
043	T32	Object – Boat
048	T3	Human
049	T2	Human
050	T2	Human
054	T54	Holes – Group
055	T7	Human
056	T27	Object – Horned Altar
057	T12	Animal – Bull Heads with Hooves
066	T34	Object – Boat
073	T36	Object – Textile (with 168)
074	T1	Human – Figure with Bow
078	T11	Animal – Ram of Amun
079	T24	Animal – Birds
080	T6	Human – In Worshiping Posture
082	T13	Animal – Horse
083	T14	Animal – Horse
084	T22	Animal – Bird
092	T47	Symbol – Ankh
093	T16	Animal – Giraffes
103	T8	Human – Seated, Possibly with Staff or Scepter
112	T17	Animal – Gazelle
126	T48	Symbol – Linear Designs, with Ankh
168	T36	Object – Textile (with 073)
183	T42	Symbol – X in a Box (with 184)
184	T42	Symbol – X in a Box (with 183)
296	T45	Symbol – X in a Box
318	T53	Holes – Group
498	T40	Object – Sandal
560	T51	Symbol
567	T33	Object – Boat
572	T49	Symbol
576	T30	Object – Offering Table
577	T43	Symbol – X in a Box
578	T46	Symbol – X in a Box
579	T18	Animal – Dog Chasing a Hare

By Kurru Graffito ID Number (cont.)

Kurru Graffito ID No.	*Catalog Graffito No.*	*Description*
592	T41	Architecture – Church
599	T9	Human – Rider on Horse (with 602)
600	T26	Plant – Papyrus Frond or Lotus Bud
601	T52	Holes – Group
602	T9	Human – Rider on Horse (with 599)
604	T15	Animal – Giraffe
614	T55	Holes – Group
627	T28	Object – Offering Table (with 628, Palm Frond)
628	T28	Object – Palm Frond (with 627, Offering Table)
630	T19	Animal – Dog Chasing a Hare
638	T44	Symbol – X in a Box
646	T21	Animal – Quadrupeds
647	T29	Object – Offering Table (with 033, Palm Frond)
648	T25	Animal – Horned Viper
P_001	P16	Object – Boat, Type 3
P_002	P8	Object – Boat, Type 2-3
P_004	P12	Object –Boat, Type 3
P_006	P15	Object – Boat, Type 3
P_008	P13	Object –Boat, Type 3

Kurru Graffito ID No.	*Catalog Graffito No.*	*Description*
P_009	P6	Object – Boat, Type 2
P_010	P14	Object – Boat, Type 3
P_011	P7	Object – Boat, Type 2-3
P_012	P11	Object – Boat, Type 3 and Rowboat
P_014	P17	Animal – Camel
P_015	P9	Object – Boat, Type 3
P_016	P3	Object – Boat, Type 2
P_017	P4	Object – Boat, Type 2
P_018	P5	Object – Boat, Type 2
P_019	P2	Object – Boat, Type 2
P_020	P21	Animal – Quadruped
P_021	P23	Animal – Ostrich?
P_022	P24	Symbol – Octagon
P_023	P25	Symbol – Triangles
P_024	P26	Symbol – Cross Potent
P_025	P27	Symbol – Cruciform
P_027	P1	Object – Boat, Type 1
P_028	P19	Animal – Camel
P_029	P28	Monogram
P_030	P18	Animal – Camel
P_031	P20	Animal – Camel
P_032	P22	Animal – Quadruped?
P_033	P29	Monogram
P_034	P10	Object – Boat, Type 3